МЭМО 2

Soviets Examine Foreign Policy for a New Decade

МЭМО 2

Soviets Examine Foreign Policy for a New Decade

Edited by

Steve Hirsch

The Bureau of National Affairs, Inc., Washington, D.C.

Library of Congress Cataloging-in-Publication Data

MEMO 2: Soviets examine foreign policy for a new decade /
edited by Steve Hirsch.
   p. cm.
   Translated from Russian.
   Produced through collaboration with the Institut mirovoi
ekonomiki i mezhdunarodnykh otnoshenii and editors of
Mirovaia ekonomika i mezhdunarodnye otnosheniia.
   ISBN 0-87179-681-3
   1. Soviet Union—Foreign relations—1985- 2. Soviet
Union—Economic policy—1986- 3. Socialism—History. 4.
World politics—1985-1995. I. Hirsch, Steve, 1952- . II.
Bureau of National Affairs (Washington, D.C.) III. Institut
mirovoi ekonomiki i mezhdunarodnykh otnoshenii
(Akademiia nauk SSSR) IV. Mirovaia ekonomika i
mezhdunarodnye otnosheniia. V. Title. MEMO two. VI.
Title: Soviets examine foreign policy for a new decade.
DK289.M464   1990
327.47—dc20
                                      90-45432
                                         CIP

Published by BNA Books, 1231 25th Street, N.W., Washington, DC.
International Standard Book Number 0-87179-681-3
Printed in the United States of America

Foreword

To the reader:

You have in your hands a collection of analytical works put together at the initiative of The Bureau of National Affairs, Inc., by Soviet scholars, experts, and specialists working through the U.S.S.R. Academy of Sciences' Institute of World Economy and International Relations (IMEMO). Staff editors of the Institute's publication, the journal *World Economy and International Relations* (*MEMO*), also took part in preparing the collection.

We believe that this collection represents a significant step forward compared to the first book of this series, *MEMO: New Soviet Voices on Foreign and Economic Policy*, which BNA published in late 1989. That book was simply a translation of a number of articles that had appeared in *MEMO* from 1987 through early 1989.

What are the fundamental differences between the new book and the first, and what occasioned the change in the book's concept and the criteria for selecting articles?

First. The articles in this book are significantly more relevant and up-to-date. Some of them were specially commissioned through IMEMO by the book's editor, Steve Hirsch, based on the specific needs and interests of potential U.S. readers. Other articles that were written or published earlier in the Soviet Union have been critically assessed and more or less substantially reworked in accordance with the realities of the present day. Why did we and the book's editor believe it imperative to do so?

The fact of the matter is that events in the world are quickening their pace before our very eyes. History is like a tightly wound spring that has suddenly been released. The situation changes rapidly in the course of a few months, weeks, or sometimes even days. Naturally, only the daily press can stay on the heels of events. That is something we did not aim to do, since we wanted to offer the reader assessments of a more general and conceptual nature. But the pace of world development is forcing us to reconsider even some assessments of that sort, assessments which seemed axiomatic just a year ago. (Suffice it to

mention a concept such as the "unshakeable socialist commonwealth.")

The extremely short deadlines that BNA proposed for producing
the book would not solve the problem, if one adds to it all the steps an
article goes through in being edited and prepared for publication at a
Soviet journal, plus the time that articles sit waiting in the editor's
portfolio. In other words, if unrevised articles were simply translated
and published, they would be like last year's snow, which no longer
interests anyone. That is why we decided to revise a number of articles
for the American edition.

Second. A large section of this book is devoted to the Soviet
Union's problems in the part of the world that until recently was
customarily referred to as socialist. This is due to the upsurge of
interest in events in Eastern Europe and the U.S.S.R., and in the
processes of society's renewal and profound transformation along the
path of democratization.

Third. This book, in our view, reflects a new stage in the development of Soviet economic, political, and sociological thought, which is
more and more decisively repudiating dilapidated ideological models.
In a single collection, it is difficult to show the whole variety of these
changes. Therefore, we agreed with the U.S. editor's proposal to
provide a wide, still far from complete, panorama of Soviet experts'
opinions and judgments on various problems. In our opinion, the
articles in this collection indicate the sometimes contradictory nature
of the views that reflect the atmosphere of pluralism in Soviet social
science.

We hope that this collection will arouse interest among various
types of American readers, and we would be glad to receive their
comments, including critical ones. They will help us in our further
work. We also ask exacting readers to act as our clients by pointing out
new topics that might become the basis of the next collection. That
would fully accord with our desire for collaboration and a deeper
knowledge of one another.

We express our deep gratitude to BNA's president, William
Beltz, for his continuing support for our collaboration, and to the
company's vice president and executive editor, Hugh Yarrington, for
his optimistic consent to undertake the cost and trouble of preparing
the book, and for his constant assistance at all stages of the work. We
particularly want to thank the book's editor, Steve Hirsch, for his high
degree of competence and exceptional energy, which conquered both
the distance between Washington and Moscow and time, which he
compressed to a minimum that to us in our country seems nearly

unthinkable for the translation and preparation for publication of such a book.

We thank the translators for their hard work and skillful ability to convey all the nuances of the authors' thought, and all the BNA staff members whose efforts have permitted you to hold this book in your hands. We believe that the fruits of these efforts will not disappoint you.

Herman H. Diligensky

Moscow   Sergei V. Chugrov

June 1990   Valery A. Slavinsky

Preface

This is the second collection of Soviet foreign policy essays BNA has published in cooperation with IMEMO, the Soviet Institute for World Economy and International Relations, and the editors of its journal, *MEMO*. I had thought publication of the first volume, *MEMO: New Soviet Voices on Foreign and Economic Policy*, would provide a formula for publication of successive volumes. But although this book is in some ways a sequel to the first collection, it is different in many ways, chiefly because changes are occurring at such breakneck speed in the Soviet Union that we had to make some changes to avoid being left behind.

Most significant, the reader will find that many of the articles in this book were first published in *MEMO* in 1990, several articles have been revised for this book, and two articles were specially written for this collection and are published here for the first time. These changes allowed us to make the book more current than the first volume was on publication and to respond to what we felt were American readers' interests.

Inclusion of new and updated articles is not without risk though. When we began the *MEMO* project in 1988, I ruled out revision of articles or specially prepared pieces for American publication because I felt strongly that such a volume should not imply greater freedom of expression than actually existed in the Soviet Union or reflect greater diversity of opinion than was allowed in Soviet publications.

Times change though, and it seemed to me that in 1990 these earlier risks had faded, and that by refusing to bend we might miss an opportunity to provide English-speaking readers with the most current Soviet thinking. Moreover, I think that in including two new pieces, Dr. Lev Delyusin's article on China and the article on interest groups by *MEMO*'s editor in chief, Dr. Herman Diligensky, we have done both the authors and our readers a service by publishing some truly novel scholarship.

This book is also shorter than the first volume and published in paperback instead of hardcover. There are a couple of reasons for this change, but the major reason relates to the speed of changes occurring in the Soviet Union. By cutting the number of articles we published in the first volume by more than half, we were able to shorten substantially the time required to put the book together. We agreed on a list of articles in March and completed translation, editing, and publication before the end of the year, not a mean feat.

A number of people deserve thanks for helping to bring this book out, including BNA's president, William Beltz, and its executive editor, Hugh Yarrington, who gave their continuing support for this project. *MEMO*'s editors again were able partners in this enterprise. Herman Diligensky, *MEMO* editor in chief, and Sergei Chugrov and Valery Slavinsky, his deputies, provided invaluable contributions, as did Oleg Kuchkin and Boris Bolotin.

As *MEMO*'s editors mention in their preface, we tried to compress the amount of time needed for preparation of the book as much as possible and I am grateful for the extraordinary efforts put forward by all on the Soviet and American sides to meet the extremely short deadlines.

Camille Christie here at BNA deserves special thanks for editing the manuscripts and is as responsible as anyone for preparation of this book. We are again grateful to Gordon Livermore and his colleagues, Robert S. Ehlers, Bruce Collins, and Elizabeth Hewitt, for both translation and expertise.

Washington   Steve Hirsch
June 1990

Contents

Part Three. The U.S.S.R. in the World Economy

Part One

The Crisis of Socialism:
What Next?

Introduction

This section of the book examines certain aspects of the dramatic changes taking place in the U.S.S.R., China, and the countries of Eastern Europe. Today hardly anyone would deny that the established economic and political systems in those countries are undergoing a profound crisis. This crisis started developing long ago, but only in the context of perestroika and glasnost has public opinion been able to recognize its true dimensions and see the impasse to which the totalitarian bureaucratic system brought society. Naturally, for Soviet scholarly and political thinking today the chief questions are: what are the causes of the crisis; what are the ways out of it; and what are the prospects for restoring health to economic and social life. One can say that these questions are becoming increasingly acute and difficult as perestroika develops.

When M. Gorbachev put forward a program of reform in the spring of 1985, he and many of his followers supposed that all that was needed were certain changes in the existing system of economic and social management. The subsequent experience of perestroika, however, has shown that it is impossible to limit ourselves to isolated adjustments, and that the very foundations of the system must be restructured. The American reader obviously knows that during the years of perestroika, Soviet society's economic and social difficulties have not been mitigated but, on the contrary, have become even further aggravated. It is hardly right to blame perestroika itself for that. Society's transition from one state to another, and the attendant search for better solutions, the vacillations, mistakes, and destabilization of former mechanisms before developing and testing new ones—all have exacerbated accumulated problems during the initial stages and made them even more painful for many people.

In Soviet society the most contradictory opinions and judgments about principal questions of its past, present, and future, are clashing today. A good many people, especially from the older generations, believe that all their problems can be blamed on bad leaders—Stalin, Khrushchev, and Brezhnev—and on those leaders' pursuit of personal power, and political mistakes they made. All that is needed is to replace authoritarian leaders with more democratic and competent ones, correct the mistakes, and everything will be fine. There are also people who are certain that the crisis has been brought about precisely by abandonment of the rigid power system created by Stalin—though surely, the advocates of such right-wing, conservative views are only a relatively small minority of Soviet society. There is also a diametrically opposite opinion (which for the most part coincides with concepts typical of Western political science): The cause of the crisis lies in the socialist choice that was imposed on the country as a result of the 1917 October Revolution, and the way out of it is to resolutely abandon socialist mythology and utopias and return to the path of "normal" capitalist development and the "Western model."

Such "antisocialist" views are not shared by either the majority of the population or by official political circles. Therein lies one of the main differences between our, and possibly China's, political and sociopsychological situation, on the one hand, and that existing today in most East European countries, on the other. In those countries the ideas of socialism have been strongly disavowed, largely because a Stalinist-type regime was imposed on them by an "outside force." For Soviet people, probably the most typical belief is that we should not repudiate socialism but improve and "humanize" it. That we should do so, in particular, by relaxing rigid party and state diktat in the economy, instituting democratic elections, distributing goods more fairly, eliminating the privileges of the political elite and the bureaucratic apparatus, decentralizing administration, and recognizing the independence of republics, regions, and local communities. But within the framework of such a "moderate," reformist course, there is also a great deal that is vague and contradictory.

Much of this is natural and objective in nature. Life is urgently demanding a shift to a market economy and competition—without it, it will be impossible to increase production, improve product quality, and create effective incentives for both enterprises and employees. But at the same time an abrupt shift to the market threatens to cause price increases, inflation, and unemployment. Yet Soviet people have grown accustomed to a way of life in which the scarcity or absence of prime necessities, low incomes, poor social services—including medical care—and unsatisfactory working conditions are combined with firm guarantees of a modest living standard and of employment, and with very low—barely more than symbolic—rent, and in which good and poor work are paid approximately the same. In Soviet society the taste for risk and initiative that is so typical of Western societies has largely been lost. The state's domination in the economy is regarded by many as a necessary and natural condition of economic and social security. Therefore, in public opinion the desire for profound changes is combined with the fear of change, and the fear of losing the state's protection as a result of the privatization of the economy is particularly great.

In one form or another and to one degree or another, the question of how to combine the market with public regulation of the economy, and competition with social justice is the key question in the reform process in the U.S.S.R., the East European countries, and China. In Soviet scholarly and political circles the view is widely held that the experience of the industrially developed Western countries is extremely important in answering this question.

Another equally acute problem is the relationship between economic reforms and political democratization. The experience of the U.S.S.R., China, and other countries shows that attempts to sever the connection between those two areas of reforms can have extremely negative consequences. Economic reforms carried out while preserving an authoritarian bureaucratic system sooner or later encounter the resistance of the all-powerful bureaucracy, while they simultaneously intensify the aspiration for democracy among broad strata of the population. On the other hand, democratization that is not linked to broad economic reforms and a fundamental improvement of the economic situation leads to a rise in discontent and protest, and may be accompanied by destabilization of the governmental system: that is approximately the sort of situation that began to develop in the Soviet Union in late 1989 and early 1990. In both cases, social and political tension in society increases, and its crisis deepens.

Such is the socioeconomic backdrop of the ongoing debates in the Soviet Union over the future of socialism. The nature of those debates and the positions taken by the disputing parties are influenced significantly by the ideological stereotypes that were instilled in Soviet people's minds over the course of generations and assumed the nature of religious dogma. In accordance with those stereotypes, socialism and capitalism are not simply different but radically antithetical types of society that are antagonistic in all respects: the capitalist system, based on private property and the market economy, is inseparably bound up with the exploitation of man by man and fatally doomed to decay and wither away, and it will sooner or later be replaced by socialism. And although the new thinking proclaimed by M. Gorbachev has in many respects undermined such notions, they still live in the minds of many people in our country, and not just in our country alone. Understandably, the influence of ideological dogma seriously clouds and distorts the meaning of debates about socialism.

To clarify the essence of this problem, it is important first of all to stop identifying socialism with the absolute power of the state in the economy and sociopolitical life that is characteristic of a Stalinist-type regime. Such "socialism" has no future. But that conclusion is far from equivalent to the contention that we are witnessing "the end of socialism and communism." After all, socialism and, especially, communism are not some sort of society that has actually existed in either the past or the present, but ideas and values. And if they are purged of dogma that is not supported by real life, and of bureaucratic, police-state "socialism," their humanistic essence will be revealed: It includes the ideas of social justice, universal material well-being, the free development of the individual, and solidarity and cooperation among people. These ideas have already played a significant role in the progressive evolution of many, many societies, and they are scarcely likely to grow obsolete any time in the future. People will always strive for a more perfect, more humane society.

The real essence of the problem of socialism is whether and how a society can be created that will attain a qualitatively different, higher degree of humanism, liberty, and democracy than any that presently exists; and furthermore, a society in which there will be no place for utopian projects or for violence against the natural course of things and the imperatives of economics and human behavior. The terms of this problem are difficult, and we do not yet have a solution today. The articles published in this section of the book to some extent indicate the directions that the search for that solution is taking.

Herman H. Diligensky

The Domestic Situation in the U.S.S.R. and Interest Groups

HERMAN HERMANOVICH DILIGENSKY*

Group Interests in a Totalitarian-Bureaucratic Society

In societies with a market economy and a pluralistic parliamentary political system, group interests are formed in the free play of social and political forces. The existence of a civil society, that is, of inter-group relations independent of the state and its policies, creates broad opportunities for identifying and defending those interests, and turns them into the decisive factor in the autonomous organization of large social groups. It is in the practice of these everyday relations that groups recognize their own interests, create their own organizations and movements, and influence the activities of parties that are either exercising political power or fighting for it, as well as the policies of state institutions.

The situation is different in totalitarian societies, in which all areas of life—production and consumption, information and culture, even the determination of where citizens live within the country—are directly controlled and regulated by an all-powerful state, or more precisely, as was the case until recently, and is largely still the case in the U.S.S.R., by a party-state apparatus. Under such a system, there are no direct, independent relations among the vast majority of groups; they are replaced by relations between people and their ruling party-state regime. Under such conditions, the differences in groups' status and the social differentiation of society are determined primarily by a status hierarchy regulated by the state.

It is extremely difficult, if at all possible, to analyze this hierarchy using concepts developed under totally different social conditions—for example, such concepts as "working class," "peasantry," "office employees," and "middle class." Of course, in the Soviet Union, as

---

*Doctor of history, professor and editor in chief of *MEMO*. This article is appearing for the first time in this collection.

everywhere, there are large social groups distinguished by various characteristics of their employment and way of life; obviously, they also possess certain objective group interests. However, such interests are in large part transformed and distorted by their group situations and differences created by the institutions of the regime.

The working class, for example, is represented in official statistics and ideology as a unified whole, but is really divided into groups of utterly different income and social status; workers in the defense industries have much greater earnings and social benefits than employees in light industry (textile workers, garment workers, and so forth). It is not just a matter of differences among industries, however. There are privileged enterprises that provide their employees with living conditions (including access to scarce consumer goods) that are considerably better than average for their industry, and such privileges often stem from the special favor that these enterprises enjoy with their ministries, rather than from their economic successes. A similar system of privileges exists in agriculture. Local party authorities consider it necessary, in the interest of prestige and political advertisement, to have under their jurisdiction a certain number of "leading" farms (collective farms or state farms), "beacons" that are artificially put in more favorable circumstances than the rest of the farms.

The total dependence of a group's situation on the arbitrary will of the state is well illustrated by the example of people working in science. After World War II Stalin considered it necessary to increase drastically investments in science to eliminate U.S. military superiority, as well as to strengthen scientists' ideological loyalty. At that time the wages of those in the sciences were raised to the highest possible level in the country. Once atomic and hydrogen weapons and missile and space technology had been developed, the regime's interest in theoretical science diminished considerably. Consequently, earnings in the sciences today are among the lowest in the country, and the low level of investment in science and education has caused a growing lag behind development of science in the West.

Thus, group interests under a totalitarian system are reduced, in practice, to competition among groups for unofficial status within the framework of the bureaucratic social hierarchy. Since success in that competition largely depends on the personal influence of leaders of varying power, and on their proximity to both central and local authority, group interests inevitably grow petty and degenerate into the corporate interests of individual occupations, territorial administrative units, enterprises, and bureaucratic institutions.

The totalitarian system effectively prevents recognition and identification of group interests, and hence the formation of large social groups as real actors in social and political life. Even the organizations that are supposed to protect those interests—the trade unions, the Komsomol, the unions of the creative intelligentsia (writers, artists, and so forth)—have actually taken entirely different functions and turned, during the years of Stalinism, into appendages of the party-state bureaucratic system.

While that system reigned, only the groups that directly ensured the stability of the totalitarian regime could defend their interests. This is particularly true of the party and state apparatus (especially its top levels), the top military brass, and the state security agencies. Over the years of the Soviet regime, the real relative status of these "elites" in the power structure have repeatedly changed. Under Stalin the NKVD and MGB [People's Commissariat of Internal Affairs and Ministry of State Security, forerunners of the KGB—*Trans.*] gained almost unlimited influence, and the fate of party, state, and military leaders effectively depended on their whims. Khrushchev put an end to this "disproportion," sharply limiting the power of the KGB. Under Brezhnev the power and influence of the party apparatus, as well as of the military, grew considerably. The years of his rule were marked by an unprecedented enrichment of many representatives of the party, state, and military elite, and were accompanied by growing corruption in that milieu. The KGB retained considerable political influence (especially during the period in which it was headed by Yu. Andropov), but in contrast to the Stalin years, it could no longer seriously compete with the power of the party apparatus.

During the Khrushchev and Brezhnev years, when the system of state terror that Stalin had created was considerably weakened, certain, if extremely limited, possibilities were created for the manifestation of real social interests.

Sporadic labor conflicts broke out; they were usually suppressed and carefully concealed from the public. Urban and rural working people reacted to poor living and working conditions and poor pay by leaving for industries and regions with more favorable conditions, depopulating many agricultural regions and causing manpower shortages in many industries. Mechanisms of a shadow economy developed, and the stratum of underground businessmen, which was usually closely associated with the corrupt element of the party and state apparatus, expanded.

Under the influence of the Khrushchev thaw, a real ideological and cultural pluralism arose. It manifested itself during the Brezhnev years in far more ways than the dissident movement and samizdat publications. During these years many groups of the intelligentsia—writers, critics, journalists, scientists—tried to gain greater creative and intellectual freedom, and a struggle among opposing tendencies developed in literature and art, and in economic, philosophical, and

political thought. Although this struggle, thanks to the powerful ideological censorship, could not become open and free, much less could it
undermine the official ideology's dominant position, it nonetheless
exerted considerable influence on the minds and attitudes of the
educated segments of society. It unquestionably created certain preconditions for the radical changes that have taken place in public
attitudes since 1985.

Despite the significance of these events, it could hardly be said
that during this period the vast majority of Soviet people have acquired
any developed group awareness or clear understanding of the connection between their individual interests and group interests. In
essence, the individual's situation has depended little on his affiliation
with any sort of large social group, or even—insofar as we are speaking
of the majority of citizens—on his place on the hierarchy of formal
social status, for example, on formal qualifications or diplomas. It has
been determined much more by the material benefits, additional
sources of income, and privileges associated with specific occupational
situations. A capable engineer in industry or research often finds
himself in a less favorable position than his colleague who is employed
in trade or has received a lengthy assignment abroad, and even in a less
favorable position than a worker at the same enterprise. Individual
"luck," the ability to get "set up" or "find a good spot" are the factors
that determine the status of most employees. Consequently, in a
society that has collectivist values inscribed on its banner, individualism may determine the psychology and behavior of many people
even more strongly than in societies that prize competition among
individuals.

Under social conditions that make recognition of specific group
interests extremely difficult, only one form of group identity has been
readily and naturally reflected in people's consciousness—the
national-state identity. This form of identity—the "Soviet people"—
has been the subject of intensive propaganda by the monopolistic
official ideology. Ideas about the elimination of fundamental social
differences in socialist society and about "socialist patriotism" as the
only possible form of group consciousness have been drilled into the
Soviet people.

The ideological myth of the "leading role of the working class" has
also influenced the formation of workers' group awareness. Since it
does not reflect real relations of any sort, it has served chiefly as a
means of psychological compensation for workers' unsatisfactory material and social position. Meanwhile, it has bolstered ideological conformism and conservatism among them, along with a mistrust of non-
working-class social strata and of dissident heresies emanating from the
intelligentsia.

Under the conditions of ideological confrontation with the West, the "class" mythology essentially nourished a great-power, nationalist, imperial mind-set that was a far cry from the original Marxist internationalism. Resistance to rotten capitalism and to the dissidents and "liberals" who had been infected by its influence supported a traditional Russian nationalist syndrome that helped unite the Soviet people around the values of the official ideology.

By their inclination toward a bipolar view of the world, the opposition of "we" and "they," and the attribution of all problems and difficulties to the "intrigues of enemies," the masses showed considerable receptivity to the stereotypes of this ideology. The historical traditions of national political culture, based on the subordination of social interests and needs to national-state interests embodied by a central political authority, also contributed. Even in the Brezhnev period, however, this sort of mythological image of society and its corresponding type of group consciousness were increasingly displaced by more realistic and de-ideologized ones. An outward display of loyalty to official values was combined with contempt for them in real life.

Under the conditions of the state-bureaucratic system and, as I have attempted to show above, the chaotic social structure of the working population that was created by that system, this realistic (or empirical) image of society is naturally based on the opposition between the bulk of its members and the representatives of authority—the "bosses" of various levels and ranks, the nomenklatura [the nomenklatura, which technically refers to the list that is maintained of persons approved by the party for appointment to positions of authority at various levels, has come to be a collective term for people belonging to that bureaucratic class—*Trans.*]. Such a division of society into two main social groups fully accords with the principles of the statist system, in which political-power relations dominate over diverse social relations.

The life of each of these groups is built on laws of its own. Within the nomenklatura, the individual's principal motive is his career, his advancement up the hierarchical bureaucratic ladder. The popular masses that make up the majority of society are extremely fragmented socially and psychologically. They are only united by the general awareness of their lack of freedom and their dependence on the bosses. The leading motive within this group, as noted above, is the individual search for a relatively favorable material and social situation. If such a situation is found, a person's behavior in the socioeconomic context becomes more or less automatic. He has only to observe the "rules of the game" developed by the system; nothing motivates him to take any sort of individual initiative or undertake any sort of creative activity.

Consequently, passive, inert behavior at work and in public life becomes the most typical trait of many members of mass social groups. Those who strive to break into the nomenklatura and have the opportunity to do so are the main exception. However, as this social structure stabilizes and ossifies, such opportunities become fewer and fewer. The nomenklatura, although it draws on the mass groups to one degree or another to replenish its ranks, surrounds itself with increasingly high social barriers, and the social structure increasingly becomes stratified into classes.

Thus, a bureaucratically organized society is characterized, first, by the undeveloped and amorphous nature of group interests and group consciousness. Second, by a universal, deeply rooted sense of dependence on the state for status and fortune, and by the sort of social behavior that tends to adapt to existing social relations rather than join together into like-minded groups that recognize and independently defend their interests. And third and last, it is characterized by a more latent than overt, but nonetheless profound, antagonism between those who wield power and the masses who are completely alienated from it. These distinguishing features of social relations in a total-itarian-bureaucratic society have had a strong influence on the course and nature of the contradictory processes that have been unleashed by perestroika.

The Ideology of Perestroika: The End of Monopolistic Society

It is well known that the five years of perestroika have not resulted in any sort of positive changes in the economy or in the social and environmental situations in the Soviet Union. In fact, the situation in all these areas has clearly deteriorated. So far the democratization process and changes in the system of political power have also been rather limited in nature. The real revolution that perestroika has accomplished has been in a different area—the area of people's political psychology and thought.

Critics of Gorbachev's domestic policies frequently criticize them for a gap between words and deeds. It is impossible not to see, however, that words expressing new concepts and principles that were previously inaccessible or forbidden are also a great force: Society's ills cannot be cured with words alone, but one can instill in people a totally different attitude toward those ills and drastically change the social climate.

The impetus for the revolutionary changes in public attitudes has come, on the one hand, from the development of glasnost and the increasing flow of truthful social and political information and the struggle among differing opinions in the mass media; on the other, it has come from the turnabout in official ideology and its gradual, but on the whole fairly rapid, radicalization.

The significance of the second of these factors is usually underestimated. Yet in Soviet society, in which ideological and political conformism are deeply rooted and people are accustomed to listening to what is said "at the top," the degree of rigidity or liberalism in the ideas of the top leadership largely defines the realm of what is "permitted" in the opinions of ordinary people, and either impedes or, conversely, stimulates development of free thinking. Over the five years of perestroika this "realm of the permitted" has expanded, step by step. The ideas proclaimed by Gorbachev following his election as general secretary look extremely modest and timid compared to the policy that was formulated in early 1990 of developing a multiparty system, free competition among political forces and concepts, pluralism in forms of ownership, and a market economy.

Of course, I do not mean to imply that the changes in Soviet public attitudes are confined to the limits set by official ideology. On the contrary, the longer the changes continue, the further they go beyond those limits. Whereas socialism and the Communist Party's vanguard role continue to be supreme, indisputable values for Gorbachev, many political trends today in the U.S.S.R. directly or indirectly reject the ideas of socialism and communism, and a negative attitude toward the ruling party is spreading among broad segments of society. Changes in public opinion are no longer controlled by the regime, and official ideology is becoming increasingly contradictory and going through a growing crisis. Nonetheless, it still plays a significant role in the dynamics of public consciousness. In essence, all the tendencies in social thought start with this ideology in one way or another, attempting either to somehow adapt to it, or to propose alternatives to it. In this sense, it continues to determine the *directions* of changes that are occurring, and the process itself of these changes represents a kind of mutual exchange between the theses of the official ideology and those that emerge outside its limits. It is the products of this mutual exchange that ultimately determine the intellectual atmosphere of present-day Soviet society, or at least its most typical and essential characteristics.

I shall cite what in my view are the most important of these characteristics, which express the impressive changes in Soviet public thinking. The first is a sharply critical attitude toward the existing economic system in the U.S.S.R., and toward the moral and ethical dimensions of social relations. The next is a rejection of the principle of unanimity and monolithic ideology, and a recognition of diversity and contending opinions as an essential component of societal life. The third is Gorbachev's "new thinking," which was originally conceived only as a change in foreign-policy priorities but in fact has caused profound changes in the structure of Soviet social and political mentality. In essence, it marked a revolution in the deeply rooted system of social values. It is no longer "class interests" and the demand that the individual subordinate himself to the totalitarian state in the name of the struggle against a hostile capitalist world that are proclaimed to be the supreme imperative of public life, but the interests of the individual himself, no matter what country he might live in, and the common interests of humanity.

This change in values has radically changed the socially accepted, legitimized motives for people's behavior in society and the foundations of the individual's social identity. The individual has acquired freedom from integration into the state-organized social entity that dominated him and appropriated the name "socialism" for itself, and has gained the right to enter into the kind of relations and the kind of community with other people that are determined by their true common interests, rather than dictated by "class ideology." Understandably, this has created fundamentally new conditions for the formation and recognition of such interests, and for their consolidation on the basis of groups at various levels and of various dimensions.

Specialists know quite well that group interests are a fairly complex and many-sided phenomenon. Depending on the specific situation, the principal place in the hierarchy of such interests may be dictated by their economic, social (group status), or political content; by their direct and immediate, or more long-term, aspects; by an abstract, symbolic, and ideological understanding, or the reverse, a rational, concrete, and pragmatic understanding of them.

The real significance of interests in group behavior is inseparable from the process of their *recognition*. For authors taking the position of dogmatic Marxism, interests exist objectively, independently of the awareness of their subjects, and the recognition of interests by people or groups depends only on their "correct" understanding of this objective reality. Accordingly, true interests, that is, correctly understood interests, are contrasted to false interests that arise from errors in cognition.

In my view, matters are somewhat different. Of course, any and all interests depend on certain characteristics of people's real situation in society and, in that sense, have an objective basis. But the recognition of them does not simply reveal what exists in and of itself (the way that anatomy and physiology reveal the structure of the human organism), but to a significant extent *forms* the very content of interests, their hierarchy, importance, and so forth. In addition, the more complex these interests, and the further removed they are from the basic needs, such as food and shelter, the truer this is. Unrecognized interests are something ephemeral, since they have no influence on people's actual behavior.

The same thing can be said about groups that do not recognize themselves. It is the recognition of interests and the forms that such recognition takes that give them substance and turn them into real motives for action. At the same time, recognition of such a community of interests among a number of people is what makes them a real group, that is, a collective unit of action.

Under the totalitarian regime, group interests simply were not recognized (except for those mentioned above), by the vast majority of people and groups. Such interests existed only in the heads of certain of the most perceptive and bold-thinking individuals. Perestroika, by virtue of the characteristics of the psychological and intellectual climate it created—social criticism, free thinking, the destruction of ideological stereotypes—provided a powerful stimulus for recognition of group interests and, consequently, for the formation of real social groups. The inception of political democracy and recognition of the possibility of autonomous group action in defense of interests have also played an extremely important role in this process. The pluralism of values and plans for economic and political reform that perestroika has given rise to have resulted in the differentiation of group interests.

In the first stage of perestroika (approximately 1985 and 1986) differentiation manifested itself relatively weakly and was expressed in rather vague and indistinct forms. On the level of mass consciousness, reactions to Gorbachev's new course vacillated between more or less active approval and indifference. A sense of profound social crisis and discontent with the economic situation and authoritarian regime and its growing ineffectiveness prompted the most educated segments of society to support the new course. The critical, reformist spirit of the new leader's declarations was in tune with these attitudes.

The relatively young and energetic general secretary looked particularly attractive against the background of the protracted gerontocracy that preceded him. People were also impressed by the new style of leadership, the emphatic democratism and ability to communicate. If all this did not provide any guarantee of major changes, it at least inspired hope. At the same time, a sizable segment of society showed no particular interest in these innovations, seeing them as the familiar routine change of titles with little bearing on ordinary people's lives. Mistrust of the regime, no matter what its representatives said and did, was deeply rooted in public consciousness.

At first Gorbachev enjoyed the support, or at least loyalty of the bulk of the party and state apparatus. Seeing the scope of the crisis, its most intellectually developed and socially responsible representatives understood the need for some sort of changes, while the majority perceived the change in course as a routine political maneuver that posed no serious threat to the existing system of power. The traditional ideological discipline and habit of repeating any and all slogans that came down from above also figured in the early reaction to Gorbachev.

At the same time, in the first months of perestroika an opposition began to develop between two groups of rather limited size that were subsequently to become the opposite poles of the differentiation that society was to undergo. It was no accident that they emerged in the same social and occupational milieu of "intellectuals"—writers, journalists, artists, scientists, and university and institute instructors. By the nature of its occupations, this milieu is the most highly ideologized, and it could not remain indifferent to the genuinely radical changes that the new leader made in public thinking.

For many Soviet intellectuals the new ideology gave the green light to ideas they openly or secretly shared, and even more important, they saw the new course as holding out prospects for the collapse of ideological censorship and for realization of that which is of supreme value to people who work with their minds—freedom of creativity. A relatively broad social outlook and an inclination toward nonconformity and social criticism is characteristic of any intelligentsia, and in Soviet society, where the intelligentsia's activities had always been subjected to particularly rigid and degrading control, distancing oneself from official ideology had become a means of self-preservation for its members. It was among the intelligentsia that an island of the culture of free thinking and opposition to the authoritarian system had developed during Khrushchev's de-Stalinization; that island, moreover, had been populated not only by people in the humanities and social sciences, but by a significant percentage of those in the natural sciences. Unquestionably, this opposition had been primarily of an intellectual and covert nature, and the intelligentsia, by and large, had been unable to overcome fear of repression and to move to active resistance to the regime. Nonetheless, it was the milieu in which people had most listened to foreign radio broadcasts, read samizdat, and sympathized with dissident human-rights activists. With the development of glasnost, it became a source of ideas that, in terms of radicalism and liberalism, went far beyond the adjustments that had been made in the official ideology.

Another segment of the professional "intellectuals" perceived these adjustments as undermining the foundations of their existence. They included writers and journalists who had devoted themselves to extolling the regime and professing Stalinist ideology, many instructors and scholars in the ideological disciplines, and finally, employees of the party agencies' ideological apparatus. For these people, Gorbachev's "cultural revolution" meant a crushing devaluation of the content of their work, and for many it also meant the real prospect of losing profitable positions and immense press runs of their works. So in this case ideological motives were closely interwoven with material motives. Because of the hierarchical relations in the country, the conservative intellectuals were at first unable to openly oppose the ideas of the top party leadership, and they were forced to pass themselves off as supporters of perestroika. This caused them to attack their opponents outside that leadership with all the more fury. The literary and scholarly battles that developed as a result became the harbinger and first act of the political struggle that subsequently split Soviet society.

The Priority of Political Interests

In the first four to four-and-a-half years of perestroika (roughly until the end of 1989), the formation and differentiation of group interests developed most intensively in ideology and politics. At first glance this assertion seems paradoxical. After all, it was in the exacerbation of social and economic problems—the low living standard, the scarcity of consumer goods and services, the poor housing conditions, and the inefficiency of centralized economic planning—that the crisis in Soviet society manifested itself most painfully. The vast majority of Soviet citizens perceived these problems as being the most urgent and as having the highest priority, and it was their solution that was proclaimed as the goal of perestroika. Economic interests, unquestionably, were an important motive force in stepping up the political struggle under way in Soviet society. Nonetheless, by the end of this period, the divisions in the society that replaced the former monolithic unity were primarily political and ideological.

The most elementary and obvious reason for this paradox lies in the nature of the economic and social system. When there is total state control of the economy, the social sphere, and the culture, no group interest can be realized without a change in state policy and in the nature of the political regime. That was the situation before perestroika, and so it remains, by and large, to this day. Gorbachev evidently had come to genuinely understand this a few years after April 1985, when he stated that economic reform could not be carried out without political reform.

Politicization of interests was also caused by the psychological atmosphere that developed under the influence of processes unleashed by the policy of perestroika. An analysis of the evolution of the country's political and ideological life in that period is beyond the scope of this article; we are interested here only in its influence on the formation of interest groups and on the struggle among them. In this connection, one can say that it stimulated mass recognition of political interests far more than it did economic interests. The problems of moving from the Soviet Union's existing economy to an efficient, intensive-type modern economy free of administrative diktat are extremely complex in and of themselves; an understanding of effective strategies and mechanisms for accomplishing this shift is largely beyond the average person's grasp. It must be said that neither the government's economic policies nor discussions of the problems of economic reform in the press and in the scholarly literature have facilitated that understanding in the least.

The country's leadership was unable to work out any clear and consistent economic policy; it combined bold general declarations with timidity and vacillations in political practice. The new laws aimed at changing economic relations either were not implemented or were soon amended by acts that contradicted them. The bitter struggle of opinions in the press provided no clear perspective on the transformations, either; it was more ideological than pragmatic. Many public affairs writers and economists who supported radical reforms persuasively criticized the existing system and argued for the advantages of a market economy, but they did far less to explain specifically how to improve the situation and what the ordinary person could expect from a shift to the market. Their opponents argued that that shift would mean universal impoverishment, unemployment, and exploitation.

Consequently, the increasing chaos in the economy was accompanied by a chaos in thought and opinion that made rational recognition of economic group interests extremely difficult. In public opinion, the desire for reform clearly prevailed over faith in the traditional administrative methods of management, but public opinion was not prepared to lend firm support to the specific measures proposed by specialists. That is indicated by a survey conducted in the fall of 1989: Only a few respondents (7 percent) favored strengthening centralized management of the country and state planning, but the opposing, reformers' positions did not receive majority support either. Thus, only 29 percent agreed that economic independence ought to be granted to state enterprises. It is highly typical that, whereas the percentage supporting "new forms of economic management" was relatively high (43 percent), considerably fewer respondents favored specific measures to implement that general position, such as the development of the leasing of enterprises, individual farms, cooperatives, individual businesses, and the enlistment of foreign capital.[1]

----

[1]*The Population's Attitude Toward Economic Reform: An Express Report* [*Otnosheniye naseleniya k ekonomicheskoy reforme. Ekspress-otchet*], All-Union Center for Public Opinion, Moscow, 1989, Table 6.

If the economy seemed confusing and incomprehensible to Soviets, they had an entirely different perception of political activity. The striking contradiction of the initial period of perestroika increasingly influenced their attitudes. On the one hand, the political climate in the country was drastically changing, and speeches by top political leaders, articles in the press, and television programs were becoming increasingly democratic and radical, while at the same time, actual relations in society for the most part remained just as they had been prior to 1985. Party committees, party first secretaries, ministries, and other bureaucratic departments continued to show the same monolithic power and arbitrariness and the bulk of the ruling stratum continued to display an obvious unwillingness to implement perestroika. The mass media, glasnost, and cultural liberalization were persuading Soviet people that they lived in a drastically changing society, but they did not feel these changes in their daily lives, while they did directly experience the further aggravation of the critical problems in the economy, the social sphere, the environment, security, and law and order.

The experience of perestroika's first years formed in the average person's mind a simple and clear-cut notion of the crisis's causes. The chief blame was placed on the bureaucratic system of power and the stake that leaders and "bosses" of all ranks had in preserving their privileges and unlimited influence. The mobilization of anti-bureaucratic attitudes was fostered both by the increasingly harsh criticism of the nomenklatura in the press, and by the democratic ideas of the leader of perestroika. Although Gorbachev generally refrained from distancing himself from the bureaucratic stratum and condemned only certain conservative leaders, his calls for democratization and for turning power over to the soviets were perceived as hostile to the country's ruling partocracy. For the time being, public opinion trusted the sincerity of the general secretary's reformist aspirations, believing that it was only the bureaucrats' resistance that prevented him from carrying out his plans. As data from the fall 1989 survey indicate, people saw the chief threat to perestroika as the resistance of the bureaucratic apparatus (44 percent); far fewer (14 percent) saw it as the incompetence of the country's leadership.[2] Such ideas resulted in politicization of the interests of mass social groups. One can say that as of 1989 the antagonism between the masses and the power apparatus had incorporated, as it were, numerous interest conflicts that had come to a head in Soviet society.

---

[2]*Ibid.*, Table 8.

At approximately the same time, the structure of the social forces that were clashing in that struggle became defined. The intensified criticism of the bureaucratic regime in the mass media contributed significantly to the formation and consolidation of the conservative camp. A large role was also played by the rise of unofficial social movements—the vast majority of which, for all the diversity of their goals, makeup, and influence, were essentially directed against the existing power system. An alternative democratic ideology began taking shape that was far more radical than the innovations of perestroika's leaders. The party and state bureaucracy and the social groups and segments connected with it started to feel a serious threat to their positions.

One sociological survey conducted in 1988 illustrates the process of divergence between the new official values, which the party apparatus at least publicly professed to support, and the values that were being developed in radical democratic circles. In this survey, three groups of highly educated people were questioned: participants in unofficial movements, lower-level specialists, and party functionaries. The survey attempted to determine their attitudes toward the changes that perestroika might bring. Party workers supported its officially proclaimed goals—"socialist self-government by the people," "a socialist state based on the rule of law," and "the power of the soviets"—to a greater extent than the other two groups. With respect to goals that had not yet received official sanction but were being advocated by the democratic movements, the groups' positions diverged sharply. Thus, 51.4 percent of the members of unofficial movements, 40.4 percent of the specialists, and only 23.6 percent of the party workers supported for a multiparty system, while 64.2 percent of the unofficial-movement members, 44.7 percent of the specialists, and 33.3 percent of the party workers favored elimination of monopolistic control of the mass media.[3]

These figures confirm the divergence of political and ideological orientations within the party apparatus, but they also show that the majority of its members, while displaying conformist loyalty to the most abstract democratic slogans, took a negative view of practical democratic reforms that directly affected their power. At various party forums there were invariably speeches demanding a curb on the press and the unofficial movements that were sowing "antisocialist attitudes"; the speakers obviously saw such movements as new parties in embryonic form. Nina Andreyeva's famous letter "I Cannot Forgo Principles!" which was published in the spring of 1988 in the news-

[3]V. Amelin, "Unofficial Groups, the Intelligentsia, and Party Activists: Political Orientations," *Obshchestvennyye nauki* [*Social Sciences*] No. 4, 1989, p. 201.

paper *Sovetskaya Rossiya* [*Soviet Russia*] and widely distributed and discussed in many local party organizations, became a kind of zenith of this ideological counteroffensive. In essence, this all-out manifesto of neo-Stalinism was directed not just against democratic movements and trends but against the whole Gorbachev policy. It also showed that the nomenklatura, in defending its chief interest—monopolistic economic, political, and ideological power—had no reform platform of its own; its ideals lay entirely in the past, in the restoration and bolstering of the Stalin-Brezhnev system.

The opposite, *democratic camp* is much more difficult to characterize. First, because it has no clearly defined boundaries of any sort. Whereas its leading center is formed by radical-democratic, extremely politicized and highly ideological groups, on its periphery lie large segments of population that are opposed to the existing system but have no clear political orientation, or are simply politically indifferent. Second, this camp is extremely heterogeneous being divided by diverse economic interests and ideological, political, and cultural attitudes and preferences. To a certain extent, it can be compared to the French third estate on the eve of the Great Revolution; while encompassing the bulk of society, it too is socially and culturally heterogeneous. But, to continue the analogy, one can say that, like the third estate, these large and heterogeneous segments of the population are capable of uniting against authoritarian power.

This unification could not be achieved on the basis of a concrete and rational economic and political program. Because of the heterogeneous nature of the Soviet "third estate," its movement had to assume a populist cast initially. In the contemporary literature, the term "populism" is frequently used in a pejorative sense that is akin to demagoguery. The original "American" meaning of the concept was different: The defining principle of the populist movement was "a consensus among heterogeneous mass social groups" in the struggle against forces monopolistically dominating society.[4] It is no accident that the most popular slogan of the growing democratic movement became the call to revoke the privileges of the nomenklatura: special food supply, medical care, dachas, and so forth. But the total redistribution of nomenklatura benefits would not substantially improve the level of mass consumption, and the primary significance of that slogan was to make it possible to identify the enemy clearly. For a totalitarian society, populism is a perfectly natural and predictable stage in the dvelopment of a democratic movement.

---

[4]M.I. Novinskaya, "What Is Populism? (The Populist Tradition in the United States," *Rabochiy klass i sovremennyy mir* [*The Working Class and the Modern World*], No. 2, 1990, p. 143.

The intensity of the political confrontation was seen most clearly in the first elections in the Soviet Union's history (held in the spring of 1989) to offer a choice of candidates. Among the most politicized segments of the electorate, especially among the population of the big cities of Russia and certain other European republics, candidates who harshly attacked the power of the apparatus received the greatest popular support. It was this factor—and to a far lesser degree, personal moral and intellectual qualities, or competence—that was responsible for the popularity of a number of figures who became opposition political "stars." For example, Boris Yeltsin, who won 90 percent of the vote in Moscow, owed that success largely to his Central Committee and Politburo colleagues who had publicly ostracized him for voicing criticism. The investigators of the Uzbek mafia case, T. Gdlyan and N. Ivanov, who had come into conflict with the top officials of the prosecutor's office, acquired hero status in the struggle for justice, in spite of using highly questionable methods of investigation, mainly because they had accused Ye. Ligachev and certain other high party functionaries of taking bribes.

The elections accelerated the consolidation and political definition of the opposing camps. A direct struggle between them unfolded at the First Congress of U.S.S.R. People's Deputies and in the Supreme Soviet elected by it. At the same time, the parliamentary debates demonstrated with new persuasiveness that the confrontation was based on the conflict between the authoritarian regime and its populist opposition. The bitterest debates focused not so much on specific problems in the country's development, as on the principles and values of public life. The speakers representing the opposing camps did more to denounce their opponents and proclaim their own ideological and ethical creeds than they did to propose specific ways out of the crisis.

At the congress a de facto bloc formed between the conservative element of the party and state apparatus and the ideologists of imperial Russian nationalism. In the final analysis, the nationalists' anticommunism and negative attitude toward the October Revolution have proved to be of little importance to them compared to their hatred of Western-style democracy and of the democratic and liberal intelligentsia—a hatred with a heavy dose of anti-Semitism. For the conservative apparatchiks, the nationalistic ideology and the appeal to great-power values represent practically the only means left of preserving some sort of influence among the masses. Although party functionaries try to frighten the people with the hobgoblin of the restoration of capitalism, and the nationalists try to frighten them with the prospect of a Russian sellout to the West and the destruction of Russian traditions, they have essentially the same thing in mind: the prospect of economic and political democracy and of the move to a pluralistic society. In short, they too are united by the struggle against a common adversary.

In late 1989 and early 1990 the struggle continued to intensify. The democrats were unable to win a majority in the parliament, but their moral prestige in the country grew. Academician A. Sakharov, whom the right-wing majority ostracized in the congress, became a national hero. The leftists' influence was augmented by a factor that assumed growing importance in political life—the rise of the *mass movement*. In a number of big cities in Russia and the Ukraine (Volgograd, Tyumen, Sverdlovsk, and others), so-called provincial revolutions unfolded—movements of broad segments of the population forced the resignation of local party leaders. *The verbal "revolution from above" started to grow into a popular movement and a real struggle for power*. This prompted the conservative apparatus to shift from covert sabotage of perestroika to open resistance to Gorbachev's domestic and foreign policies, and to the organization of actions and movements under a neo-Stalinist banner.

The rise of the democratic movement prevented the party apparatus from taking political revenge. Official acceptance of the multiparty principle and revocation of Article 6 of the Constitution, which proclaimed the Communist Party's monopoly of power, were a major victory for the democratic forces. Republic and local party elections in the spring of 1990 in Russia and, in part, the Ukraine, confirmed the broad scope of the leftists' influence: In Moscow, Leningrad, and other big cities they won majorities in the soviets.

Despite this influence, an impasse has developed since these elections. The leftist offensive has stalled, since neither their electoral success nor the democratic revision of the Constitution removed the party apparatus and state bureaucratic institutions from power. Unquestionably, this power has been weakened and destabilized, but for the most part the party and state apparatus has held on to its positions in Moscow and most of the country's regions. There are three main reasons for this:

First, development of the masses' democratic activism across the country has been uneven. Rural areas, small cities, and many union republics (especially the Central Asian republics) have been relatively untouched by the democratic movement. The average person there still feels political indifference and impotence toward the partocracy. In these places the apparatus manipulated the elections fairly freely, which naturally affected the correlation of forces in the union and republic parliaments, and in the local soviets.

Second, the worsening of interethnic conflicts, and the rise of nationalistic and separatist movements in the republics have dealt a powerful blow to the democratic camp. These movements and their social and political contexts differ widely from region to region, but their general consequences have included not just a critical destabilization of the country's political situation, but a fragmentation of the democratic camp and a narrowing of its geographical boundaries. In many republics exacerbated ethnic problems, the struggle for republic sovereignty, and bloody ethnic conflicts have pushed the goals of internal democratization into the background. Since the proclamation, in one form or another, of the Baltic republics' secession from the union, their democratic forces have effectively ceased to take a direct part in the political life of the country as a whole. Russian conservatives have taken advantage of the increasingly complex problem of preserving the union and its boundaries, and of the real or imaginary threat to the rights of the Russian minority in the republics to kindle nationalistic attitudes and campaign for a return to a strong, authoritarian state. This has significantly complicated the activity of Russia's democratic forces and forced them to shift their attention to the nationalities problem. Consequently, at the Congress of Russian Republic People's Deputies, the central issue has been the question of Russian sovereignty, which is devoid of any clear and specific social and political content.

Third, the democrats' main problem is their internal weaknesses. Their critical weakness is their organizational, political, and ideological amorphousness and fragmentation, which in many respects reflect the democratic movement's populist nature. As a complex conglomeration of voter blocs, parliamentary groups, clubs, small parties, committees, and so forth, it has been unable to create an effective nationwide political organization to unite them or to identify a sufficiently prestigious team of leaders. The Interregional Group of People's Deputies, torn by internal conflicts, could not become such a team. For all the power of their mass base, the democrats have thus been unable to assume the role of a truly alternative political force capable of vying for state power.

Of course, M. Gorbachev's political tactics and his relations with the opposing blocs have fundamentally influenced the situation. For a time he managed to "outplay" the conservative apparatus while actually relying on the strength of democratic sentiments in the country. One would think that the logic of his policy would have led him into an alliance with the democratic politicians, but in reality their relations were increasingly marked by conflict. There was evidence not only of fundamental political disagreements—on the issue of Lithuania and reform of the Federation, and on the pace and means of moving to a market economy—but also of an emotional background of mutual offenses and suspicions. At the time of the first Congress of U.S.S.R. People's Deputies, certain leftist leaders assumed a rather contradictory position, aspiring at the same time to an alliance with the initiator of perestroika, and to the role of an alternative political force to him (for which they hardly had serious grounds).

Gorbachev has been striving to maintain a position between or, more precisely, above the two warring camps, a goal he has achieved, aided by the narrowness of the conservatives' political influence and the weakness of the leftists. He faces considerable risk with this tactic: In March 1990, at the time of the vote on establishing the presidency, he could perfectly well have lost power if he had not received last minute support from some leftists who were frightened by the threat of a right-wing coup in the party Central Committee. By freeing Gorbachev from strict dependence on either the partocracy or the Supreme Soviet, the presidency has given him new opportunities to play the role of supreme arbiter. At the same time, balancing between the two camps was becoming increasingly difficult. The need to find solutions for the worsening economic and political problems and to carry out urgently needed reforms, and the growing political polarization in society—all this was making a middle line increasingly impossible and forcing a choice between alternative tendencies. In questions pertaining to Lithuania and to the attitude toward the leftist opposition within the party, and in the struggle of opposing tendencies at the first Congress of Russian Republic People's Deputies, the president, in effect, took the rightists' side and remained loyal to the partocracy's caste solidarity. By sticking to that position, he undermined his own ability to carry out his promised radical reforms. Such reforms cannot be carried out with the help of the existing party and state apparatus.

A new turn in Gorbachev's policy has been motivated by the Constituent Congress of the Russian Communist Party, and by the 28th CPSU Congress. Both congresses showed that party and state apparatus (especially at the regional and local level), as well as the army generals, on the whole are aggressively hostile toward the domestic and foreign policies of perestroika's leader. At the 28th Congress, Gorbachev managed to get the upper hand over his opponents from the right who wished to strip him of the highest party office, and managed to force Ligachev to retire. Reasons for this included the balance of forces in the country in general and the rightists' lack of an alternative leader capable of challenging the president. The conservative majority of the delegates realized at the end that ousting Gorbachev would effectively put the party into total isolation. By making his first public rebuff to the conservatives, by stripping the Politburo and the Central Committee of their position of supreme authority, and by winning the Congress' approval of his main policies, the president undoubtedly obtained greater independence from the apparatus.

But his victory was neither complete, nor final. The conservative apparatus has remained a significant and potentially hostile force, and has not at all given up on its sabotage of perestroika. At the same time the left-wing opposition has significantly increased its influence: it began to draw support from the Russian government and parliament headed by Yeltsin, and from the soviets of a number of big cities.

The example of Russia augmented the separatist feelings in the national republics. In Moldavia and Armenia nationalists came to power, and even Byelorussia, which had been obedient up to now, has decided to organize its own army. One republic after another proclaimed the precedence of their legislation over the union laws. The central state bodies found themselves facing the prospect of being effectively degraded into merely symbolic institutions with no power over the major part of the country.

In this situation the search for some kind of consensus with the left and with the new leaders of Russia became imperative for the president. His opponents from the left shared that interest, as Yeltsin could not allow himself to destroy the union. The first important step toward such a consensus was taken in the summer of 1990, when Gorbachev and Yeltsin jointly set a commission for drafting a new pattern of radical economic reform.

It is evident that the status quo, based on maintaining the present central executive power structures, personnel, and methods, and on continued maneuvering between the opposite sides, cannot bring about solutions to the problems that are shaking society, or prevent the rapidly declining influence of the ruling party and the country's leadership. Maintaining the status quo is more likely to contribute to a deepening crisis, which could have unforeseen consequences, including an abrupt change of power (as in Eastern Europe). The alternative for political development lies in a relatively peaceful regrouping of political forces with the active involvement of the president, a regrouping that would open access to real executive power to the new "political class"—the people and groups that have entered politics on the groundswell of the popular movement.

The feasibility of this alternative, which in my view is the optimal one, does not depend entirely on the will of the president. Another important condition for its realization is a more clear-cut structuring of the democratic camp itself, the identification of the specific interests and goals of all its components, and the formation, on that basis, of a unifying, integral, and inherently logical program. Such a development would enable it to overcome its weaknesses, the proclamatory, populist nature of many of its actions, and to become a constructive political force. A crucial element and condition of this whole process is the clearer recognition, differentiation, and integration of society's group interests. After all, it is ultimately those interests that form the basis of the fundamental political conflict between the people and the regime, and that determine the best means of resolving that conflict.

Classes, Segments, and Group Interests

The conflict between the people and the regime, between the advocates of change and those who want to preserve the old system, represents the most generalized form of the expression of group interests. In the context of this conflict, economic and social interests are poorly differentiated and identified, and the recognition of them is fed more by the emotions of protest against the existing state of affairs, or conversely, by a sense of threat to individual status, than by a rational interpretation of reality. Therefore, interests are recognized in their immediate rather than their long-range dimension. Defining the image of the enemy predominates over clarifying one's own situation and the factors that determine it, and symbolic ideological formulas predominate over pragmatism and rational understanding of socioeconomic problems. Thus, the democratic movement's opponents are able to counter its populist slogans with the "principles of socialism."

This situation could be maintained only until the problem of rational economic reform was put on the agenda in practical terms. The idea of moving to economic pluralism and a market economy did not acquire the right of citizenship until 1987, and for a time it remained no more than an idea. Attempts to implement it in practice—the introduction of cooperatives and joint ventures, partial changes in the status of state enterprises and in the distribution of their earnings—had little effect on the dominant economic system, but certain of these attempts, especially cooperatives, actually helped to ideologize economic problems. Operating in an economy of scarcities and having an uncertain legal status, cooperatives inflate the prices of their products, and some of them engage in ordinary speculation. All this, together with the cooperative members' rather high earnings, has turned part of public opinion against them, and conservative circles have made extensive use of cooperatives' track record in their campaign against the idea of a market.

That the idea of a market has been put forward at all has served to differentiate group interests, but not until late 1989 and early 1990, when the party leadership, government, and parliament actually took up reform of the property system, did this differentiation and its shift from the ideological to the practical plane become inevitable. In essence, every member of society was confronted with the question of what he stood to lose or gain as a result of the anticipated reforms, and which of the proposed measures accorded with, or ran contrary to his interests. The search for an answer to these questions gave a strong impetus to the emergence of active interest groups and, at the same time, to the formation of a genuine (not purely verbal and pro forma) attitude toward the perestroika process on the part of these groups.

The group interests awakened or intensified by perestroika are making sense of, and giving form to, the conflict between those in positions of authority and the broad segments of the population that are alienated from it. Those interests are intensifying the political struggle over the problems of perestroika, but at the same time they are serving to de-ideologize those problems, and the focus in relations among groups in shifting to comparison and contrast of pragmatic socioeconomic and social interests. As a result, conflict is ceasing to be the sole means of expressing group interests; in addition to conflicts, there is a widening basis on which various groups can identify common goals, and the possibility and need for compromise are becoming clear. The simple "us" and "them" dichotomy is gradually giving way to a more complex range and continuum of interests.

Of course, these tendencies have only been able to develop widely as the result of extensive democratization, and the complete or partial loss of power by the groups that previously monopolized it. In that respect, developments in the Moscow City Soviet, where the opposition Democratic Russia bloc won the majority in the spring 1990 elections, and in the Congress of Russian Republic People's Deputies, where that bloc succeeded at the end of May in electing B. Yeltsin as chairman of the republic's parliament, are highly indicative. These events have not ended the confrontation between opposing tendencies, but by addressing themselves to the actual problems of Moscow and Russia, the democrats have considerably expanded the possibilities of agreement with their opponents.

In what follows, I shall attempt to characterize the principal interest groups in Soviet society of the late 1980s and early 1990s, and their attitudes toward perestroika. The picture that is offered is in many respects schematic and approximate, which is due both to the incompleteness of existing information, especially the shortage of specific sociological studies, and to the fact that many such interests are still not sufficiently formed.

The groups to recognize their interests most readily and quickly have been those with political and economic power. They have something to lose, and as in any society, their main interest is to preserve the sociopolitical status quo. The highest place in the Soviet hierarchy is occupied by the *party apparatus*, and as I have already noted above, the deepening of perestroika (the development of glasnost and pluralism, and the prospect of radical reforms) reinforced its inherent conservative character.

Relatively few representatives of the apparatus permit themselves to publicly condemn Gorbachev's policies, but they are increasingly calling into question its most radical aspects, especially those that pertain to the problems of property and the market, that is, those that affect the "principles of socialism." The apparatus's most effective form of resistance to perestroika has been to sabotage practical steps to carry it out. Still possessing immense power at the center and, especially, at the local level, the party functionaries have broad opportunities to manipulate elections, block the development of new economic forms (cooperatives, leasing arrangements, individual peasant farms), curb an insubordinate press, and impede the work of the new democratic soviets. It is hard to draw the line here between deliberate sabotage and mere habit, between corporative group solidarity and psychological rejection of the old system's collapse.

At the same time, the loss of its monopoly on power and the regime's growing destabilization are increasing divisions within the apparatus. A good number of its members are confused, disoriented, and uncertain about their prospects. These feelings have been further intensified by events in the Baltic republics and the East European countries. Some members, especially functionaries belonging to the intelligentsia, have joined the internal party opposition (the Democratic Platform movement), or nationalist movements in the republics. The differences between "hardline" and "flexible" members of the apparatus have increased. The latter more or less actively support the Gorbachev line, the moderate, "centrist" version of perestroika. Many of them understand the need for and inevitability of major changes in the economic and political structure and want to somehow adapt to them, and the most honest and thoughtful of them are even promoting such changes.

At the same time, the goal of the apparatus as a whole continues to be the preservation, if not of monopolistic power, at least of the party's leading role in society. Such hopes are based on the fact that the CPSU is still the country's most powerful organized political force, and that a real alternative to its rule is far from taking shape. However, it is becoming harder and harder to use these advantages. Because of their conservatism and authoritarian mentality, most members of the party apparatus, especially of its middle level, are incapable of taking hold of the reform process and ensuring the party's leading role in perestroika. Anticommunist sentiments are rapidly gaining strength in society. There are signs of the party's moral deterioration as a political organism, and one gets the impression that many of its elements are more concerned with preserving the apparatus's material privileges and party property than with long-range political goals. The large wage increase that party functionaries received in 1989 was obviously a means of reducing the exodus from the apparatus and overcoming the difficulties of recruiting qualified and capable personnel. Making use of the huge party funds, apparatchiks have been increasingly moving into business, creating banks, cooperatives, and joint ventures of their own.

Evidently, the only thing that could prevent a further decline in the party's role would be a radical renewal of its membership and a revamping of its entire structure and its operating methods on the basis of democratic principles. However, it looks as though the party leadership is more concerned with blocking the development of a strong social-democratic tendency within the party, which it believes would lead to the party's collapse. This line and the departure of dissidents that it implies are unquestionably strengthening the conservatives' position in the party.

What has been said about the interests of the party apparatus can also be applied, for the most part, to the *apparatus of state agencies*, especially since the two are closely interrelated and are continually exchanging personnel. By virtue of their mentality, *military circles*, especially the generals and other top officers, side with them closely. The military has special reasons for dissatisfaction with perestroika: Their interests and traditional status are being damaged not only by the recognized need for military reform, but also by the policy of demilitarization and disarmament, press criticism of the situation in the Army, and the movement formed by democratically minded officers in opposition to the military leadership. The military's actions during the well-known tragic events in Tbilisi evoked a wave of antimilitary sentiment in the country.

At the same time, I think the prospect of a military coup, often mentioned in the Western press, is unlikely. Politically, today's Army is by no means a unified force: Most of the officers are dissatisfied with their material living conditions, and they have as much a stake as other citizens in improving the country's economic situation. Soviet generals bear little resemblance to Latin American or African generals, and the Army has never played an active political role in the Soviet Union. By and large, military circles maintain a passive loyalty to the political leadership. The same is true of the KGB, which has been forced to rethink its functions, with political repressions a thing of the past and with the emergence of ideological and political pluralism. That does not deter them from acting as an influential conservative pressure group, of course. The role of the Army, security agencies, police, and internal troops could become decisive only in the event of a split in the top political leadership: In that situation their ties with the conservative element of the party apparatus would most likely manifest themselves.

Economic executives of various ranks form special and highly distinctive interest groups. This segment encompasses numerous levels of the social structure: from ministers to enterprise directors, collective farm chairmen, foremen, and brigade leaders. Thus, it is part of both the state apparatus and the production sector. This is the segment that can be considered the backbone of the state bureaucratic system. It completely determines the specific characteristics of Soviet management, characteristics that make it radically different from its counterparts in countries with market economies.

The basis of these distinguishing characteristics is the fact that economic activities are independent of consumer demand and totally dependent on state authority. The financing of industries and enterprises, the prices of their products, their supply of equipment and materials, and the economic status of their executives and employees depend entirely on the higher levels of the management system. Freedom from the consumer is bolstered by the shortages of most types of goods and services, as well as by the fact that most of the economic ministries and the enterprises under them enjoy monopolies in their production sectors.

Naturally, in this system of relations, every executive's primary interest is to "earn" the highest possible evaluation of his performance at higher management levels. His financial position, status, and career prospects depend directly on that evaluation. The corporative interest of ministries, production associations, and enterprises consists of securing allocations of funds, material resources, bonuses, and so forth from the higher levels. There are two main mechanisms for realizing these interests.

First, a department or enterprise attempts to "prove" to state agencies the special need for its production goals. Since in most cases the consumer's view is in no way taken into account, the procedure for providing such proof and making the corresponding decisions is purely bureaucratic. On the whole, the more an entity strengthens the state's power and creates symbols of the state's grandeur, the greater its material status. Therefore, it is more advantageous to produce weapons than food, clothing, or medicine, and more advantageous to build the "world's largest" electric power plants or chemical combines than it is to build housing, schools, and hospitals. The maximum for the state, and the minimum for the human being. That is the principle of the totalitarian economy.

Second, a Soviet manager's performance evaluation depends on his fulfillment of the plan directives. Since all-encompassing centralized planning is unable, especially in such an immense state, to take the dynamics of real demand into account, it is oriented primarily toward increasing the quantity of output. In the absence of market mechanisms that would provide incentives for production efficiency, production results are measured using artificial indicators devised in bureaucratic offices. To fulfill its plan, an enterprise has no need whatsoever to introduce new technologies that save labor, energy, and materials; to the contrary, it finds it "profitable" to expend as much of those resources as possible. Every level in the hierarchical system has an interest in reporting the most favorable results to "the top." This bureaucratic game of "plan-report" gives rise to a system of universal deception (so-called "pripiski"* that the strictest sanctions are incapable of eliminating).

The economy of totalitarianism and of centrally allocated resources encourages the production, in enormous quantities, of unnecessary products or products that are harmful to society, and the construction of gigantic, "high-prestige" facilities that destroy the environment. (The press has written about a railroad costing immense sums that has nothing to transport, and about tens of thousands of harvesting combines that cannot be used in the fields—there are many known cases of this kind.)

The struggle for state money and resources creates a specific type of "competition" characteristic of the totalitarian system. Before perestroika this struggle was hidden from the public eye. To a certain extent, glasnost revealed the real mechanisms of the activity of many "economic" ministries, and the disastrous consequences of that activity for the economy, the environment, and the social sphere. Under the pressure of public opinion, it was possible to bring about the abandonment of some of the projects that were most costly and dangerous to the country's future (such as the project to divert Siberian rivers to the south).

The interests that are called "departmental" interests in the Soviet Union cannot, however, be eliminated as long as bureaucratically managed state property continues to play a decisive role in the economy. "In and of itself the word 'department,'" notes economist V. Yaroshenko, "masks the broad social context that its existence supports. The interest parties serve the vital needs of many millions of people, and the only way their dominion can be eliminated, or at least limited, is if the state and society can meet those needs by means other than through the present structures."[5]

This conclusion is confirmed by many examples from the perestroika period. The departments are finding new ways of protecting their interests that have been adapted to changing conditions. In

---

*Falsifying financial documents to receive additional rewards.—Ed.
[5]V. Yaroshenko, "Interest Parties," *Novy mir* [*New World*], No. 2, 1990, p. 115.

particular, they are taking advantage of the liberalization of foreign trade and price setting, and they are relying on the still-powerful centralized management apparatus to thwart attempts by legislators and the public to subordinate their activities to real public needs.

The shift to a market economy would require the Soviet managers to undergo a total revolution in thinking, habits, and practices. Their deeply internalized "rules of the game" are fundamentally different from those dictated by market competition. That is the reason for enterprise executives' contradictory attitude toward the economic reform. On the one hand, they support measures that weaken the diktat of the State Planning Committee and the ministries and that reduce the deductions from their profits that are paid to the state budget. On the other hand, only 35 percent of the executives questioned in 1989 favored granting economic independence to state enterprises.[6] Thus, for the majority the fear of independence and the "escape from freedom" prevail over the desire for freedom. In essence, the middle manager's ideal comes down to preserving the guarantees of the planned state supply of resources and marketing of output, while receiving greater freedom in setting prices. Such is the pseudo-market, the "planned market" economy that has been proclaimed in a number of programs and that an influential element of management is, in effect, putting forward as an alternative to a real market.

Such a position reflects the conflicts of interest between middle and top management, between enterprises and central management; at the same time, it reflects their common interest in preserving the monopolistic structure. It seems that this common interest is having a strong influence on the implementation of the economic reform. Enterprises have taken advantage of the greater freedom granted them to inflate prices on the domestic market and, if possible, earn hard currency on the foreign market without improving their productivity or the quality and assortment of their products. At the same time, the corporative interest of the state management system has been effectively blocking the shift to genuine market relations. The plan for economic perestroika that the government proposed to the parliament in May 1990 envisaged a sharp rise in prices, but included no specific measures for reducing the size and powers of the economy's centralized management. The unstinted declarations from the country's top political leadership concerning the transition to a market are in practice being reduced to nothing by the people in charge of implementing them—functionaries in the economic-management agencies.

---

[6]*The Population's Attitude Toward Economic Reform*, note 1, above, Table 6.

It would unquestionably be wrong to apply what has been said to all of economic management. In many respects, perestroika has served as a stimulus to those members of management who have abilities, an inclination toward genuine freedom and initiative, and an entrepreneurial spirit. In this population segment, as in others, the process of internal differentiation is deepening. But in today's conditions, the initiative of such enterprising and creative managers is still often suppressed.

As V. Yaroshenko rightly notes, "the only way the departments' influence can be abolished is by profoundly splitting off the interests of primary-level enterprises and their employees, by separating their interests from those of the bureaucrats."[7] Obviously, it is impossible to realize that prospect without eliminating the foundations of the state functionaries' dominant position in the economic system. But that requires radical political decisions.

The interests of groups that operate in the realm of the *shadow economy* are in many respects linked to the interests of the bureaucratic management apparatus. For understandable reasons, it is very difficult to identify the specific makeup and boundaries of those groups. Existing in the cracks between legal economic mechanisms, they are extremely heterogeneous. The shadow economy includes underground industrial enterprises, cooperatives engaged in speculation, various mafias and racketeers, and ordinary speculators in scarce goods and hard currency. A large part of the work involved in building rural homes, repairing apartments, furniture, and private cars, and so forth is done outside the framework of the "official" economy.

Divergent views on the shadow economy are expressed in the press and public opinion, depending on people's ideological and political biases. Conservatives claim that it brings together powerful forces that operate through their own lobbies in the state apparatus, among congress deputies, and in academic circles and the mass media, and are striving to steer the country toward the path of capitalism. For some radicals, the "shadow economy" represents the ready-made structure of a future "normal" market: we have only to legalize its activities and we will acquire perfectly respectable entrepreneurs.

I think that both these views are mistaken. Among the operators in the shadow economy, there are probably people who really are capable of entrepreneurial activity in the context of a free market, but the shadow economy's distinguishing feature is that it represents a natural offshoot of the totalitarian economic system and feeds on its fuel. Its conditions for existence are a shortage of goods and services, and the monopolistic economic power of the bureaucratic state appa-

---

[7]V. Yaroshenko, note 5, above, p. 117.

ratus. Big underground business can flourish only to the extent that it corrupts some part of that apparatus. Corrupt bureaucrats are not the agents of that business but its direct participants. The trade mafia, which is in practice the most powerful and influential sector of the shadow economy, consists of employees of state institutions, storage depots, and stores who steal goods and sell them at speculative prices on the underground domestic market or to foreign clients.

The shift to a genuine market and an abundance of goods would undermine the foundations of the Soviet shadow economy. Many or most of the underground capitalists would hardly be able to adapt to the conditions of free competition. I was told about a king of Odessa underground business who accumulated millions in assets and then emigrated to the United States. Now not a trace of his wealth is left; he went bankrupt and now does odd jobs in a small store in the Bronx.

One can hardly doubt that the most influential groups associated with the shadow economy are putting up bitter resistance to perestroika and economic reform. There is probably some basis for the opinion that the aggravation of economic difficulties during the years of perestroika, especially in the areas of supply and distribution, is attributable, in more than a small way, to sabotage by the trade mafia. Other former underground "businessmen" are organizing speculation-oriented cooperatives that do not create real goods and services, thereby compromising the cooperative movement in the eyes of the public.

*   *   *

The process of the recognition of group interests has been most complicated among the major segments of the working population—among the workers, peasants, and ordinary office employees. Perestroika has unquestionably provided a strong stimulus to that process, but at the same time it has revealed its difficulties and contradictions—above all, intellectual and cultural difficulties. The least educated social groups do not have the capacity for systematic economic and political thinking that is needed to understand the optimal reform strategies; they are the ones that alternative values and concepts—those different from official ideology and the existing system—have the most difficulty in reaching. According to a survey conducted in early 1988, only 15 percent of workers supported the principles of pluralism, 29 percent supported the deideologization of international relations, and 42 percent supported the priority of universal human interests over class interests. Among the more educated groups—technical specialists, members of the intelligentsia, and students—the percentage of supporters of the new values ranged from 65 to 90 percent.[8] These data confirm the fairly well-known correlation of a low educational level and manual labor with intellectual conservatism.

Perestroika's success depends to a critical extent on the working class's attitude toward it, although not in the mythological sense in which official Marxism asserts the "working class's leading role in social development." In today's society, such mass social groups are so heterogeneous and differentiated that they can scarcely play a "leading role" in social processes of any sort. The role of the Soviet working class in perestroika is determined primarily by the fact that it forms the largest social group capable of mass actions in the social and political arena. In that respect, its potential contribution to perestroika can be compared to that which the working people of the capitalist West (especially in Western Europe) made to the evolution of 19th-century "classical capitalism" into the welfare state or "social market economy." Workers did not directly carry out the political, legal, and ideological transformation that turned capitalism into a more democratic and humane society, but without the working class movement, and without its pressure on the bourgeoisie and social institutions, that transformation obviously could not have been carried out.

Perestroika, which was originally conceived of and supported by rather limited groups in society, cannot become a real possibility without fairly substantial working class support. That is why the struggle of various political and ideological forces over the problems of perestroika is, to a significant extent, a struggle for the working class.

Conservative, antiperestroika forces have several trump cards in this struggle. First, the emotional substratum of workers' psychology that is called "class instinct," the sense of belonging to a group that differs in its status and interests from all who are free from manual labor in factories and at construction sites. In Soviet society, the traditional social and psychological barrier between blue- and white-collar employees has always been reinforced by official propaganda and the doctrine according to which the working class naturally has its own special political line. Now efforts are being made to direct the workers' class feelings against the liberal intelligentsia, which lends impetus to perestroika and provides its ideas.

Second, the Russian conservatives are whipping up nationalism among the workers; here, as everywhere, nationalism is most widespread among the relatively uneducated segments of society. Lately, the separatist movements in the republics have provided nationalist propaganda with additional arguments: One must bear in mind that in the Baltics, the Ukraine, Moldavia, and Central Asia ethnic Russians

---

[8]*The Sociology of Perestroika* [*Sotsiologiya perestroiki*], Moscow, 1990, p. 182.

constitute a significant part of the working class in major industry. The prospect of losing national territory through secession of republics from the union; the bloody ethnic conflicts in the Transcaucasus, from which the local Russian population and soldiers and officers of the military contingent stationed there have suffered; and finally, the withdrawal of Eastern Europe from the orbit of the Soviet Union's political influence have all served to intensify Russian nationalism among workers.

Third, practically the strongest trump card of conservative propaganda is the attempt to frighten workers with the woes that the shift to a market economy will bring them—the prospects of price increases, unemployment, and the revival of "capitalist exploitation." Soviet workers have an incomparably lower living standard than their Western colleagues; they suffer from poor working conditions and a de facto lack of rights on the job; and many lack any sort of satisfactory housing and live in regions where deterioration of both the environment and the health of their inhabitants has reached disastrous proportions.

These phenomena are giving rise to anger among the working class, an anger, however, that until recently had little to do with the principles of the statist economic system. With guaranteed jobs in a state enterprise, Soviet workers are accustomed to dependence on the state Moloch, and often regard the state as the natural patron and arbiter of their destiny, as the only force that ensures the relative stability of their existence. This psychological dependence recalls the psychology of the peasant serfs who could hate their landowners but could not imagine life without their protection. No matter how hard the workers' working conditions, no matter how few their rights may be in relation to the all-powerful bosses, the bureaucratic systems' "rules of the game" do not demand of them any real production discipline, the sort of discipline which presupposes a high degree of job motivation and concern for the productivity and quality of their work. Low-paid, poorly organized work that is poorly geared to real social needs inevitably demoralizes some elements of the working people, gives rise to cynicism and indifference, and makes them marginal in terms of their social psychology. Workplace theft, other forms of crime, and alcoholism are widespread among workers. At the same time, a certain element of the relatively highly skilled and better paid workers that is linked to privileged (especially defense) branches of the economy has been drawn into the sphere of the monopolistic corporative interests that engender the fiercest opposition to the market.

The worker who has been shaped by the totalitarian economy is poorly prepared psychologically for free-market conditions, for tough job competition that demands both harder work and greater psychological involvement in the work process. Naturally, many workers are put off by that prospect. Relying on these sentiments, the conservative party and trade-union apparatus and its ideologists are attempting to channel the workers' discontent and protests in support of a right-wing "statist" populism. They are proposing to solve the problems of the working class by rejecting market experiments and establishing a firm "class-based" state authority—in the area of economic management, among others—that could supposedly ensure order in production, a rapid growth in output, and the redistribution of material benefits in the spirit of egalitarianism and social justice. Such neo-Stalinist ideas formed the basis of the platform of the United Working People's Front (UWPF) that the conservatives created, and of a number of other right-wing organizations aspiring to mass influence. In addition to a thinly veiled totalitarianism, they usually are also characterized by a nationalistic orientation and appeals to combat Russophobia, pernicious Western influences, and the enlistment of foreign capital in the economy, an act that is interpreted as "selling out the country to the Western capitalists."

To what extent is this ideological operation succeeding? Unquestionably, there are many signs of worker opposition to radical economic reform and hostility toward the intellectuals who defend the need for it. The speeches of some worker deputies have repeated the motifs of right-wing conservative propaganda. They claim that the development of cooperatives, the leasing of enterprises, and their possible privatization are contrary to the interests of the working class, and beneficial only to the operators of the shadow economy. The high incomes of cooperative members and high prices for cooperatives' products arouse particular anger among workers. Some workers are inclined to believe that the price increases, deterioration of the consumer market, and disorganization of the economic mechanism that have occurred in the years of perestroika are attributable to the continuing alienation of the working class from power, and to the fact that there are far fewer workers than representatives of the apparatus and members of the intelligentsia in the new elective bodies—the Congress of Deputies and the Supreme Soviet. The idea that "professors can't represent workers' interests" has been a persistent theme in many speeches in parliament and statements in the press.

In one such item, an article written by the Moscow worker A. Lyashenko, the author takes an extremely negative view of the process of democratization taking place and claims that it is leading to a new form of "elitist democracy" and the power of professional intellectuals. "Like the administrative-command form of management, it is aimed at expanding and reinforcing the privileges, above all, of the circle of people who are taking the place of the former nomenklatura."[9]

---

[9]A. Lyashenko, "Under the Cover of Democracy," *Pravda*, May 28, 1990.

And of course, elitist democracy and the laws adopted by it serve the interests of the "underground millionaires" and the shadow economy operators. Lyashenko insists on the need for the development of an independent working-class movement to defend the working class's specific interests, but offers no explanation of what those interests are, and how they differ from the programs put forward by the "elitist democrats."

I think that such positions reflect a certain type of mind-set that is widespread in the working class. It is characterized, on one hand, by rejection of the existing system of economic and political relations and the desire to change it in the workers' interests, and on the other, by an inability to conceive independently of a specific plan for such changes, an inability that fosters mistrust in plans that come from a different, "alien" social milieu. Recognition of class interests is limited to the context of immediate economic and social needs and to protests against authoritarian relations and alienation from power, but everything beyond that framework, including radical solutions that would change the foundations of the economic and political system, is rejected with alarm. For it is impossible to get a clear sense of the consequences of such solutions by relying only on the sort of concrete empirical thinking that is typical of a significant part of the working class.

The psychological defense mechanism prompts one to perceive problems that are beyond one's understanding as alien problems imposed by other, potentially hostile social groups. This type of "closed," sectarian class consciousness is well known from the history of the Western workers' movement.

It is not always easy to gauge the extent to which antimarket and anti-intellectual incantations reflect the actual thoughts of the workers who utter them. They are often heard from people with direct ties to the party and trade-union bureaucracy, people selected by it for working-class "representation" on elective bodies. Nonetheless, one can say that they represent certain mass attitudes.

In the fall 1989 survey, only 38 percent of the workers—fewer than all other groups of the employed population—favored the development of new forms of economic management (54 percent of the specialists, 45 percent of the executives, and 48 percent of the office employees favored it). Even less popular among them were such forms as leasing arrangements and individual farming (32 percent), the use of foreign capital (13 percent), and especially, cooperatives and small individual businesses (6 percent). At the same time, 43 percent of the specialists supported leasing agreements, 11 percent favored cooperatives, and 25 percent favored the use of foreign capital.[10] Public

---

[10]*The Population's Attitude Toward Economic Reform*, note 1, above, Table 6.

opinion still reflects a persistent conviction that the workers will suffer
the most from the move to the market. Thus 69 percent of the Moscow
residents questioned in April-May 1990 believed that under market
conditions the workers' situation would deteriorate (48 percent shared
this pessimistic forecast among or about the intelligentsia and 18 percent believed it would hold true for managerial personnel).[11] This fear
of the market, private property, and economic pluralism should probably be regarded as an extremely important sociopsychological asset for
right-wing, conservative trends, for the only alternative to the market
that is being proposed as a way out of the economic crisis is a strengthening of the "principles of socialism" and the planned economy, that is,
a return to the old authoritarian system. In May 1990, 31 percent of
those questioned in a survey of Russian Republic inhabitants favored
"strengthening the planned economy in all branches of the national
economy."[12] Obviously, the plan that the government proposed in
May for the "transition to a market economy," a plan which put off the
practical implementation of radical reforms until the future, while
promising the public a sharp increase in prices in the coming months,
constituted quite an important "argument" in favor of conservative
ideas. A more effective means of compromising the idea of the market
could hardly have been found!

Is it correct, on the basis of all this, to assert that the working class
for the most part shares the right-wing conservative beliefs and is
prepared to support the platform of those who advocate a statist
sociopolitical system? I think that the facts argue against such a conclusion. Bear in mind, for example, that the people's deputies who make
up the radical leftist group in the all-union, Russian Republic, and
other parliaments and in the city soviets were elected in the large
industrial cities and regions. The vast majority of those deputies are
not workers but professors, journalists, lawyers, and engineers. A
survey conducted in a number of big cities of various republics in
July 1989 showed that only 15 percent of those questioned would
prefer to vote for a candidate who is a worker, and for 74 percent the
chief criterion was the candidate's "business" and personal qualities,
rather than the social group and occupation to which he belonged.[13]
Neither the complaint that workers' are poorly represented on elective
bodies, nor the "class approach" to politics on which the right-wing
ideologists and party and trade-union apparatus have insisted has
found a broad response among major population groups, including the

[11]*Moskovskiye novosti* [*Moscow News*], No. 19, May 13, 1990, p. 10.
[12]*Argumenty i fakty* [*Arguments and Facts*], No. 21, May 26–June 1, 1990.
[13]V.G. Britvin, "Who Will Become a Deputy?" *Sotsiologicheskiye issledovaniya*
[*Sociological Research*], No. 6, 1989, p. 23.

working class. It is equally characteristic that the 1989 and 1990 elections in Russia's industrial cities and regions brought defeat to the representatives of right-wing nationalist tendencies.

Thus, in a *political* sense the workers, at least the working class in major industry and in Russia's cities and industrial regions, do not set themselves apart from other groups that oppose the authoritarian power of the apparatus, and are joining the mainstream of the democratic struggle. The contradictions described above manifest themselves chiefly in workers' recognition of their economic and social interests. In that area they have a keener sense of the specific nature of their own group situation, feel mistrust for the groups and social tendencies that are demanding radical reforms, and are afraid that they will sacrifice the workers' interests to their own ambitions and desire for power. A. Lyashenko, the worker quoted previously who was once a member of the Moscow People's Front, claims that "the more seats the 'professionals' gained in the 'parliaments,' the clearer the line was drawn between them and the workers and ordinary people. All my attempts to call their attention to the problems of the ordinary working people drew only a condescending smile from them."[14] There may be grounds for this observation. Judging from their statements, many radical economists and representatives of the liberal intelligentsia, in general, are not particularly interested in the specific problems of the working class, nor in the consequences for it of a rapid shift to the market.

The revival of the workers' movement is critically important to the process of workers' recognizing the connection between their economic and political interests, and to the evolution of their attitude toward radical economic reform. In the strikes that have become widespread in the years of perestroika, primary emphasis, naturally, has been placed on questions of wages, working conditions, pensions, and the supply of basic necessities to industrial regions. But fundamentally new developments emerged in the powerful miners' strike movement that shook the country when it was launched in the coal regions of Russia, the Ukraine, and Kazakhstan in the summer of 1989. In addition to material demands, the miners' strike committees put forward a program of radical economic reforms: calling for complete independence for the enterprises from their Moscow ministry, and for granting them the right to sell a substantial portion of their output themselves and keep part of the profit. This unquestionably represented a step toward market relations. At the same time, the movement had nothing to do with sectarianism and went beyond a narrow class framework:

[14]*Pravda*, May 28, 1990.

Although the miners reacted with mistrust to attempts by the members of various unofficial groups to take part in the movement, they included engineers, specialists, and management employees on their strike committees. In some regions the strikers demanded replacement of the local party and soviet leadership, and the removal of Article 6 of the Constitution.[15] This merger of the economic and political struggle, of opposition to the ruling bureaucracy and to the statist economic system, marks a new stage in the working class's recognition of its own long-range interests, and the beginning of its assimilation of the market-economy principles.

Of course, tendencies of this sort have developed very unevenly in various regions and segments of the working class. As in other developed countries, the Soviet Union's working class is extremely varied in social, occupational, and cultural respects. Sociological studies conducted back in the preperestroika period established fundamental differences in mentality, educational and cultural level, work motivation, and social behavior between relatively unskilled workers engaged in routine work and workers associated with modern, technically advanced production.[16] The local cultural environment also has considerable influence on the level of workers' economic and sociopolitical thinking. From this standpoint, Moscow and Leningrad differ greatly from many provincial regions. According to some data, conservative groups such as the United Working People's Front are mainly supported by the least skilled and least educated workers, while the younger and better-educated workers usually favor radical economic and political reforms.

The independent and organized workers' movement has not yet assumed nationwide scope, and it operates within a relatively narrow occupational and regional framework (mainly in the coal industry). Since the strikes in the summer of 1989, the official trade unions have actively attempted to co-opt it. This has not been easy for them. For many decades the trade unions unquestioningly subjugated themselves to party and state authority and completely degenerated into a bureaucratic institution, a kind of ministry for social affairs. Now the trade-union leadership is trying to change its image and assume the role of defender of the working people's interests. It has disputed several government decisions that have hit the workers' pockets, and it has taken the initiative in proposing a draft law on labor conflicts. A significant number of trade-union functionaries are highly conser-

---

[15]See H. Diligensky, "Strikes and Perestroika," *Novoye vremya* [*New Times*], No. 32, Aug. 4, 1989, pp. 29, 30.
[16]See L.A. Gordon and A.K. Nazimova, *The U.S.S.R.'s Working Class: Trends in and Prospects for its Socioeconomic Development* [*Rabochiy klass SSSR: tendentsii i perspektivy sotsialno-ekonomicheskogo razvitiya*], Moscow, 1985.

vative and share the views of the United Working People's Front and of reform opponents from the party apparatus. The top trade-union leadership has been taking a more moderate line. It has demonstrated simultaneously its support for Gorbachev's course and its relative autonomy with regard to specific issues of economic and social policy. On the whole, the trade-union bureaucracy understands quite well that in the event of the privatization of the economy, entrepreneurs, management, and workers could all get by perfectly well without its services. Therefore, it has a stake in preserving the state sector's dominant role in the economy, and in maintaining a model of industrial relations that would secure its monopolistic right to represent the working people in relations with the patron state. In defending such a model, the trade unions rely on statist economic conservatism and the social passivity of a significant portion of the workers.

All the organizations and movements claiming to represent the interests of the working class are forced to consider, in one way or another, its growing urge to struggle for its own rights and the improvement of its life. But since the workers themselves have an extremely disparate and contradictory understanding of the connection between their interests and the ownership and economic-management system, ideological and political polarization is inevitably growing in the workers' movement. The workers' organizations that emerged on the wave of the strike movement are becoming radicalized.

Thus, in November 1989 the Kuznetsk Basin Union of Working People proclaimed that its goals would be to eliminate the bureaucratic-command system in the economy and to establish the equality of various forms of ownership, including cooperative, joint-stock, and "private-labor" ownership, as well as the right of labor collectives to choose among such forms. [17] The First Congress of Independent Workers' Movements and Organizations, which met in Novokuznetsk in May 1990, formed the Confederation of Labor and adopted a declaration proclaiming the goal of the workers' movement to be "the elimination in practice of the diktat of the CPSU and its apparatus," and "the establishment, from below, of fully empowered agencies of self-management" that would perform the functions of parallel structures of authority. The declaration's authors refer directly to the experience of Poland's Solidarity. [18]

---

[17]L.A. Gordon and E.V. Klopov, "Perestroika, the Independent Workers' Movement, and the Renewal of Socialism," in *The Phenomenon of Socialism: Essence, Regularities, and Prospects* [*Fenomen sotsializma. Sushchnost, zakonomernost, perspektiva*], Moscow, 1990, p. 102.
[18]*Argumenty i fakty*, No. 22, June 2–8, 1990.

Thus, the development of the workers' movement is drawing it closer to the radical leftist flank of the political spectrum, and is enhancing its role in perestroika. However, one must also not fail to consider the possibility that opposite tendencies could grow in the movement. Disappointment with perestroika, from which the working person has yet to receive any real gain, could bring a growing number of workers to the point of alienation from the political struggle and to a strengthened corporative class consciousness that is focused exclusively on their own immediate material interests. That would inevitably increase the influence of conservative, antiperestroika tendencies among such workers. In the event that the radical economic reform succeeds, the working class's group interests will obviously develop in the mainstream of the dialectic of conflict and partnership with the technocracy and entrepreneurs that characterizes industrial relations in the developed Western countries. For the time being, however, that prospect seems rather remote.

* * *

Among the Soviet *peasantry* the development of group interests has followed an even more complex and difficult path than it has among the working class. The rural population is more fragmented and less capable of independent collective action than the urban population, and a substantial segment, especially the young, has weak psychological ties with the interests of its group and many aspire to move to the city. The rural inhabitant's dependence on local authorities and farm executives is even greater than the urbanite's dependence; it forces him to adapt to existing relations and suppresses protest and independence. Factors that erode work motivation and ethics operate even more strongly in the countryside than the city. The existence of many state and collective farms, and their employees' income depend not so much on their production performance as on state subsidies. Rural inhabitants take little part in political life, and in elections they submissively vote for representatives of the apparatus.

All this does not mean that perestroika has had no effect in the countryside. Democratization and the emergence of new elective bodies have given impetus to peasantry's formulation of specific demands and its defense of those demands in the political arena. In the first Congress of People's Deputies and then in the Supreme Soviet, peasant deputies organized their own group and proposed a program of perestroika in agrarian policy. Its main points: the freeing of agricultural enterprises from the diktat of the party and state bureaucracy, higher purchase prices and reduced mandatory deliveries, increased state investment in the agricultural sector, an improved supply of modern machinery for agriculture, and elimination of the scandalously backward infrastructure and the social and cultural spheres (services, medical care, schools, roads, housing) in rural areas.

These demands no doubt reflect the interests of the entire rural population, and its desire to improve its material and social status. At the same time, it is obvious that the demands do not address the basis of the agrarian relations created by collectivization—the collective farm and state farm system that has turned peasants into dependent, hired workers and has destroyed the independent peasant farm. Scholars and journalists have said and written a great deal about the ineffectiveness of these relations, which have brought about a food crisis; official representatives of the peasantry have had the least to say about that. The radical agrarian reform that has now been legislated by the Supreme Soviet providing for the development of rural leasing arrangements and individual farms is an act by the highest political authority that was taken without the least pressure to do so from the peasantry itself.

This paradox is fairly easy to explain. The peasants' representatives in parliament are for the most part farm executives—state farm directors and collective farm chairmen. They are prepared to defend the countryside's interests, but only as far as this is in their own group interest, which consists of maintaining their authoritarian power. Widespread privatization of agriculture would eliminate the need for this rural elite. As for the bulk of the peasantry, for the most part it has not yet shown the ability and will to oppose the relations of hired labor that have been imposed on it. The bold ones who attempt to take advantage of the new laws often encounter bitter resistance from the local authorities and from those same farm chairmen and directors, and consequently, peasants' faith in the effectiveness of those laws is eroding. The social and psychological consequences of the breakdown of the peasantry's class identity also take their toll here: The younger generations of the rural population have largely lost their taste for independent labor, and many prefer an income that, although low, is guaranteed by the state, as opposed to the difficulties and hazards that face the independent farmer.

Lately there have been signs of a differentiation and struggle among various group interests in the agricultural sector. Separate organizations of leaseholders and independent farmers are beginning to form, and the rural elite, for its part, has been toughening its stand and shifting to open criticism of the reform and its instigators. The Peasant Union established in June 1990 has the clear goal of preserving the elite group's monopoly in the representation of peasant interests. In a situation in which an independent peasant movement in support of radical agrarian reform is scarcely possible, the evolving balance of forces clearly does not favor such reform. Evidently, the only thing that can change this situation and activate peasant group interests that coincide with reform goals is a decisive radicalization not just of legislation, but of the state's overall agrarian policy, the creation of favorable economic conditions for the peasant farm, and the abandonment of support for money-losing collective farms and state farms.

Today the Soviet Union is rightly being called a transitional society. In terms of its potential and goals, perestroika is a genuinely revolutionary process, the replacement of one type of society by a fundamentally different one. If this transition is really accomplished, not only will certain situations enjoyed by the social groups that make up society be changed, but the groups themselves will be transformed. Managers and workers, peasants, specialists, and political figures will live and act under conditions that require different vocational and psychological qualities than before, and will follow different "rules of the game." A process is already under way of developing groups that Soviet society has not known for six decades, especially groups of entrepreneurs in various areas and professions. These circumstances are leaving a strong imprint on the recognition of group interests: after all, such interests need to be projected into the future, and to most people that future seems vague and ill-defined. In addition, it is much harder to change one's brain than to change jobs or even habits.

As Academician T.I. Zaslavskaya notes, "among the representatives of every class or social segment, one finds people with differing attitudes toward perestroika." At the same time, she shows that "the ratio of perestroika supporters to opponents differs rather sharply from one social segment to another." Zaslavskaya attributes these differences both to the level of different groups' real interest in the changes, and to specific psychological characteristics of the individuals who make up those groups.[19] One should add yet another fundamental factor: the lack of a clear picture of the alternatives for social development that perestroika is creating. This lack of clarity is in many respects being aggravated by the sluggishness of the perestroika process. Its goals are more often proclaimed than realized in practice, and the degeneration of the old structures is not being accompanied by a sufficiently rapid emergence of new ones: so the crisis condition of society is deepening.

This lack of clarity is slowing the recognition of group interests and causing people to vacillate between different positions and decisions, to demand changes while simultaneously clinging to the familiar forms of life. It seems that society is seriously tiring of this state of affairs and

---

[19]T.I. Zaslavskaya, "Perestroika as a Social Revolution," in *The Sociology of Perestroika*, note 8, above, p. 28.

is feeling a growing desire to cross the Rubicon. This is evident, in part, from the shift in public opinion in favor of moving to a market economy. In May 1990, 58 percent of the Muscovites questioned favored a move to market relations, and of the urban and rural inhabitants of Russia who were polled, 28 percent favored "a complete shift to a market system of operating the economy," and 36 percent favored "the development of market relations in the service sector and in the production of consumer goods." And most of those surveyed did not expect any immediate improvement of their situations as the result of introducing the market.[20] In other words, progress toward fundamentally new relations, and an escape from uncertainty have become psychologically even more important to the majority than has the solution of their own economic problems, a solution which in practical terms is impossible today.

The prospects for such progress are not being realized because of the preservation of the bureaucratic system of power, and the indecisive and inconsistent domestic policies of the country's leadership. This situation is increasingly moving the problems of politics and power to the forefront of Soviet people's interests. The new group interests taking shape are also concentrating on those problems. Obviously, only radical democratic changes in the political area will enable Soviet people to define finally the interest group to which they belong and specifically what those interests are.

---

[20]*Moskovskiye novosti*, No. 19, May 13, 1990; *Argumenty i fakty*, No. 21, May 26–June 1, 1990.

Western Experience and Our Economic Reform

First Article

Viktor Ivanovich Kuznetsov*

"Life shows that planned management that ignores the market criterion and control by the market is just as deficient as a market that is unregulated by a plan" (M.S. Gorbachev, Pravda, *November 16, 1988*).

I was prompted to turn to this topic by an uneasiness that grew as I became acquainted in the general and scholarly press with documents and proposals concerning ways and means of carrying out the radical economic reform in our country. My uneasiness stems from the fact that, as it seems to me, our economic thought is now repeating, at the new stage, a mistake that it has already made once: In specific proposals for introducing new forms for the organization and functioning of the economy, it continues to rely on abstract logical constructions while paying little heed to world historical experience in the successful development and operation of intensive-type national economy. Soviet economists continue to underestimate economic institutions that have been tested and proven in Western practice, despite their seeming recognition that, in addition to the specific laws of the development of production, there are also a whole series of general laws common to different systems.[1]

What is most unsatisfactory is the treatment of such categories as the market and, in particular, the relative importance in it of *a priori* and *post factum* methods of regulation; centralized planning; price formation and prices, including inflation; and monopoly production.

*Chief research associate at the U.S.S.R. Academy of Sciences' Institute of World Economy and International Relations. This article appeared in the March 1989 issue of *MEMO*.
[1]In *Political Economy [Politicheskaya ekonomiya]*, a textbook for higher educational institutions published by Political Literature Publishing House in 1988, the first section is devoted to the general laws of economic development.

Market?

Production relations among lower-level economic entities in the modern developed capitalist economy—corporations, small and medium-sized businesses—are not readily described in market terms. In defining the most essential feature of that economy, Western scholars increasingly use the adjectives "contractual" or "organized," although they also continue to refer to it as "market."[2]

Our own published works either do not deal with the category of "market" or define it in extremely vague terms, and most important— and this is the most misleading thing—they define it, as a rule, as being opposed to planned forms of regulating the social economy. Given our standard economic education, which is based on a more or less thorough "study" of K. Marx's classic *Das Kapital*, the word "market" invariably brings to mind the image of the Nizhnyy Novgorod fair, where craftsmen who had been working all winter would come together in the spring from the entire surrounding region in hopes of finding buyers for their *already produced* goods. It equally brings to mind the stereotype according to which the market is invariably accompanied by uncontrollable forces and anarchy. And that, understandably, is a highly dubious recommendation for proposals that we move to a market form of organizing our economy. So the public at large becomes irate when reading the writings of many of our esteemed economists from the 1960s; that, in part, may explain why it is common practice in our radical reform for favorable statements about the market and decentralization[3] to coexist calmly alongside a de facto ban on direct ties among enterprises if such ties have not been sanctioned in advance by central government bodies.

Just how are direct ties among enterprises organized in the Western economy, and to what extent is the term "market" applicable to them?

The chief principle of the present-day Western market is that a potential producer first finds a buyer for the commodity that he, in principle, is able to and prepared to produce, and only then, after the appropriate and necessary preparation, does he begin production. This principle is directly contrary to the principle of the archaic market-fair: first produce, and then find a buyer. Practically every buying-and-selling transaction between corporations is presently preceded by

---

[2]In one of the latest French textbooks on economics recommended to schoolchildren preparing to enter economic higher schools, the term "market" is defined as "the *organized* meeting of supply and demand for a given type of economic good."

[3]". . . It is impossible to restore normal economic life functions while bypassing or circumventing the socialist market," writes A. Yakovlev (*Pravda*, Dec. 17, 1988).

a written or oral contract that has legal force. This means that the sides assume mutual commitments to fulfill the contract's terms, and any violation of it may entail court-ordered sanctions.

A contract radically changes the state of affairs where market relations are concerned and turns them into a realm of direct ties between producers and customers. The risk of producing without selling practically disappears. Discrepancies between the specifications of products brought to market and the requirements of the buyer are reduced to a minimum. Matters of quality and price, the forms and dates of deliveries and payment, and so on, are spelled out. The contract, to all intents and purposes, is an order to be filled by the contractor. It makes it possible to draw up advance production schedules; plans for procurement of the necessary raw materials, equipment, and manpower; in some cases, plans for research and development; and in all cases, enterprise financial programs. The production process is almost completely removed from the sphere of operation of uncontrollable market forces and anarchy. At the enterprise level it becomes predictable, that is, planned.[4]

The reduction of risk does not mean that all aspects of enterprises' economic activities become predictable. Market forces continue to operate in the form of producers' and customers' competition with one another. Competition affects the level of price and quality, on the one hand, and the extent to which individual enterprises' production capacity is utilized, on the other. The risk of not selling commodities produced is replaced by the risk of being left with underutilized capacity while your competitors are operating at full capacity.

Thus, the contractual form of relations does not weaken the potential for economic compulsion that is inherent in competition. Competition continues to compel producers to improve production, seek new markets and new customers, and reduce unit costs by all means possible. In addition to its negative role—increased unit cost—unused reserve capacity also plays a positive role. It can readily be put into action in the production process at the first sign of a favorable change in market conditions.

Of course, the contractual economy is not devoid of the market economy's negative features either: Enterprises can still go bankrupt or shut down. Nonetheless, experience shows that the social losses in the contractual economy, which combines elements of both plan and market, are less severe than in a pure market economy or purely planned one.

----

[4]S. Otsu, professor of economics at Kyoto University, who was invited to *Izvestia's* editorial offices, said: "Such phenomena as the last-minute rush to meet output targets, or downtime caused by breakdowns of machinery and equipment or the lack of raw materials, are practically unknown in Japan" (*Izvestia,* Jan. 11, 1989).

Major corporations are not the only ones to establish direct ties. Small and medium-sized business also get into the network. Subcontracting relations between large and small companies have become a structural component of Western practice. Simple agreements on deliveries of precisely specified products are complemented by various forms of assistance on the client's part: technological, credit, financial, and organizational assistance. Dictated by big capital, these forms of relations are rapidly becoming standard for subcontractors.

However, relations of the contractual type (let us call them planned- or organized-market relations) have extended beyond the limits of relations among enterprises. In the same or somewhat different form, they also exist in the mass consumer-goods markets.

The process of converting purely market relations between enterprises and the mass consumer to planned-market relations advanced considerably in the 1970s and 1980s, thanks to the computerization and automation of production and the shift to flexible production systems. The increased capability of computer technology made it possible to process huge amounts of information and apply them directly to the management of technological and production processes. Thus, the first qualitatively new harbinger of things to come appeared in the automotive industry. While preserving the assembly-line organization of work, it has shifted partially to working on the basis of individual orders: Every vehicle is assembled and equipped differently on a single assembly line in accordance with its future owner's orders. There are many hundreds of possible variants, given the 20 to 40 types of finish and equipment the buyer can choose from. Before it even begins its existence, the vehicle already has a specific buyer. His requirements are incorporated in the program for the assembly line's operation. People, robots, and automated equipment operate in accordance with that program. A hybrid that was unthinkable relatively recently is being created: standardized mass production, each model of which is built according to an individual order. Of course, this type of service for the buyer is an exception, and it has yet to prove itself and demonstrate its economic feasibility on a larger scale.

Another way of creating quasi-market structures is associated with the improvement of forecasting. Expansion of the volume of information now circulating in Western society, and development of new technical and theoretical methods for its processing and rapid transmission are making it possible to make rather reliable forecasts of consumer demand for specific types of goods and services. Such a forecast, supplemented by a dependable feedback system between producer and seller, provides a basis for effective planning of production of individual consumer products. With this form of organizing production and marketing, the risk of overproduction and accumulation of unsold stocks of finished products is reduced to a minimum. Stocks of finished products that stand for many months, or even many years, have become a great rarity for the Western economy. It has been a long time since that economy has known anything like what occurs in our country, where stocks of goods have reached 1.5 trillion rubles, or 2.5 times the U.S.S.R. national income.[5] The practice of operating with minimal lead time has become widespread in the capitalist countries, not only in the sphere of relations among producers but in producer-merchant relations. Sales costs have been substantially reduced.

The term "self-organizing economy" has appeared in recent publications by Soviet economists: It designates approximately the same sort of intercompany relations described above under the term "contractual economy." Granted, the term has been used in conjunction with terms characterizing various states of the market sphere— monopoly, oligopoly, competition.[6] That does not change things, since the main idea—the possibility of the stable existence of a regularized quasi-market or quasi-planned system of production and marketing based on the autonomy of economic entities at the micro level—is present in both approaches.

The category "self-organizing," however, does reflect a tendency to turn the regulation of process into an absolute, a tendency which is not characteristic of the real Western economy. As an integral system, that economy includes more than the "self-organizing" principle. It necessarily includes a second principle—the centralized regulation of economic and social processes, including the self-organization process itself. Failure to take the mechanism of centralized regulation into account, may give rise to the illusion that in our day highly developed economic systems can dispense with continuous observation and monitoring by the state. At present the world of industrially developed capitalism has no such systems based on a single principle of self-organization or self-regulation.

Some general considerations force one to think that the absence of systems lacking centralized regulation (or of systems having centralized regulation, but of the sort that has developed organically and entirely from the lower economic level—from the base—rather than being at least partially "imposed" by the upper, noneconomic, superstructural levels of the social infrastructure) is no accident, and that the absence of such systems is not evidence of the historical immaturity of the social-production system, but a normal and natural fact.

---

[5] The figure is cited in A. Yakovlev's speech at the Perm Province Party Conference (*Zvezda* [*Star*], Dec. 17, 1988).

[6] See, for example, Ye. S. Popov, "Monopoly and Competition: The Evolution of Capitalist Society's Economic Mechanism" (*Rabochiy klass i sovremennyy mir* [*The Working Class and the Modern World*], No. 1, 1988; No. 1, 1989).

People's production relations constitute what may be the main form of their social relations and interests, but they are not only form. Singling out economic activity from the entire range of human actions has indisputable analytical value and makes it easier for science to grasp social realities. However, turning such an approach into an absolute and applying only economic methods of analysis go against the observation that the closest, unbreakable connection exists among all types of social relations—economic, social, political, cultural, personal.

All contemporary centralized institutions of economic regulation are by origin political in nature; all in one way or another have been created and initially put into action by the state.[7] Contradictions and regular malfunctions (crises) in the economic sphere, and its natural inability to completely "know itself"[8] and effectively overcome its own contradictions have forced society to resort to "outside intervention" and the use of noneconomic methods to rectify economic shortcomings. Moreover, in acting politically, man introduces broader goals and motives into economic dynamics than are inherent in those dynamics themselves. Economic entities' motivation becomes more complex and assumes a more well-rounded, "human" nature than is characteristic of the abstract *homo economicus*. That has always been the case, in all socioeconomic systems. Probably the only difference between present, highly developed production systems and historical systems is that cases of the involuntary oppression, subversion, and even destruction of the economy for the sake of political goals or realizing the narrow social interests of a single group have become more rare. The Western theory and practice of state compulsion and intervention have advanced far enough to understand and take into account the need not to violate economic laws in the name of any political goal whatsoever—not to knock society's principal source of support out from under it.

Centralized regulation is just as essential a constituent of today's social production as is the "contractual economy." Only in organic interaction do they form a dependably and efficiently functioning organism.

---

[7] I think that in the context of present-day credit and monetary systems even the central bank is an institution with a goodly measure of political content.

[8] This inability is natural, since the assertion that no object can be described (defined) completely if one remains "inside" it and uses only internal coordinates of measurement is correct in a general sense. This follows from theorems concerning the incompleteness of formal systems, or from Goedel's theorems concerning the impossibility of proving the noncontradictory nature of a formal system using the means of the system itself (see *Philosophical Encyclopedia* [*Filosofskaya entsiklopediya*], Moscow, 1960, Vol. 1, p. 338). With respect to cybernetic systems, this consequence has been formulated in St. Bir, *Cybernetics and Production Management* [*Kibernetika i upravleniye proizvodstvom*]Moscow, 1963. See also: N. Ya. Petrakov, *Cybernetic Problems of Economic Management* [*Kiberneticheskiye problemy upravleniya ekonomikoy*], Moscow, 1974, pp. 44–52 (thanks to Candidate of Economics Ya. Pappe for help in selecting references.—V. K.).

It is important to stress that the dependability and efficiency of the social system of reproduction as a whole is ensured by a clear-cut division of functions between the centralized and the self-organizing subsystems. As a rule, the center (in the person of the parliament, government, institutions with macroeconomic influence, and/or central bank) very rarely interfere directly in decision-making by individual entities. When the need arises to influence the state of affairs in the lower levels, i.e., when an assessment, based on macrolevel criteria (according to state criteria) of how those affairs are going shows a deviation from the economically, socially, or politically desirable objective, that is when state agencies change certain universal conditions influencing economic activity. These are precisely the factors that company executives usually take into account when making decisions on current operations or investments.

The universal factors include the volume and structure of the flow of credit and money into the economy, the rates of income or sales taxes, the amount and structure of state budgetary expenditures, and the legal norms regulating economic activity. The universal nature of state measures—neither damaging nor advantageous to particular groups of microentities—nonetheless produces differing economic reactions among those subjects. Differences arise because the economic entities differ among themselves in terms of production capacity, financial situation, degree of dependence on one another, and so forth.

Take, for example, an increase in the cost of credit that is undertaken to prevent the "overheating" of the economy and halt the development of inflation. All other conditions being equal, an increase in interest rates results in a drop in the effective demand for investment goods and consumer goods. At the same time, the universality of that measure, or—what amounts to the same thing—the fact that it is mandatory for everyone without exception, guarantees that the new credit terms will force a reconsideration of investment programs by precisely those firms whose estimate of prospective profits from capital investments is not very high. As for businessmen who are confident that their products can be marketed even if they become more expensive (prices will have to be raised to compensate for increased financing costs), they will pay no attention to the government measures. But that is precisely what the center is trying to achieve. After all, only if such a diversified reaction occurs "from below" will attainment of the societal (macroeconomic) goal—elimination of the inflationary boom—not come into contradiction with the need to continue carrying out the promising production projects that society needs.

The basic principle of present-day Western centralized regulation—stimulate or restrain everyone without hindering or helping anyone individually—gives the economic system as a whole additional stability and dynamism.

Central regulating agencies not only monitor and adjust the economic behavior of microentities, they can create artificial "rules of the economic game" for the latter that will prompt them to act along the lines that the center wishes. Antitrust legislation, for example, can slow, stop, or even reverse a tendency toward monopolization, stimulate competition, orient corporations toward reducing unit costs through technological innovation, increase innovation, and so forth. In Western theories of economic regulation, the ability to create artificial market structures is regarded as one of the real methods of implementing state policy.[9]

And so, present-day Western economy cannot be adequately described in either market or planned terms. It represents a centrally regulated system of interaction among autonomous corporations and enterprises that are based on the right of private ownership, and of interaction between all of them taken together and the political and economic upper level. Such a form of organization and self-organization, while giving stability to reproduction processes, does not deprive the system as a whole of the necessary freedom to maneuver, and does not prevent the exercise of initiative "at the local level" by individual economic entities.

The system of regulation of the Western economy can be depicted in the following schematic chart:

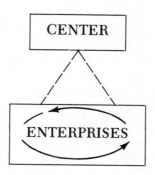

---

[9] Ch. de Boissieu, *Principles of Political Economy* [*Principes de politique économique*], Paris, 1978, p. 88.

Our administrative economy is structured in a fundamentally different fashion:

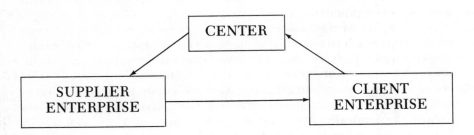

Upon receiving a signal from the user of a final or intermediate product (an enterprise or individual) and deeming it valid, according to its own criteria, the center (the State Planning Committee or other appropriate government agencies) issues a command to producers, after first racking its brains over the problem of providing them with the necessary resources. According to calculations by knowledgeable people, the average period of time it takes to fill an order that has not been provided for in the plan varies from 18 months to two years.[10] In practical terms, this means that by the time the commodity is delivered, it is often either unneeded or no longer meets the client's requirements, which have changed in the meantime. Immense losses that are hard to measure arise because of this rigid, triangular system of decision-making. They in fact constitute the bulk of all losses in our national economy.[11] What society gains from increases in the productivity of equipment at the level of the machine-tool operator is squandered in the exchange process between the producer and the final sale. Hence the plausibility of calculations by some of our economists showing that in some years the entire Soviet economy has worked not for final consumption, but to increase operating capital and stocks of finished and semifinished products.[12]

Nonetheless, a change in the principles governing the exchange and marketing of output—our economy's central problem—is still only in the field of peripheral vision. Moreover, the U.S.S.R. State Com-

[10]This figure was cited by V. Kabaidze, director of the Ivanovo Machine Tool Association, in a report delivered at IMEMO explaining the mechanism whereby statements of requirements for the production of new products are coordinated with the ministry and the U.S.S.R. State Planning Committee. This figure is not at variance with the average time required for the "compilation" and confirmation of an enterprise's five-year plans.

[11]An idea of the scale of combined losses is provided by the figure of 240 billion rubles (40 percent of the national income), a number cited by Yu. Brovko at a round table conducted by *Literaturnaya gazeta* [*Literary Gazette*] (November 11, 1988, p. 10).

[12]"In certain years increases in national income have not even covered the increase in material stocks" (V. Selyunin, *Sotsialisticheskaya industriya* [*Socialist Industry*], January 5, 1988).

mittee for Material and Technical Supply, which is preparing the reform, views such change primarily in terms of wholesale trade, which it understands to mean precisely direct ties among enterprises and the development of a network of economically independent enterprises serving as wholesale middlemen. The administrative, centralized approach to determining which products are best distributed directly and which through middlemen does not guarantee that an optimal balance will be found between contractual sales and trade-based methods of selling. Rather, an emphasis on trade threatens to result, along the way, in the growth of a cumbersome intermediate level of economically autonomous wholesale and retail offices that will, for all intents and purposes, feed parasitically on production. Yet in the Western economy wholesale middlemen service only a relatively small part of the total turnover of goods. In the United States, for example, only one-third of all industrial output is marketed through wholesale trade in the direct sense of that word.[13] The nature of the ties permitted among enterprises will also be of fundamental importance for us. As the first steps in this area have shown, it seems that even deliveries imposed outright by the U.S.S.R. State Planning Committee at prices set from above will be considered wholesale trade. This procedure has nothing in common with the contractual practice, whereby, in the first place, it is primarily the commitment to deliver output, rather than output proper, that is sold, and in the second place, all the terms of a contract, including amounts, quality, and so forth, are agreed upon directly and solely by the two contracting parties.

Given the relatively high level of concentration and centralization of production (there are fewer than 47,000 industrial enterprises in our country),[14] the establishment of a reliable system of direct ties among all enterprises[15] would solve the problem of their developing reliable production and delivery plans over a period of several weeks, and would free the U.S.S.R. State Planning Committee from this thankless task once and for all.

However, the problem of the transition to a contractual market arrangement for the exchange of goods and services is not limited to the reliable exchange of information, which is just one aspect of it. It

---

[13]S. Komlev, *U.S. Domestic Trade: Organizational and Structural Changes* [*Vnutrennyaya torgovlya SShA: organizatsionno-strukturnyye sdvigi*], Moscow, 1987, p. 13.

[14]*The USSR National Economy in 1987* [*Narodnoye khozyaystvo SSSR v 1987 g.*], Moscow, 1988, p. 81.

[15]If desired, such a tie could be established very rapidly. The French program for the development of a network of "minitels" (a keyboard, a CRT, a printer and a telephone) linked through a central processor has garnered more than 3 million users in the less than 10 years that it has been in operation. By the time it is completed, there will be 5 million users. A "minitel" makes it possible not only to seek and distribute information and to enter into direct contact with a partner, but also to call up all documents in written form, exchange them, carry out payments, and so forth.

also comes up against a key aspect of implementation of our economic reform—the reluctance to change or fear of changing the existing procedure for setting prices.

Price

A market, organized or not, cannot exist without market prices. They can be monitored from the center, regulated, temporarily frozen or raised, but for all these and many other manipulations to be carried out, the prices must originally result from an encounter between demand and supply, and the clear-cut expression at that moment of the free will of contracting parties. In short, any price must begin its subsequent existence, in all of its potential metamorphoses (intermediate, monopolistic, administered, fixed, etc.), as a market price.

Is that really so necessary? Should the proposed thesis be formulated in such a rigid and uncompromising fashion? After all, we have lived with planned prices that have been set once and for all![16] Lived poorly, perhaps, but lived.

We do live, of course, trying not to notice that the lack of market-oriented production and a market worthy of the name has deprived our country of a mechanism of equivalent exchange based on the law of value. That this has caused our economy hard-to-repair damage in the form of imbalances, which have gotten far out of hand, between production and consumption, savings and investments, the material-production and the services sectors, effective demand and available goods, and so forth. These imbalances have gotten so far out of hand that one does not know how to approach the task of setting them straight without risking economic collapse or social outrage.

In order to understand the importance of market prices, one must have a clear conception of their economic function.

In a living, real economy in which the interests of all producers of goods and services and of all consumers with earned incomes at their disposal encounter and complement one another without impediment, all of the components of such an economy are constantly changing: labor productivity, structure of unit costs, incomes, demand. The task of market prices is to react to those changes as quickly as possible and to transform them into quantitative magnitudes, that is, to measure them by determining the proportions of the exchange of the commodity equivalent for the monetary equivalent. A sound market price constantly fluctuates, thereby seeking out the true monetary-

---

[16]Prices, of course, change and are revised. But this happens every time as though it were independent of the will of the central economic authority, under the pressure of insurmountable objective circumstances, which, moreover, have the bad habit of not following subjective orders from above.

value proportions between outlays of individual (isolated) labor and social need. If you forbid fluctuation of market prices or, in general, deprive the act of buying and selling of its essential content—the conflict between the interests of the producer and the interests of the consumer—myriad small changes occurring on the supply side and the demand side will start to accumulate and create conditions for the development of a black market, speculation, fraud, theft, shortages in some places and surpluses in others—in short, the familiar conditions of an unbalanced economy.

What other agency, what office, besides the market, can cope with the task of taking prompt and complete account of all those countless changes without which people's economic activity is unthinkable, and of bringing them, with the help of prices, within the limits of the dynamic equilibrium of the economic system as a whole? If such an agency were created, its staff would number at least as many employees as there are economic entities acting in the economic arena. And in that connection, a strange situation would arise: in order to endow bureaucratic personnel with the right to establish equilibrium prices, it would be necessary to deprive producers and consumers of their inherent economic functions, leaving them only the legal duty to work and the legal duty to consume.

Only the joint participation of all producers and all consumers in acts of mutual exchange of the products of their labor for the monetary equivalents of those same products in the form of earned income can accomplish the task of maintaining the planned and proportional development of social reproduction. Such participation presupposes the existence of a market mechanism.

For a long time our economic science proceeded from the postulate that the worst directive plan was better than the best market. Within the framework of that postulate, "invariable" prices established by directive were considered not only a natural attribute of a planned economy, but one of socialism's great achievements. Yet the initial postulate itself was never put to either a strictly logical or dispassionate empirical test for absolute validity.

The postulate was based on at least two widely accepted theses. The first was a logical conclusion drawn on the basis of observing the process of development of the social nature of labor, in the course of which isolated and routine production processes are transformed into socially combined and scientifically directed ones. In other words, this is a matter of the replacement, at a fairly high stage in the development of machinery production, of commodity relations with rigid, technologically determined relations among workers performing various types of labor.[17] Given a fairly advanced state of the socialization of

---

[17]See, for example, K. Marx and F. Engels, *Collected Works* [*Sobraniye sochineniy*], 2nd edition, Vol. 23, pp. 642, 397, 431, 497, 641, etc.

production, and on the condition that private property has been converted into public or state property, the theoretical possibility is created of calculating the volume and structure of social consumption *a priori* and *in natura*, without resorting to the subsequent use of market relations to verify the social validity of the correlations that have been obtained in this calculation. V.I. Lenin also wrote about organizing social production according to the principle of a single large enterprise.[18]

History, on the one hand, confirmed the truth of this thesis in the course of World Wars I and II; on the other, it radically corrected it in the course of the normal development of a highly intensive economy during the postwar period. As it turned out, market mechanisms underwent an extremely powerful transformation, but on the whole they maintained their role in regulating the proportions of social production. Moreover, even when the achieved level of concentration of capital and its power over production have provided every reason for moving to directive planning in vast spheres of the economy (for example, within the framework of large, diversified corporations), businessmen under the pressure of the laws of the efficient organization and management of large systems have created within the economic formations subordinate to them artificial conditions of competition among individual units, endowing those units with economic independence and the authority to make decisions that require the exercise of initiative.

As for the experience of the wartime economy, it served for Russian Marxists and Soviet economists as a second powerful argument in favor of introducing directive planning and abandoning market-type regulating levers. The war showed that "monopoly capitalism is turning into state-monopoly capitalism, and by virtue of the pressure of circumstance, the social regulation of production and distribution is being introduced in a number of countries. . . ."[19]   That really was the case, and World War II confirmed the tendency that had first appeared from 1914 to 1918. But in the conclusion drawn about the universal significance of the processes that had been noted, two circumstances were overlooked: the brevity of the war periods, and the disastrous impoverishment of the assortment of end products produced.

---

[18]"The entire national economy, organized like a post office—that is our immediate goal" (V. I. Lenin, *Complete Works*, Vol. 31, p. 449). Lenin's thinking was always concrete and historical. Hence it is not surprising that the change in the conditions of social production in 1918 to 1920 led him to the conception of the New Economic Policy, which was based on the principle of the use of a planned market mechanism for regulating the economy. However, that did not prevent Lenin's earlier propositions from the period of War Communism from being turned into absolutes during the Stalin period and later.

[19]V.I. Lenin, *Complete Works*, Vol. 31, p. 449.

Neither World War I nor World War II lasted beyond four or five years. Therefore, the genuinely rigid framework of directive management and centralized planning and regulation, which arose after a state of war existed and full power was concentrated in the hands of the central executive offices,[20] "worked" effectively for too short a time to make it possible to recommend, with confidence, the extension of that experience to a longer historical period.

In postwar Soviet economic literature, the transition from wartime nonmarket economy to postwar market economy was always treated as the natural consequence of the historical immaturity of the capitalist system, in which social production is controlled by private owners of the means of production, who favor the market and its anarchic freedom from all restrictions. No one rose to the level of analyzing that transition from the standpoint of the growth in the efficiency and rationality of social production that was achieved as the result of decentralization. Even raising the question in such a way was frightening because of its "obvious anti-Marxism" and the fact that it contradicted the established convictions of the majority.

Yet even a cursory glance at the specific features of the wartime economy, both ours and that of the capitalist countries, indicates that the effectiveness of direct, command methods of central management and planning was always inseparable from a reduction in the number of items produced. The state authority controlled all the constituent parts of final demand: weapons and everything necessary for the army, and the volume and structure of the civilian population's consumption (the rationing system). It also distributed scarce resources, and all of them, from raw materials and machinery to manpower and scientific and technological research, rapidly became scarce, as soon as the war or forced preparations for it began. Food was reduced to a few basic products; clothing, to military or military-type uniforms; housing, to available stocks; medical care, to surgery and measures to prevent epidemics; and so forth. The wartime economy is social production simplified to the utmost, an economy of survival and poverty.

What the notorious efficiency of the wartime years' centralized planning rested on was maximum simplicity; the practical possibility of encompassing all social relations from above; the deliberate refusal, for the sake of the survival of at least some social structures, to take into account interreactions between those responsible for implementing directives and those who were in their charge (wartime coercion and absolute discipline); in short, on the reduction of the self-developing

---

[20]The planned nature of the wartime economy of 1939 to 1945 is examined, using the example of France, in my book *The Mechanism of the State-Monopoly Regulation of the French Economy* [*Mekhanizm gosudarstvenno-monopolisticheskogo regulirovaniya frantsuzskoy ekonomiki*], Moscow, 1979.

and self-organizing civil society to a barracks. A mandatory feature of the wartime economy was prices that were set once and for all. The law of value practically ceased to operate, making its hidden existence known only through the black market and covert speculation.

Any production is efficient and rational only so long as its end result is socially useful products. Only the free marketing of products can determine social necessity. "The market . . . performs the function of spontaneously keeping account of commodity producers' socially necessary expenditures of labor."[21] Free exchange between autonomous economic entities is the central feature of a normally functioning economic system. The lack of it sooner or later deprives social production of such qualities as rationality, efficiency, technological progressiveness, and ultimately, social progressiveness as well.

These statements about free exchange should not be interpreted as an appeal for a pure or perfect market.

In real Western life prices, of course, are not determined in the course of each separate deal. The haggling that leads to agreement on price between seller and buyer has become a relative rarity. Most goods are sold at advertised (marked) or list prices; many are sold at prices that are legislatively fixed and regularly, but relatively infrequently, revised. Such a practice is convenient and does not raise objections among buyers. At the same time, since the seller reserves the right to revise prices at any moment, marked and listed prices do not prevent a flexible reaction to the constantly changing conditions of supply and demand. They quite reliably perform their assigned economic function as the representatives of market prices.

As already emphasized, political institutions can, if they so desire, introduce their own rules governing economic operations. Joining the series of other economic factors that every economic entity takes into account when making decisions, these rules influence the configuration of the buying-selling transaction: the amount of supply, the magnitude of demand, the level of prices. State goals are thereby achieved without direct interference by the center in the exchange process. This being the case, the form of the market and the number of enterprises operating in it are not of fundamental importance. Whether the market is free, oligopolistic, or even, under certain circumstances, monopolistic, the very fact of a clash of interests between contracting parties belonging to the two great economic camps—production and consumption—produces the desired effect.

---

[21]*Economic Encyclopedia: Political Economy* [*Ekonomicheskaya entsiklopediya: Politicheskaya ekonomiya*], Moscow, 1979, Vol. 3, p. 524.

Of course, deviations of price from value are inevitable. Only through its constant deviation from value, Marx noted, can price realize the law of value.[22] Deviations may be transient, stable, and even fixed in the price structure on a long-term basis—in any case, the incessantly repetitive nature of the acts of exchange, and the participation of all economic entities in them guarantees the genuinely social nature of the assessments[23] better than any surrogate proposed by government agencies.

The tendency to replace the functional approach with a statistical approach manifested itself early in our administered economy. In the case of price formation, it expressed itself in the practice of using average outlays for a given industry as the basis for calculating price levels. In this practice, the fundamental differences between the process by which the real market prices of goods lead to an average industry price, on the one hand, and the operation of calculating the average industry price on paper by adding up all industry costs, on the other, were dismissed as insignificant. Those costs, increased more or less arbitrarily by several percent, were called production prices, although the main condition for the formation of production prices—competition within the industry—was lacking. In such a calculation of prices, living economic activity is represented by only one of its sides—the production side. That production acquires meaning only after its product has won the acceptance of all members of society is ignored. And if that condition is not met, nothing guarantees that the production process will not turn into the senseless expenditure of materials and people's energy.

The statistical method of dealing with economic magnitudes harbors a constant danger. At present the press is writing a lot about a reform being prepared in the depths of the State Prices Committee. And what is being written does not inspire optimism. The clearest formulation of the content of the reform has been provided by I. Gorbachev, deputy chairman of the U.S.S.R. State Committee on Prices, in a round-table discussion published in *Literaturnaya gazeta* [*Literary gazette*]. Noting that "our present prices have lost the function of assessing real value and turned from a planning and measuring category into an accounting and distribution category," he cited what in his opinion were two fundamental differences between the retail-price reform now in progress and previous such reforms: (1) the fact that it is to be carried out in conjunction with a reform of wholesale and procurement prices, and (2) the intention of the State Prices Commit-

---

[22]See K. Marx and F. Engels, *Collected Works*, 2nd edition, Vol. 25, Part I, pp. 189-218.
[23]*Ibid*, p. 194.

tee to turn the price system "into an objective measurement of the results of economic activity that consistently reflects, in prices, socially necessary expenditures of labor for the production and sale of products, those products' consumer properties and quality, and the effective demand for them; and to structure prices in accordance with the requirements of objective economic laws."[24]

The passage cited arouses profound concern. Every word in it reflects a claim to genuinely divine omniscience, omnipotence, and total license. The things that the Western economy, with its proven effectiveness in matters of prices, does automatically through market trade and direct ties among enterprises, the State Prices Committee intends to accomplish through the efforts of several thousand specialists. In the West there are hundreds of millions of people carrying out billions of transactions every day, thereby fairly reliably monitoring the economic validity of prices. Here we have a handful of technocrats who aspire to accomplish tasks that cannot, in principle, be accomplished by bureaucratic methods: the measurement of socially necessary expenditures of labor, and of the consumer properties and quality of goods. All this is a typical case of attempting to reform a living social organism in accordance with yet another abstract scheme. It will be impossible to make that reform successful. The central government simply will not have the necessary information and data-processing capacity to do so. And the initiators of the radical reform clearly recognized that. After all, the very understanding of the need to carry it out grew precisely out of a recognition of the central government's increasing helplessness in the face of the growing avalanche of information that the modern developed economy generates.

With depressing inevitability, the position taken by the State Prices Committee will lead the country along the same path that it has followed so far—the path of the maximum simplification of economic ties. And first and foremost, the simplification and standardization of the structure of consumption.

And so, "let's agree on the main point," as A. Levikov concludes his article "Prices and the Market," "the economy that ignores the law of value is incapable of providing its citizens with a selection of goods at fair prices. It guarantees only one abundance—the abundance of shortages."[25] We urgently need to look constantly at real historical experience, temporarily putting aside the invention of new abstract schemes, no matter how fine they may seem to their authors and to those who commission them.

---

[24]*Literaturnaya gazeta*, Nov. 9, 1988, p. 10.
[25]*Literaturnaya gazeta*, Dec. 14, 1988, p. 10.

However, at this point I am sharply interrupted by V. Stepanchenko, deputy chairman of the U.S.S.R. State Committee on Prices. He sets forth the principles for the development of a new price system based on industry normative unit-cost; he promises "to expand the rights of enterprises in the area of price setting, democratize that process, and prevent it from resulting in a price increase"; and he projects the use of three levers: a unified methodology of price setting, uniform economic normative rates to be applied in developing prices, and stronger control over price discipline at the local level. The critical remarks of O. Latsis, who, in his own words, was "flabbergasted" by the thesis concerning the three levers, and suggested the desirability of taking world economic practice into account, drew a categorical rejoinder: "I must say, in all seriousness, that I simply see no other ways to resist a rise in prices."[26]

The above passage is not cited to try dispute or refute it. It speaks for itself. What is important is something else. Hovering invisibly over the roundtable conducted by *Kommunist*, as it has over many other discussions, was the key word in our entire discussion of the principles of price reform: inflation, an increase in the general level of prices. Most theoreticians and practitioners of reform have strived not to allow this evil into our country, and if they cannot succeed in doing so, to at least reduce its destructive effect to a minimum and rapidly neutralize it. To this end, they are prepared to sacrifice the heart and the point of the whole radical reform of our economy: the development of a market and the creation of a system of direct ties.

As we know, inflation is a characteristic feature of the present-day capitalist economy. Just how does the West get along with it, while managing in the process to preserve a high level of efficiency and speed up the intensification of production? Doesn't the phenomenon of inflation have some aspects that are commonly ignored by our economic science? This question deserves special analysis, analysis that is as unhurried as possible.

---

[26]*Kommunist*, No. 18, 1987, p. 29.

Western Experience and Our Economic Reform

Second Article

Viktor Ivanovich Kuznetsov*

In one of his interviews, O. Latsis compared the state of our economy in the fourth year of perestroika to an airplane that had broken out of a spin and gone into a controlled dive. If we used the same image to assess the discussion of price reform, we would get the reverse sequence. T. Zaslavskaya spoke rather emphatically in the magazine *Kommunist*[1] of the need to revise the price structure by raising prices of unprofitable products. She was supported by specialists and almost unanimously rejected by the broad public. By the end of 1988 the discussion had turned into a set of contradictory views united by the common reluctance to admit that without a rise in prices, that is, without inflation, it would be impossible to restructure our neglected economy. And although the inflationary component of the growth of our production had reached 4 to 8 percent,[2] the discussion turned in the direction of seeking noninflationary versions of reform. The former supporters of raising prices started to move into the camp of the "stabilizers."

Having noted the obvious fear of the word "inflation" among specialists and the public, I asked myself: Just how has the West managed over the entire postwar period to combine the "absolute evil" of a practically continuous rise in the general level of prices with an improvement in the workers' living standard and the accomplishment of effective, intensive-type economic development? The West has succeeded where our economy, with its system of rigidly fixed, unchangeable prices—that is, an economy that is noninflationary in the formal sense—has stumbled.

*Chief research associate at the U.S.S.R. Academy of Sciences' Institute of World Economy and International Relations [IMEMO]. This article, which is a sequel to the preceding article on the same subject, appeared in the July 1989 issue of *MEMO*.

[1]*Kommunist*, No. 13, 1986, pp. 61-73.
[2]*Literaturnaya gazeta*, Nov. 9, 1988, p. 10.

This is not an easy question, and the answer to it will require time and the reader's patience.

Inflation

Inflation is currently understood as the combination of several symptoms that characterize a specific state of the economy. An economy can be called inflationary if it exhibits a steady rise in overall prices; if that rise is not haphazard but self-sustaining (cumulative, as the specialists say) in nature; if it is caused by serious macroeconomic disproportions in the principal macroeconomic relationships (such as the ratios of supply to demand, accumulation to consumption); and if the economic entities acquire an inflationary type of behavior, assuming in their decision-making an inevitable rise in prices in the near future. Two types of inflation are distinguished, "creeping" and "galloping." In this connection, some Western economists are inclined to regard the increased amount of money in circulation usually characterizing an inflationary economy as a consequence of the credit and monetary system's passive adaptation to the changing demand for money by economic entities. Others consider that the main supplier of money is the state, which is capable of regulating the amount in circulation.

In this definition, focus has been shifted from the formal condition for development of the inflationary process (too much paper money in circulation) to the causes for its development and the mechanism sustaining it. It is thereby emphasized that the sources of inflation must be sought in the disturbance of the economic balance, while inflation itself is only the economy's spontaneous reaction to the violation of the law of value. Sooner or later, ignoring the law of value inevitably means the use of coercion by the government against all the creative forces of society. Overt inflation at least makes the problem generally accepted, demanding elimination of the processes that have caused and sustained the disproportions in the economy.

Current theories of inflation cite several main factors giving rise to monetary disproportions in the economy:[3] imbalance between revenues and expenditures of the government, especially if the deficit is covered by compulsory loans from the central bank or by the printing of money; similar methods of financing investments—withdrawals from today's product with the promise to compensate for them in the future through new production; monopolistic price-setting or price-setting by administrative fiat, which under the conditions of developed

---

[3]See "Present-Day Inflation: Sources, Causes, and Contradictions [Sovremennaya inflyatsiya: istoki, prichiny, protivorechiya], Moscow, 1980.

credit and monetary transactions results in so-called one-sided price elasticity; a rise in production costs, including labor costs, outstripping the increase in labor productivity; a rise in the prices of imported goods, and so forth.

The mechanism whereby inflation develops can be illustrated using the diagram of the "three P's" proposed by the French economist R. Courbis.[4] Without including all the inflationary factors, it relies on three postulates that fairly accurately reflect the behavior of economic entities. The "principle of productivity" is based on the observation that, as a rule, the wages in an industry rise in proportion to the growth in the industry's labor productivity. The "principle of parity" states that wage earners of equal qualifications endeavor to achieve equal compensation for their work, regardless of what industry they work in. The "principle of purchasing power" reflects the fact that, in the struggle to maintain their living standard, wage earners generally seek regular increases in their money incomes that keep pace with the rate of increase in prices of consumer goods and services.

If all three postulates are correct, one can construct the following diagram of the cumulative growth in the general price level:

CUMULATIVE GENERAL RISE OF PRICES

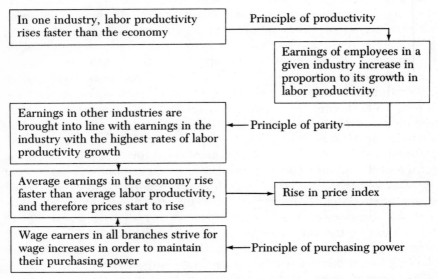

According to the diagram, inflation arises and is sustained as a naturally developing, continuous process. The inflationary effect arises

---

[4]J. Bremont and A. Geledan, *Dictionnaire économique et social*, Paris, 1981, pp. 213-214.

from the interaction of two different laws: the law of the growth of labor productivity, and the law of the value of manpower. The first expresses the distinctive features of scientific and technological progress, the economic effect of which is differentiated by industry. The effect of the second is universal, and if it is differentiated at all, it is differentiated among countries and regions. The inflationary effect arises, in particular, because a rapid growth in productivity in one industry is not necessarily attributable to increased efforts by the workers in that industry. In fact, it is more likely that the growth is due to an increase in the technical productivity of equipment developed and produced in other industries—in particular, in the research and development area, where there is no adequate yardstick for measuring labor productivity. The socioeconomic mechanism compensates for the "unfairness" of an increase in wages proportional to the rise in technical labor productivity in one industry by bringing into line the rate of wage increases in other industries, where the rate of labor productivity growth is lower. The result of this leveling process is a general increase in prices.

The structural nature of the factors that give rise to inflation make this process an integral part of the modern, highly developed social economy, and a characteristic feature of the current stage in the development of capitalism. By now the process of the socialization of production has gone so far that it has resulted in a narrowing of the sphere of operation of the law of value in all markets—commodity, money, and manpower—and in the multiplication of various sorts of nonmarket forces. In Western economics, this phenomenon has been termed institutionalization.

The concept of institutionalization retains a certain vagueness. "Nonetheless," write Canadian economists G. Breton and C. Lavasseur, "employing the category of institutional forms is extremely useful, since this category marks a break with the idea of the economy as some sort of pure essence, as the economy of a balanced and harmonious world . . . that has been purged of precisely everything that gives it the fullness and richness of societal life. . . ."[5]

Institutionalization has encompassed practically all aspects and forms of markets. Thus, the labor market has been fundamentally transformed since collective contracts covering wages and procedures for organizing the work process have become common; since a minimum wage has been legislatively established and become the point of departure for calculating the whole wage scale; since the practice of indexing the growth in nominal wages to price increases has been

[5]G. Breton and C. Levasseur, "Etat, rapport salarial et compromis institutionnalisés: rappels élémentaires sur l'impossibilité de penser l'Etat en dehors du politique" (Conférence prononcée à Barcelone, dans le cadre du Colloque international sur la théorie de la régulation), Barcelona, June 16-18, 1988, p. 8.

introduced; since a system of social assistance and social security has been established; and finally, since the government has taken over the financing of certain extremely important forms of social services (health care, education).

Institutionalization has made fundamental changes in the process of the reproduction of capital. If all the institutional forms that have been enumerated are translated into the language of production costs, it is not hard to see that those costs have become relatively fixed, practically independent of the level of demand for the commodity being produced. The level of the market prices in a heavily institutionalized economy is predetermined by costs.

When outlays are to a certain extent fixed, any weakening of demand for a specific item results either in a reduction in its supply (loss of market share) or, if the producer decides to lower the price, in a disproportionately large reduction in profits and rates of profitability, which severely disturbs the process of the reproduction and accumulation of fixed and working capital. (For example, given unit costs of 90 percent of the price of a product and, accordingly, a 10-percent profit,[6] a one-percent reduction in the price of a product produces a 10-percent reduction in the amount of profit; a 10-percent price drop leaves the businessman without any profit at all.) If one considers that business profits include both fixed revenues and revenues that can hardly be reduced,[7] it becomes clear why voluntary reduction of the nominal price of goods is practically gone as an element of market behavior in the strongly institutionalized economy. Price increases, on the contrary, are becoming customary. Our economic scholarship traditionally interprets this trend as a sign of the monopolization of the exchange sphere and, accordingly, as a deliberate, if not malicious, strategy on the part of monopolies.[8] Yet in the institutionalized economy this phenomenon, while remaining monopolistic in nature, does not always owe its inception to a producer's monopoly. Its sources may lie in other types of monopoly, including a government monopoly on the establishment of production and economic relations in the form of mandatory legal norms. In this case the businessman himself is more the victim than the initiator of the monopoly.

---

[6]Ten percent is a very high rate. In 1958 to 1982, average before-tax profits for the U.S. processing industry amounted to 7.9 percent of price, while after-tax profits amounted to 4.9 percent (*Profit Rates and the Transfer of Capital* [*Norma pribyli i pereliv kapital*], Moscow, 1987, p. 207).

[7]As an example, one can cite dividends on preferred stock, the amount of which is fully defined. It is extremely dangerous for a corporation to pay dividends on common stock that are lower than expected, since that may cause the value of the corporation's stock to drop below the value of its real assets, and it will become the victim of stock speculators. It is practically impossible to avoid major losses if one terminates the financing of previously undertaken investments merely because profits drop.

[8]See *Bourgeois Economic Scholarship on the Problems of Economic Cycles and Crises* [*Problemy ekonomicheskikh tsiklov i krizisov v burzhuaznoy ekonomicheskoy nauke*], Moscow, 1988, p. 26.

If inflation was made inevitable by the process of the all-encompassing institutionalization of economy, it was made possible by the shift from the gold standard to paper money.

Outwardly (historically), paper or, more precisely, credit-based money[9] resulted from the forced abandonment during World War I, and then in the period between the wars, of the circulation of gold-backed bank notes. Later it became clear that, in doing so, humanity had made one of its most brilliant discoveries—one it was led to by the objective laws of economic development. Not only had the fantastically costly "gold corset" increased the cost of operating monetary systems, but poorly managed inward and outward flows of the metal in circulation channels were detrimental to the regular reproduction of capital, created or significantly deepened economic crises, and resulted in a tremendous waste of social labor.

Credit-based money made it easier to mobilize money and finance investments, and it brought possibilities of accumulation beyond the limits of the discretionary saving of monetary capital, creating or reviving on a new basis numerous forms and methods of compulsory borrowing from present generations for the benefit of their descendants—methods ranging from the primitive (printing more money) to the most refined (the liquid forms of long-term investments of money that became widespread in the 1980s).[10]

Credit-based money made it easier to mobilize money and financing in relation to the amount of money in circulation and, by making financing dependent on the demand for money exhibited by economic entities, made it possible to maintain price competition in the context of an all-encompassing institutionalization of economy. The purchasing power of credit-based money is readily subject to erosion, and for that reason it can, without disturbing the course of real reproduction, service the exchange of goods and services whose prices are increasing. At the same time, inflation permits business executives to continue using price as a means of competition by simply regulating the rate at which their prices increase. In contrast to price reductions, slowing the rate of price increases does not require them to accomplish a suicidal task of attacking the fixed revenues included, indeed, into production costs as outlays. Against the backdrop of "creeping" inflation, without violating laws on minimum wages, on fixed rates of deductions for social security, or on tax payments to central and local governments, and without requiring the early revision of collective-bargaining contracts previously concluded with employees—in short,

[9]See, for example, G.G. Matyukhin, *Problems of Credit-Based Money Under Capitalism* [*Problemy kreditnykh deneg pri kapitalizme*], Moscow, 1977.

[10]See, for example, A. Aninkin, "The Structure and Functioning of Present-Day Financial Capital," *MEMO*, No. 11, 1987.

while continuing to adhere in a law-abiding fashion to all the restrictions imposed on business by society—the executive of an enterprise retains the ability to compete in the market. It makes no difference that all prices rise. What has always been important for successful price competition are not nominal but relative prices—how they compare with those of other sellers in the market.

The preservation of price competition (and any competition can ultimately be represented as price competition) means preserving the market instrument for comparing social (effective) demand with individual production costs of the goods and services that satisfy that demand. Preservation of competition and of the market mechanism, albeit in transformed form, means the continued operation of the main factor that motivates producers to make technological progress and actively introduce its advances into production. It is precisely in that sphere that the West has demonstrated its advantage over the administered economy of "real socialism."

Income

The dislike of inflation by broad segments of the public and by specialists has to do with its social consequences. Erosion of the purchasing power of money means, at the same time, devaluation of fixed incomes and of savings in monetary form. In our country the dispassionate discussion of questions of price setting and price reform is made more difficult by the long-cultivated myth that general price increases are incompatible with the principles of socialist economic management. Consequently, any technical and professional discussion of prices automatically takes on ideological and political overtones, forcing specialists to be so cautious in their statements that their very positions often become incomprehensible.

The problem of the compatibility of price increases with the stability of incomes exists in the West, too. As of the present, it can be considered to have been more or less solved, at least in the industrially developed countries.

How has this been done? The negative social effect of inflation has been minimized, if not completely eliminated, through two types of state policies: (1) implementation of measures to prevent "creeping" inflation from turning into "galloping" inflation (anti-inflationary policies), and (2) indexation of the rise in incomes to the rise in retail prices of the "basket" of consumer goods that define the consumption pattern income of a typical family (an element of incomes policy). The mechanisms of both types of policy are far from perfect, but on the whole, especially during the 1950s and 1960s, they have proven their effectiveness and social usefulness.

Since World War II the capitalist world has experienced two great waves of inflation: during the transition from a military economy to a regulated, market-type economy (1945 to 1952) and in the 1970s following the two oil shocks, which shook the whole structure of world and national wholesale and retail prices (1974 to 1981). In both cases, it took several years to stop the cumulative inflationary processes and calm the spontaneous forces that had gotten out of control. During the years of fighting inflation, severe drops in rates of production growth were caused by the effect of government measures.

The dilemma of anti-inflationary policy is that the main controls used to stop the cumulative effect of inflation simultaneously retard economic growth and curb consumer purchasing power.[11] Indeed, suppose that, following the classical view that the cause of inflation is a "surplus of money in circulation," the experts recommend "shutting off the flow of excess money that is overflowing the circulation channels."[12] But as soon as you examine that flow, you discover that it does not simply pour mechanically into certain channels through which goods and services circulate, but, before entering those channels, forms and creates a continuously reproduced effective demand among vast social groups of the population. What is more, the latter most often occupy an economically or politically important place in society; otherwise, the government would not consider violating the principles of sound money circulation. For those groups of people, "shutting off the flow of excess money" is a life-or-death matter. Mere discussion of the question of diminishing their income is unacceptable to them, since they are utterly blameless for the fact that their life is financed by the printing press.

At the basis of any inflation lies a disturbance of fundamental economic proportions. Therefore, combating inflation, too, is also no simple matter of "shutting off channels," but a matter of serious and long-term *structural* policy aimed at overcoming economic disproportions. They cannot be eliminated through one-shot reforms that "set everything straight once and for all."

The Western postwar economy (and this has been apparent in our country, too) generated inflation through several channels simultaneously: an imbalance in government spending, with the difference between expenditures and revenues being covered by compulsory loans in the banking sphere; a high rate of real accumulation combined with a low rate of monetary savings on the part of the public and

---

[11]For more details, see The Paradoxes of Regulation [Paradoksy regulirovaniya], Moscow, 1988, pp. 114-126.

[12]From statements made by Ye. G. Yasin, deputy director of the Central Institute of Mathematical Economics, at a round table organized by the magazine Kommunist (No. 18, 1987, p. 31).

businesses; and a rate of wage growth, due to a manpower shortage, that outstrips the increase in labor productivity. That is why anti-inflationary measures have provided for lowering the rate of growth in state spending, raising income taxes, restricting bank credit, slowing the rate of wage growth, and freezing prices and, sometimes, income.

The point of the entire strategy, and of the complex maneuvering in carrying it out, has been to do so without stumbling over the fine line that separates a lowering of effective consumer and business demand, and with it, a reduction of the inflation rate, from a halt in the growth of real production, whose rate depends on the stability of that same effective demand. To that end, governments have generally introduced different forms of restraints on the growth of consumer incomes, on the one hand (more rigid restraints), and of business revenues allocated for the financing of capital investments, on the other. A number of West European countries, realizing the seamless connection between inflation and the structural defects of their economies, have not limited themselves to regulating the circulation sphere and the mechanism for the distribution and redistribution of income, but have also drawn up major investment programs and implemented them on a centralized basis.

The socially negative aspect of inflation constitutes the chief obstacle to successfully combating that same inflation using economic methods. There is only one reliable means of neutralizing the income-eroding effect of inflation, and that is to link the growth of fixed incomes to the rise in the general level of prices. But that means that the state, whose job it is to prevent the formation of conditions conducive to the development of "galloping" inflation, is itself creating the first round of a cumulative inflationary process: a cost increase leads to a price increase, which leads to an earnings-cost increase. (The second round is the development in society of an inflationary psychological climate, which creates a basis for price increases under the influence of a demand that constantly outstrips supply.) Nonetheless, in practically all the Western countries, albeit in various forms, the principle of indexing incomes to prices became firmly established in postwar economic and political practice. Subsequently its institutionalization in the form of continuously renewed collective agreements between trade unions and employers (the United States, Canada), state laws (France, Italy), and the participation of worker representatives on enterprise management bodies (the Federal Republic of Germany) served as the chief target of neoconservative attacks aimed at deregulating labor relations and giving them greater "flexibility," i.e., lowering them to the level of "free" bargaining between two owners of goods.

As for the neoconservative period in anti-inflationary policy, it is, so to speak, a different story, which has to do with the special conditions of the "great crisis" of the 1970s and 1980s. In our country, the problems and contradictions are closer to those that characterized the capitalist economy during the first postwar decade. Then and later, in the 1950s and 1960s, indexation of incomes to prices played a generally positive role. High growth rates in production and labor productivity, combined with a developed system of social security, allowed the industrially developed capitalist countries to substantially increase their living standards while maintaining moderate rates of increase in overall prices. By indexing incomes to prices, they eliminated one of the most volatile factors that had aggravated social and political contradictions.

Drift

Among reforms now being outlined and discussed, price reform is most important to the prospects of perestroika. From every known indication, the proposed version of this reform being developed in the depths of the U.S.S.R. State Committee on Prices deliberately ignores the sad results of the prolonged operation of the system of "stable" state prices. The unshakable certainty that they are right displayed by the authors of this departmental "reform" would evoke nothing but respect if it had any real ground beneath it. Unfortunately, in science opinion is not proof, and practice has repeatedly and cruelly punished attempts to base rational economic activity on faith.

In support of the position taken by the State Prices Committee [stated at the end of V. Kuznetsov's first article—*Trans.*], which sees the application of its "three levers"[13] as the only means of preventing a price increase ("I must say, in all seriousness, that I simply see no other ways to resist a rise in prices."), V.F. Stepanenko argues as follows: "As for references to world experience, vying for the consumer (competition—*V.K.*) is unrealistic today. Look around you! Until the necessary material reserves have been created in the country, there will continue to be an acute shortage of even the most essential material and technical resources, and there can be no serious talk about any sort of freedom on the part of the consumer."[14]

If this sentence indicates anything, it is a complete unwillingness to understand the nature of our economy's chronic scarcities. Why, one wonders, has the U.S.S.R. State Planning Committee been trying

---

[13]A uniform method for setting prices, uniform economic normative rates, and stronger monitoring to ensure price discipline.

[14]*Kommunist*, No. 18, 1987, p. 29.

for 60 years to solve the scarcity problem by increasing the production first of one set of products and goods and then of another, while shortages have expanded uncontrollably, and we find ourselves on the threshold of stores with empty shelves,[15] and have reconciled ourselves to the familiar phenomenon of enterprises standing idle because of regular shortages of raw materials and parts? The answer would seem to be clear: because of disproportions in the cost structure, the individual elements of which are formed by multiplying the amount produced by the price of a unit of output. And as we can see from data on stocks of raw materials, other materials, and finished products in our country, the relative amount of which greatly exceeds the comparable figure for the capitalist countries, the disruption of proportions is attributable not to inadequate quantities, but to intolerable price distortions. And if, following V.F. Stepanenko's categorical demand, the shift to the price-setting principle that has been adopted in all countries whose economies are free of shortages should be deferred until our own shortages are eliminated, the futility of that undertaking can be guaranteed in advance.

But can it be that the price reform being prepared will, with the help of "scientific price-setting,"[16] also create the conditions for eliminating the shortages? After all, experiments with prices for gold, rugs, and crystal have shown that any shortage can be instantaneously turned into a surplus if prices are sharply increased.

Faith in "scientific price-setting" is widespread, even among competent economists. "The whole trick is to calculate a price for milk. . . ." Or: "Suppose, based on the requirements of the country's population (for milk), we were to calculate. . . ."[17] But how, one wonders, does one "calculate" in practical terms? In practice it is done by determining the actual, established outlays for the production of a given product—more often, a large group of similar products—and factoring into the results of those calculations normative adjustments for quality, level of demand, the size of consumers' incomes, and so forth, that are more or less hypothetical. The problem, however, is that outlays are calculated on the basis of actual outlays in existing prices. And since all outlays ultimately come down to outlays of labor, what emerges as prices are current levels of wages or of producers' revenues. These are levels that are the result of the economy's pro-

---

[15]"The All-Union Research Institute for Market Conditions and Demand monitors 211 groups of foodstuffs. And it turns out that only 23 of those can be acquired without difficulty" (*Literaturnaya gazeta* [*Literary gazette*], Dec. 14, 1988, p. 10).

[16]In the course of a discussion carried under *Literaturnaya gazeta's* rubric known as the "Position Club," L. Yevenko quite rightly called for us to rid ourselves as quickly as possible of the illusions created by that concept (*Literaturnaya gazeta*, Dec. 14, 1988, p. 10).

[17]From an interview with Academician A.G. Aganbegyan in the magazine *Ogonyok* [*Flame*] (No. 29, 2987, p. 3).

longed operation under the conditions of an administrative system and command-type management, and therefore no one knows how far they have ranged from the assessments that are characteristic of a proportional economy.

According to the State Statistical Committee, from 1940 to 1987 the following tendencies were apparent in the U.S.S.R.: (1) an increase in the relative valuation of construction workers' labor (on the average, a relatively low-skilled category of manpower), (2) stability in the valuation of labor in mining and manufacturing, and (3) a lowering of the valuation of highly skilled labor of physicians, teachers and higher-school instructors, people in culture, the arts, and science, and government office employees. That resulted, first of all, in making construction workers the highest-paid employees (more than twice as high as people in culture). And secondly, between 1960 and 1987 the dispersion of earned income among the various branches of the economy dropped sharply.

Construction workers' high wages are in no way related to the intensity of their work or its high level of productivity: The Zlobin and Travkin experiments [in creating incentives for construction brigades to boost productivity by relating members' pay more directly to their productivity—*Trans.*] showed that simple rationalization of labor and pay, without any radical technical innovations, assures increased productivity of construction crews by a factor of from two to four. Just let anyone try to perform the same trick on the assembly line at the Likhachev or Togliatti automotive plants, in brigades of machine-tool operators, or in weaving shops, where the intensity of labor is close to the limit of physical endurance!

AVERAGE MONTHLY EARNINGS IN VARIOUS SECTORS OF THE U.S.S.R. NATIONAL ECONOMY (IN PERCENTAGES)

	1940	1960	1987
National economy as a whole	100	100	100
Industry	103	114	109
Construction	110	115	127
Agriculture	70	68	98
Transportation	105	108	118
Health care	77	73	71
Public education	100	90	82
Culture	67	61	60
Art	118	79	74
Science	142	137	107
Public administration	118	107	93

Calculated on the basis of *The U.S.S.R National Economy in 1987* [*Narodnoye khozyaystvo SSSR v 1987 g.*], Moscow, 1988, pp. 390-391.

As for the decline in the index of dispersion and the reduction of differences between wage levels in different economic branches, that is also an unpleasant symptom—a symptom of a tendency toward wage-leveling, toward distribution according to the principle of "a little for everyone," rather than according to the actual work performed. This is the source of the decrease in the motivation to work because no matter where or how one works, the results will be approximately the same; it is also the origin of the incentive to seek sources of improving one's income in "shadow-economy" activities.

That, then, is the structure of the distribution of earned income that will serve as the basis for calculating a new price structure that is supposed to stimulate perestroika processes, or at least not interfere with them. That approach is fraught with considerable potential danger. The prices will "incorporate" the plainly antieconomic realities of the present administrative system.

A number of economists propose taking the structure of world prices as a model.[18] That is not as uncontroversial as it might seem at first glance. In each country the level and structure of prices reflect the level and structure of production and consumption in precisely that country. As a rule, both objective and subjective "filters" exist between prices on the internal market and those on the world market. The first filter: The products exported to the world market are primarily those whose relative production costs are lower than in most other countries. Not all products are exported, at least not in the proportions in which they are sold within the country.[19] The second filter: In practically every Western country, despite GATT prohibitions, exported and imported products are subject to certain restrictions or incentives. The purpose of such manipulations is usually to improve the competitiveness of national products in foreign markets and weaken the competitiveness of foreign products in domestic markets. In most cases the manipulations include measures affecting the price level of goods concerned. In that sense, world prices represent a kind of special design that serves commodity exchange above all in world markets. Taking it as the basis for the national price structure would be nearly as wrong as prescribing the prices in some bureaucratic offices.

---

[18]N. Shmelev, "Advances and Debts," *Novy mir* [*New World*], No. 6, 1987, p. 151.

[19]Thanks to this effect, according to the assessment of a French publication, Japan, for example, managed, while the official exchange rate of the yen rose to 120 to 130 yen per dollar in 1987, to preserve the yen's parity, which was calculated on the basis of purchasing power at the level of 270 yen per dollar, and calculated on the basis of relative wage costs at 360 yen per dollar; that is, it managed, in effect, to maintain the rate of its foreign-trade yen at the 1972 level in the first case, and at the 1950 level in the second! (*Paribas conjoncture*, December 1988, p. 168).

Yu. Izyumov made an apt statement at a round-table discussion in *Literaturnaya gazeta*'s offices: "It is not prices but the mechanisms by which they are set that need to be reformed."[20] And, as world experience indicates, the only realistic mechanism for determining prices is the market in one form or another, including a socialist form. Why resist the obvious? Out of fears of inflation?

It would be naive to believe that one could move immediately from a false price structure to an ideal one, or even one that is simply more acceptable. In any case it will take years of gradual movement from one structure to the other, years of slow drift, in the course of which the disproportions will be straightened out, and the balance between commodity and money flows will be restored. And since it is impossible, in the process, to abstract ourselves from the realities of the normative and cost-based economy, it would be utter head-in-the-sand naiveté to suppose that such a transitional period of drift is compatible with stable prices. We must look economic truth in the eye, recognize that experience of other countries is instructive and worthy of copying—not as evidence of the ignorant naiveté of apologists for the bourgeoisie who reject the true theory—and build our economic strategy not on the sand of groundless hopes or "maybes," but on strict and precise calculation. One element of such strategy, in my view, should be controlled and regulated inflation.

Given a sufficiently serious approach and appropriate preparation and resolve on the part of the central political and economic authorities, the danger of uncontrolled inflation can be eliminated, the rate of "creeping" inflation fixed, and its negative effect on the population's real income neutralized. It will be necessary, of course, to prepare and carry out a number of measures, which will take no more time than the calculation of prices by bureaucrats. The actual experience of the Western countries that successfully accomplished a similar transition during the postwar years indicates the main features of the objectives and content of the reform of the price mechanism.

First, we must accept as a natural and scientific fact that a self-regulating economy cannot exist without at least minimal freedom to set prices in the sphere of the exchange and sale of products, without "trade-offs" and debates between producers and consumers.

Second, we must abandon the false notion that one must choose between opposites: either stable prices or the anarchy of inflationary processes. Not only is inflation subject to restraint; it can and should be regulated by government authorities in the interests of the economy and of society. In the 1940s and 1950s West European enterprises were not forbidden to raise prices on specific items, but a "ceiling" was

---

[20]*Literaturnaya gazeta*, Nov. 9, 1988, p. 10.

established (from 3 to 4 percent annually) above which the average price of all the output they produced was not supposed to be raised, under the threat of financial sanctions. That gave an enterprise the necessary freedom of maneuver and allowed it to regulate the profitability of individual items in its product mix. That made it possible to avoid the situation in which Soviet enterprises were caught in 1988 with the shift to full cost accounting and to the practice of contracting for purchases and deliveries: lacking the right to change the price of a single item they produced, they took the route of abandoning unprofitable items and increasing the production of profitable output. The country was on the threshold of a collapse of the existing structure of the division of labor, and newspaper pages were filled with indignant remarks concerning the "immorality" of the economic bureaucrats who were trampling society's interests for their own gain. Yet everyone striving for his own gain is precisely what the common interest is based on in the self-regulating economy! That means that an appropriate reaction should consist not in appealing to conscience but in providing every condition for the effective operation of the incentive mechanism.

Third, along with recognizing the naturalness and necessity of a regulated inflationary drift of prices, it is necessary to institute the indexation of all incomes, regardless of size, to the real increase in the prices of consumer goods and services. To this end, the subsistence income of a standard family is calculated, and standard packages of goods and services ("baskets") that are actually consumed by families of various sizes and in various regions of the country are determined. This is done on a democratic basis (i.e., with the involvement of representatives of the working people, consumers, enterprise executives, government administration, and experts).[21] The rate of increase in the subsistence income serves as a guide for the regular revision (from one to four times a year) of minimum earned income (wages plus monetary payments in the form of social assistance and social security). If their financial situation permits it, the management and employees of enterprises are permitted to revise, by the same or a lesser percentage, the incomes of workers and office employees that exceed the subsistence income.

---

[21]At present the definition of "subsistence income" and "consumer basket" is entrusted to the U.S.S.R. State Committee on Labor and Social Questions, together with the All-Union Central Council of Trade Unions (see *Izvestia*, Jan. 16, 1989). This task is too important and socially significant for it to be accomplished in a bureaucratic fashion, partly behind closed doors. The utmost democracy and glasnost are not only desirable but simply essential in this matter in order that the public not doubt the social fairness and appropriateness of the basic indices of their living standard. Especially if it is proposed that they be made into operative indices—that they serve as the basis for determining the amount of monetary compensation for increased prices.

Fourth, as world experience has shown, it is desirable, in the interests of combating runaway inflation, that special-purpose supplements to families' monetary income be given preference over forms of aid that entail maintenance of low prices for consumer goods. Practice has shown that subsidizing the production of inexpensive goods, or providing free services to all strata of the population is usually economically costly and far from always socially just. Not only do whole areas of subsidized production arise (which is directly contrary to the principles of rational economic management and to the proclaimed goals of the radical reform), but their products only partially reach their intended recipients, while the rest is bought up by the high-income strata of the population or serves as industrial raw material to be processed into other articles. When its object is a specific family or person, local social assistance, in the first place, efficiently accomplishes a specific task, and in the second, is cheaper for the society.

Fifth, life under the conditions of an economy with mobile prices presupposes the establishment of agencies for monitoring and effectively controlling price changes, as well as a mechanism of severe, mainly financial punishment for violating legislatively mandated prohibitions—in particular, the prohibition against raising the established "ceiling" for price increases. Appropriate legal norms and forms of sanctions are needed. The work of monitoring and control agencies should be as democratic as possible and should be carried out in close contact with consumers' associations and People's Control agencies.

Sixth, the most complex and subtle task of income policy is to prevent "creeping" inflation from turning into "galloping" inflation. A central aspect of the mechanism for combating cumulative inflationary effects is the macroeconomic, societal attitude toward the connection between nominal income and labor productivity at every enterprise. According to the considerations presented above, this connection cannot be as primitively simple as it is currently interpreted in our press and our schoolbooks. Given such an interpretation, there would be no escaping the cumulative effect of price increases. The growth in labor productivity depends on many factors, some of which are beyond the control of the enterprise. It is these factors that should influence allocation of additional income that is realized from the sale, at unchanged prices, of commodities produced with the new and more productive technology.

What I have in mind is not introducing special obligatory ratios for such distribution, but simply granting economically independent enterprises the right to resolve this matter themselves, in accordance with specific circumstances. At the same time, within the framework of nationwide income policy, it is perfectly appropriate for quantitative restrictions (a "ceiling") to be placed on the increase in wages paid out by individual enterprises. This is a difficult question and demands a thorough analysis of all of its grounds and prerequisites—of course, under conditions of openness and democracy. But that is the central question of any price policy.

General and specific measures aimed at preventing "creeping" inflation from turning into "galloping" inflation will produce an effect only if measures are simultaneously implemented to eliminate the structural disproportions that cause inflation. That is the duty of the central government in the person of the legislative and executive authorities. In developing a strategy of social development, they should take into account not only short- and long-term goals, no matter how important, essential, and urgent they may seem, but also the realistic possibilities of the self-regulating economy. Given a state budget deficit that amounts to several percent of national income, demanding rational economic behavior of economic managers and the working people would simply be socially unjust.

There needs to be a general purge of everything that currently produces what O. Latsis has called "nongoods." "It is important to understand the complexity of the task that must be accomplished," Ye. Gaydar, the editor of *Kommunist* magazine's department of political economy and economic policy, quite rightly emphasizes. "A serious and real reduction of state expenditures must entail a large-scale redistribution of material resources in favor of industries working for the consumer market, a change in the content of the work of millions of people, the resolute curtailment of inefficient production facilities, the radical perestroika of the whole economic structure, and the turning of the economy toward the human being. The scale of financial disproportions is such that the only way it will be possible to rapidly rectify the situation and impede inflationary processes is by accomplishing serious changes in three key areas: cutting back on the number of construction projects and reducing centralized government capital investments, reorienting the mix of imports, and reducing the defense burden on the economy.[22]

If we take everything from the economic experience of the industrially developed capitalist countries that pertains to the methods and forms for the efficient organization of social production, place it at the service of socialist ideals, and turn it to the benefit of the working person, that experience may become a powerful factor in the acceleration of our perestroika, and may save us from perfectly avoidable mistakes in the course of the experimentation being pushed on people in the practical realm by the outwardly correct and logically irre-

---

[22]*Kommunist*, No. 2, 1989, p. 30.

proachable, but essentially ruinous, theory-bound recommendations of those who argue for the uniqueness of everything socialist. The history of human communities, especially the history of such complex systems as the system of social production, does not start anew with every new system. It is based on everything positive and of general significance that has been achieved by hundreds of generations since people first entered into relations with one another for the purpose of the collective reproduction of their own life.

Where is Eastern Europe Headed?

LILIYA FEDOROVNA SHEVTSOVA*

1. The Essence of a Social Turning Point

Political scientists and historians will return for some time to the events that occurred in Eastern Europe in 1989. These events altered—altered fundamentally—not only the destiny of individual countries and regions but also ideas about socialism, the present world order, and future paths of social progress. The consequences of the East European revolution have yet to manifest themselves fully, and some of them will only be revealed over time. There are already grounds for comparing this revolution, in view of its all-European and global significance and implications, to the Great French Revolution of 1789, the 1848 "Spring of Nations," the 1917 October Revolution, and the emergence of the people's democracy system in the 1940s.

But there are also substantial differences from these earlier events. The earlier people's revolutions took place under leftist banners. Current East European events, on the contrary, are associated with a decline in the prestige of leftist forces and with their removal from power in a majority of countries, lending a special complexity, a contradictory character, and drama to the situation in Eastern Europe.

The masses that took to the streets in East Germany, Czechoslovakia, Bulgaria, and Romania put an end to a system of administrative, statist socialism, which in some places took the form of a cruel feudal tyranny. We should point out, however, despite the fact that these actions were seemingly unexpected, the groundwork had been laid to a certain extent by completely peaceful events that occurred in other countries somewhat earlier. We refer to the attempts made in Hungary, Poland, and to some extent, Yugoslavia and China to restructure authoritarian socialism. These attempts ultimately failed. But they left their mark, leading largely to abandoning any hopes that the old system could be renewed without rejecting its basic principles. The mass demonstrations at the end of the 1980s marked the collapse of these illusions.

---

*Doctor of history and section head at the U.S.S.R. Academy of Sciences' Institute of the Economics of the World Socialist System. This article appeared in the April 1990 issue of *MEMO* and has been revised for inclusion in this collection.

Of course, one cannot indiscriminately deny the utility and expediency of the intrasystem reforms (reforms implemented within the framework of a specific social system and aimed at improving, not destroying, it) that were carried out in Hungary, Poland, Yugoslavia, or China. At earlier historical stages, these reforms had a certain effect, in some cases enhancing the well-being of society and facilitating the neutralization of social conflicts. In the 1980s, however, all efforts to renew the administrative-authoritarian institutions by means of such reforms were either forcibly broken off or perverted. Reformist attempts even exacerbated the developing crisis in society—leading to the collapse of the old mechanisms without creating anything in their place. This proves the validity of the conclusion that there are limits to the duration of certain social structures; on reaching those limits, these structures lose their capacity to develop and can operate only to the detriment of their surroundings. Moreover, they become dangerous to world development as a whole. In all the socialist countries, including the reformist countries, by the end of the 1980s social tensions had deepened, and anarchy and inability to govern had emerged. The idea of reforms under socialism was discredited. In various social strata, the possibility that socialism could be renewed became increasingly doubtful. Moreover, even the possibility of creating a different, just, and democratic structure on the basis of socialism came to be doubted. The masses' confidence in the ruling parties plummeted disastrously.

In countries that tried to avoid change—the G.D.R., Czechoslovakia, and Romania—explosive tensions accumulated. And the deeper the dangerous maladies were driven inward, the more likely their sudden and violent eruption became.

In light of the events that occurred first in the G.D.R., then in a wave of explosions in Czechoslovakia, Bulgaria, and Romania, it became clear that a partial restructuring of the existing system would no longer suffice. A gradual, evolutionary transition to a new social system also proved impossible. The task of completely dismantling all the old party-statist institutions as quickly as possible, and molding a new kind of social order based on different principles and norms became an urgent priority. Not long before, many reformers in East European countries had been preoccupied with whether the transition to a new system should be made all at once or gradually. There had been much debate over how opposite forms should coexist, and how reforms could be pursued without upsetting social stability. In theoretical terms, these problems were never solved. Events in most countries proceeded rapidly, and in some cases unexpectedly for their participants themselves (for example, the jailed Havel could hardly have imagined that he would be president of Czechoslovakia six months later) and there was no time for reflection. The foundation and roof of the old building started to collapse before a clear blueprint of the new building had been drawn up. Under these conditions, the "revolutionary" countries—the G.D.R., Czechoslovakia, and Romania—could not avoid dual sources of power, emergence of several decision-making centers, and even periods in which no one held power and anarchy reigned. In all the countries, radical changes at the top were accompanied by preservation of the old system at the middle and lower levels.

The Polish example is instructive. In the summer of 1989, new supreme bodies of authority were formed there and began to implement their policies while the old lower-level political structure—not to mention the economic foundation—remained in place. The lower-level political structure began to change later. In short, not one country managed to effect a clean transition to democracy. In many countries, that transition began spontaneously. In others, events confounded all the reformers' plans by giving rise to many unforeseen developments. Ultimately, all the countries entered a highly unstable transitional state in which previously ruling forces had already lost or were losing their power, while the institutions they had created temporarily remained intact; in which new forces had entered the arena and begun governing while still lacking legal levers of influence.

How, then, does one characterize the events that occurred in Eastern Europe at the end of the 1980s? Do they constitute a revolution, and if so, what kind? Or were they coups? Without answering this question, it will be difficult to understand the present nature of development in individual countries, as well as to foresee its future prospects. Of course, it will still take time and we will need to see the final form of various trends that are still vague and indistinct before a definitive assessment of the events that occurred is possible. With respect to the G.D.R. and Czechoslovakia, revolutions evidently did take place, leading not only to the fall of the ruling clique but also paving the way to power for new public and political forces. However, they were peaceful revolutions and were not at all like the bloody mass uprisings of the past. Bulgaria is a somewhat special case. There the fall of the dictatorial Zhivkov regime was brought about by the actions of a reform-minded group within the top party and state leadership. But this very fact triggered phenomena of a revolutionary order in society. I continue to have very serious doubts as to whether the events in Romania constituted a popular revolution or simply a coup organized by certain forces—forces close to the ruling center, incidentally—that decided to topple a regime everyone despised. In any case, there is a lot that suggests the second possibility. The popular disturbances most likely facilitated that coup. We will have to wait a little longer to see what it brings—gradual development of democratic structures, or yet another authoritarian regime, albeit in a different ideological wrapping.

On the whole, however, the transformations in Eastern Europe force us to rethink our traditional notions about the nature of social transformations, and especially our ideas about revolution and reform and their content. In part, these transformations raise doubts about the validity of rigidly distinguishing between such types of social change. Consider, for example, the processes taking place in Hungary and Poland. In those countries, radical forces in the communist parties that ruled at the time adopted a course of reforms that led to a revolutionary change in the countries' social structures. On the other hand, we know from history that in most cases revolutions have not led to the immediate emergence of a new social order. Let us recall earlier revolutionary events that occurred in various socialist countries: in the G.D.R. in 1953; in Hungary in 1956; in Poland in 1956, 1970, and 1979 to 1981; and in Czechoslovakia in 1968 to 1969. In no country did these revolutions—which, to be sure, were dissimilar in content and forms of development—lead to the creation of a new social system.

The world has also seen revolutions that marked a retreat or halt in social development. The formation of some social systems have required more than one revolutionary attempt. With regard to any previous order, revolutions are primarily destructive. Creation of a new order, on the other hand, requires a series of reforms. The East European revolutions were also the first, and perhaps not even the most decisive, step toward forming more progressive social institutions, something which involves a number of reformist efforts. Today we are apparently observing the birth of a new type of social transformation in which revolutionary and reformist elements are mixed. T. Ash has dubbed this transformation a "ref-olution." It is impossible to draw a clear distinction between them. The more developed a country is socioeconomically, the less polarized its society, the stronger its traditions of civic activism, and the greater the foundation for setting revolutionary goals and for achieving them through evolutionary means.

It would be a considerable oversimplification, however, to draw direct parallels between the reformist model characteristic of Western society and the social transformations in Eastern Europe and in the U.S.S.R. Such attempts are frequent today, yet there can be no direct analogies between reformist processes in East and West. In Eastern Europe, the world is seeing an attempt, which has never been made anywhere before, to move from a party-state system of a communist type to a pluralistic, market-oriented organization of society. In a society of statist socialism, it is necessary to destroy the old foundations and to build new ones. In Western society, reforms are aimed at improving its qualities. This compels the conclusion that the social changes taking place in the East European countries are unique.

Now let us ask, what is the nature of these changes? People's-democratic? Socialist? Antisocialist? Anticommunist? Interpretations of East European events vary—they are viewed both as the collapse of socialism and communist ideas, and as the formation of a new socialist model. The content and orientation of these events can be ascertained, first of all, through analysis of the social forces behind them and the basic aspirations of these forces. In the G.D.R., Czechoslovakia, and Romania, and subsequently in Bulgaria as well, the detonator and chief participant in all the mass actions was the young, especially students. In that respect, these actions are in many ways distinct from protest movements in previous decades, movements in which the working class played the leading role. In the early 1980s in Poland, when Solidarity first arose, workers were both the initiators and main force of the mass actions. Today we are seeing social movements lose their former class character and assume a broader social shape. New social groups are coming to the fore in these movements and their ideological orientation is changing. Before, workers took to the streets with the slogans "Socialism Yes, Distortions No!" This time one sensed many people's disbelief in the possibility of building a just society on the basis of socialist ideas. Only yesterday, people were chiefly demanding the resignation of ruling party discredited leaders. Today the overwhelming majority of society has come out against the leading role of the communist party in general, refusing to place its political confidence in it. "We're tired of 'communist experiments'!"—it would be a mistake to view this theme, which was heard during 1989's actions and is still heard today, as an attack or provocation by a narrow group of antisocialist elements. The masses' disenchantment with socialist ideas—but most important, with the people who represent them—has become widespread in all the countries, encompassing a sizable part of even the working class, the traditional base of communists. And this fact must be taken into account in analyzing the East European revolutions.

In general, there appear to be grounds for not interpreting these revolutions from a purely ideological standpoint, that is, from the standpoint of their relationship to communist ideals. In such a framework, some of them could be viewed as only anticommunist, although a great many rank-and-file communists took part in them. It would be more accurate to characterize them from the standpoint of political criteria—as antitotalitarian and democratic. Still, it cannot be ruled out completely that in one or another country that lacks traditions of civic activism and experience in grassroots political action, the revolutions will boil down to a change in power and political regime that leaves intact the basic authoritarian structure, which might take on a different ideological form.

The East European revolutions were not just a protest against local cults and dictatorships. They were simultaneously society's protest against the artificial development scenario that was once imposed on it by the Soviet leadership, and against prescriptions for "happiness" introduced from outside that were at odds with the national and historical traditions and true interests of the various states. It is undeniable that in most East European countries statist socialism did not arise spontaneously, but was exported to them, and with an iron hand. Historians have yet to reveal the tragedy of the violent end to the people's democracies, and to show the mainsprings of the ultraleftist coups that occurred throughout Eastern Europe. The Soviet Union also bears responsibility for the failure of repeated attempts to reform the administrative system in Poland, Hungary, and Czechoslovakia. At the same time, we recognize that the European countries also had committed followers of Stalinist ideas, some of whom, in terms of their criminal designs and their implementation, were little better than the "father of peoples." There were also certain social groups that were impressed by the spirit of egalitarian-style authoritarianism. And there were political forces that viewed the statist socialist system as the most effective means of acquiring and retaining personal power.

The East European countries' experience demonstrates the possibility of two alternative ways to transform the authoritarian-administrative system: one peaceful, the other revolutionary. The first was embodied in Poland and Hungary, where reformist circles in the ruling communist parties themselves—of course under pressure from society—initiated movement in the direction of a new social system. The second was embodied in the actions of the popular masses in the G.D.R. and Czechoslovakia.

Still, it was Polish reformers who were the first to transcend the bounds of the authoritarian system.

As recently as 1988, relations between the Polish leadership and Solidarity were characterized by acute hospitality. However, the rapid development of the crisis in the country, the declining prestige of the PUWP [Polish United Workers' Party, i.e., the communist party— *Trans.*], unsuccessful economic reform, and the mounting discontent of the masses, which was approaching a critical point—all forced Polish leaders to urgently seek ways to prevent an explosion that could have dramatic consequences for both the country and the entire region. The 10th plenary session of the PUWP Central Committee in early 1989 was a turning point. It was there, after many hours of heated debate, that W. Jaruzelski and his supporters, under his threat of resignation, secured a decision that was to change the country's destiny—a decision that called for the party's voluntary self-limitation, and for talks with Solidarity. For many members of the ruling party, this decision was unexpected and led to disorientation and even resistance. This is understandable. For so many years they had spared no effort in the struggle against Solidarity, which was regarded as a counterrevolutionary force, and suddenly they were faced with a 180-degree turn. As then Prime Minister Rakowski has recounted, the plenum's decision also took foreign observers by surprise. One Western statesman even said to him anxiously, "I'm afraid you are jumping the gun." However, the situation was such that there was no time to reflect or try to persuade doubters—a way had to be found to prevent the people from taking to the streets en masse and to forestall uncontrollable events. And this required surmounting the previous political and ideological barriers.

Subsequent events unfolded at a rapid pace. The "round-table" talks with the opposition began in the spring of 1989. At first things were difficult, and understandably so. Sitting face to face were those who had imposed martial law and directed the internment—General Jaruzelski and General Kiszczak—and those who had been jailed or gone underground—Walesa, Bujak, Gwiazda, and their advisers. A fair amount of hostility and mistrust had accumulated, and it took the intervention of a third force—the church and the mediation of Polish Primate Cardinal Glemp—to enable the sides to take their first step toward rapprochement. That process, which took two months, was dramatic. An outside observer might have expected more intransigence, heated passion, and mutual recrimination. But most of the round-table's participants evidently sensed their civic responsibility to the country, which looked to them not for mutual accusations, not for haggling, but for an agreement. And an agreement was reached, which put an end to open hostility. Solidarity was recognized as an equal political partner and received 35 percent of the seats in the Sejm, as well as the right to take part in a campaign for seats in the second chamber—the Senate. It was agreed that in four years' time, elections in Poland would be free. This was a major concession for the communist party, but not to have made it would have meant putting the country once more on the brink of national disaster.

The next stage was the elections in the summer of 1989. They led, for the first time in a socialist country, to the formation of a new government that included opposition forces. This was a breakthrough of enormous importance, marking the beginning of the end of the authoritarian party-statist system. But for the PUWP itself, the radical change brought about with its assistance and participation proved fateful. To be sure, the party got the seats in the Sejm that had been reserved for it in advance, but Solidarity won complete control of the Senate. Something happened that many people in Poland and abroad had never expected: Even the army, internal troops, and diplomatic corps voted for Solidarity. It must be said that the country's leaders, that is, the very people who had initiated the change, were also defeated. "The reform's victory is the reformers' loss," some Polish newspapers wrote.

We have dwelt on the Polish experience in great detail because the Polish leftist forces were the first to go beyond entrenched patterns, the first to take the risk of renouncing their monopoly on power, and the first to sit down at round-table talks with the opposition. Today we can debate whether that step was merely a tactical move by the Polish leadership at the time, and to what extent it was forced. But the fact remains that the Polish leaders at the time found the strength to forgo narrow party and selfish interests and reach a compromise with opposing forces in the name of saving society. One could conclude now that the consensus reached between the PUWP and Solidarity gave the leftist forces a certain political advantage. It not only helped avoid a revolution that would hardly have been as peaceful as those in the G.D.R. and Czechoslovakia, but also enabled the leftist forces, despite their overall negative showing in the elections, to remain in power temporarily in a coalition, and to retain for some time the national presidency. Subsequently, the Polish scenario was repeated in one variation or another in all the East European countries. Round-table talks between the leftist forces and the opposition were convened everywhere, and everywhere attempts were made by the recent ruling and opposition forces to come to an agreement that would ensure a peaceful transitional stage. In every country, however, the communist party decided on such a step only when it was already too late, when it was already under outside pressure and its prestige and influence in society had seriously declined. Under these circumstances, the communist parties in those countries were no longer able to ensure themselves a place in the new system of power taking shape.

The East European events of this year and last show a surprising synchronism of development in separate, completely dissimilar countries. This is essentially the first time in world history that we have observed the almost simultaneous fall of cult regimes in so many countries at once. Certain general trends in the individual countries' development, the directions in which their principal forces have evolved, and the dominant processes in their public opinion all coincide. At the same time, it would be rash to lump all these countries together. Already, as the old system is liquidated, the distinctive national, historical, and other characteristics of the individual countries are becoming increasingly apparent. Some countries are beginning to show a distinctiveness in new social forms, or in the pace of various transformations. For example, Hungary and Poland were the first to set about creating a new system. But the G.D.R. and Czechoslovakia, which followed them, completed in a matter of weeks a process that took the trailblazers years to accomplish. In view of their higher level of socioeconomic development, the absence of sharp social divisions, certain qualities of their social psychology, and the traditions of civil society that they have managed to retain (and, in the case of the G.D.R., the role of the F.R.G. as well), one cannot rule out the possibility that these countries will soon take the lead in building a new order. Tasks of a completely different nature confront Romania, for example, where elementary conditions for the development of society had been disrupted. There the question is to stabilize the very foundations of life of the country. "The country is in chaos," said one Romanian leader. "And chaos cannot be reformed."[1] At the same time, it is also clear that overcoming chaos without dismantling the totalitarian system that spawned it is equally impossible.

To what extent are the processes taking place in Eastern Europe characteristic of the development of the community of states that, until recently, was commonly referred to as the "socialist commonwealth"? Is there reason to speak of the collapse of the system of statist socialism as a whole? Clearly, such an unqualified conclusion would still be premature. All the countries that made up the socialist system can be divided—somewhat schematically, to be sure—into three groups. In most of the East European countries, whether as a result of the struggle between democratic forces, on one side, and Stalinist and neo-Stalinist forces, on the other, or in the course of popular movements, the foundations of the administrative-authoritarian system have collapsed. We cannot assume, however, that an identical future awaits all these countries. In most of them, there is no sure guarantee that the social processes are irreversible. Granted, a return to the Stalinist or even a milder—say Kadarist—model of the party state is hardly possible here. But relapses into authoritarian tendencies of a different variety, even on the part of the former opposition forces, cannot be ruled out entirely. Another group of countries, including China, the U.S.S.R., and Yugoslavia, are still trying to carry out a moderate perestroika. Let us begin with the U.S.S.R. At the time of this writing, at least, the Soviet leadership had not exceeded the bounds of the perestroika variant of renewal, that is, it was still trying to restructure the party-statist system without repudiating its basic operating principles. Yes, liberalization and glasnost had developed in

---

[1]*Novoye vremya* [*New Times*], Jan. 18, 1990, p. 7.

society. At the same time, however, one sensed a strong effort on the part of the center to preserve the party's vanguard role, the need to introduce private property was being denied, a real transition to a market had been put off indefinitely, and attempts were being made to preserve the domination of Marxism-Leninism in ideological life. The maintenance of this perestroika variant of development had only deepened destructive tendencies without creating anything new.

And what was taking place in China during this period? With certain variations, the same thing. China had gone somewhat further than the Soviet Union in creating economic incentives for production. But the principles of the party-state regime remained firmly intact, in contrast to the U.S.S.R., where this regime had already been seriously shaken. On the whole, however, in the case of China we are dealing with the same perestroika model, or more precisely, with a modification of it. A similar model of sprucing up an authoritarian system— albeit a milder system than some others—is also being followed in Yugoslavia for the time being. What is all this leading to? To a deepening of the contradictions between the old mechanisms and their efforts to survive, on one hand, and the new requirements of society, on the other. The 1989 events in China on Tiananmen Square confirm this. The lagging of restructuring processes intensifies the crisis in society and spawns conflicts and anarchic phenomena and disintegration, as shown by the present development of Yugoslavia, and of the U.S.S.R. as well. Finally, there are a number of countries—Cuba, North Korea, Albania—that continue to cling stubbornly to the old path, permitting no democratic indulgences. Lately the leaders of some of these countries, to preserve their regimes of personal power, have been trying to channel public discontent in the opposite direction, by creating an image of the "enemy" out of not just capitalists but also former friends—the European reformist countries. It is difficult to gauge the internal temperature of these closed societies from outside. Therefore, it is unclear just when social ferment there will reach a critical point, and exactly how their dictatorial regimes will fall—under public pressure or in the course of a political coup. However, one can be sure that the logical outcome of these regimes will come, and evidently it is not too far off.

2. The Fate of Leftist Forces: What Lies Ahead for Them?

The East European revolutions of 1989 demonstrated one thing in no uncertain terms—a crisis of confidence in the former ruling communist and workers' parties by broad segments of society. Strictly speaking, the revolutions themselves were in many respects a consequence of that crisis. More or less clear indications of the ruling parties' declining authority in various countries had long been apparent. In the late 1980s, these parties and their role in society aroused open discontent among the working people. The command-style, coercive nature of their operations came into direct conflict with a long-standing and urgent need to emancipate public life. A profound internal crisis in the ruling parties also became evident: ideological chaos among their rank and file, a gap between the rank and file and the party elite, bureaucratization of the elite, the development of leaders' cults, and corruption and moral degradation among those leaders. In some countries, especially Romania and Bulgaria, the ruling parties had become obedient tools of dictatorial regimes, something that decisively discredited the institution of the communist party in the eyes of the masses. The last hopes in the ability of these parties to renew themselves were dispelled. Life itself forced both society and rank-and-file communists to draw a relentless conclusion: The monocentrist-type party (this type of party is also characterized as mobilizational, statist, and administrative) constituted the backbone of the authoritarian system, and therefore all attempts to destroy the system while leaving the party untouched were senseless. It also became clear that party structures had become the basic obstacle in the path of social reforms.

During the stormy events of the late 1980s, ruling communist parties in the East European countries found themselves isolated and in an atmosphere of ever-growing distrust, rejection, and even hostility and anticommunist sentiment. "The parties were unwilling, unable, and did not know how"—that is how one party leader characterized the ruling organizations' inability to engage in a dialogue with the masses that had taken to the streets. V. Mohorita, a leader of the Czechoslovak Communist Party, said bitterly: "The avalanche of popular indignation toppled the CCP from the administrative-leadership throne on which the party had installed itself, the right to which it was unable to confirm through its actions."[2] Most of the ruling communist parties effectively lost their monopolies on power in the course of the popular movements. This was a severe shock for them. The centrist structure that only recently had seemed stable suddenly began to collapse before their eyes: The top party bodies and apparatus became paralyzed, the lower-level structures ceased to function, and a mass exodus from their ranks—involving no longer tens of thousands, but hundreds of thousands of members—intensified. The harshest fate befell the Romanian Communist Party, which had completely discredited itself in the eyes of society by its support for the tyrannical Ceausescu regime. For all intents and purposes, that party has ceased to exist, and the possibility of its revival is rather dubious. Similar

---

[2]*Literaturnaya gazeta* [*Literary gazette*], Dec. 12, 1989.

tendencies of declining prestige and diminishing party ranks, although not in such devastating forms, have affected the leftist parties in Hungary and Poland, parties that had already embarked on a reformist path and voluntarily given up their monopolies on power. Last fall, radical forces in the HSWP [Hungarian Socialist Workers' Party], having been the first to see that the old party had exhausted its potential, set about creating a new socialist organization. However, even that resolute step has been unable to halt the narrowing of the leftist forces' positions in the country.

What happened in Eastern Europe to organizations that only yesterday were the most influential and, let us emphasize, powerful can be characterized as a political defeat. In some instances, however, it is no exaggeration to call what happened a disaster. The question arises: was this process inevitable? Was there any possibility at any point of halting the communist parties' downward slide? Or were these organizations truly incapable of reforming themselves in a timely way, as many assert today, and doomed to proceed to their end? This question troubles many people, Marxists and non-Marxists alike. It cannot be said that there was no understanding in the ruling communist parties of where they were headed, that there was no realization of the consequences of their alienation from the masses, or of the danger of their becoming a conservative force and guardian of an anti-democratic order. In some parties, there were forces that recognized this threat. In the HSWP, for example, those forces grouped themselves around Nyers and Pozsgay, and in the PUWP—around Jaruzelski and Rakowski. Lilov and Mikhailov, members of the top echelon of the Bulgarian Communist Party, were not afraid to protest cult tendencies in that party. Even in Romania, a few RCP [Romanian Communist Party] leaders were able to raise their voice in protest against the party's transformation into a blind tool of Ceausescu's will, speaking out in their now-famous "Letter of the Six." In Hungary, Poland, and Yugoslavia, repeated attempts were made to renew the party, to cut the umbilical cord that tied it to the state, and to turn it into a political force that would fight for influence. But all these attempts ended in utter failure. The party machine continued to blindly follow the old course that had been programmed into it decades earlier, trampling even its own reformers underfoot or casting them aside. Some of them, realizing the futility of their restructuring endeavors, fell silent or defected to the other camp; others quit the party ranks. It is not without interest that many present ideologists of the opposition movements in neighboring countries are former communists who lost faith in the potentials of the parties to which they once belonged. For example, five members of the Polish government who now represent Solidarity once carried red party cards.

What, then, accounts for the repeated failures that befell attempts at party reform? There are apparently several reasons. In most cases, the communist reformers were not strong enough, or they did not dare to go beyond the bounds of familiar but long-obsolete ideas. Perhaps they were unable to renounce a part of themselves, and so stopped halfway. But these explanations do not fully answer the question of why. Why were the ruling communist parties in Eastern Europe never able to change the garb that inhibited and restricted their own movement? The conclusion is fairly clear that the problem lies in monocentrist, statist-type parties per se. It is understandable that these parties rejected any profound reforms; in doing so they merely exhibited their survival instinct and that of the groups that served them, the inner urge for self-preservation, even to the detriment of society. After all, the renewal of the party that we inherited from the distant past—the party as a special order and as a quasimilitary organization—inevitably demanded a radical change in its foundations and principles. That meant one thing: the creation, in effect, of a new party. However, the importance of internal party mechanisms in transforming the ruling communist parties into conservative forces, into supercentralist organizations serving primarily to pass down decisions made at the top, should not be overestimated, either. These mechanisms themselves were effects, rather than causes. Here we have come to the main cause, to the source of both the rise of statist-type communist parties and their historically inevitable fall. We are speaking of the parties' total and absolute monopoly on power, a monopoly guaranteed both constitutionally and by the full might of the state. That is what suppressed the need in the ruling parties to fight for their authority, and doomed them to bureaucratization and alienation from society. Absolute power deprives a political organization of both the internal urge toward, and external sources of, self-development in light of society's changing needs. That is the truth that the ruling communist parties' travails have now taught them, if much too late and at too high a price.

The fact that these parties never succeeded in changing themselves still does not mean that no such possibility ever existed in the history of real socialism. Let us recall the "Prague Spring." What distinguishes it from the recent "Prague Fall"? Above all, the fact that back then the renewal movement of Czechoslovak society was led by reformist forces within the CCP. It appears that in 1968 and 1969 certain conditions existed in that country for a democratic transformation of both the party and the system as a whole. Society still had faith in the possibilities of socialism. Within the party itself, there were influential forces capable of effecting a democratic change. During that period reciprocal movement "from below" and "from above" could have created real preconditions in Czechoslovakia for the party's voluntary renunciation of absolute power and its development into a new, pluralist structure as one of several political forces. It is entirely possible that two or more parties could have emerged on a socialist platform, parties that would have provided the basic system of counterbalances that the society of real socialism was so lacking in. In any case, the ideas of one reformist party leader, Z. Mlynar, and his "team," which drew up plans for political reform in Czechoslovakia, were developing in precisely that direction.

At that time, as we now know, the chance to transform the ruling party was missed. All attempts by communist parties to democratize themselves, not just in the past but today as well, have ended in utter fiasco. As a result, quite a few scholars, including scholars in Marxist circles, have concluded that statist-type parties are incapable of reform, that it is impossible to reconcile their activity with the requirements of a civil society. Needless to say, it is very difficult to disprove this conclusion.

From the 1970s on, it was difficult to stop the erosion of the ruling communist parties' moral and political positions: they were heading straight to their defeat. That defeat was no accident, but the natural outcome of attempts to preserve a political organization that had outlived its time.

In late 1989 and early 1990, that is, after the revolutionary events, the communist and workers' parties in virtually all the East European countries held extraordinary congresses to decide their future. The congresses took place in an extremely complex political atmosphere—amid deepening crises in the parties themselves and intensifying attacks by the opposition forces, which were gaining in popularity and influence. The communist party congresses failed to become turning points in the parties' revival, and were unable to consolidate them on a new basis. This was impeded by continuing division within party ranks and the absence of new ideological reference points.

Despite the contradictory situation persisting in the parties in early 1990, two tendencies can be identified in their development. Some communist parties embarked on the path of creating leftist parties of a new type. Others tried to confine themselves to moderate changes. The first to set about shaping a new party were reformist forces in the old HSWP, which founded the Hungarian Socialist Party. The next to do so was the PUWP, which summed up its past and adopted a decision to liquidate itself. A new Social Democratic Party of the Republic of Poland arose on its foundation. The decision to create leftist parties of a new type is one of the most important results of the current stage. This decision signaled liberation from illusions about artificially extending the life of an organization that belonged to a completely different era. In creating the new parties, communist reformers were also seeking to accomplish more specific tasks, especially to distance themselves from the hard-core elements that still held strong positions in the parties, to break down the obstruction of the apparatus, and to cut off the line of responsibility for past mistakes and deformations. Formation of new leftist parties, however, did not proceed painlessly in either Hungary or Poland. There was no avoiding a split in the leftist forces. In Hungary, a social democratic party and a communist party emerged from the former HSWP. In Poland, the PUWP gave rise to two social democratic parties, one of which includes Christian democratic ideas in its program.

In other parties—the Bulgarian Communist Party [BCP], the Czechoslovak Communist Party, the Party of Democratic Socialism [PDS] (the former Socialist Unity Party of Germany), and the league of Communists of Yugoslavia—a tendency to pursue limited transformations and to preserve certain previous ideas and ties with their historical past initially prevailed. However, it gradually became clear that reforms of this type no longer satisfied many rank-and-file communists.

The massive exodus from party ranks continued, and in society itself, the reforms in these parties failed to inspire confidence. Steps taken in the PDS, the CCP, and the BCP to purge their leadership and to uncover corruption and malfeasance among their former leaders not only failed to enhance these parties' prestige, but actually intensified the opposite process.

The only party that managed for a time to avoid such wrenching upheaval was the League of Communists of Yugoslavia [LYC]. However, the split that occurred at its Extraordinary 14th Congress indicated that it, too, had difficult times in store. The LYC had long been torn by conflicts among its individual republic organizations. Recent events show that efforts to preserve the League of Communists as a centralist nationwide organization will not succeed. The process of the party's federalization has gone so far that it will be very difficult to stop it, given the buildup of nationality and ethnic conflicts in the country as a whole. In addition, the uneven nature of reform processes in the individual republics seems likely to lead to the future emergence of dissimilar party structures based on incompatible principles and having differing programs. This unevenness in the development of republic organizations is already being felt. For example, the Slovenian and Croatian Communists have given up their power monopolies and called for the development of political pluralism. The communist parties in a number of other republics continue to adhere to their former principles. Clearly, one cannot rule out the emergence of various types of leftist parties in Yugoslavia in the near future.

On the whole, late 1989 and early 1990 were for all the East European communist parties, as one Bulgarian party leader was forced to admit, a "time of lost opportunities." On the threshold of the first free elections, these parties could not articulate programs that could meet the aspirations of broad segments of the populations. They failed to restructure themselves, to throw off the continuing burden of the past, and to overcome internal discord. Today, even moderate reformers are forced to admit: Yes, partial restructuring has failed once again; yes, it is necessary to form a new type of party. In an attempt to overcome the negative stereotype of the communist party that exists in society, their successors have begun changing the parties' names, electing new leaders, and reorganizing the parties' structure. But overcoming the widespread public lack of confidence in the communists is proving difficult. Incidentally, even the parties that embarked on a reformist path much earlier are finding themselves in a difficult situation. For example, the new leftist party in Hungary, the HSP, has also failed to win broad support in society. "We have made quite a few mistakes lately, and they [the mistakes—L. Sh.] are taking revenge on us," said one HSP leader, L. M. Szabo. "We should have dissolved the party and formed a new one a year ago, and not tried to give the impression that we were united. We did this too late, at a time when people no longer believed us."[3] Yes, "too late"—this pessimistic conclusion with respect to the communist parties is heard rather often, sometimes in Marxist circles. Indeed, the crisis of the East European communist parties or their successors has not been overcome and has even deepened.

At present, a completely new situation has arisen in the various East European countries. In the past, a single party claimed to represent socialist ideas in each country. Today a diversity of schools, movements, associations, and parties proclaiming socialist ideals is gradually taking shape in certain countries. Some of them are still in an amorphous state. Both the new and the old leftist forces lack sufficient clarity in their program concepts, and their social base has yet to settle. Still, certain embryonic tendencies can already be discerned in this rather chaotic development. Thus, one can more or less clearly differentiate three new schools: socialist, communist, and mixed. Groups and parties belonging to the first school seek to develop social democratic concepts, drawing on the theoretical and practical experience of both Western social democracy and the nationally based socialist movement that was cut off in the late 1940s. The second group of parties and groupings seeks to preserve a link with the communist

---

[3]*Polityka*, Jan. 1, 1990.

heritage. It emphasizes the need to maintain the purity of Marxist ideology and to defend class principles and the masses' egalitarian sentiments, and it seeks to preserve the communist parties' old foundations, especially democratic centralism. Finally, the third group of parties is trying to synthesize certain Marxist-Leninist precepts and social democratic ideas. Through ideological and organizational compromises, they are trying to avert a split and to unite both leftists and rightists in their ranks.

In Western Europe, one rather often hears the view that, of all the present leftist forces in the East European countries, only the social democrats have a future. A comment made by the prominent West German Social Democrat Oskar Lafontaine is popular: "There is a specter roaming Eastern Europe, the specter of social democracy." Social democratic ideas have indeed struck a chord among the intelligentsia and some young people. But for the present, at least, their attraction should not be exaggerated. Thus, the Hungarian and Polish Socialists (the communist parties' successors) have yet to succeed in attracting the masses with social democratic slogans. Perhaps the social democratic parties that are forming on a completely new basis and are not linked in any way with the former communist parties will enjoy greater popularity, as the experience of the G.D.R. and Czechoslovakia indicates.

However, it cannot be said that the communist-oriented parties have lost their social backing altogether. They have supporters not only among the older population, which finds it difficult to abandon former precepts and loyalties, but also among part of the working class, especially among workers at large enterprises. In some countries, radical leftist traditions are still alive. But in most countries these parties can hardly become mass organizations.

On the whole, the new types of leftist parties in the East European countries are still in the formative process, a process characterized primarily by rejection of both ideological and organizational rigidity. Most of the new and transformed parties are trying to take a critical approach to their Marxist-Leninist heritage. Their attempt to divest their activity of excessive ideology and to formulate more pragmatic programs is noteworthy. Virtually all the leftist parties propose programs of democratic socialism in which they attempt to combine traditional socialist values with the concept of transition to a market economy. But there is also diversity in their understanding of the democratic socialist formula. For example, the ideologists of the Party of Democratic Socialism interpret it as a third path of development between capitalism and authoritarian socialism. In a number of other parties, including the Hungarian Socialist Party and the Polish Social Democratic Party, there is a very strong view of democratic socialism as a program that permits a return to the values of world civilization, and integration with Western countries. Thus, the Slovenian Communist Party's new program is titled "For a European Living Standard." The document specifies ways to incorporate the republic in all-European structures. For its part, the Bulgarian Socialist Party is developing a platform called "The Bulgarian Path to Europe." Its leader, Mitev, observes: "It is essential to move away from the 'bloc society' that arose in our countries. We must restore the severed ties between East and West, that is, carry out a reintegration."[4] Many ideologists with a liberal view of democratic socialism are trying to overcome the old rigid ideological schemes and to appeal to the entire spectrum of the leftist intellectual movement. They interpret socialism itself as a school, movement, or tendency in the development of humanity. They usually regard the Scandinavian model of development as the ideal social system.

By contrast, among circles that are increasingly called the "traditionalists" or "fundamentalists," the notion of "democratic socialism" is being used in an effort to preserve the tenets of Marxist-Leninist ideology. But these circles no longer play a decisive role in the leftist movement.

Not only are the leftist forces' ideological platforms changing, the organizational principles of their activity are changing as well. A number of parties have abandoned the principle of democratic centralism and are trying to base their activity primarily on the principles of democratic unity or consensus. Thus, conditions are expanding for the development within parties of a pluralism of views, positions, and interests, as reflected in the formation of party clubs and various tendencies and platforms. In some parties, factions have begun to emerge, which is in itself no longer considered seditious. At the same time, we should point out that so far these parties have no mechanism for reconciling different positions. Hence it is very difficult for the new parties to reach common decisions, and they also lack sufficient internal consolidation to wage an active political struggle.

Most of the leftist parties have embarked on a fundamental restructuring of their central bodies, which are now more akin to party parliaments than secretive military headquarters. Their apparatus has been cut substantially (by more than half, and in some parties by 70 to 75 percent), and it now performs purely technical functions. Internal party activity is becoming largely voluntary. The center of activity is shifting to the lower-level party organizations, which now have a strong set of rights and can form horizontal structures at their discretion.

---

[4]*Narodna mladezh*, Jan. 16, 1990.

The separation of communist parties from the state has occurred, and this process ultimately concluded with the formation of new governments in free elections. In spite of some resistance, most leftist parties in the individual countries have already left the army and the justice and internal affairs agencies, which will now be ideologically neutral. The communist parties were forced to abandon their orientation toward the production principle of activity, which ensured party organizations' ability to interfere in economic life, and from every indication, this abandonment became universal. The leftist parties are quitting the enterprises and shifting their activities to territorial entities, where the main political struggle is now taking place. These parties are trying to reestablish a mechanism through which they can indirectly influence society—through the creation of discussion clubs and various associations. This process, however, is proving difficult: The parties' loss of the elementary skills required to exist without state "props" is taking its toll. The leftist parties' development is in the direction of becoming loosely organized movement-type parties in which there is room for both ideological and organizational diversity.

For now, the process of establishing a new structure of leftist forces and of organizing each such individual force has only begun and may assume the most diverse forms. One cannot rule out the departure of some leftist parties from the political arena and the emergence of others. The splitting of some existing parties into several groups or parties is also possible. A number of factions and platforms in various parties could at any moment turn into independent parties. In other cases, several platforms or movements will probably coalesce into a single party. Establishment of more or less stable party structures, especially following such a severe upheaval, will take considerable time.

The first free parliamentary elections were a serious test for the leftist parties. What was their outcome? In the overwhelming majority of East European countries, the elections resulted in the defeat of the communists, and of leftist forces in general. In those countries, coalition governments were created, but without communists or representatives of other leftist forces. For the first time in a long time, these forces were forced to go into opposition. In most countries, it is unlikely that socialist forces will exert a dominant influence in politics in the near future. In fact, in many of the region's countries, it is doubtful that any leftist parties will play a substantial role in the foreseeable future. Such is the price that these forces are being forced to pay for their long years of absolute power. A leader of the former Polish communist party speculated, "One cannot rule out the possibility that rightist governments will rule throughout Eastern Europe in the coming decade. This will be a reaction to the communists' past failures—both real and exaggerated."[5]

In this connection, there is mounting skepticism in the East European countries with regard to the prospects of leftist forces, especially those of communist parties. Many Western Marxists have expressed the same view. "It's the end of the system spawned by 1917," said M. Jacques, editor in chief of *Marxism Today*, the theoretical journal of British communists. "It's the end of the road for those systems based on single-party states, highly centralized planning, authoritarian systems cut off from the Western world."[6]

How justified are these conclusions? How is one to explain what is happening to the communist parties of Eastern Europe: as the crisis of their final collapse, or a crisis leading to rebirth? It seems that essentially the same process is taking place in both the East European and Western communist movements—the gradual departure from the arena of authoritarian political organizations that sought to bring about an oversimplified communist utopia. Some of these parties will disappear tomorrow. Others could linger in political life for an indefinite period, but eventually they too will likely become a marginal force.

Does this mean the end of the leftist vision of social development? By no means! Our own experience as well as Western experience shows that civilization cannot exist and renew itself without alternatives. An absolute monopoly by rightist neoliberal or conservative forces could lead to no less grievous consequences than the absolute power of leftist doctrinaires. Even Walesa, one of the most famous leaders of the noncommunist movement today, recently declared that society can "stand only on two legs—its right and its left." However, only the socialist forces that succeed in creating a truly democratic organization and in combining the ideals of equality and social protection with the demands of social and, above all, economic progress have a future. The social atmosphere now in most of the countries would not favor a revival of the leftist parties—they are burdened by the mistrust created by their predecessors. But in the next few years, the need for such parties will obviously grow in all these countries. This is inevitable as these countries move to market economies, when the problem of social justice will become especially acute. But it is quite possible that at such a moment the leftist forces will face a serious new threat—the danger of becoming political organizations representing the interests of a populist movement. As market economies are established, how

---

[5]*Polityka*, Jan. 13, 1990.
[6]*Newsweek*, Dec. 11, 1989, p. 60.

can they avoid the temptation to become representatives only of the neglected segment of society? How can they avoid an egalitarian bias, and how can they keep from becoming parties of the social groups that are on their way out and have now become conservative? This is a question that all the leftist parties will eventually face, and their future will depend on how they resolve it.

In any case, one should probably not oversimplify the picture of political life in Eastern Europe, as some Western observers do when they speak of the final defeat of socialist ideas in the region. Everything is far more complex. There is a paradox in that these ideas have a sizable social base and apparently will continue to have one in the future, and yet their former spokesmen and representatives have lost public support. Their very understanding of socialist ideals has also been discredited. But when the real transition to market economies takes place in the East European countries, a reinvigoration of the leftist forces and their ideology is inevitable. At the same time, it is clear that socialist organizations of various shades will no longer be the sole force in the political arena. They may not even be a very influential force. It all depends on the specific situations in the various countries. In some of them, socialist organizations have so discredited themselves that they may be forever confined to secondary or even tertiary roles. In other countries, they may acquire a larger social base, especially if tendencies toward the development of lumpen groups are strong in the society. The authority and influence of leftist forces will largely depend on their ability to unite (for the present, internal strife is tearing them apart) and to win allies, for example, among democratic movements, and especially among Greens, pacifists, and so forth.

3. The Dialectics of Political Pluralism

For the first time after decades of leveling, or of strictly rationed diversity controlled from above, Eastern Europe has embarked on the path of real political pluralism. Public life in the individual countries now represents a Brownian movement of dozens and perhaps even hundreds of associations, groupings, tendencies, and parties. In most countries, this process has been legalized by appropriate legislation. It is unlikely that anyone could imagine the elaborate mosaic of diversity that has suddenly sprung up in all the countries: Some political organizations emerge, while others suddenly disappear or change their names and orientations. Most are still shaping or clarifying their programs and organizational principles and searching for their social base. But no matter how confused the incipient new political structure of society may be, several types of political associations can already be distinguished.

Let us first consider the noncommunist parties that existed under the administrative system. Such parties operated in Bulgaria, the G.D.R., Poland, and Czechoslovakia. Granted, most of these organizations could be called a party in name only—they had all become rubber stamps for the ruling parties, essentially branches operating under different names. In the context of the current political reinvigoration, however, it has suddenly come to light that forces aspiring to independent activity, to a life free of the leash, have survived in these parties.

The Polish noncommunist parties—the United Peasants Party (UPP) and the Democratic Party (DP)—were the first to embark on the path of revival, but their first show of independence had painful consequences for the communists. The UPP and the DP began by abandoning the PUWP and siding with the opposition at a crucial moment, when the fate of the new Polish government was being decided. From a moral standpoint, this step can be assessed in different ways, but politics has its own logic. Evidently these parties, having long played the unenviable role of tools of others' will, felt that the past had released them from any further obligations to the PUWP. This example only demonstrated the utter unreliability of coalitions and multiparty arrangements based on coercion and inequality. Following the Polish noncommunist parties' lead, others soon embarked on an independent path, including the Czechoslovak People's Party, Czechoslovak Socialist Party, Slovak Freedom Party, Liberal Democratic (LDPG), National Democratic Party of Germany, Democratic Farmers' Party of Germany, the G.D.R. Christian Democratic Union, and the Bulgarian Agrarian People's Union (BAPU). Many of them adopted a critical, opposition stance toward the communists. It is noteworthy that in many of these parties, the renewal of both program and organization started to proceed much more rapidly than in the communist parties. Many of the ideas these parties espouse—liberal democracy, individual freedoms, the rule of law, antimonopolist guarantees, mixed forms of property ownership, the defense of free enterprise, and transfer of the land to the peasants—have struck a certain chord in society. It should be pointed out that some of Eastern Europe's surviving noncommunist parties have long-standing progressive traditions. The Czechoslovak People's Party and Czechoslovak Socialist Party have carried on the democratic movements of the late 19th century; the LDPG traces its origin to the German People's Party and German Democratic Party, which were liquidated by the Hitler regime; the BAPU arose early this century. These parties' rich historical past and traditions are a significant factor in their activation today. At the same time, many of them also feel the burden of a past marked by inglorious obedience and withdrawal from independent activity, which hinders their efforts to expand their popular base. For this reason, the noncommunist parties that survived the administrative system are trying to make the most drastic changes in a bid to create a new image for themselves in society. Granted, they do not always succeed in doing so.

In addition to the old parties, a great many new movements, associations, and parties have emerged in the East European countries. Their membership varies—from a few dozen to tens of thousands. Particular mention should be made of the revival of parties that once existed in the people's democratic countries, but whose activities were forcibly terminated. They include the National Peasants Party and National Liberal Party of Romania, the Smallholders Party in Hungary, and the Polish Peasants Party. Once-liquidated social democratic parties are being revived everywhere. For example, the newly organized Social Democratic Party of Czechoslovakia has already overtaken the Czechoslovak Communist Party in its membership. There are many indications that these resurrected "historical" parties, which once enjoyed considerable prestige and popularity, could become an influential political force today.

Nevertheless, most of the new associations and parties in the region's countries are appearing for the first time. It is these new parties, unburdened by any responsibility for the totalitarian perversions of the past, that have the greatest prospects in the East European countries. In contrast to the cadre-style parties, they represent a completely new type of party that has a flexible organizational structure; usually lacks intermediate organizational bodies, or has them only in the form of coordination centers; and permits broad pluralism of views. For these parties, the institution of membership is far less important than the ability, at critical times (for example, at election time), to influence the electorate. A distinctive feature of the G.D.R. is the formation there of a multiparty structure analogous to the one that already exists in the F.R.G.

Now, however, the largest and most influential organizations in the East European countries are not parties at all, but broad democratic movements that have no rigid institution of membership and include representatives of various social strata and ideological and political schools. These include Civic Forum in Czechoslovakia, the Union of Democratic Forces in Bulgaria, the National Salvation Front in Romania, and Solidarity in Poland. These movements arose on a wave of protest against authoritarianism and dictatorial regimes. For the time being, they are amorphous in nature, but the political struggle is forcing them, little by little, to acquire certain organizational structures. In Romania, prior to the elections, the National Salvation Front became a provisional institution of power, which created very favorable conditions for its participation in the elections. In Czechoslovakia, also prior to the creation of a new parliament, Civic Forum, which had succeeded in assuming the leadership of the popular movement, essentially took on the basic functions of governing the country. In other countries, alternative movements were somewhat weaker at first. But in early 1990, opposition forces began joining forces on a common platform in those countries too. An example is the growing popularity of Bulgaria's Union of Democratic Forces, which has become a serious opponent of the communist party.

At the same time, one cannot overlook contradictions in the mass movements' development. These movements were a decisive force in the destruction of the outmoded social mechanisms. They cleared the way to power for new political forces and new leaders. But under conditions of peace, especially if they are not opposed by a serious political force, their role inevitably declines, centrifugal tendencies begin building in them, and the factors that divide the diverse social and national groups come to the surface. Such was the fate of the former popular fronts in the people's democratic countries.

To a certain extent, this pattern is being repeated in the development of Poland's Solidarity. It began as a mass movement protesting administrative socialism and, according to some estimates, enjoyed the support of nearly 10 million Poles. In the past few years, its supporters have not exceeded 2 million people, and their number continues to fall. Solidarity's assumption of power intensified the divisions in its ranks, and naturally so, since Solidarity's leaders had to choose one of the numerous orientations within it, creating a camp of discontented members. Subsequently, the struggle within Solidarity among its various tendencies—especially between the syndicalist and political-party tendencies—has become an obvious fact. It is obvious that the once powerful movement will split in the near future into several parties, or into a party and a trade union. It will be hard for diverse social tendencies, forces which in some cases represent opposing interests, to live under the same roof. In the past, they were all united by a common opponent—the PUWP. Now new socialist parties have emerged. An interesting situation has developed: Certain forces in the socialist parties and in Solidarity have a far easier time reaching agreement with one another than with colleagues in their own organizations. This could become the foundation for new political alliances in the future. A similar blurring of the boundaries between separate groupings in the leftist parties and among alternative forces is taking place in other countries too. Thus, new groupings and parties will inevitably emerge from the noncommunist mass movements in all the East European countries.

Despite the existence of mass movements in the various countries, the pluralism that has arisen in these countries is fragmented, and, as mentioned earlier, the mass alternative movements themselves are highly unstable and could splinter into a number of parties and groupings in the future. In a situation of fragmented pluralism, any force that has political ambitions has to look for allies.

Let us now try to see the overall picture of political life in the East European countries. For all their differences, we can identify one set of characteristics that is common to all the countries: a weak center; relatively active movement on the right, to which the activity of most of the newly formed associations is shifting; and a highly diffuse field on the left, which for now is characterized by less political vitality, and is much less populated. Some parties, like the Christian Democratic Party in the G.D.R. and Democratic Forum in Hungary, are clearly trying to take centrist positions and become moderators of sorts in relations between left and right. However, it must be said that the "center" exhibits a clear tilt to the right, possibly because of the leftist parties' continuing weakness. Noncommunist forces were particularly active in forming blocs in the East European countries on the eve of the 1990 elections. This was a natural manifestation of their struggle for power. Once they had won power, however, centrifugal tendencies began to emerge in the coalitions. New centers of political struggle arose, this time in the victors' camp. Thus, the first act of the political play has ended. The second act has begun; it will be marked by the development of a new correlation of forces and the appearance of new political actors aspiring to power.

What political tendencies have appeared in the East European countries? There is a great multitude: leftist, including social democratic; neoliberal and Westernizer national-patriotic; populist and agrarian (narodnik); ecological; anarchist; and Christian democratic. There are also manifestations of other orientations, including fascist, and even monarchist. In addition to the secular political forces, all manner of religious organizations and associations, as well as the churches themselves, are active in certain countries—granted, often behind the scenes. In the G.D.R., it was the Evangelical Church, long in opposition to the former regime, that gave shelter and refuge to dissidents, in effect creating a foundation for the formation of the opposition movement. It also initiated the round-table talks between the opposition and the communists, without which it would have hardly been possible to accomplish the painless transition to the new system of power. In Poland, the assistance of the Catholic Church also made it possible to carry the dialogue between the PUWP and Solidarity through to conclusion, and it was that dialogue that resulted in the new political structure's emergence in the country. The powerful, though veiled, influence of the Catholic hierarchy and Catholic social doctrine on society's political course can be felt in that country even now. It would be no exaggeration to conclude that no significant decision can be taken in Poland if the country's Catholic Church opposes it. Religious circles are exerting growing influence on political life in Hungary, Czechoslovakia, and certain republics of Yugoslavia. Given the division and hostility in relations between certain forces and political blocs, the church often plays a restraining and conciliatory role, trying to neutralize conflicts. But in the process its own influence and importance as a political arbiter and spokesman for certain moral and ethical values also increases.

In the multinational states—Yugoslavia, Czechoslovakia, and Romania—extremist nationalistic political groups are also forming. For the present, most are small, but rather militant. For example, one of the nationalist parties that has recently emerged in Yugoslavia, the so-called Serbian National Renewal, is calling for the creation of an independent Serbian kingdom. Along with attempts to revive the Chetnik movement that existed in the 1940s, attempts are being made in the country to organize "Great Croatian," "Great Albanian," and similar associations. In view of the intensity of national and ethnic conflicts—and not just in Yugoslavia—it is entirely possible that such movements will assume a mass character.

It is a disturbing fact that often perfectly justifiable disenchantment with former political parties develops into an unwarranted idealization of alternative movements. In these circumstances, new disenchantment is possible, and could come very soon. Of course, the new forces' leaders include people who have great moral authority in society, such as Havel, Walesa, and Zhelev. But in a number of countries, the new forces have yet to put forward charismatic figures who could unite society at such a critical time. In no country do the alternative forces have enough cadres capable of administrative work, and hence they will be forced to rely largely on the old apparatus. It must also be said that yesterday's opposition leaders are neither Martians nor ideal people raised in test tubes. They are flesh of the flesh of the society in which they were reared, and have therefore absorbed its stereotypes. It can be said bluntly that some of them are children— even if illegitimate children—of the system, who happen to be on the opposite side, but are just as disposed to intolerance and Bonapartist ways as the dogmatic communists. This is borne out by the implacable attitude many noncommunist leaders and their associates take toward the leftist forces.

It would be dangerous at present for society to become disenchanted with the new forces that have entered political life. In some countries, indications of such disenchantment are already appearing.

But if the masses lose hope in both the old and the new movements, a dangerous vacuum could form. This vacuum could be filled either by spontaneous, unorganized forces, or by the far-from-democratic forces waiting in the wings.

On the whole, political pluralism in Eastern Europe right now is highly unstable. That is understandable considering that its formation has only begun. The habits of political discourse, dialogue, and compromise that are so vital for the development of a multiparty system have been lost (and in some cases were never developed). One sees the results of the social and ethnic polarization of society, and the preservation—and in some places intensification—of an atmosphere of mutual intolerance among various groupings. However, this process is largely inevitable: The initial phases in the development of a pluralist structure are nercessarily dominated by a tendency toward division, the separation of the parts from the whole—from the masses—and the intensification of individual and collective selfishness. That is how independent political entities develop. Under these circumstances, it is difficult to avoid an intensification of political struggle and the emergence of extremism, which lends the newborn pluralism an explosive character. In any case, for now the desire to get rid of one's opponent at all costs, rather than to reach agreement, often predominates. Usually this line of conduct is pursued with respect to the communist parties or their successors, which, incidentally, complicates the process of their renewal and limits the possibilities for leftist reformers.

In all the countries, the development of pluralism in late 1989 and early 1990 was influenced by the fact that this was a period of preparation for elections. This added even greater intensity to the political clashes. All the participants in public life, without exception, strove not so much to clarify their programs or fine-tune their organizational arrangements, as to win votes, and to win them by any means. Attempts to discredit rivals became frequent, and the approach of the elections forced some organizations to adjust their programs accordingly, strengthening their populist appeal, and shelving anything that the average voter might not like. And what happened after the elections? A new stage in the political development of Eastern Europe began. In the overwhelming majority of countries, this stage will be defined by noncommunist forces, but one should not exaggerate their maturity. Their maturation and clarification of their programs and political goals are just getting under way. During this transitional period, there may still be major shifts in the activities, tactics, and strategies of all the noncommunist—i.e., liberal, national-patriotic, and Christian democratic—forces, until they solidify their new political role and identify their social base. This will take a good deal of time.

There are objective, as well as subjective, reasons for the diffuse ideological and political life in various countries. Society retains its former social-class structure, which only yesterday was supporting the edifice of statist socialism. Moreover, the crisis that persists in all the region's countries not only has not resulted in more progressive features in that structure but, on the contrary, has intensified its conservative attributes. Formation of new social groups has been suspended; the beginning tendencies toward social integration have been disrupted; differences among the masses, and irreconcilable conflicts between various social strata have intensified. In short, the attributes of the structure of an archaic industrial society have appeared. At a time when society's democratic impulse has not yet abated, and society as a whole is still experiencing a certain euphoria over its triumph, this fact is not yet discernible everywhere.

But in the countries that embarked on a reformist path earlier—in Hungary and Poland—it has already become clear just how hard it is to build a new political life on the old social foundation. Yet the formation of more dynamic social groups and interests that could become the source of new political movements is impossible. After all, the foundations of the command economy are still intact, and they continue to support the old interests and the old ideological and political stereotypes. The result is a vicious circle: The shaping of new political reality is held back for want of the necessary social and economic conditions, but the latter cannot be created without the appropriate political policies, without a change in the very substance of politics. In principle, political forces can be based not only on social differences but also on a platform of certain common interests, as shown by the development of the Greens movement. But the problem is that the persisting social structure, that of a pre-market-economy society, and that structure's characteristic system of interests and aims also complicates integration on the basis of universal human values. Consequently, even the new pluralism is firmly attached to the surviving foundation of the half-destroyed authoritarian edifice.

What might this lead to? Anything could happen. As long as the social and economic foundation of administrative socialism exists, it is difficult to eliminate a duality in society's interests, which could assume an opposite orientation. And that inevitably would affect political life, making it unpredictable. Thus, the forces that advocated democracy yesterday could suddenly make a 180-degree turn tomorrow and espouse the idea of strong government. Stalinist totalitarianism could give way to right-wing authoritarianism. The latter might be more humane and pragmatic. Nevertheless, we must admit that it is not real democracy. It is hard to predict political development that is not supported by a social and economic base. In any case, one cannot mechanically apply Western models of pluralism to the East European countries. We can already see a great many paradoxes there that would be simply unthinkable in the West. For example, a syndicalist-inclined Solidarity forms a neoliberal government that, for the first time, tries to carry out economic reform, and does so à la Thatcher, despite the egalitarian disposition of the movement's rank and file. Some leftist forces can prove further to the right than the opposition. For example, the Hungarian Socialist Party goes further in its demands for economic liberalization and the introduction of a private sector than, say, the Democratic Forum.

The formation of new parliaments and governments in Eastern Europe, which was completed by the summer of 1990, will bring a certain stability to political life. Even in the best of circumstances, however, it will take several years for the correlation of political forces in some countries to take on even a relatively stable character. We will still see repeated changes of government, the collapse of some alliances and coalitions, and the formation of others. One must also consider that a variety of fundamentally rather weak movements that can hardly as yet pursue a stable course is emerging in many countries.

What contribution will the alternative forces make to the new character of public life in these countries? Considering the coalitional character of the new governments, one can assume that society's political course will be based on compromises among various parties and movements. The existing correlation of forces in the East European countries and the nature of the dominant ideologies permit us to assume that the near future of these countries will be defined by struggle and cooperation among the neoliberal, leftist, national-patriotic, and populist political schools. These schools can form various combinations with one another. Depending on the content of such political alliances, three basic options are possible for the East European countries' further development.

Let us begin with the neoliberal option, since Poland has already begun to implement it, and other countries are leaning toward it. The essence of the neoliberal course is as follows: political and ideological pluralism, that is, competition among all forces and their programs of development; broad-based, Western-style democracy with its characteristic system of separation of powers, a state based on the rule of law, and emphasis on citizens' individual rights and freedoms; and an immediate transition to a market economy, with limits on the protective role of the state. The neoliberals believe that the only way to reinvigorate society is to return to private property and to emphasize enterprise, competition, and individualism. In effect, they reject the possibility of a "third," nonauthoritarian path of development, and propose adoption of the solutions that Western society has devised.

The essence of the neoliberal concept was described in Solidarity's newspaper in the following terms. "We will have to pass through a stage from which we once withdrew, through a stage of selfish capitalism with its struggle among people, its lockouts, and its unemployment."[7]

The fate of the neoliberal course in Eastern Europe—its victory or defeat—will in many respects depend on whether the pioneering countries succeed in carrying out the entire planned series of steps—including reprivatization, price reform, liquidation of unprofitable enterprises, and the curbing of hyperinflation—and in avoiding severe social shocks in the process. Heed should be paid to the views of observers who believe that attempts to enter the market "in one great plunge" are too dangerous to social stability. Some believe it altogether impossible to switch to a market economy amid shortages and deepening economic crisis. But even under favorable conditions, many believe that it could take 15 to 20 years to establish a market economy. In short, there are considerable grounds for skepticism about radical economic reforms. The neoliberals also have an important argument in their favor; though. So far not a single attempt, including those made in Hungary and Poland in the 1980s, to enter the market gradually has ever succeeded either. A second argument is that "shock therapy"—that is, a decisive plunge into the free interplay of market forces—has enabled Poland to create at least the initial foundation for real economic relations, and to curb hyperinflation. Poland will obviously not be able to avoid various shocks on this path, either. But I think that this risk is still much smaller than the risk entailed in slow rot.

The political forces advocating the social democratic scenario of development seek to combine the ideas of equality and social justice with the requirements of a market economy. A mixed economy, equality for all forms of property, employee participation in managing production and controlling the distribution of goods, state oversight over the development of a market economy, and emphasis on social policy—these are the main features of their program. The social democratic path takes more fully into account our region's social complexity and the widespread unpreparedness in the population for life under market conditions. Only the future will tell which means of treating the patient is better—surgery or medication. Yet world experience indicates that the social democratic model of development is more suited to a period of prosperity and social stability; periods in which efforts are made to overcome crises and to search for new growth incentives have

---

[7]*Tygodnik solidarnosci*, Nov. 17, 1989.

always been accompanied by the conservatives' assumption of power. We will soon see whether Eastern Europe rejects this pattern or follows it.

In this context, one must mention another option for development—the authoritarian option. Unfortunately, it has not yet been ruled out completely in most of the countries. Depending on each country's national and other distinctive features, authoritarianism could take various forms—a dictatorship ruled by one or several political forces, or quite possibly, even by the army. A purely administrative or party-controlled authoritarianism is theoretically possible. A relapse of authoritarianism is likeliest to occur in the event that the neoliberal or social democratic options for development fail. It cannot be ruled out if the ruling political forces prove unable to form constructive coalitions, in situations where there is an incessant power struggle and a deepening crisis in society. Authoritarianism can appear as a result of populist or national-patriotic movements. However, it is always hard to separate them.

Let us emphasize that the potential social base for a regime of "strong-authority" exists in all the countries. It is possible that in one country or another such a regime will prove to be a forced means, or the only possible means of maintaining stability in a society torn by social and national conflicts. But in any case, such a course of events would only complicate and slow the transition to a new society.

4. The Complexities and Contradictions of Transition

It would be an error to assume that a new society is already developing in the East European countries. They are in various phases of transition from authoritarianism to democracy. This period has its own logic and characteristics—although they are still not entirely clear—and it will inevitably take a long time. So far there has been no historical experience in transforming a party-statist system of the pseudosocialist type. Therefore, we have set out on an uncharted course along which many surprises await us. It is important here to try to analyze the problems arising in the East European countries today.

The fact that a mass protest movement directed against the administrative system emerged in all these countries does not yet mean that all obstacles on the path to forming a democratic society have disappeared. The braking mechanism continues to operate in these countries, but it is changing somewhat. In most of the neighboring countries, Stalinist or neo-Stalinist forces have been isolated and removed from power. Yet all the countries still have a very broad social base for conservatism of a different sort, conservatism mingled with nationalism, chauvinism, egalitarianism, and stereotypes and prejudices inherited from authoritarian socialism. In addition, as individual countries move from destruction of the old to creation of the new, they will increasingly feel the effects of the absence or underdevelopment of the traditions of civil society, the limited political sophistication of many of the working people, the uneven development of various regions, the multinational nature of some of these countries, and so on. They are feeling ever more keenly the disruption of historical continuity that previously occurred in socialist society, the severing of connections with universal civilization, the loss of traditions, and the weakening of the role of spiritual and moral ideals—in short, the loss of everything that might provide for the internal integration of society and help cushion social shocks.

Under these conditions, the breakdown of external administrative connections increases the danger of disintegration and uncontrollable events. It is very difficult and even risky to erect a new structure on soil that is crumbling underfoot. Let us add to this the fact that in all these countries, the transition to a democratic system is taking place amid social and economic crisis, which also limits the possibilities of reform. After all, one must avoid exacerbating the already explosive situation and, to this end, postpone adoption of various radical measures for improving the economy.

Many of the complexities in the reformist countries result from lack of a clear vision of the new society that is to be built, and of proven tactics and strategy for the transition period. The old concepts have been discarded, but the resulting theoretical vacuum has yet to be filled. Therefore, social movement is now proceeding more by trial and error, and is often utterly unplanned. There is nothing inherently wrong about unplanned development; self-regulation was precisely what the old society so badly lacked. But the logic of the transition period requires political will and possibly strong pressure, clear ideas and goals, and a vision of the future, without which the creation of new structures could be delayed or even stopped. Western society is where reform has become a continuous process of spontaneous self-renewal, although forceful methods sometimes have to be used there too. In our countries, the internal source of self-regulation has been lost, or more precisely, destroyed by the administrative system. Therefore, society still needs an outside push to get moving. The new forces coming to power are sometimes weak and inexperienced, lack clear goals, or are simply afraid of taking unpopular but often unavoidable action for fear of losing support among the masses.

An antiauthoritarian movement has emerged in all the countries, but not one has developed a sufficiently broad social base for a specific political course. The need to adopt tough measures to introduce economic regulators may narrow the reformers' public support. The problem of consolidating the supporters of the emerging democratic, market-type system is now appearing in all the countries. In this connection, it is essential to reconsider the old notions about leading social forces. Accordingly, many people are now reflecting on the role the working class will play in the impending transformations, and whose side it will take—the side of the social democrats, the communists, the syndicalists, the neoliberals, or the populists? The situation in the working class is complex, and differentiation within it continues. There are groups of workers who support the policy of democratization and a market economy, but a substantial number still fear reforms. The first attempts to introduce market mechanisms in Hungary and Poland have already provoked open discontent and demonstrations by workers, especially the employees of large enterprises and workers employed in heavy industry. Will the working class be able to voluntarily adapt to new forms of activity? The fate of East European reforms will largely depend on this. It should be noted, however, that the reforms are supposed to lead to the creation of a "service and information society" in which the traditional proletariat and its class ideology will simply disappear, and in which the workers will be fated to play a completely different role. In light of this, there is no country where one can completely rule out the emergence of worker opposition to the new structures, or even an alliance between that opposition and neo-Stalinist or populist forces.

Among the obstacles to the creation of a new society, one can also distinguish certain illusions about restructuring. One of them concerns the possibilities of pluralism, democracy, and self-government. Their attraction for masses that long lived under totalitarian laws is fully understandable; however, there are no grounds for turning these principles into absolutes or for viewing them as the sole regulator of development, as some noncommunist forces do. World experience shows that pluralism, democracy, and self-government can function only in combination with a certain amount of centralization, with reconciliation mechanisms in place. The emphasis that is being placed in some countries on just one side of the balance has seriously complicated not only restructuring but also efforts to bring elementary order to the life of society.

The East European countries' further development can also be complicated by extremes in determining paths of renewal. In most of these countries, the politically active part of society has split into supporters of a national path of development and "Westernizers." In some cases, this division overshadows all other political differences. For example, supporters of both orientations, Western and national, can be found among both leftist forces and alternative groupings. Life is demonstrating the possibility of the most unexpected shifts. Proponents of the "national path" can be found both in the communist parties and among the recent opposition forces; they stress the need to consider the distinctive nature of the East European region and of their own countries; they emphasize their uniqueness and independent logic of development; and they argue that implanting "alien" mechanisms is impossible. They propound the idea of a third, independent path of development and urge that national social forms be devised. Some of them question the possibility of integrating their countries into world relations. The views of extreme East European proponents of the "native-soil" approach* approximate those of our own "native soil" or "pro-unity" advocates, who are fond of saying: "Russia cannot be grasped through reason, nor measured by the common standard."

Of course, one cannot apply the same standard to all proponents of a "third path." They do include outspoken nationalist conservatives who oppose a market economy and pluralism in general and are prepared to accept a "patriotic dictatorship." But they also include influential moderate forces that are trying to find a new social path of development and are seeking to combine traditional market mechanisms and West European democracy with specific national characteristics. This is precisely the orientation of Hungary's Democratic Forum.

For their part, proponents of incorporating society into West European integration mechanisms and of making direct use of Western developmental experience are to be found among Bulgarian Communists as well as members of Bulgaria's Union of Democratic Forces; among Slovenian and Croatian Communists and the local opposition; among members of Hungary's Alliance of Free Democrats and the Hungarian Socialists; and in Czechoslovakia's Civic Forum, the socialist wing of the Polish leftists, and Solidarity. They, too, have considerable differences in their understanding of social goals and the pace at which they should be pursued. They can be divided by personal ambition and the logic of the struggle for power. But there is also something else that unites the "Westernizers." They argue that all attempts to find a third path will inevitably lead society to a new impasse. "It's not necessary to reinvent the bicycle, even a six-wheeled one," they say. "What is necessary is to get onto the road that Western society is taking." Hungary's Alliance of Free Democrats is a typical representative of the Western orientation. "There can be no third path

---

*[The author calls these people *pochvenniki*. Derived from the Russian word *pochva*, or "soil," *pochvenniki* was the name originally adopted by a group of 19th-century Russian intellectuals, including Dostoevsky, who believed that social institutions must be grounded in national tradition, or the native "soil."—*Trans.*]

of social development," its program declares. "Our goal is to return to European civilization. We are moving from one social system to the other. No third system is possible."

Only experience can provide the most compelling argument in favor of any given path of development. It is clear, however, that extremes—both the refusal to see the logic of development that applies to civilization as a whole, and the unwillingness to take into account the characteristics and level of development of individual countries—can lead only to the creation of new artificial constructs that ignore the wealth of approaches and tendencies to be found in real life. Eastern Europe has already begun to turn toward societal forms that do not belong to any single class but have been worked out in the course of human development. But it is clear that institutions tested and proven under one set of national conditions will operate differently under other national conditions. In some countries, the universal, civilizationwide laws of development are already beginning to take on rather unique forms. This is reflected in the development of pluralism, market relations, parliamentary democracy, and approaches to the problem of nationalities. The East European countries are beginning to embark on the common road of progress, but with their own baggage of traditions, experience, and stereotypes. Granted, before joining the developed societies, they will have to get through a highly complex and drastic transition.

The main trials for the East European countries still lie ahead, and the decisive trial will be the transition to a market economy. For the time being, the development of democracy and pluralism is suspended in midair, as it were. Only new economic relations and a market economy, with its complex system of forms of ownership, can guarantee the irreversibility of changes. If efforts to create it fail, the entire superstructure will collapse like a house of cards. That is why the problem of establishing a market economy has now become the key problem in building a new society. Few now doubt, at least openly, the need to shift to economic regulators. Debates over how to effect the transition to a market economy—all at once or gradually—and where to begin are becoming secondary. From every indication, the new forces coming to power do not intend to put off this transition.

Today, the question of the transition's political forms is proving more important. As we know, Western Europe and world civilization as a whole took the path of first creating a market base; this base was often formed under authoritarian or semiauthoritarian regimes, on which later democratic institutions were imposed. A distinctive feature of Eastern Europe has been the accelerated course of political reforms and democratization of society. This is no accident, but rather the logical result of development according to an inverted pattern. In the socialist authoritarian societies, politics supplanted all of societal life, including economics, which simply did not exist for us in the traditional sense. Under these conditions, government reform and a fundamental change in the content and role of politics are the key precondition for all other transformations.

However, the accelerated pace of political changes is already creating considerable problems in all the countries. These problems are a direct consequence of the discrepancy, and often contradiction, between the tasks of democracy and the requirements of economic efficiency. In some countries, the state is finding it increasingly difficult to withstand the onslaught of consumer interests sparked by liberalization, interests that are very hard to channel in the direction of production. Under these conditions, calls for the establishment of authoritarian government are beginning to be heard here and there, even among new ruling circles.

Unquestionably, both Hungarian and Polish experience already shows that it is very difficult to introduce a market under the conditions of democratization. However, the authoritarian regimes that existed until recently in all the countries of the "socialist world" hardly led to the creation of a market economy. On the other hand, comparisons with South Korea, post-Franco Spain, or Chile after Pinochet, which did achieve economic upturns under dictatorships, are wholly inapplicable to us. Even under totalitarianism, all the aforementioned countries had something that we do not have to this day—a real market. Attempts to resort to authoritarian government in a society that has only just cast off the chains of dictatorship could trigger a protest movement that would sweep away everyone—including the "nonauthoritarians." At the same time, it is entirely possible that circumstances may arise during the transition to a market that will force the leadership of a given country to resort to a certain amount of forceful pressure—for example, to grant the government extraordinary powers with which to carry out essential economic measures. Such a policy can succeed only on two conditions: that the economic reform program enjoys the support of the majority of society, and that all democratic institutions (parliament, an independent press) remain intact, serving to block any unjustified increase in personal or group power.

There is yet another factor that could not only seriously affect events in Eastern Europe but also distort their development. We are referring to long-submerged national and ethnic contradictions and conflicts that are now coming to the surface. They could have the most serious consequences in the Balkans.

The most explosive ethnic cauldron is Yugoslavia, where long-standing conflicts among nationalities and republics have reached the critical point, threatening to destroy the entire federation. The example of that country is very instructive for the U.S.S.R. Delays in implementing much-needed reforms have led to a situation in which insoluble social and economic problems in Yugoslavia have begun assuming the form of conflicts among nationalities, especially since there are historical grounds for this. Today, irreconcilable differences among nationalities has become a factor impeding countrywide changes. The most developed republics, such as Slovenia, are attempting to abandon the listing ship in an effort to find their own course. An exacerbation of interrepublic conflicts is possible and, in fact, is already occurring in Czechoslovakia, where there have always been latent frictions between the two republics. To this let us add mounting nationalistic and chauvinistic sentiment in other multinational countries. The problem of the Moslem minority in Bulgaria has come to the surface. Steps that the country's leadership took to restore justice with regard to the Turkish population have triggered an upsurge of Bulgarian chauvinism there, which could affect the political situation in the country as a whole. The fate of the Hungarian and German minorities in Romania remains unresolved, which is also provoking constant conflicts.

There are compelling grounds to conclude that a period of division, during which various nations and nationalities acquire a certain degree of sovereignty or even statehood, is unavoidable along the way to the new integration. In any case, the time of unitary multinational states is past.

A variant of their development along the lines of an "asymmetrical federation" cannot be ruled out. As proposed by some Yugoslavian republics, this would be a rather free association of republics with varying structures and different levels of development. The formation of confederations, and not just in place of the former multinational countries, is highly likely in Eastern Europe. In the long run, the formation of confederations among independent states is also possible, but the tendency toward convergence will be preceded by a quest for individual identity. Let us recall that Western Europe, too, embarked on the path toward integration only after the resources of independent national-state development had been exhausted. But this process— the meeting of national interests—will yet entail a good many contradictions, conflicts, and confrontations, which could be dangerous to the security not just of individual countries but of Europe as a whole.

The character and direction of social processes in the region depends in many respects on the overall international backdrop and on the position of the world powers. In the era of socialist isolationism and the Iron Curtain, these factors did not play such a significant role. Today they can critically affect the domestic political situation in any given country. The movement that has begun toward unification of the two German states, for example, will soon lead to the emergence in the center of Europe of a power with a population of nearly 80 million and enormous intellectual and economic potential. The emergence of such a power will alter the course of all European and even world processes. This fact will also affect domestic life in the neighboring countries, especially Poland and Czechoslovakia, and even in the U.S.S.R. Old fears associated with the existence of a neighbor that has twice started world wars have already begun to revive among the Polish population, which has always been very sensitive to the "German question." This is all the more true in view of the fact that revanchist attitudes are resurfacing on the other side of the border. Such apprehensions are not without consequences for domestic life; they can lead to increased conservatism, autarchic tendencies, and populist sentiment.

Analyzing events in Eastern Europe, *The Times* wrote: "We are seeing not only a broadening of freedoms but also the emergence of new dangers." In the Western press, one often sees the recent enthusiasm over East European events giving way to concern. Misgivings are being expressed about a possible expansion of a zone of national and ethnic conflicts, and the likely social explosions that will accompany the transition to the market. F. Heisbourg, director of London's International Institute for Strategic Studies, even raised the question: "How can we avoid another world war as a possible consequence of the current destabilization in the East European region?"

The main phase of tectonic shifts in most of the countries may still lie ahead. In this connection, there is already a need to formulate an international "stability strategy" in Eastern Europe as a whole that would help minimize potential conflicts (including conflicts between countries) and create conditions for less painful changes. The development of such a strategy should be a collective undertaking of Western and Eastern states. The situation today requires a shift to a transbloc policy and to shaping an all-European consensus. This is the first time, in any case since World War II, that the interrelationship, intertwining, and interdependence of European and world processes have shown themselves with such urgency. Today Eastern Europe can hardly solve its problems without Western help, but the fate of the latter also depends to a certain extent on how processes develop in the Eastern part of the continent.

What kind of system is taking shape in Eastern Europe? It would hardly be proper to call it democratic socialism, especially if one considers the assumption of power by noncommunist forces in many countries, the development of reprivatization processes, and finally the very fact that the concept of "socialism" is starting to be removed from constitutions and other state documents. But it is also impossible to call the inchoate society capitalism—an assessment opposed even by the noncommunist movements' leaders. "The fall of communism is by no means the victory of capitalism," said B. Geremek, one of the leaders of Poland's Solidarity. It must be borne in mind that despite the communist parties' fall, the influence of socialist ideas is still very strong. Even many alternative and noncommunist forces are influenced by socialist ideals, though they may be interpreted in different ways.

A dichromatic image of social development, whereby it is divided into orthodox socialist and capitalist development as traditionally understood, is obsolete. This may be the chief lesson of the events in Eastern Europe. The bipolar development of civilization is giving way to a pluralism of societies that are difficult and even impossible to assign to one system or another. The society taking shape in the East European countries will be fundamentally different from Stalinist or neo-Stalinist society, but it will not completely resemble Western society either. This society, at least in the foreseeable future, will be characterized by a much greater regulatory role for the state, maintenance of certain restrictions on a free market, and policies significantly influenced by egalitarian attitudes. However, the question is not one of some third path of social progress, but of national and specific historical forms of realizing its universal principles.

We should also note that, like the Soviet Union, Eastern Europe—or as it is now being called, Central Europe—has just embarked on the path of building a new society. However, the term "new society" requires considerable qualification. After all, what is involved is an entire region's return to the bosom of world civilization, but with its own baggage of traditions. Some countries are already moving resolutely along this path, although their main problems and difficulties obviously still lie ahead. Other countries are only contemplating whether to take this step and when, or whether to wait. We must not overestimate slogans calling for renewal, or the ability of these societies to live by new laws, or even the restructuring of administrative systems in these countries. The moment of truth for this region still lies ahead. By the same token, neither should we underestimate what has been accomplished, for a movement toward civilization has now begun.

But various turns, stops, and reverses are still possible along this path. And so Eastern Europe is rushing to meet Western Europe. The new meeting on the Elbe is taking place more than 40 years after the first. Let us not forget what happened after that first meeting. One need not entertain illusions that the process of our rapprochement will be easy, quick, or painless. Its result will depend not only on the efforts of Eastern Europe itself, and on the position of the Soviet Union, but also on the help of the entire world community.

What Kind of Socialism Are We Rejecting? What Kind of Socialism Are We Striving For?

This was the theme of a discussion organized by the journal MEMO. Its participants included prominent Soviet social scientists and a number of Western scholars. The discussion was opened by Prof. Yu. Krasin, rector of the CPSU Central Committee's Institute of Social Sciences.*

Yu. Krasin: First of all, we must clearly define what sort of society exists in our country. One can say that in the seven decades since the Great October Revolution a typical model of "state socialism" has been established in our country, but with serious deformations in the periods of Stalinism and stagnation. On the whole, the development of the model of state socialism took place in accordance with the Marxist notions of that time. In the period before October and in the first postrevolutionary years, Lenin, too, espoused such notions. Granted, it must be noted that in his last works, usually called his political testament, he took other approaches that went beyond the boundaries of state socialism and contained elements of a model of socialism of a higher order. Unfortunately, after Lenin's death this direction of theoretical thinking was not developed.

While admitting the possibility that theoretical notions of socialism can develop ahead of social reality itself, one can nonetheless assert that the model of state socialism was in keeping with the early stages of socialist society's development, especially in a country where there was no developed mechanism for measuring labor and consumption against a common standard. Therefore the task of bringing labor and consumption into balance fell to the state, and that was one of the most important functions Lenin assigned to it in his work *State and Revolution*.

---

*The full discussion from which this article has been condensed originally ran serially in the May, June, August, September, October, and December 1989 issues of *MEMO*. The condensed transcript of the discussion was prepared by Yuriy V. Krasheninnikov, department head of sociology at MEMO.

State socialism provided for effectively mobilizing the country's resources for the modernization of social production. The assumption of state control over the basic means of production, and centralized state management of the economy, made it possible to carry out the country's industrialization in a historically short time.

I think that one can draw the conclusion that, historically, state socialism was objectively necessary. It is another matter that there could have been different versions of it. The "despotic version" that was established in the 1930s was not inevitable. No references to historical necessity can justify the Stalinist deformations of state socialism that exaggerated the state's role, placed it above civil society, and erected a bureaucratic barrier to the development of democracy and popular sovereignty. It was precisely these monstrous deformations, which were contrary to the nature of socialist society, that prevented the state socialism model's normal development, and its timely transition to a model of a higher order.

Therefore perestroika, which signifies a revolution in socialism, that is, Soviet society's movement to a qualitative change and movement to a new model of socialism corresponding to society's present level of technological and cultural progress, has been confronted with the need to accomplish an additional, complex task—that of freeing socialism of the deformations of the Stalinist and stagnation periods.

At the present stage of Soviet society's development, state socialism has become obsolete and should yield to a different model of socialism. But what sort of model? There is a temptation to give a technocratic response to the needs of society's economic development. The advocates of such an approach employ the categories of "economic rationalism." If a solution is economically rational, they reason, it must be implemented, regardless of its side effects. Questions of social justice, which are of paramount importance for socialist society and are part of the socialist ideal, are relegated to the background. Some advocates of economic rationalism even admit the possibility of unemployment in our society, propose transplanting the mechanisms of capitalist competition in socialist soil, and, citing the objective laws of pricing, insist on raising retail prices. Lenin, as we know, spoke of the primacy of politics over economics, the primacy of the political approach to the accomplishment of economic tasks. But in this case the political and social consequences of the actions proposed are not even considered.

The abandonment of the administrative-command system does, indeed, bring economic methods of management to the foreground. But to distance ourselves in this process from the social consequences of the adopted solutions would be to take a position that can be defined as a kind of analogue or socialist version of neoconservatism. On this course, there is a real danger of creating knots of social tension in society, and an even more serious danger of losing the important socialist values that society has gained—values such as the social protection of the individual, collectivist solidarity, and the like. That would be a technocratic response to the challenge of our time. But perestroika is called on to find a democratic response.

I think that such a response should be sought not in the direction of curtailing state forms and state regulation of the economy, but along the lines of combining state levers for the management of society with the broad development of a self-management system. In other words, the time has come to move from the state socialism model to a combination state- and self-management model.

State levers are needed to ensure the economy's functioning and development as an integral national-economic complex. This, of course, does not mean preserving the obsolete administrative-command system, which is based on depersonalized state ownership embodied in a single owner—the state. Within the framework of the combination state- and self-management model, public, socialist ownership should be developed into an economic system of interaction among a multiplicity of owners of both state property (relatively independent enterprises and associations) and nonstate property (various types of cooperatives and individual enterprise). The socialist state's regulating role in this complex system can be carried out only by economic—not administrative—methods: taxes, loans, subsidies, capital investments. Such a pluralistic system of socialist ownership has been gradually developing in the course of perestroika as cooperatives and leasing arrangements have spread, and cost accounting, which incorporates self-management principles in the activities of relatively independent units of the state economic complex, has developed.

This entire system, as a whole, is based on the combination of state planning and the socialist market. State planning reflects the unity and integral nature of the economy. It is used to ensure a general direction of progressive development in the interests of society as a whole. The socialist market provides for bringing the activities of enterprises into accord with social requirements, and measuring labor costs and the results of labor against a common standard. As a result, self-management initiative is unleashed, and the alienation of the producer from property that arose in the bosom of state socialism is eliminated. The combination state- and self-management model of socialism creates the conditions in which every producer and the employees of every enterprise can act as co-owners and co-managers of public socialist property.

The move from "state socialism" to combination state- and self-management socialism requires thorough economic reform, which is being carried out in our country. But by its very nature, perestroika cannot be limited to the economy. It also inevitably encompasses the political system.

One can point out a series of fundamental reasons explaining why the economic objectives of perestroika cannot be accomplished without carrying out radical political reform.

First, the strongholds of bureaucratism that are resisting perestroika are located precisely in the state system. To break up these strongholds and eradicate bureaucratism, fundamental, qualitative changes need to be made in the state structure. The state apparatus must be subordinated to the civil society and placed under the control of democratic bodies.

Second, the difficult search for new economic and managerial structures that meet the requirements of social development as nearly as possible must entail the broadest discussion of these issues, and the proposal and comparison of alternatives for economic development. All this demands broadening of democracy, glasnost, and the free discussion and expression of nontraditional views that are often contrary to those that are commonly accepted.

Third, bringing economic levers of economic management into play requires the broadest possible development of democracy at the enterprises. And that is a question of general politics, a question of the democratization of society and the introduction of popular self-management into the economy at various levels, starting with the primary level of the production team and the shop, and going all the way up to the national level of state planning and regulation.

Fourth—and this is evidently the most important thing—the employee of socialist enterprise cannot develop into a conscious subject of socialist production relations, and a fully empowered co-owner and co-manager of socialist property solely in the realm of economic relations. Activeness and initiative in the workplace are inseparable from a person's participation in state and public affairs. The political awareness and habits of the citizen are an essential prerequisite for the employee's recognition of his vanguard production tasks.

In conclusion, I shall dwell on one more general issue. One aspect of the technological revolution taking place in the world is the internationalization of economic life. An increasingly dense network of worldwide production relations is being formed. No country in the world can avoid being included in this network of world economic relations, which constitutes a kind of economic basis for the unity of today's contradictory world.

From this follows the inescapable conclusion that socialist society, for all of its particularities, is an inseparable part of the world community. Acknowledging this conclusion requires that we put aside narrow ideas of socialism and capitalism as absolute antitheses. Such ideas developed in the 1920s following the victory of the Great October Socialist Revolution. It seemed—and this viewpoint was shared by most Marxists, including Lenin—that the victory of the world revolution and the universal triumph of socialism were close at hand. Because of the bitterness of the class struggle and the lack of historical experience in this area, the transition to socialism was thought of as entailing the complete destruction of the capitalist system. Revolutionaries of that time shared a belief in the words of the proletarian hymn, the *Internationale*: "We will destroy the whole world of violence down to its foundations, and then we will build our own world, our new world." In accordance with these views, socialism and capitalism were regarded as "world" and "antiworld." The increasing bitterness of the class struggle in that period left a strong imprint on the communist movement's subsequent development, and in many respects it determined the ideas about the transition to socialism that became widespread in that movement.

Yet capitalism had already begun to stabilize by the 1920s. There is no question that in his last works Lenin took note of that change, which was reflected in his statements about the objective necessity, independent of the will of classes, parties, and states, for establishing and developing economic ties between the two social systems. Unfortunately, following Lenin's death theoretical thinking did not pick up those ideas but started developing in a different direction. The oversimplified and romanticized ideas of the 1920s were turned into absolutes, which did great damage to the development of Soviet society. It is precisely the habit of mechanically opposing socialism and capitalism as two absolute antitheses that explains the negative attitude toward commodity-money relations, the concept of a state governed by the rule of law, and universal human moral values.

Today the groundlessness of such views is glaringly apparent in the light of the new political thinking. In this area a drastic change is needed in both public attitudes and the social sciences.

The realities of the late 20th century confirm that the two socioeconomic formations, capitalism and socialism, are developing on a common, civilizationwide basis. This conclusion is in no way contrary to Marxist theory. The socioeconomic formation is the cornerstone concept of the materialist understanding of history in the Marxist world view. But for all the concept's theoretical importance, it characterizes the stages and social forms of the development of a single human civilization. It is in these formations, which succeed one another and sometimes exist simultaneously and interact for long periods of time, that the accumulation, development, and enrichment of universal human material and moral values take place. These values include human mastery of the forces of nature; society's discovery of its own creative forces; the social activeness of society and the individual; democracy, which is measured by the degree and depth of participation by society's members in the political process; lasting spiritual values embodied in works of art and in science; and finally, the human being himself with his world view, psychology, morality, norms of human decency, and measure of freedom in decision making and behavior. The development of these universal human values runs clearly through all socioeconomic systems. Their continuity forms the core of world history.

From this perspective, social progress is seen as a constant process of the accumulation and enrichment of the values of civilization, and not simply as a succession of social systems and "breaks," which characterize mainly the *forms* of societal development.

We are forced to reflect on all this by the technological revolution and the processes developing from it, which represent the fundamental modernization of our civilization. All this prompts the democratic and progressive forces of all contemporary societies to search for a future model that will adequately reflect the new technological and international realities. As M. S. Gorbachev said in a speech during his visit to India, "humanity needs to rethink the values of its own existence."

In the search for answers to the many questions of the times, we must take the utmost advantage of the potential for the social systems to mutually enrich one another, despite their profound differences and inevitable competition. But competition must not and cannot exhaust social systems through the senseless waste of economic and intellectual resources; rather it should mutually enrich them. After all, competition is first and foremost rivalry in solving universal human problems, and not confrontation that threatens the stability of the world order.

In the process of the complex and contradictory search for paths to the future, socialism is making its own worthy contribution to social progress. No one can deny that such socialist values as democracy in the social realm, the social protection of the individual, and the collectivist principles of human community represent a qualitative enrichment of universal human values.

It can be said that at the end of the 20th century one finds an increasingly distinct urge to create the model of a complex social system that will combine the maximum economic effectiveness with the maximum conditions for ensuring the individual's freedom and comprehensive development and self-expression.

Such a prospect for the future fully accords with the socialist ideal and the goals of Soviet perestroika. In this sense, the basic direction of the search for the future in Soviet society coincides with the aspirations of democratic forces in the developed capitalist countries, despite the differences in the specific tasks that face different socioeconomic systems. On this platform, it seems to us, there is a possibility for constructive dialogue and broad cooperation among all the forces of the worker and democratic movement.

Prof. F. Burlatskiy (CPSU Central Committee's Institute of Social Science, currently editor in chief of *Literaturnaya gazeta*: First I would like to say a few words in connection with certain general problems touched on by Prof. Krasin. It seems to me that at the present time we can reevaluate historical experience in order to find answers to many of the questions that concern us. We have involved ourselves in the process of perestroika, of reconstructing our society, and we are seeking a concept of its development. The first prerequisite for a fruitful search, in my view, is complete rejection of theoretical doctrinairism and theoretical intolerance, because the entire experience of our century, of both capitalism and socialism, has shown that no single doctrine is capable of answering all the questions raised by actual historical processes. Of course, Marx has had tremendous influence on the development of contemporary thought and the emergence of many social structures. But it may be that Einstein, or Fermi, or Wiener, or many other scientists who laid the foundations of modern science and thereby created an absolutely new basis for the development of modern societies have had no less influence. It is no accident that the concept of the technological revolution has now become key for both Marxists and non-Marxists. That is a recognition of the fact that historical development proceeds according to its own laws. Attempts to force this process have distressing consequences.

I think that the chief gain of glasnost and our theoretical thinking—perhaps a very small gain, but a gain nonetheless—is that we have opened our eyes to the real picture of the contemporary world and started to compare our development not with the situation before the October Revolution or in the prewar period, but with what has been taking place in other countries and civilizations—in the United States, Japan, and the Common Market countries. We have started looking realistically at the nuclear threat, the environmental threat, and our own place in the contemporary world, a place which has turned out to be less grand than we used to think.

In this connection, it seems to me, we must return anew to the idea of convergence. I was never a supporter of that idea in its "pure" form, that is, I never believed that any sort of single model of human society would ever emerge. I do not know, maybe in a millennium such a model really will emerge, but there are no signs of one in the foreseeable future. But I am profoundly convinced that the present scientific and technological revolution is having a similar effect on all social systems and all civilizations, giving rise to a number of problems that are common to them all—the environmental problem, the threat of unemployment as the result of new technologies, and so on. New forms of economic management are emerging in both the capitalist and the socialist world.

From this standpoint we need to rethink the key questions of contemporary social development: What is contemporary capitalism, what is contemporary socialism, and what are contemporary humanity and civilization? And the main thing here is not a search for new terminology, not playing at words and definitions, but analysis, serious and unbiased analysis.

And so we are presently arguing about what socialism is, and throughout society a bitter and, for the time being, bloodless struggle is being waged over this concept and its interpretation. Every step forward along the path of perestroika creates even greater doubts, not just among individual conservatives, bureaucrats, functionaries, or moss-grown teachers of the history of the CPSU, but among a tremendous mass of the population: Are we following the path of socialism or straying from it?

I personally believe that about one third or, at the most, half of the society we have created has to do with Marx. The rest we inherited from Russian civilization in the form in which it had developed after several centuries of existence. From Marx our society took the idea of destroying private property, although no one answered the question of what private property was (for example, an automobile may be a means of producing services; nonetheless, that form of property was allowed in our country). On the other hand, from precapitalist Russian traditions we inherited the notion of a strong state authority that controls everyone and everything. The emergence of what Prof. Krasin quite rightly called state socialism is related to that notion. To this day the vast majority of the population is convinced that the state should distribute everything.

We are presently trying to work out a concept of the transition from state socialism to what we call a "socialist civil society." But there are still a lot of unclear questions. The first is what sort of economic model we should follow if the state ceases to play the role of central regulator of economic relations. Another related question is what sort of correlation should there be between planned state regulation and market regulation. Since the overall concept has not yet been developed and remains unclear in practical terms, the legislative process tosses back and forth between Scylla and Charybdis.

The fact that economic reforms have been lagging behind political reforms, and the asymmetry between glasnost and democratization, on the one hand, and real economic changes, on the other, are one reason for the difficulties and contradictions that have arisen in the course of perestroika. As the experience of Poland and a number of other East European countries has shown, this situation is fraught with the potential for crisis. The way out of the situation lies not in narrowing glasnost and applying the brakes to the democratization process as a whole, as the conservatives propose, but in more vigorous and decisive movement along the path of structural economic reforms, and the development of economic, as well as political, pluralism. Such pluralism is based on different forms of ownership that vie or, if you like, compete with one another. They include state ownership (transformed into public ownership), cooperative ownership, other forms of group ownership, and individual and family ownership. If there is no diversity in forms of ownership, there will be no political pluralism, either, because nowhere in the world does political democracy exist without an appropriate economic basis.

Another acute problem that has arisen in the course of perestroika is, as you well know, the nationalities problem. Here we must study the experience, both positive and negative, of other countries. In this connection I want to quote a statement by a Belgian political leader with whom I recently spoke. I thought it was sensible: "We also have our nationalities problem," he said, "and we used to have a desire to solve it. But then we realized that we had to learn to live with the problem."

And so we, too, are learning to live with new problems and to seek answers to questions raised by reality. Indisputably, the way out of the situation lies in expanding autonomy—economic, political, and cultural—and granting greater independence, not only for the republics, but also for all the nationalities that have no state structures. Simultaneously, it lies in the development of our federation. This, of course, is too general an answer. It is impossible not to see that this process is taking place amid acute struggle, and no one can predict to what excesses it may lead, because the general background of all our democratic transformations is an authoritarian and patriarchal political culture that is far from being eliminated in the minds of our functionaries, and even less so in the mass consciousness.

And finally, the last thing I would like to say. The West has missed two historical chances to promote democratization in our country. The first was in the 1920s, when we moved to the New Economic Policy. I even think that if our country had not found itself in isolation, and if we had managed to arrange highly active economic cooperation with the West at that time, we probably would have managed to avert the emergence of Stalinism. A second chance was missed in the Khrushchev period. At the present time, the West is turning toward supporting perestroika. I am convinced that a great deal in the course of our domestic perestroika will depend on how decisive that turning proves to be.

L. Shevtsova (Doctor of history, Institute of the Economics of the World Socialist System): It seems to me that perestroika is undergoing a complex, maybe even dramatic, period. The stage of the "cavalry attack" on the administrative system has ended, and the system has stood firm. Moreover, the antireform forces have even managed to consolidate themselves, while a serious social basis for the reform movement has not yet been created. We are facing what may be an even more difficult and dangerous stage of perestroika, because reforms will now take place in a situation in which the masses are feeling a certain disenchantment.

Moreover, whereas at the initial stage of the reform of political institutions, certain superficial factors of renewal were brought into play—factors which may have even existed in the administrative system itself—those factors have now apparently been exhausted.

In this connection a question arises: To what extent are the reforms being carried out within the context of the administrative-command system strengthening it, and to what extent are they destroying it? This is the question of the correlation between reform and revolution.

One often hears the opinion that one reason for the difficulties arising in the course of perestroika lies in the asymmetry between economic and political reform. In my view, the problem is not so much that the political reform has gone further than the economic reform, but that the political changes—greater freedom of expression, glasnost—are of a "nonsystemic" nature. On the other hand, the power system itself remains practically unchanged.

All the concepts that we are putting forward for renewing the system basically amount to the rudiments of ideological positions that have remained unchanged for decades. There are many stereotypes that we have yet to abandon. Take, as just one example, the practice of contrasting bourgeois democracy to socialist democracy. Or socialist pluralism to bourgeois pluralism. For me that is the equivalent of discussing socialist versus bourgeois railroads. Either democracy and pluralism exist, or they don't—that's reality, freed of myths. The form that democracy takes is another matter; here differences are inevitable. But regardless of the form, the invariable attributes of democracy are the possibility of choice, and pluralism. And choice exists where there are alternatives. And if we admit the need for alternatives, we should take the next step and admit that alternatives presuppose the existence of parallel decision-making centers, that is, abandonment of the existing monocentric sociopolitical system, and movement toward a multipolar society. The problem now is to "fit" the Communist Party into such a society.

Or take another problem: the opposition under socialism. If democracy cannot exist without pluralism, pluralism, in turn, cannot develop without elements of dissent and opposition, without the expression of views that contradict the position of the leadership and the official line. How can that minority be protected? The path that Poland and Hungary have taken, in which efforts have been made to find a niche for a constructive opposition, seems fruitful to me. You know the maxim: If there were no opposition, one would have to be invented to strengthen the regime. In any case, dissent will always exist. But it is more dangerous when it is driven inward. And, conversely, the controlled existence of an opposition within a legal framework makes it possible to find optimal solutions. In general, the presence or absence of an opposition is the criterion of whether a society is democratic, for democracy means not only the power of the majority, but also the protection of the minority and of the individual, including protection against the majority.

In both theory and practice we very often reduce democracy to decentralization. In doing so we fail to take into account the experience of a number of countries, including China and Yugoslavia, that shows that decentralization and the expansion of local authorities' powers often produce negative results: Centrifugal tendencies appear, the integrity of society is weakened, and the positions of the local bureaucracy are strengthened.

Yet another problem is the relationship between political and economic democracy. That is, should democratization in the political realm be accompanied by the same processes in the economic realm? In theory this may look attractive, but in practice the criteria of democracy in politics and in economics are different and, what is more, may contradict one other. Democratically adopted decisions are not always economically effective, and the requirements of democracy do not coincide with the requirements of prompt reaction to changing situations. There are other drawbacks, as well. For example, with democratic decision-making procedures, marginal group interests may dominate over the interests of society as a whole. And we are presently encountering that contradiction. The democratization of political life is resulting in opposition to needed radical economic measures by a substantial part of the population, and is thereby delaying the country's development. In the West the problem of economic democracy is evidently different, but economic laws are in operation there. In our country, in contrast, they are not yet working, and politics calls the shots in the economy.

In other words, while rejecting one extreme—excessive centralization—we should not rush to the other extreme— universal decentralization. We must find an optimal correlation between them.

Prof. H. Diligensky (editor in chief of *MEMO*): I would like to return to the questions that Prof. Krasin raised in his remarks, as well as to questions of a more general nature. They involve clarifying the nature of the system that has been established in our country, and the contribution that socialism has made to world development. I think arguments over whether we can call the society that has been built in our country socialism are pedantic. Why? When a phenomenon is being classified, it is always compared to an existing class of phenomena. If, for example, a new animal hitherto unknown to specialists is discovered in the ocean depths, it is studied in accordance with the existing classification system and assigned to either the fishes or the mammals. But when the new system emerged in our country, socialism did not exist as an established class of phenomena. And it was decided to call the new social organization socialism. That term entered into the language both in our country and abroad. Therefore, I think, the essence of the matter lies not in the name—whether it is socialism or not—but in clarifying the inner nature of the social formation we are talking about.

In principle I agree with the definition of socialism that Prof. Krasin gave. But I would like not to end it with that, but to go a little further, because that definition itself leaves a number of questions unanswered. First, the state exists everywhere. Often it plays an active role in regulating socioeconomic processes. One example is Sweden, which one could also say has state socialism, but it is entirely different from what exists in the U.S.S.R.

I shall permit myself to propose a theoretical hypothesis for your consideration; its essence is that what was established in our country following the Revolution was not just some sort of authoritarianism or, as it is presently called, administrative-command system, but a new, hitherto unknown *mode of production*—in the most orthodox Marxist sense—a mode which, for want of any other suitable term, I would call the *statist* mode of production.

To understand how that mode of production arose, one must recall that the new society did not emerge in the process of the spontaneous development of productive forces and production relations, but was built in accordance with an existing design. Socialism as an idea that appeared in the heads of 19th-century thinkers—first the utopian socialists, and then Marx and Engels—preceded socialism as a reality.

In this connection, a question arises as to what extent Marxism bears responsibility for everything that subsequently took place, that is, for the specific character of the society that was built in this country. It does not bear complete responsibility for it, since by and large, Marxism formulated the historical possibility of the new system's emergence and its most general features, but not its specific character. Marxism formulated, first and foremost, the socialist system of values, the socialist ideal, and the possibility of attaining that ideal, and it defined the new system of ownership in principle. At the same time, Marxism does bear a certain responsibility for what has taken place in our country and other countries, a responsibility I would call methodological, because Marxism, like all 19th-century thought, proceeded from the assumption that one could first design a new society in one's head and then build it in accordance with that plan. That is, building a new society was considered a process like building a new house: One must first draw up the blueprints, then, on the basis of those blueprints, get together the appropriate building materials and then build the house. The historical experience we have gained has demonstrated the fallacy of such an approach.

Since words and ideas formed the basis of the process of building socialism, a great opportunity presented itself for voluntarism in the course of that process. A voluntaristic approach presupposes the existence of a kind of Demiurge (which, naturally, can only be the state, united with the party) that has at its disposal all the capability and all the powers required to attain the goals that have been set.

Such is the general pattern of development that gave rise to the statist mode of production. As I see it, the paradox of that phenomenon is that its existence absolutely refutes the very laws of the evolution of society that Marxism itself discovered. For example, the law of the interaction between the base and the superstructure. Whereas, according to Marxist ideas, the base gives rise to a corresponding superstructure, and the superstructure serves the base, in practice just the opposite occurred: The superstructure itself, by dint of its will, built itself a base and production relations that accorded with its plans and interests.

What did that mean? It meant that the leading, definitive role was played not by economic or class interests, but by the interests of state power as such. That is the objective basis of Stalinism. Stalin's repressions can be viewed as a distortion of the original model of socialism, but the fact of all-encompassing state power itself cannot be viewed as a distortion of that model. And if we analyze the chief distinguishing features of the existing economic system from that viewpoint, we will see that it does not work and is not supposed to work for the satisfaction of people's needs. Its functions are wholly subordinated to its main purpose—strengthening the power of the state. That is the reason for the excessive development of the military industries and the constant expansion of the production of coal, steel, oil, and so forth—that is, of everything with which the growth of the state's power has been identified. The extensive type of economic development and the use of the "leftover" principle in allocating money and resources for social needs are also directly bound up with this.

The type of economic, social, and political system that was established in our country was essentially a violation, not just of the objective laws of a specific system, but of universal historical laws, one of which, it seems to me, is that no matter what the mode of production, and no matter what the level of productive forces, normal economic activity is impossible if the participants in that activity lack independence. Therefore, for us today the return to a normal economic situation means restoring the elementary independence of the economic entity, an independence which, given today's productive forces, is even more important than it was in the past.

A few words, for the sake of discussion, about the problems of democracy. I think that in analyzing these problems, we do not take changes in public attitudes sufficiently into account. It is there that the democratization process has gone the furthest—much further than in the economy or in political relations. And that is no accident. In essence, the preconditions for our current perestroika were created back during the period of so-called stagnation. Even during that period, the elements of free thinking that became possible after the 20th CPSU Congress (1956) were preserved in public attitudes and in the realm of culture.

In general, the type of social system that we want to reject is characterized by a profound contradiction to which I do not think sufficient attention has been paid. In the most general sense, this contradiction can be defined as a contradiction between existence and consciousness; more precisely, it is a contradiction within public consciousness itself.

In the West, totalitarianism of the Stalinist model is often compared and even identified with totalitarianism of the Hitlerist type. In many respects that is warranted, and superficially they are very similar. But there is a profound difference. National Socialism [Nazism] was, in its own way, an internally noncontradictory ideological system: Its inherent principles—the cult of the leader, racism, and the rejection of democracy—were carried to their logical conclusion and constituted an internal unity. In contrast, the ideology that became established in our country was contradictory in the highest degree. The statist system was based on the personality cult and authoritarian state power. But the paradox was that this system could not cut off its ideological roots, could not repudiate the basic democratic and humanistic principles contained in the original socialist ideal. Despite the personality cult, Soviet people were still able to read not only what was written by Stalin, but also the products of world thought; it was impossible to prevent that. Or take such a fact as the adoption in 1936, when the repressions were already in full swing, of "Stalin's" Constitution, which was very democratic in content. That step should not be regarded merely as an attempt to give a democratic semblance to a terrorist regime; it was, at the same time, a forced concession to the system's democratic roots.

If we do not take that paradox, and the profound internal contradiction built into the ideology into account, we will not be able to understand how perestroika arose at all. As I have already said, the preconditions for it in terms of public attitudes emerged during the "stagnation" period. But for all the importance of those processes, perestroika was still not initiated by a mass movement, but by those members of the party and state apparatus for whom devotion to socialist values and to their democratic and humanistic foundation was not a mere concession to prescribed norms of conduct. And such people have always existed in our society.

Finally, the last thought I would like to express pertains to the stages of the democratic process. I think that one can see a positive tendency in our social sciences: The unrestrained euphoria that existed at the beginning of perestroika regarding the prospects for democratization of public life is giving way to a more sober approach and an understanding that in certain areas we cannot attain the desired level of democracy without going through a number of intermediate stages.

I do not fully agree with Prof. Burlatskiy in his assessment of the significance of Russian traditions. Traditions, of course, always leave an imprint on any contemporary phenomenon in any country. British conservatism carries the imprint of British traditions, but that does not mean that Mrs. Thatcher's conservatism is a recurrence of something old. The same thing is true of our country. But we should also take into account the actual level of political culture in our country, as well as the historical law that was noted a long time ago by Pushkin: the government has always been the bearer of enlightenment in Russia.

The development of a civil society and of its attendant culture is still at the initial stage, although the process is proceeding very fast. In such circumstances, I cannot help agreeing with an opinion expressed by one participant in a discussion of the problems of democratization that *MEMO* recently carried: the opinion was that we are presently at the stage of *managed democracy*. The distinguishing features of this stage are, on the one hand, that it is characterized by a sharp increase in mass initiative and the emergence of mass democratic movements, and on the other, that because of the contradictory nature of these processes, there continues to be an objective need for them to be managed by the state leadership.

Prof. V. Loginov (CPSU Central Committee's Institute of Social Sciences): I do not know what to call Prof. H. Diligensky's position—maybe liberal-conservative, and maybe something else—but I would like to support it. In the specific situation that exists in our country today, the step-by-step movement toward democracy, which many people in the West and in this country, too, perceive as reflecting inconsistency and a half-way approach to political reform, is the only constructive course.

Yes, it represents a certain deviation from the principles of "high democracy," but such is the situation. The vast mass of the population does not yet possess a sufficiently high level of political culture. Under these conditions, the differentiation taking place in society, a differentiation often based on false distinctions (ethnic distinctions, the opposition between "Stalinists" and "anti-Stalinists"), is creating the danger of uncontrollable processes and may result in crisis situations. To prevent such a turn of events, we must establish some sort of system of counterweights that will ensure that the forces leading perestroika have the advantage.

Unfortunately, the level of legal awareness in our country is such that it gives rise to unrestrained faith in formal legal norms and laws. Sometimes it is even proposed in the press that a law be adopted prohibiting any deviation from perestroika. Yet that is naive. There has been the experience, for example, of Germany's Weimar Republic, whose constitution met the highest requirements of a state based on the rule of law, but did not prevent the establishment of a fascist dictatorship. The outcome of the real political struggle is determined by the correlation of the struggling forces. Today that correlation is rather complex. That is why I believe that we have acted correctly in embarking on a course of step-by-step movement toward democracy.

Prof. G. Karasimeonov (the magazine *Novo vreme* [*New Time*], Bulgaria): It seems to me that one of the basic obstacles to developing a dialogue for the purposes of solving the problems of civilization is black-and-white thinking, or the traditional system of approaches. It is the product of the Cold War period, and possibly of an even earlier period. Whatever the case, we continue to speak about the two systems as though each of them represented something monolithic, and they had nothing in common with one another. But such an approach ignores the tendency toward differentiation within each system, a tendency that is especially noticeable in the political culture and traditions of different countries belonging to the same system. In Western Europe, for example, a powerful influence is exerted by the Social Democrats, and to a lesser extent, the Communists. In the United States, on the other hand, the bourgeois parties enjoy practically unchallenged hegemony. Or take political culture: There is an anticollectivist culture (United States) and a paternalistic culture (Japan), while a number of countries have a synthesis of both these cultures. Fundamental differences also exist among the countries of Eastern Europe.

On the other hand, there has been a tendency toward the growth of interdependence—not between systems, but between nations, peoples, and states. A new type of cooperation is developing between different countries, parties, social groups, and political leaders. New societal interests are emerging, and on that basis new social blocs are being formed that go beyond the limits of the two systems. In both the West and the East a search is under way for the model of a new, humane civilization.

One of the most serious obstacles along this path is the resistance of conservative forces in both systems, forces that are striving to preserve confrontation and thereby protect their own interests and defend their own privileges. On this basis, the possibility arises that the interests of conservatives in the East and the West may coincide.

Prof S. Peregudov (IMEMO): What worries me is that, given a broad consensus in society regarding the goals of political reform—the establishment of a genuinely democratic political system—there are different understandings of the sequential order of its stages and their specific content. What is especially troubling is the fact that neither among specialists nor among the top leadership, to judge from published projects, has any final concept of the new political system been developed. And the fundamental question which has not been clarified is how powers should be distributed between the party and the soviets. On the one hand, there is talk of giving full power to the soviets, and on the other, it is stressed that political leadership is provided by the party. We have a clear contradiction here: What is more, this is not just a superficial contradiction but one that permeates all relations in the political realm. The danger of such a situation, in our view, is that without a clear concept of the distribution of power between the party and the soviets, the incipient process of transferring power to the latter is at risk of being broken off at some stage, or even of being reversed.

Prof. A. Galkin (CPSU Central Committee's Institute of Social Sciences): I agree with what has been said here about the need to "incorporate" into the democratic institutions being created certain regulating elements that will maintain the orderly functioning of the entire system. Unless that is done, then regardless of our subjective intentions, instead of democracy we will get anarchy, and instead of moving toward a new stage in the development of socialism, society will be set back.

Now a few words about the state's role in the process of building socialism. Justifiable criticism concerning the excessive assumption of state control should not turn into the opposite extreme, into a tendency to depict the socialist state as being the sole source of negative tendencies. Disparaging the role of the state will inevitably result in destroying the system of social protection for the working people. Moreover, under the conditions of the technological revolution, the state's role should increase, since under socialism only the state is capable of carrying out the structural reorganization of social production.

And one more observation concerning the distinctive features of our historical development, and particularly about the distortions that have caused our country tremendous damage. I liked the image Prof. Diligensky proposed of the statist phenomenon that crushed the rest of society under itself. But I have serious doubts as to whether that image can be used as a research tool. After all, if one follows the proposed model, what emerges is a kind of mystical phenomenon that, lacking any social basis and somehow hanging suspended in midair, managed to turn all the laws of the historical process upside down. Such a mystical phenomenon cannot exist; it has to have a real basis.

Granted, this is more a superficial than an inherent contradiction, and it disappears if one recalls that the proposed concept contains the thesis concerning a dualistic ideology. But the point, it seems to me, does not lie only in this dualism, which seemingly existed apart from societal life. The state's power did not lie solely in its taking advantage, for its own interests, of the masses' desire to create a just society that was based on their acceptance of socialist, humanistic values. To a certain extent, albeit far less than it should have, and often in a deceptive and distorted form, the state actually did express the interests of the masses themselves. If that had not been the case, there would have been no explosion of enthusiasm, no tremendous spurt forward, and a backward country would not have turned into a great power. That is, the statist state, if one may use that term, distorted social processes, but since it nonetheless relied on them, it could not ignore them in its policies.

Prof. K. Kholodkovsky (MEMO): I would like to join in discussing the question of what sort of society has been built in our country. Should it be defined as state socialism or statism? I think that the classification proposed by Prof. Diligensky takes us closer to understanding the phenomenon that we observe. Theoretically one can draw a line separating state socialism from the Stalinist perversions, but in real life it is hard to do. It is no accident that right now, when we are setting the goal of putting an end to the deformations of socialism inherited from the past, we are simultaneously discussing the question of what the alternative to state socialism should be. An analysis of the administrative-command system (or the command system, or the statist system, or whatever it is called) shows that an inseparable element of that system is the fear of repression; without it, the system loses the ability to function in any satisfactory way—something, incidently, that the period of Brezhnev's rule graphically confirmed.

As for statism itself, I agree with Prof. Diligensky that its emergence is related to the fact that socialist thought has an inherent tendency to regard the state as an absolute Demiurge. But it seems to me that it is quite wrong to link this phenomenon—at least, to link it directly—with the traditions and methodological approaches of Marxism. In 19th-century Marxism there was a statist tendency whose origin went back to rationalism, the Enlightenment, and Jacobinism; but there was also another tendency that was in many respects the opposite: historical determinism. A constant struggle went on between them, a struggle in which first one, then the other tendency won.

In Russia the outcome of that struggle was in many respects predetermined by the fact that the process whereby social thought developed, and the distinctive features of that development, greatly intensified the Enlightenment-Jacobin tendency. And that, it seems to me, was not only due to the nature of the social struggle, the intelligentsia's considerable separation from the people, and its desire to overcome that gap and place itself at the people's service. There was something else that was equally important. When we attempt to understand how it happened that it was our country in the 20th century where the state turned into a force that could transform the base and rebuild society in accordance with the ideas that ruled the minds of the people in power, it is obvious that one should recall national traditions, especially the traditionally great role of the state in society's life. In Russia the state established the first enterprises (often in order to subsequently turn them over into private hands), provided for the country's defense, and managed and disposed of a substantial part of the available land. As early as the time of Peter the Great the state created a powerful administrative apparatus, which grew extraordinarily over the following two centuries.

I think that all this indicates that the statist system did not emerge in a vacuum, and moreover, that its emergence was in many respects predetermined. That is, not only did the superstructure create the

base, but certain elements of the base itself also formed the superstructure. If one regards the laws of the development of statism from that
standpoint, I think that the contradiction with classic Marxist theory
looks less absolute than in the pattern proposed for discussion. As for
statism itself, I think Prof. Galkin is absolutely right when he says that
the state itself took advantage of the revolutionary impulse that existed
in the broad masses, transforming that impulse in a deceptive form into
practical activity. But one must not forget that in doing so its main goal
was not so much to build a just society, as to overcome historical
backwardness and create conditions for a leap in economic development that would place the country in one of the world's leading
positions. However, for all that—and here I agree with Prof. Diligensky—in both ideology and public attitudes a continuity with old
revolutionary traditions and a revolutionary impulse were preserved.

They are what provided the foundation on which our society could
fall back when the bankruptcy of statism and the need to return to the
sources, to the ideas of the October Revolution, became obvious.

Prof. Yu. Krasin: I would like to reply to certain critical remarks
made in the course of the discussion. First, concerning the influence of
state traditions in Russia. That is a fact that one cannot dispute. But is
that exclusively a distinctive feature of Russia? One could cite other
examples, such as Prussia, where there were equally deep state traditions. Therefore, if one is to speak of statism, one either should regard
that phenomenon as a general regularity of development that is unre-
lated to specific national features, or one should not accord it excessive
importance.

Another question is whether it is correct or incorrect to draw a
distinction between state socialism and the deformations that occurred
during the Stalinist period. That such a distinction should be drawn, I
am profoundly convinced. Otherwise it turns out that Stalinism was
inevitable and, consequently, that the deformations themselves were
inevitable. Agreeing with that would mean not only justifying Stalinism politically, but also admitting that there were no alternatives to
it. Yet, as writings that have recently been published show, such an
alternative did exist: Up until the 16th Party Congress, political development had taken a different direction. It was broken off in 1929 to
1930, when Stalin, for all intents and purposes, carried out a coup
d'état, violating the decisions adopted by the congress and Central
Committee plenums, and then using administrative levers to reinforce
his regime of personal power. Our society's tragedy is that the despotic
version of state socialism won.

Prof. H. Diligensky: I would like to clarify several aspects of my proposed concept that drew critical comments. The question of the sociopsychological basis of the statist regime, which I did not touch on in my remarks, is indeed important for understanding the processes taking place in our society. As for the essence of the question, I see no points of disagreement with Prof. Galkin. If one takes the 1930s and 1940s, it's true that there were both mass enthusiasm and a devotion to socialist ideals that persisted, no matter what.

But that's only one side of the matter. The other was shown in Kholodkovsky's remarks: Repressions played no less important a role than mass enthusiasm for the statist regime. A kind of mixture of enthusiasm and fear developed that was paradoxical but understandable. Fear stirred up enthusiasm, which operated, in part, as a psychological mechanism of adaptation to an uncomfortable situation; and enthusiasm, in turn, helped people forget their fear.

Is it possible, from this standpoint, to explain the situation in the post-Stalin and, especially, Brezhnev periods, when the enthusiasm had already disappeared, and the fear had disappeared too, yet the regime held on, and rather firmly at that? A schematic explanation comes down to the following:

When an individual, group, or society sees no real alternative to the existing state of affairs, it adapts to its environment—at least the majority does. This is a law of human psychology—both personal and group psychology. How did that adaptation occur in the specific situation of the 1960s and, especially, 1970s? Most of the population regarded the official ideological values precisely as the official and only possible values. That is perfectly natural. After all, adaptation of this sort is not just outward in nature; it also takes place on the psychological level. People have to somehow justify to themselves the conditions under which they live, otherwise the mind breaks down, and unbearable frustration develops.

But while accepting official values, people completely separated that loyalty or ideological conformism from the psychological attitudes that determined their behavior on the job, in the family, and so forth. That is, the result of adaptation came to be a dual consciousness, a consciousness that was conformist at its basis and oriented toward the sociopolitical status quo, toward a certain social contract, the essence of which was that a person was prepared to acknowledge that the state system was right and its ideological values true in exchange for the possibility of doing what he wanted in his private life. That ideological conformism, which is closely bound up with sociopolitical passivity, is one of the obstacles to perestroika.

And a final observation concerning the influence of national traditions in the process of building the new society. After all, it is a fact that the personality cult and the whole system of ideas associated with that phenomenon, and also with the role of the state, became widespread far beyond our country's borders—in some cases in countries with different political cultures and traditions. The corresponding ideology put down deep roots in the entire communist movement; even in countries with rich democratic traditions, communists were for a long time disciples of that ideology.

All that, in my view, indicates that statism has some basis other than national culture. And I think that basis is related not to the theory of Marx himself, but to the notions and ideas that became widespread in mass Marxism in the late 19th century, ideas that bore a strong imprint of Hegelianism. The Hegelian idea of the absolute spirit that is the creator of history not only does not contradict determinism but coincides with it. It stems from the same premise that development is predetermined once and for all, and alternative possibilities, if not ruled out entirely, are at least not considered. After the October Revolution the Soviet state became the embodiment of that idea, just as the Prussian state had been for Hegel.

Socialist Orientation:
A Restructuring of Ideas

VLADIMIR ILYICH MAKSIMENKO*

The discussion of the problems of socialist orientation (non-capitalist development)[1] that developed in 1987 and 1988 in the journals *Aziya i Afrika segodyna* [*Asia and Africa Today*], *Rabochiy klass i sovremenniy mir* [*The Working Class and the Modern World*], and *MEMO*[2] is noteworthy as a sign of its times. The attentive reader will find everything in it: a real increase in theoretical knowledge, and a semisubconscious desire to return scholarly thought to its "pre-perestroika" level; an honest attempt to rethink the problems within the confines of old methodological approaches, and a mixture of obvious ignorance of the classical legacy with "antidogmatic" rhetoric. In short, a great deal of material has been accumulated in the course of the discussion, but it is clearly too early to generalize it, since the discussion itself, it seems to me, has reached the point where it can be continued only if the arguments are shifted from the limited context of the problems of developing countries and placed in a broad, global context.

---

*Candidate of history, lead research associate at the U.S.S.R. Academy of Sciences' Institute of Oriental Studies. This article appeared in the February 1989 issue of *MEMO*.
[1]I use the terms "noncapitalist path of development" and "socialist orientation" synonymously, since no strict differentiation has yet been made between them on the basis of property relations and nature of regime.
[2]See G. Mirskiy, "The Liberated States: Paths of Development," *Aziya i Afrika segodnya*, No. 3, 1987; G. Mirskiy, "On the Developing Countries' Choice of Path and Orientation," *MEMO*, No. 5, 1987; V. L. Sheynis, "The Developing Countries and the New Political Thinking," *Rabochiy klass i sovremenniy mir*, No. 4, 1987; V. Li and G. Mirskiy, "Socialist Orientation in Light of the New Political Thinking," *Aziya i Afrika segodnya*, No. 8, 1987; Yu. Aleksandrov and V. Maksimenko, "Once Again, On the Problem of Socialist Orientation," *Aziya i Afrika segodnya*, No. 10, 1987; N. Simoniya, "Lenin's Concept of the Transition to Socialism, and the Countries of the East," *Aziya i Afrika segodnya*, No. 4, 1988; A. Kaufman and R. Ulyanovskiy, "The Question of the Liberated Countries' Socialist Orientation," *Aziya i Afrika segodnya*, No. 5, 1988; N. Simoniya, "Conduct a Scholarly Discussion Honestly!" *Aziya i Afrika segodnya*, No. 6, 1988; I. Zevelev and A. Kara-Murza, "The Afro-Asian World: The Contradictions of Social Progress," *Aziya i Afrika segodnya*, No. 7, 1988; Yu. Ivanov, "Some Questions Concerning Noncapitalist Development," *Aziya i Afrika segodnya*, No. 8, 1988; V. Maksimenko, "Lenin's Political Testament and Some Problems of Socialist Orientation," *Aziya i Afrika segodnya*, No. 9, 1988; A. Kiva, "Socialist Orientation: The Concept's Theoretical Potential, and Practical Realities," *MEMO*, No. 11, 1988; G. I. Mirskiy, "Socialist Orientation in the Third World," *Rabochiy klass i sovremenniy mir*, No. 4, 1988.

Soviet scholarship has already fully recognized the need to expand the boundaries of the discussion of socialist orientation in the Third World, and here I can only second the opinion of V.L. Sheynis, who noted that understanding the essence of the "socialist alternative for economically backward countries with non-European historical and cultural traditions" requires that countries such as China and Vietnam be included among the states under consideration on the same footing as the developing countries.[3] The same point has been made by Yu. M. Ivanov, whose own analysis of noncapitalist development has sought to encompass not only the Third World countries, but also China, North Vietnam, North Korea, Mongolia, and Soviet Central Asia.[4]

What dictates such an expansion of the context in which this set of problems is considered? First, there is the long-standing argument as to whether it is possible to go from social relations based on a relatively undeveloped commodity exchange and the predominance of "identical but by no means common interests,"[5] to socialism as a system of socialized property in which the working people exercise real power over their working conditions and means of production, and whether such a transition can be made by a "shortcut" (in comparison to the West European route), thus bypassing the full cycle of capitalist development. Second, expansion of context in which these problems are considered is necessitated by the global dimensions of the problems that arise, since what is at issue is the feasibility of a socialist system (and the content of the socialist ideal) in economically undeveloped countries that occupy a vast part of the planet. I am convinced that the course of events in the world, and especially the demands of working people who are cognizant of a "natural" right to be the masters of their own lives, will not allow the politicians to evade this argument and put off to some relatively distant future the questions that it raises.

In this connection, it is necessary to take yet another step to expand the framework in which noncapitalist development is analyzed, and to include in that framework multistructural [*mnogoukladnaya*]* Soviet Russia's experience from 1917 to 1929. In this case, the principal points of departure and sequence of theoretical analysis could be approximately as follows: the nature of the New Economic Policy [NEP] as an alternative to War Communism and, at the same time, the ways in which both the NEP and War Communism belonged to a *common* post-October legacy, that is, to the practical experience of

---

[3]V. Sheynis, note 2, above, p. 80.

[4]Yu. Ivanov, note 2, above, pp. 15–16.

[5]K. Marx and F. Engels, *Works* [*Sochineniya*], 2d ed., Vol. 18, p. 544.

*[A *mnogoukladnaya* country is one in which several different socioeconomic structures or *uklady* exist simultaneously. For example, Lenin spoke of patriarchal, small-commodity, capitalist, state-capitalist and socialist *uklady* functioning simultaneously in Soviet Russia in the early 1920s.—*Trans.*]

making the transition to socialism by a "shortcut" that "bypassed" the developed capitalist phase; the crisis of the NEP policy, which resulted from the lack of adequate political underpinning for its bold economic initiatives; and the Stalinist option for escaping the crisis by forcibly ending the NEP and destroying the peasantry as a class of independent agricultural owner-operators.

There is an endless amount of research to be done in this area, and it is just now getting under way. One cannot predict what course that work will take, and what results it will produce, but it is possible and necessary to avoid *pseudoproblems* that are characterized by raising such questions as: "Do you recognize or deny noncapitalist develop-ment?" To ask the question that way is to strip it of its real content and divert the discussion into the realm of ideological phantoms. The real, fundamental difficulty of updating the socialist ideal and socialist prac-tice today is increasingly being focused in the question: *What kind* of socialism? *What kind* of socialism do the participants in the discussion have in mind when they speak of socialist orientation, and *what kind* of experience, what tradition, are they drawing on in framing their arguments in the debate? Until such matters are clear and explicit, as long as they remain unspoken and in the subconscious, it will always be possible to take the reader "by fright" with statements such as, "unsubstantiated criticism of the policy of socialist orientation, criti-cism which goes so far as to actually reject it, is tantamount to a repudiation of the Marxist-Leninist theory concerning the possibility of economically backward countries' making the transition to socialism by bypassing or interrupting capitalist development. . . ."[6] It would apparently be useless to try to get the authors of this quoted passage to clarify which "theory concerning the possibility of transition" they are operating with. And of course, it is no longer so easy to take readers by fright, but nonetheless, in reply to such statements one constantly hears people deny that they are "rejecting" or "repudiating" anything.

I.

Thus, the task of expanding the framework of the discussion of socialist orientation is both timely and complex. It is complex if only because it requires taking into account the multiplicity of views of socialism and the diversity of the historical experience of the states and movements that call themselves socialist. In particular, any scholarly (as opposed to propagandistic) approach to the questions that arise in this connection requires that the political language in which the prob-lems of socialist orientation are formulated today be squared with the

---

[6]A. Kaufman and R. Ulyanovskiy, *op. cit.*, p. 23.

classical Marxist legacy. It hardly makes sense, for example, to carry on a debate about the noncapitalist development of Third World countries without pointing out that the problem of "bypassing" capitalism has a long-standing intellectual tradition; that it arose not on the periphery of Marxist thought but in the mainstream of its philosophical inquiry in the final two decades (1875-1895) of the creative work of Marx and Engels; and that a new stage in the development of that tradition was marked by Lenin's political testament, which outlined the contours of the dispute with a different tradition (but one that had also developed in the Marxist mainstream)—the tradition that was most fully expressed by War Communism (or distributive, or egalitarian communism) in Russia and that continues to produce ideological "spinoffs" to this day. The unity of these contending traditions, which nonetheless coexist in the bosom of Marxism, stems from the fact that both are geared toward *worldwide* revolutionary transformations; the opposition and contention within that unity stem from the difference in their understanding of the paths to what Marx called the world-historical "result,"[7] as well as in their interpretation of that result.

According to the *Manifesto of the Communist Party* (1848), the prerequisite for communism as a world-historical "result" is the world's transformation into a unified society with a capitalist mode of production. The *Communist Manifesto* portrays the bourgeoisie as a class that cannot exist without continuously revolutionizing the totality of social relations, and that therefore draws all the world's peoples into the sphere of capitalist civilization, or in other words, "creates a world for itself after its own image and likeness."[8] In the logic of the *Communist Manifesto*, the world's movement toward a unified capitalist mode of production is taken as a given and is not subject to question. But it is precisely the axiomatic nature of this premise that Marx and Engels disputed over the course of their own theoretical development, and one sign of the way they recast the bases of their theory is their proposed idea of a "shortened process of development"[9] whereby countries that were economically backward by West European standards would arrive at a socialist system by "bypassing" the complete cycle of the separation of producer from the means of production.

The inner logic of that evolution is superbly disclosed in M. Ya. Gefter's article, "Russia and Marx."[10] For my part, I want to single out just one aspect of it. The admission of the possibility of "bypassing" capitalism (that is, of development by a fundamentally different path

[7]See K. Marx and F. Engels, *Works*, 2d ed., Vol. 46, Pt. I, p. 47.
[8]K. Marx and F. Engels, *Works*, 2d ed., Vol. 4, p. 428.
[9]K. Marx and F. Engels, *Works*, 2d ed., Vol. 22, p. 446.
[10]See *Rabochiy klass i sovremenniy mir*, No. 4, 1988, pp. 152-170.

from that which Western Europe took) redefined the framework of what we call classical Marxism: The substantiation of a different path of development that was potentially an alternative to that of Western Europe, and hence the denial that progress was a one-way, "linear," movement toward a uniform result known in advance, became equally as "classical" as the ideas of the *Communist Manifesto*. Marxism formulated the new understanding in terms of a methodological prohibition against the use of a "universal passkey" in the guise of a deceptively profound-seeming theory "of the universal path that all peoples are fatefully doomed to follow."[11] Equally important, however, is the fact that the world historical perspective of the *Communist Manifesto* not only was not negated by the new understanding but, to the contrary, was strengthened by a more concrete notion of development as *unity in diversity*. And conversely, the understanding of *unity as standardization*—an understanding fed both by a commonplace urge to order the surrounding world, and by the indomitable revolutionary will of those guided by the conviction of having discovered the law and goal of development once and for all—became the opposing side in the dispute that arose within the Marxist theory.

The thought of the possibility of "bypassing" the capitalist stage entered Marxist theory through contact with Russian peasant socialism. In the ideal of a harmonious society based on communal collectivism not yet destroyed by capital, Marx and Engels saw reflected a "moment of truth": the fact of the existence of production cooperatives within the framework of the peasant commune, and the impossibility of ignoring that fact without doing violence to reality by trying to make it artificially conform to preconceived theoretical patterns. Hence K. Marx's agreement with N.G. Chernyshevsky, who saw the possibility, in Russia's situation, of bypassing the vicissitudes of the capitalist system and harvesting all of its fruits by developing "our own historical givens." Moreover, for Marx in the late 1870s and early 1880s, such a possibility looked like "the best chance that history has ever granted any people."[12] The best (let me note this as emphatically as possible, to underscore the nontrivial relationship between "utopia" and "science" in classical Marxism), since that "chance" would allow Russia to avoid the "plague of proletarianism" that had stricken the people and that frightened not only Chernyshevsky. In contrast to the Russian socialists, however, Marx formulated his conclusion with due caution and made it highly conditional in nature: If Russia continued to follow the path that it had followed after the elimination of serfdom (that is, the path of a rapid development of

---

[11]K. Marx and F. Engels, *Works*, 2d ed., Vol. 19, pp. 120, 121.
[12]*Ibid.*, p. 119.

commodity-type capitalist relations in the city and countryside that
was destroying the peasant commune), the possibility of "bypassing"
capitalism would be irrevocably lost.

The archaic peasant commune with its production collectivism
figures in the late works of Marx not as a synonym for backwardness,
underdevelopment, and stagnation (stagnation of the commune was
the result of its parasitic exploitation by Russian capitalist promoters
encouraged by a despotic state), but as a prototype of future worldwide
cooperation among working people. However, the possibility that was
outlined could become a reality only under two indispensable conditions, which Marx formulated strictly and unequivocally (if those conditions were absent, the very possibility was excluded). First, the
"shortened" process of development was possible, as already noted,
only in the event that it began *before* the capitalist environment had
completely undermined communal production relations. Second, that
path to socialism was conceivable only if it became a path for assimilating the immense productive forces already accumulated by capitalist
society. Between these two "ifs" lay the whole dialectic of the pos-
sibility-impossibility of "bypassing" capitalism.

In connection with such an unconventional development of his
and Marx's theory, Engels considered it necessary to recall the "basic
truths of socialism": The creation of a society that destroyed class
distinctions required the existence not only of a proletariat, but also of
a bourgeoisie as the class that had first managed to raise social production relations to a "very high" level of development. Only a level that
high, Engels stressed, could ensure that the elimination of class distinctions would be of a lasting nature, and that genuine progress would
occur. Otherwise, the attempt to eliminate private property and
classes would have catastrophic consequences: It would become the
cause of "stagnation or even decline in the social mode of
production."[13]

Thus, it is an elementary fact that the founders of historical
materialism conceived of the transition to a society in which the free
development of each would become the condition for the free development of all as entailing the consistent assimilation of the totality of
productive forces developed by the capitalist mode of production. And
in this light, the genuine theoretical service of Marx and Engels was
their ability to discern, in the rapid development of postreform Russia
as a country that was backward in capitalist terms ("there is no other
country in which, for all the original savagery of bourgeois society,
capitalist parasitism has been developed to such an extent"),[14] a point

---

[13]K. Marx and F. Engels, *Works*, 2d ed., Vol. 18, pp. 537, 538.
[14]*Ibid.*, p. 540.

of fundamental historical novelty: *backwardness as an advantage*. But to the revolutionary socialist consciousness, Russian backwardness could have seemed an advantage only in a strictly defined sense: the fact that communal collectivism, with its whole complex of work habits and popular customs had survived, held out—in theory—the possibility of a *synthesis* of that structure with material and nonmaterial productive forces on the level attained by the industrially developed West. But why a *synthesis?* And precisely what was it considered possible to "bypass" or "shorten"?

It is clear from the texts that what was meant to be "bypassed" was such an integral element of the historical development of capital as the separation of producers from the means of their production (land, craftsmen's tools, etc.), and what was meant to be "shortened" was the practical European historical experience that had included a centuries-long process whereby the sufferings of the expropriated masses had accumulated at one pole, and all the material and human elements of societal wealth had undergone an unprecedented concentration in the form of "capital" at the other pole. Indeed, as Marx informed the editor of [the Russian journal] *Otechestvenniye zapiski* [*Fatherland Notes*], "bypassing" and "shortening," if they were possible, would be "the best chance that history had ever granted any people!"

In that light, one can understand how the idea of synthesizing the archaic collectivist experience that had become part of the genetic code of the human race with the highest achievements of European industrialism emerged in classical Marxism. Neither the Russian peasant commune, nor the workers' artel, nor any other archaic, primitive form of production cooperative could become the *direct* basis for the socialist socialization of production on a national scale. And the simple reason it could not was that it did not have an inherent source of development: It was nondevelopment (Nicht-Entwicklung, in the terms of the "German ideology") as a fundamental feature of the natural merger of working individuals with the main condition of their production, the land, that accounted for the remarkable stability of the agricultural commune's forms over the course of millennia.

As Marx explains in that same letter to *Otechestvenniye zapiski*, a most important historical mission of West European capital was that it had provided "an extremely great impetus *simultaneously* (my emphasis—*V.M.*) to the growth of the productive forces of social labor and to the full development of every individual producer."[15] If one does not take that simultaneity literally, its internal dialectic is such that it was precisely the liberation of the individual producer from "natural" attachment to the archaic collective, as well as from noneconomic

---

[15]K. Marx and F. Engels, *Works*, 2d ed., Vol. 19, p. 120.

compulsion of the large precapitalist and early capitalist private owners who exploited the commune, that became the social source of the immense increase in the productive forces of social labor as a whole. In real history, *the progress of the freedom of the individual* (as producer and owner of the conditions of his existence) *is inseparable from the progress of private ownership*, just as it is inseparable from class polarization into a minority of private owners of "capitalized" social wealth who are free from compulsion, on the one hand, and a mass of people who are "free" from any ownership at all, on the other. To bypass the lengthy historical period of social injustice that arose from that polarization, but to borrow and assimilate the most important fruits of European freedom; to "reduce" the price of progress by paying for it with an accelerated, *revolutionary* assimilation of predecessors' experience—that is the profound humanistic point of the project for "bypassing" capitalism as it appears in the works of Marx and Engels.

II.

The negation and antithesis of that project was the practice of War Communism, in the course of which the assimilation and surmounting of private ownership was transformed into the myth concerning the "socialist" nature of the universal state ownership, and the problem of human freedom that had been the point of departure for the authors of the *Communist Manifesto* was turned into the ideological stereotype of freedom as the coercion of the minority by the majority. It is very important, however (for all the depth of present-day antipathy toward the practice of War Communism), to avoid the temptation to present War Communism as a "perversion" and "deformation." People who speak of a deformation should, following their own logic, also declare the second program of the Russian Communist Party (Bolsheviks), numerous works by Lenin, and the entire Russian Revolution to have been "perversions."

The historical roots of War Communism lie in that common understanding of the *worldwide* nature of its mission that it shares, and that marks its continuity, with the European movement. The revolutionary spirit of 1848 Europe that suffuses the *Communist Manifesto*, and the revolutionary spirit of 1917, along with the practice of War Communism that grew out of it, are historically related. They are related not only through a common sense of the universal nature of the liberating revolutionary upsurge, but also through their attitude toward the world revolution as something that was *immediate*. The "word and deed" of the revolutionaries of 1917 were based on the profound conviction that the world revolution had already begun, that it was taking place before their very eyes, and that the more radical the

Russian revolution was, the easier it would be to achieve a worldwide victory bringing liberation from exploitation and oppression. Thus, the worldwide nature of the revolutionary cause, and the notion that a worldwide task could be accomplished directly were the alpha and omega of the world outlook of War Communism. But what were its leading principles, as recorded in the documents of that time?

The chief (and, for all intents and purposes, sole) moving force of the socialist revolution was proclaimed to be the state of the dictatorship of the proletariat, which was supposed to carry out a radical social revolution by destroying not only big capitalist ownership, but also its economic base in the form of simple market-oriented production. Since capitalist society, with its class divisions, could exist only by virtue of "civil peace," or a certain commonality of interests among opposing classes—a commonality that "terribly delayed the progress of revolutions"—the proletarian state was required to wage incessant "civil war." More specifically: "The proletarian revolution is . . . the rupturing of civil peace—it is civil war."

Politics and economics in the proletarian state were "supposed to merge . . . into a single whole," and as a result of that merger, "state-proletarian compulsion" became the decisive lever of the socio-economic revolution. State violence was "economic potential" and the only means of building "full communism—communism devoid of the state" within the context of the proletariat's worldwide victory. In that connection, the greater the scope of the violence carried out by the proletarian state, "the lower the 'costs' of the transitional period would be (all other things being equal, of course), the sooner social equilibrium would be established on the new basis, and the faster the curve of productive forces would start to rise."

The compulsion on the part of the state was directed not only against the large private owners, but also against that mass force that took the form of "the speculative, unbridled behavior of the peasantry, which is the embodiment of fragmented ownership and haphazard market forces." The sense of private ownership drove the peasant "into the arms of the reaction" and was expressed "in resistance to the state grain monopoly and in the desire for free trade, which is speculation."

What was supposed to counter those uncontrolled forces? The proletariat's state plan as "socialized labor," the complete centralization of production, the aforementioned grain monopoly, mandatory universal labor service and the forced mobilization of the population to perform public works, the rationing system of distribution, fixed prices, and so forth. It was believed that the state in this case was functioning as a "social regulator," and that "goods were being turned into products and losing the character of market commodities." Thus, the period of transition from capitalism to socialism represented the negation of commodities and money, which by that logic, "ceases to be a universal equivalent and becomes a conventional . . . token of the circulation of products." And this entire policy, "from the viewpoint of a grand historical scale . . . is . . . a method of developing communist humanity from the human material of the capitalist era."[16]

These quotes, which capture the logic of War Communism, are taken from two books by N.I. Bukharin: *The Theory of the Dictatorship of the Proletariat* [*Teoriya proletarskoy diktatury*] (1919) and *The Economics of the Transitional Period* [*Ekonomika perekhodnogo perioda*] (1920). Lenin immediately studied the latter as soon as it came out, gave it generally high marks, and made numerous notations in its margins. I think it is worth looking at one of them, in particular, which pertains directly to Lenin's widely known idea that he expressed (two months after reading Bukharin's book) at the Second Comintern Congress, that figured in truncated form in a number of documents of the Stalinist Comintern of the late 1920s and early 1930s, and that later, after a hiatus of a quarter of a century, would be reproduced by Khrushchev in 1959 in his report to the 21st CPSU Congress. It is the idea of the possibility of backward countries' making the transition "to a soviet system and, through certain stages of development, to communism, while bypassing the capitalist stage of development."[17]

And so, Bukharin wrote: "Colonial uprisings and national revolutions *belong, as an integral part, to the great world revolutionary process* that is realigning the whole axis of the world economy"; the collapse of capitalist production relations that occurs in that process "*facilitates the victory* of the proletarian revolution and the dictatorship of the working class." Reinforcing Bukharin's emphasis, Lenin underscored the words "integral part" and noted in the margin: "Precisely!"[18]

In my view, this brief textological digression demonstrates the following: The formula "proceeding to communism, while bypassing the capitalist stage of development," which was transposed from the War Communism of 1920 to 1959, which then, in the 1960s and 1970s, became the basis for the notions of the "national-democratic state," "noncapitalist development," and "socialist orientation," and which has never been critically reinterpreted to this day, is a formula that is inseparable from the climate in which the world revolution was thought of as an immediate, practical and urgent matter, and the state's

---

[16]*The Path to Socialism in Russia: The Selected Works of N. I. Bukharin* [*Put k sotsializmu v Rossii. Izbranniye proizvedeniya N. I. Bukharina*], New York, 1967, pp. 121, 67, 71, 68, 114, 85, 112, 118, 119.

[17]V.I. Lenin, *Complete Works* [*Polnoye sobraniye sochineniy*], Vol. 41, p. 246.

[18]V.I. Lenin, "Notes on N. Bukharin's Book *The Economics of the Transitional Period*," *Lenin's Anthology* [*Leninskiy sbornik*], Vol. XI, Moscow and Leningrad, 1931, p. 399.

coercion of small-scale, noncapitalist private owners was thought of as a way of building socialism. And accordingly, the concept of "bypassing" capitalism as it was interpreted in our country starting in the 1960s was the result of uncritically transposing the philosophical concepts of the period of War Communism to the reality of the postcolonial world.

The persistence of the views generated by this transposition indicates that the concepts in question cannot be partially updated and modified; the only thing to do is to completely *restructure* them. Otherwise we will shamefacedly remove the word "communism" from the "bypassing" formula but continue to regard national liberation revolutions as "inevitably" going "beyond the framework of capitalism."[19] We will tone down the thesis concerning "inevitability," cease to claim that "capitalism as a system has become obsolete,"[20] and skirt the question of the socialist goals of "bypassing" capitalism and the question of the real political system in so-called revolutionary democratic regimes, but we will go on repeating that "the national-democratic state" is a pledge of movement "along the path of social progress."[21] And we will propose that same state as, if not the sole agent of the transition to socialism, then in any event, an invariable guarantee of "noncapitalism," democracy, revolutionary spirit, progressiveness, and so forth (we will be doing so in accordance with that state's ideological self-assessment, and using the language of the remote War Communism period, a language in which we often continue to speak without realizing it). And, as long as we are discussing the question of the possibility of socialist orientation and socialist policies in the Third World, the key to restructuring that language and that thinking lies in the radically renewed understanding of socialism that Lenin formulated in general outline in his political testament. Today his behest appears, in M. Ya. Gefter's precise expression, as "the Leninist revolution of reforms," the "NEP alternative to October," and—as such—as a "new world policy."[22] There is no question that these ideas of Lenin's still await interpretation and development.

III.

Just what did Lenin include in the demand to carry out a "radical change of our entire view of socialism"[23]—a demand that he made at the end of his life and addressed not only to himself but to his suc-

---

[19]*Classes and the Class Struggle in the Developing Countries* [*Klassy i klassovaya borba v razvivayushchikhsya stranakh*], Vol. 1, Moscow, 1967, pp. vi, vii.

[20]*The Paths of Development of Countries That Have Won National Independence, and World Socialism* [*Puti razvitiya stran zavoyevavshikh natsionalnuyu nezavisimost, i mirovoy sotsializm*], Prague, 1964, p. 21.

[21]A. Kaufman and R. Ulyanovskiy, note 2, above, p. 20.

[22]See M. Ya. Gefter, "Stalin Died Yesterday," in *There Is No Alternative* [*Inogo ne dano*], Moscow, 1988, pp. 319, 312, 314.

[23]V.I. Lenin, *Complete Works*, Vol. 45, p. 376.

cessors? To understand that is to reach a new theoretical frontier in our analysis of socialism's prospects for economically undeveloped countries.

What, in Lenin's eyes, required a "radical change"—a revision or restructuring—was the War Communism view of socialism, a view that measured the degree of "socialism" by the degree of state coercion of private interests, and that regarded socialization of the means of production as nothing other than total assumption of state control over the reproduction process in all of its phases. War Communism, which was fed by the sense of an imminent world revolution, and which believed in the creative mission of the centralized will of the state, turned from the utopia of world social brotherhood into a monstrous anti-utopia of the universal abolition of private interests.

It is striking how accurately the young Marx predicted this sort of metamorphosis of immature communist aspirations. In characterizing the communism that strives "to destroy *everything* that, on the basis of *private ownership*, not everyone can possess," the "communism that denies the individual *personality* everywhere," Marx wrote: "The fact that such an abolition of private property is not the genuine assimilation of it can be seen precisely in the abstract rejection of the whole world of culture and civilization, in the return to the *unnatural* simplicity of the *poor* person who has no requirements, who not only has not risen above the level of private ownership, but has not even risen to it."[24] That is something that the state can arrive at "only by a path that brings it to the destruction of lives, to the *guillotine.*" And Marx continues: "At moments of a particularly exalted sense of its own power, political life strives to suppress its prerequisites—the civil society and its elements. . . . But it can achieve that only by entering into a *violent* contradiction with the conditions of its own life, only by declaring the revolution to be *continuous*; and thus the political drama ends with the restoration of religion, private property, and all the elements of the civil society, and it does so with the same degree of necessity with which war ends in peace."[25]

The extent to which the logic of Lenin's turn away from War Communism to the NEP reproduces the logic of Marx's philosophical speculation is noteworthy: from civil war to civil peace, from the state's "particularly exalted sense of its own power" to the restoration of natural conditions for people's material life, and to the restoration of the rights of "the whole world of culture and civilization," which had been rejected in the paroxysm of War Communism. (N.I. Bukharin

---

[24]K. Marx, "The Economic-Philosophical Manuscripts of 1844," in K. Marx, *From Early Works* [*Iz rannikh proizvedeniy*], Moscow, 1956, pp. 586-587.
[25]K. Marx and F. Engels, *Works*, 2d ed., Vol. 1, p. 393.

also came, from "the economics of the transitional period," to the same point at the end of his life: In 1936 he expressed the idea of "restoring humanity" by realizing a "universal synthesis of culture."[26]

In the context of that radical reconsideration, it was by no means the fantastic side of "the fantastic plans of the old cooperationists, including Robert Owen," that revealed itself to Lenin, at a time when he assigned top priority to analyzing the possibility of "turning class enemies into class collaborators (!!!—V.M.) and class war into class peace (so-called civil peace)."[27] Lenin conceived the essence of the "radical change" in the view of socialism as a practical shift of the center of gravity of all socialist work from the sphere of politics, state power, the class struggle, and so forth, to "peaceful organizational 'cultural' work." And in the context of that shift, the "two chief tasks that define the era," were the taming of the state apparatus, which was "utterly unacceptable," and "cultural work among the peasantry, as an economic goal."[28] The collapse of the utopian notion of the transition to a stateless communist system through the use of all-encompassing state coercion made it clear to Lenin in practical terms (and not just in theory) that the attempt to "bypass," in the socialist process of socializing production, such achievements of civilization as free labor and the free exchange of the products of labor not only completely blocked the path to a more just social order, but actually led to the death of the civilized community.

In the perspective of the NEP, "that socialism that previously evoked a derisive smile and a scornful attitude on the part of people who were justifiably convinced of the need for class struggle, struggle for political power, etc.," Lenin wrote, "achieves its goal of its own accord" on condition that: (1) the state confirms in practice the nature of its regime as a regime of *workers and peasants*, regarding the future of socialism from the viewpoint of a noncompetitive "accord" between the two principal—proletarian and private-owner—working classes, the latter of which is not subject to compulsory refashioning in the process of a transition from a multistructural social reality to some sort of imagined social homogeneity; (2) the state-ownership structure [*uklad*] and the state's entire economic policy are geared to the *civilized cooperative* as the central, key figure in the socialist system being established, and the task of using planned exchange "to establish intercourse between the city and the countryside" develops into "a gigantic, world-historical cultural task"; (3) the concerted forces of the worker-peasant inspection service and the bearers of the old culture

---

[26]See *Sovetskaya kultura* [*Soviet Culture*], September 13, 1988.
[27]V.I. Lenin, *Complete Works*, Vol. 45, p. 375.
[28]*Ibid.*, p. 376.

avert the danger, which is fatal for socialism, of the bureaucratic degeneration of state authority (the situation in which "that bureaucracy does not belong to us; we belong to it!!"); and (4) the bourgeoisie, both Russian and international, admits the two working classes, "on specified terms," to cooperation with it.[29]

Thus, Lenin's alternate understanding of socialism retains the world-historical prospect of establishing a new social system, but it rejects a world communist revolution as a *direct* act of the concentrated will of the revolutionary vanguard. And in that sense the movement of Lenin's thought to the NEP is akin to the movement of Marx and Engels from the ideas of the *Communist Manifesto* to the idea of a "shortened path of development." And the "shortened" path itself appears in Lenin's political testament as a new *synthesis* of production cooperatives (the cooperatively organized free labor of independent producers) with the highest achievements of capitalist civilization in the development of productive forces. The possibility of such a synthesis, the possibility of "bypassing" such a prerequisite for the accumulation of societal wealth as the separation of the worker from the objective conditions of his labor, is revealed in *revolution*, but no revolution in and of itself guarantees progress along this path.

IV.

And so, in assessing the prospects for "socialist orientation" in the Third World, it is impossible to avoid the question, "What kind of socialism?" It is impossible even to raise it and seek to answer it without analyzing the revolutionary experience of the past—experience that is worldwide in nature and, in that sense, common to both East and West, and to Russia. But in expanding the context of the problem in this way, it is important not to lose sight of the problem itself, and here the most practical and valuable guideline is Lenin's last word in the area of socialist theory, a word specifically embodied in his political testament: socialism as a *civil society with actually socialized social relations based on multistructural modes of human activity*. We will not find the literal expression of this idea in Lenin; moreover, it is really not an idea but an image, one of the last images in Lenin's thought. And we see that this image of socialism is an alternative to the understanding of progress as standardization and the subordination of activity to any single mode of production, whether it be the utopia of capital's universal domination of labor and nature, or the anti-utopia of universal state control over people's lives.

---

[29]See *Ibid.*, pp. 369, 367, 441, 387, etc.

The updated socialist ideal that we are redesigning today is based on multistructural modes of human activity (modes of producing and reproducing people's societal life) as a historical given that cannot, in principle, be eliminated. In that understanding of it, present-day socialist orientation is a path of development between two impossibilities: the impossibility of destroying "capital" (as social wealth accumulated by history and embodied in material objects), and the impossibility, for "capital," of encompassing the entire world (that is, of entirely subordinating people's lives and destinies to "material" relations that are alienated from them). And accordingly, the positive content of socialist orientation is a *synthesis*, on the one hand, of the elements of that social system that mediates human relations through the universal exchange of products and activities of various sorts, and that, without being the product exclusively of capitalism, has nonetheless developed in the bosom of capitalist civilization and is its crowning achievement, and on the other hand, of the elements of the opposite system, which is based on unmediated, cooperative labor and traces its roots to the archaic depths of the human race's primordial existence. In that understanding of it, socialist orientation is a *planetary cause* that has no single missionary spokesman, and on which no one holds a monopoly, but that reaches above state, racial, and religious boundaries and superstitions and unites people through a common antipathy for the oppression that stems from people's alienation from property and power.

By virtue of its multistructural nature and the impossibility of reducing it to either the "First World" or the "Second World," the Third World (while integrating features and aspects of both the other "worlds") has brought into sharp focus for us the problem of unity in diversity as a world-historical norm. In turn, the focusing of that problem requires a soberly skeptical attitude toward the socialist alternative's real chances in the Third World of the late 20th century. In any case, to the extent that we try to associate socialist orientation with the all-encompassing activities of any given state, with the regimes of military bureaucratic dictatorships that are centralized as much as they need to be to prevent the working people from organizing themselves and to prevent interference with the freedom of private, parasitic accumulation under cover of the "managerial" activities of the state apparatus—to that extent we will, like the Molière character who spoke prose without knowing it, be projecting onto the real Third World the reflected light of our own War Communism past.

A "revolution of a new type" appears here as an alternative to the existing type only in the event that we recognize that such a revolution in the developing countries is not a matter of the past (as was imagined in the 1960s and 1970s), but a matter of the future. It can go beyond and lead beyond the bourgeois-democratic framework in only one sense: by positively assimilating the liberation content that history has incorporated in that framework. The fact that such a movement "beyond the framework" to universal human unity is an imperative of development in a world moving toward an irreconcilable clash of "national" ideas was already understood by the revolutionaries of 1917. It has fallen to their heirs, in turn, to realize that movement toward universal human community cannot be the apotheosis of violence, and that such movement, therefore, not only has no right to attack the real multistructural nature of the present world—both developed and developing—but faces an acute need to take the multiplicity of socioeconomic structures that have spontaneously taken shape on earth and to develop them consciously into a culture of "life-creating differences."[30]

---

[30]See M. Gefter, "From the Nuclear World to a World of Worlds," *Vek XX i mir* [*The 20th Century and Peace*], No. 3, 1988, p. 36.

Reforms in China: Problems and Contradictions

LEV PETROVICH DELYUSIN*

After the Tiananmen Square events of June 1989, when the student movement calling for social and political democratization and intensification of the campaign against bureaucracy and corruption was suppressed, many Sinologists concluded that this marked the failure of reforms in China, and the triumph of conservative forces that were trying to stop China's movement along the path of democratization and the restructuring of its economic system. In their view, China had abandoned the path of reforms and started to move in a direction opposite to the course followed by the Soviet Union and East European countries.

The opinion that there has been a departure from the course of reform can be found in China itself; evidence of its existence can be seen in the press, which has criticized as mistaken the view that there has been a retreat from the previous course of reforms and policy of openness. China's new leadership never tires of trying to demonstrate that it will continue to implement a policy of economic transformation and pursue a course aimed at deepening the reforms, and that there can be no question of returning to previous methods of economic management. Nevertheless, Chinese society is wary of official assurances and perceives actions taken to restore order and improve the economy as a return to authoritarian-bureaucratic methods of economic management.

What provided the grounds for such assessments and opinions? Why was enthusiasm over the successes of reforms in China replaced so abruptly with disappointment in their results and pessimism regarding prospects for the country's future development?

I.

If we look at the actual economic policies, they are characterized today by expansion of the sphere of centralized planning, rejection of wage reform, institution of strict price controls, and intensified super-

---

*Doctor of history, professor. This article was written for this collection.

vision of individual labor activities and private enterprise. Administrative methods have become predominant in managing the national economy.

While declaring war on corruption, at the same time the new leadership of the Chinese Communist Party (CCP), even if it did not actually abandon implementation of reforms in the political and administrative system, for all practical purposes halted the democratization process.

In the area of ideology a campaign has been unleashed against so-called bourgeois liberalism. The press has condemned many of the theoretical propositions on which the need for economic and political transformations was based. A number of articles have called the need for reforms into question and mocked those who "put their faith in the omnipotence of reforms."

"Bourgeois liberals" are being accused of allegedly calling for the restoration of capitalism by demanding complete freedom for market relations, restoration of private property, and introduction of a parliamentary system. All these charges are unsubstantiated and based on fragments of quotations from unknown, unpublished materials, which makes it impossible to judge the genuine views of those who are being condemned in the Chinese press today. In any case, the "bourgeois liberal" views that are criticized in the Chinese press appear quite cautious and moderate compared to opinions that are published in Soviet journals and newspapers, as well as in the East European countries' press.

It must be pointed out that when propaganda tries to intimidate society with the threat of the restoration of capitalism, a significant proportion of the public does not feel any fear. After 40 years of development along a "socialist" course, the Chinese, having gained the opportunity to learn about the living standard of working people in capitalist countries, and the degree of the democratization of social and political life there, realized how far they lagged behind other countries in both economic and political respects. The example of Taiwan, whose economy has developed according to principles different from those on the mainland, has had a particularly strong effect on the attitudes and imagination of the Chinese. The press condemns the statements of Chinese workers who say that they would prefer to be subject to exploitation by capitalists, but to have the living standards of workers in Taiwan, Japan, and the United States. The Chinese press calls such statements mistaken, assuring readers that the high living standard in capitalist countries is by no means evidence of the capitalist system's advantages.[1]

---

[1] *Qiushi*, No. 22, 1989.

At the same time, official propaganda is doing everything to revive the cult of Mao Zedong. The name of the soldier Lei Feng, a symbol of unthinking execution of the "great helmsman's" orders and an example of asceticism and self-sacrifice, which at one time had disappeared, is again widely held up as a model to imitate, and the country's young people are called on to follow this example. The spirit and style of Yanan, which are tied to calls for the strictest frugality in consumption and perseverance in the face of deprivation and difficulties, are praised.

The attitude toward the experience of Daqing, the oilfields that were extolled in the 1960s and 1970s as a model of industrial development according to Mao Zedong's prescriptions, is being revised.

Zhao Ziyang, former General Secretary of the CCP Central Committee, is being condemned for pandering to the ideas of "bourgeois liberalism," for violating the "four fundamental principles" (that is, socialism, the dictatorship of the proletariat, Marxism-Leninism and the ideas of Mao Zedong, and the leading role of the CCP).

As for these charges, it can be said, to put it mildly, that they falsify the positions of Zhao Ziyang. Looking at his report at the 13th CCP Congress, one can readily see that he stressed the need for faithful adherence to these four principles. As for the principles themselves, it should be pointed out that at different times they have been invested with different social, economic, and political meaning. For example, during the period of the Cultural Revolution, many leaders of the CCP, including Deng Xiaoping, were subjected to persecution under the banner of defending these principles.

The Cultural Revolution showed how easy it is, under the banner of revolutionary socialism and communism, to launch a campaign to reinforce feudal and fascist practices, suppress democracy, and engage in lawlessness, tyranny, and violence against individuals and society. It is no accident that over all the years since Mao Zedong's death, which began a new page in the country's history, polemics have focused on the question of whether the target of the ideological and political struggle should be bourgeois-liberal or feudal ideas. Conservative figures stress the importance and significance of the struggle against bourgeois ideology, while radicals stress the struggle against feudal views and institutions. Socialism is supported by both: both those who fired the shots on Tiananmen Square, and those at whom the shots were fired. So, the issue is not the principles themselves, which both Zhao Ziyang and his opponents defended, but the actual meaning invested in slogan-style precepts.

In general, it has been characteristic of China's political culture to continue to use the same slogans while the actual political course is changed. An appearance of continuity is created in policies, even though the policies may be fundamentally altered. The same slogans are invested with different social and economic meanings. This applies to the transformation of the "four fundamental principles," the spirit of Lei Feng, the "hundred flowers," and so forth. One would think that this would interfere with the proper orientation of party and economic management personnel, but it has become a tradition to use secret decisions and instructions to reveal the true meaning with which the leadership wants to invest the standard slogans, in order to avoid confusing local cadres.

Many of the theoretical propositions contained in Zhao Ziyang's report to the 13th CCP Congress are being suppressed, distorted, or criticized. The point of reference now is the appointment of Jiang Zemin as General Secretary of the CCP Central Committee, and rarely does anyone dare to refer to the decisions of the 13th Congress. Associated with the leadership change is the beginning of the policy of regulating and tightening administrative control over economic life; according to the official view, this does not mean the abandonment of reforms, but on the contrary, will result in deepening them.

If one considers the ultimate goal of the reforms to be the complete replacement of administrative-bureaucratic methods with economic market levers, a diversity of forms of ownership, and democratization of the political system, one can contend that at the present time there has been an obvious retreat from this goal. It must be recalled, however, that while proclaiming the policy of developing commodity-money relations and forming a market mechanism, the leaders of the CCP never stopped declaring that they aimed to use both plan and market principles, the combination of which was supposed to create incentives for increasing production activity and provide rapid economic growth rates. From the outset, the question of determining the most effective relationship between the plan and the market was at the center of the discussions. This question has still not been resolved.

Often descriptions of the current state of the Chinese economy call it a mixed economy, meaning that it functions on the basis of a combination (or synthesis) of plan and market mechanisms. In reality, though, one must admit that the combination of plan and market as factors regulating the process of economic development exists only in theory. It is still too early to speak of a combination or a synthesis. Attempts are being made in this direction, but for all practical purposes no effective methods have yet been found for managing the economy by using plan and market levers. Nor has any definite answer been given to the question of what the proper relationship between them should be. Actual economic policy has still not taken on consistent, stable features, and for now directive planning, from either the capital or provincial centers, still determines the direction and pace of development of the principal branches of the national economy. The plan and the market have not yet begun interacting equally, and a mechanism for such interaction has not yet been found. The old (totally planned) and the new (market) systems are not being combined and are not interacting; they are coexisting, and instead of complementing one another, they are interfering with one another. The old form of economic management retains its dominant position, and it is not giving the market mechanism the opportunity to fully determine the economic situation in the country. The bureaucracy, while recognizing the need to combine the plan and the market, actually strives to stifle the market in the cradle, or to place such restrictions on market relations that their effect on economic activity is reduced to a minimum.

While recognizing that a certain retreat took place in the Chinese leadership's domestic policies after the Tiananmen Square events, and that conservative tendencies have temporarily gained the upper hand in the Chinese leadership, we are nonetheless disinclined to share the pessimistic views regarding the prospects for China's social, economic, and political development. Reforms in that country represent long and complicated processes, during the course of which there will be some bold breakthroughs, some retreats, and some marking time.

The 10-year period of reform in China brought about major changes in the life of Chinese society. In the period following the CCP Central Committee's Third Plenum (December 1978), a great amount of theoretical and practical work was done in China to revamp the economic and political system, and one cannot simply discount everything that was achieved.

A new idea of the social and economic content of socialism and the ways to achieve it was formed. The concept of socialism with a Chinese face put forward by Deng Xiaoping, and the concept of the initial stage of socialism adopted at the 13th CCP Congress marked a departure from the Stalinist-Maoist model of socialism. Concepts such as commodity-money relations, pluralism of forms of ownership, competition, risk—that is, concepts that during the era of Mao Zedong were considered characteristic only of capitalist society and to be avoided at all costs under socialism—were given a new legitimacy.

The principle of wage leveling advocated by Mao Zedong and the extreme-left theory of the "common pot" were also criticized severely. It was admitted that the principle of wage leveling held back and retarded the development of the country's productive forces, because it diminished the work efforts of the working masses and prevented the people from displaying their creative abilities. However, even though it has been condemned at the theoretical level and in political documents, for all intents and purposes this principle has been preserved in actual practice. At the same time, in speaking of the principle of wage leveling, one should bear in mind that actually this principle was and is applied in a graduated, hierarchical fashion. Wage leveling was practiced within a given social group or official rank. Thus, employees in the same category received the same wages, but a promotion in rank meant a corresponding increase in material benefits.

By supporting this sort of hierarchical wage leveling, the bureaucracy encouraged careerism, developing a bureaucratic zeal among functionaries in the party and state apparatus; a zeal reinforced by a desire to retain their achieved rank, thus preserving their right to a larger piece of the state pie.

As a result of the reforms, people's communes were eliminated in the Chinese countryside and a contract system was established. Major changes were also seen in the cities, where leasing and contract arrangements were introduced at industrial and trade enterprises, and joint-stock companies were formed. The sphere of centralized planning was reduced, the rights of provinces were expanded, and the independence of many enterprises was expanded. These changes produced positive results and helped increase economic efficiency and boost production in both agriculture and industry.

In the opinion of Chinese economists, a further deepening of the reforms was needed, along with a search for new management methods and an expansion of market relations. The old system, however, continued to exert a strong influence on the course of events and to limit the sphere of the reforms.

In the mid-1980s serious difficulties arose in the country's economy, which affected the consumer market, among other sectors. Stagnation in agriculture, low industrial efficiency, increased unemployment, a sharp rise in prices, imbalances in the development of different segments of the economy, corruption, black market speculation—these negative phenomena all gave rise to widespread discontent in society and served as the objective basis for the student disturbances in the spring of 1989. It must be said that difficulties of this sort had also occurred in the past, but by the end of the 1980s they had reached extreme proportions.

In discussing the causes of the difficulties, some scholars and political figures blamed the excessive pace of reforms, while others blamed the sluggish pace and inconsistency of their implementation. Debates over this issue continue to this day. There was a generally accepted view that the economic reforms needed to be complemented by a radical restructuring of the political system, since the existing system of power no longer corresponded to the new forms of economic relations and impeded the progress of reforms. The issue of political reform, discussion of which had begun following Deng Xiaoping's speech in 1980 and had been interrupted after the student unrest in 1985 and 1986, became the subject of heated debates.

The new Chinese leadership formed after Zhao Ziyang's removal declares its commitment to the reforms and stresses the need to deepen them. At the same time, certain adjustments are being made in actual economic policies with the aim of improving economic conditions. Price controls have been tightened, steps are being taken to regulate the activities of the private and collective sectors of the economy, and investments in capital construction are being sharply reduced, which, the press alleges, has already led to a drop in prices and stabilization of the consumer market.

II.

In analyzing the factors hindering stable and gradual economic development, Chinese economists point out that they include excessively fast industrial growth rates, as well as an irrationally structured economy, which is upsetting the balance between industry and agriculture. In the early 1980s measures were taken to reduce imbalances among the growth rates of heavy industry, light industry, and agriculture; they resulted in creating a relatively even balance among these elements of the economy. It was deemed normal and necessary to maintain a ratio of about 2.8:1 between the rate of industrial growth and the rate of agricultural growth. This policy was soon violated, however. Between 1985 and 1987 the ratio rose to 4:1, and in 1988 it reached 6.7:1.[2] This disproportion is one important cause of the economic difficulties and the strains in the supply of energy and raw materials.

The lag in agricultural production could not but affect conditions in industry and in the economy as a whole. As a result of the drop in capital investments in agriculture, grain and cotton harvests failed to increase for four years, remaining at the 1984 level. Consequently, not only the countryside but the cities suffered.

The Chinese leadership has now reached the conclusion that the thesis that "agriculture is the foundation of the national economy" must be backed up in material terms, and that money should be invested in farming. They have recognized that to ensure a stable improvement in agriculture, it is necessary to ease the burden on the countryside, provide financial and technical assistance to the peasants, and give them a greater stake in increasing the production of grain, cotton, and industrial crops. Many Chinese agricultural specialists

---

[2]See *Renmin Ribao*, Feb. 5, 1990.

believe that the modernization of agriculture should be transformed from a slogan into reality. This will require real support for agriculture, not just lip service to the idea.

Some economists, campaigning against "bourgeois liberalism" on the theoretical level, attribute the difficulties that have arisen in recent years to a weakening of centralized planning. In their opinion, the granting of greater rights to regions, the independence of enterprises, the narrowing of the sphere of directive planning and expansion of the sphere of guideline (recommended) plans, and the increase in the role of the market mechanism have caused greater imbalances in the national economy, price increases, and other economic difficulties. These economists believe that the way out of this situation lies in strengthening the plan mechanism and weakening the role of the market, the significance of which, they say, has been blown out of all proportion. They pin their hopes for stabilizing the country's economic condition on expansion of the role of directive planning, while stressing the need to enhance the scientific basis of plans and to monitor their fulfillment more closely.

There are also some economists who, while not speaking out directly in favor of market relations, call for a combination of plan and market regulation, assigning the leading role to the planning principle.

Some scholars believe that a planned system is inherent in socialism. But China is at the initial stage of the movement toward socialism. Therefore, the objective conditions do not yet exist for direct, comprehensive planning. Public ownership, which constitutes the foundation of the national economy, makes planning possible, and planning is supposed to maintain, by and large, equilibrium among the various sectors of the economy and ensure efficient use of the work force, material resources, and energy, in order to avoid anarchy and uncontrolled developments.

Planning makes it possible to maintain proper proportions in economic development, to sustain stable growth, to utilize limited capital to develop the most essential and important branches of the economy, and to consider and combine various interests in the organization of production and distribution. But this planning should not be too centralized and too rigid. Since production remains a commodity-based operation, a market should also exist that plays a multifaceted and positive role.

Supply and demand in the market make it possible to determine the value and necessity of products. But the market reaction occurs after the fact and is blind; therefore it leads to price fluctuations and creates imbalances. Hence the need to combine plan and market principles. When the sphere of directive planning is expanded, the role of the market becomes extremely weak. When guideline planning is used, this role grows, and when centralized planning is rejected, it becomes definitive.

For the market to fully perform the role of economic regulator, it needs to be free and developed, which is not the case in China now. The task is not to limit the development of the market, but on the contrary, to promote it. In the past China suffered from insufficient development of market relations. The Chinese economy needs not just a developed market, but a relatively stable one, that is, one in which a balance between supply and demand is maintained.[3]

Some Chinese scientists do not agree with the commonly accepted proposition that under socialism demand should exceed supply, and that this is an advantage of socialism. They believe that an effort should be made to have supply exceed demand.

Describing the current situation in the country's economy, the journal *Qiushi* notes that, in the first place, the country's economy is not yet a market economy, but a planned-commodity [*planovo-tovarnaya*] economy. It is known that not every commodity [*tovarnaya*] economy is necessarily a market economy. A socialist commodity economy does not play an all-encompassing role. A market economy is not the same as market regulation, since a commodity economy can be regulated by the market without becoming a market economy. In the second place, the regulating roles played by the market and the plan should be different. These two factors can be combined in different ways when applied to the individual, private sector of the economy and the sector in which foreign capital is employed. State enterprises are regulated mainly by the plan; collective enterprises—by both the plan and the market. The production of goods that are not part of the state-plan system is regulated by the market, and also partially by the plan. There remains a need to understand the principle for delimiting the spheres in which directive planning, guideline planning, and market regulation, respectively, apply, and to determine the proper proportional relationships among them. There is also a need to learn what sort of measures are required to carry out recommendation-type planning. (Directive planning now covers one third of all capital investments.)

The journal points out that in one situation the decisive role is played by the plan, while in another it is played by the market. Right now the role of the market has become predominant.

---

[3]See *Qiushi*, No. 23, 1989.

In a speech at the All-China Conference on Economic Reform, Li Peng, premier of the State Council, stressed the need to combine plan and market principles, and said that total planning and highly concentrated management would suffocate the economy. On the other hand, a purely market economy could create economic chaos and social instability, which were not in keeping with China's specific national features. He pointed out that achieving a rational combination of plan and market regulators suitable for China was an extremely difficult task, and that efforts were being made in that direction. The most important thing, he said, was to ensure the sort of stable development of productive forces that would prevent drastic swings up or down.[4]

Discussions of this issue are continuing, but their content is being affected by incessant attacks on "bourgeois liberals," who, by promoting the advantages of a market economy, are supposedly trying to restore capitalism in China. Therefore, some scholars, in an effort to avoid using the term "market relations," speak about the advantages of economic levers as opposed to administrative and plan levers. They believe that a tightening of administrative control over economic processes, which is justified under existing conditions, can solve only superficial problems, but cannot help resolve the fundamental difficulties and obstacles that hinder economic growth. Proponents of this viewpoint stress that developing commodity-money relations and taking the law of value into account will produce greater economic results than directive planning.

In the course of the campaign against "bourgeois liberalism," attacks are being made not only against the market mechanism, but also against private property, and efforts are being made to prove the advantages of the plan system and state (so-called people's) property. The Chinese press is saying that a market and the privatization of property would mark a retreat from the principles of socialism, and would lead to the enrichment of some and the impoverishment of others, and ultimately to the restoration of capitalism. At the same time, the defenders of fundamental principles hardly touch on the question of economic effectiveness, or the question of which methods—total control or freedom—will make it possible to develop productive forces more rapidly, apply the achievements of the scientific and technological revolution, and improve the people's living standard in a short period of time.

The Chinese press gives no direct answer to the question of which is preferable: To preserve the authority of ideology and to hold fast to one's principles, *or* to make the main goal the creation of social and political conditions that will guarantee economic growth and a better

---

[4]*Renmin Ribao*, Feb. 25, 1990.

living standard for the people, even at the cost of violating ideological dogma? To keep the faith and remain poor, as Mao and the other ideologues of the Cultural Revolution demanded, or to retreat from the canons, "departing from the only correct course," and to embark on a path that guarantees attainment of a decent life?

This question, however, still stands and is the subject of debates that cannot be carried on openly today. But reports on events taking place in the Soviet Union, the German Democratic Republic, Poland, Hungary, and Czechoslovakia are reaching Chinese society, whose progressive forces are following the radical changes in those countries with hope. These changes are arousing serious concern among the present Chinese leaders. They have introduced a thesis according to which the "peaceful evolution" taking place in the socialist countries marks a slide in the direction of capitalism. These processes are supposedly taking place as a result of the pernicious machinations of imperialism, and are not the result of those countries' internal development. But not many people in China today believe in the machinations of imperialism.

It is characteristic that the top leadership, while allowing attacks on proponents of the market and of expansion of the private and individual sectors, is simultaneously declaring the need to permit those sectors and develop them as modes of production that complement the state modes.

In the debates over private versus state (and public) ownership, the thesis that "public ownership hinders the development of productive forces and diminishes the efforts of workers and peasants" is being criticized. Defenders of state ownership argue that only when it is preserved are the working people the masters of the means of production, which ensures the distribution of products in accordance with people's work. While allowing the possibility of the existence of private and collective ownership, they believe that these forms of ownership should function within the limits defined by public—actually, state—ownership. The principle of wage leveling and the "big pot," they claim, does not stem from the essence of public ownership, but is the product of left-extremist distortions of socialism. They give the same response to those who claim that bureaucratism is the organic result of the total domination of state ownership.

Theoretical arguments about the disastrous role of market relations and private property, and criticism of "bourgeois liberalism" as a whole have already had a negative effect in practice. Chinese peasants have started to worry that this might represent preparations to dismantle the contract system and return to communes.

To some extent, the alarm among the peasants can also be attributed to the fact that the introduction of the family contract system in the countryside is associated with the name of Zhao Ziyang, who, as first secretary of the provincial CCP committee in Sichuan, was one of the first to promote this form. His dismissal naturally caused some intellectual ferment and gave rise to fears about the future of the contract system.

Those engaged in individual labor activity and private enterprise have also started to think about the prospects for their existence. In this connection, the Chinese press has published a number of articles attempting to reassure public opinion, and to show that the country's leadership is not retreating from the reform program, that there can be no return to past practices, and that the only issue here is to put the situation in order.

III.

Recently CCP leaders have been making statements to the effect that the political reform will be carried out only by slow and cautious methods, so as not to disrupt order in the country. At the same time, they stress that by virtue of their specific national character the Chinese people are not prepared for the introduction of democratic forms of organizing social and political life.

Thus, writing in the pages of *Qiushi*, Zheng Hansheng and Feng Zhibin, who are on the staff of the People's University of China, remind readers that the Cultural Revolution forced people to realize that "great democracy," which recognizes neither heaven nor the law, can only undermine the process of the development of socialist democracy and violate the people's democratic rights. In their words, in the 10 years that have passed since the CCP Central Committee's Third Plenum, the following successes have been achieved: The functions of party and government-administrative bodies have been separated; power has been delegated to lower bodies of authority; public monitoring of their activities has been implemented; a system of consultations and dialogue has been established; reform of the election system has been carried out (elections are held at regular intervals and the system of lifetime appointments to office has been eliminated); and a system of direct, multiple-candidate elections has been introduced at the district level.

In 1988 changes were made in the election law, according to which all parties and public organizations can nominate candidates for deputy. Collectives of citizens (consisting of at least 10 people) can also do so. Multiple-candidate elections have increased the accountability of deputies to the people.

The authors of the article do not agree with the opinion that the political reform is proceeding too slowly. They believe that excessive haste could upset stability in society, and the maintenance of order and stability is the primary condition for successful implementation of reforms.

A handful of schemers could use the political reforms to overthrow the socialist system; according to Zheng Hansheng and Feng Zhibin, the student disturbances are evidence of this. The disease of democratic extremism can lead to anarchy and cause disruption in the economy. It will take a great deal of time and effort to instill in the people an understanding of freedom and independence, and at the same time, respect for the law.

In China, the authors contend, both bourgeois and socialist democracy are things that have been brought in from the outside, and therefore many people do not understand the meaning of democracy, and do not realize the difficulties of implementing it in China. Many people believe that democracy means willfulness, that you can do as you please, without being bound by law or discipline.

Haste in carrying out political reforms, in the authors' opinion, will also lead to the restoration of clan ties, and to a rise in sectarianism and cliquishness. The clan psychology in the countryside has weakened now as a result of the growth of a commodity economy, but in many areas clan relations still hold sway. Under these conditions, democratic alliances could legalize the activities of clans and sects, which would lead to disturbances.

Haste, they say, could also result in a rise in regionalism and revive the danger of federalist and autonomous inclinations, which would be harmful rather than beneficial. Centralized leadership is needed, or regionalist forces will rear their heads. The authors from the People's University emphasize that stability and democracy can be ensured only under the leadership of the CCP, which represents the interests of the people as a whole.

At the same time, the authors reject the view that the conditions for democracy are absent in China, and that the people are not ready for democracy. The development of the economy, science, and technology are creating the conditions for democracy, while educational reform, the spread of education, and the elimination of illiteracy will help develop the proper qualities among the people. The authors of the article in *Qiushi* conclude: "Do not hurry, but do not move slowly either."[5]

Official statements stress that the measures taken to establish order and tighten control are temporary, and that within three years (or a slightly longer period) they will produce the required effect, that is, they will gradually lower inflation, gradually reduce the rate of increase in retail prices to 10 percent or lower, decrease the money supply, eliminate the financial deficit, and so on. The desired production growth rate has been set at 5 to 6 percent. Normalization of the

[5]*Qiushi*, No. 20, 1989.

economy should also help boost agricultural production and eliminate strains in the supply of energy and raw materials. As a result of the measures being taken, it will be possible to create a system that will be regulated at the macro level, combining plan and market mechanisms. Efforts in this direction are continuing.

The country's leadership is warning the people that difficult days lie ahead, stressing that it will take several years to stabilize the situation in the country.

That means, according to the explanations from above, a tightening of control over expenditures by the apparatus and public organizations. It is necessary to limit expenses for receiving guests and buying gifts, suspend construction of hotels, show modesty in furnishing and equipping them, and discontinue construction of nonessential facilities. Directors of enterprises must prevent any increase in wages that is not tied to a rise in labor productivity.

In this connection, it is explained that the call for "extra effort" does not mean a decline in the people's living standard. However, the closing of a number of enterprises or partial reduction in their production has already affected workers' wages and resulted in a decline in their living standard. Huge sums of money are unlawfully collected from peasants and rural enterprises, which also affects their financial situation and increases their doubts as to the correctness of the policy now being pursued.

Another unresolved problem is the ratio between savings and consumption. In the early 1980s prominent Chinese economists believed that the main reason for China's economic difficulties was an excessively high savings rate. In their opinion, the development of imbalances in the country's economy and the decline in the people's living standard were due to the fact that savings constituted between 30 and 50 percent of the national income. Economists considered it unacceptable and economically harmful for the savings rate to rise above 25 percent. Now, according to information in the Chinese press, the savings rate is 30 percent. Thus, this problem is waiting to be solved. To a certain extent, this, in turn, is related to the establishment of proper relations between the center and the provinces.

Granting independence to the provinces has unquestionably helped increase their economic activity and revitalized economic operations at the local level. But at the same time, because of incompetence and a low level of economic sophistication, there has been a rise in regionalism. In the pursuit of high gross-output indicators, which local leaders associate with an increase in their own prestige, directives from the center calling for a reduction in capital construction are not obeyed, and money and materials are being invested in the construction of enterprises that are economically inefficient and produce poor-quality goods for which there is no demand among consumers, who are forced to buy them, however, under pressure from local authorities who prohibit such goods from being shipped in from other areas.

But it is not only the race for gross-output indicators that forces local leaders to expand construction of new plants and factories, contrary to appeals and directives from the center. They face the complicated task of providing jobs. Every year millions of young people join the ranks of those "waiting for work"; they need jobs, at a time when industry, transportation, and trade suffer not from a manpower shortage, but from a surplus. Therefore, for local leaders the construction of new enterprises is an important means of creating new jobs for the younger generation. In their efforts to solve the employment problem to the greatest possible extent, provincial authorities are forced to ignore directives from the center about cutting back on capital construction.

The problem of relations between the center and local authorities is not new. Heated debates over this problem occurred during the Cultural Revolution; arguments continue now, but an effective solution of this problem has not yet been found.

There are quite a few other questions in China for which answers have not yet been found. We can point to the following: the independence of enterprises and the coordination of relations among them; maintaining high growth rates and ensuring economic efficiency and product quality; campaigning against wage leveling and implementing social justice; reducing capital construction and solving the employment problem; revising the price-setting system, bringing prices into line with the law of value, and dealing with the unacceptability of a sharp decline in the people's living standard.

All these problems were discussed intensively and freely by Chinese scholars prior to the start of the campaign against "bourgeois liberalism." Now these discussions are hampered by ideological limits, which naturally makes it more difficult to find the most rational and effective methods for solving pressing problems in the country's social and economic development.

One disastrous consequence of the campaign against "bourgeois liberalism" is that, by gagging scientists who do not fully agree with official propaganda directives, it is excluding the best minds from the discussion of important problems in the country's socioeconomic and political development, and is denying them the possibility of expressing their views if they differ from those that are imposed from above. The Chinese leadership is thereby cutting itself off from using the country's intellectual potential, and it is suppressing the creative activity of those scholars who, during the period of free discussions, showed a desire to find, and interest in finding, optimal methods for accomplishing the tasks associated with modernization. The campaign being waged cannot help having an effect, a negative effect, on young people who would have liked to study social sciences. Losing faith in the possibility of freely expressing their ideas, they will either shut themselves off in their own internal worlds or take an easier path—the path of conformism, which will cost society a great deal.

That sort of thing already happened in China in the 1950s, during the years of the campaign against "rightists," and then during the Cultural Revolution, when the tormented and disgraced intelligentsia was forcibly excluded from the country's sociopolitical and cultural life. The Chinese people paid a high price for the practical implementation of the Maoist tenet that "the ignorant can lead specialists," and that "Reds" take priority over "the educated."

Today, despite the bitter fruits of previous campaigns and the obvious damage that they inflicted on the country's development, young people are being told once again that the most important thing is to be "Red," that is, to be ideologically committed, and that one's specialty or profession is of secondary importance. That is why appeals to "revive the spirit of Lei Feng," that is, the spirit of blind, unthinking obedience and meaningless memorization of quotations from the speeches of Mao Zedong, are being seen in the Chinese press today.

I would like to stress once again that recent processes in Eastern Europe are having a serious influence on the content and form of the search for ways to deepen reforms. Chinese propaganda has assumed a posture of aggressive defense in an effort to protect the public and young people, in particular, from the "pernicious influence" of "peaceful evolution" and capitalism. The press has increased the publication of propaganda about the advantages of socialism, the correctness of the course of the CCP leadership, and the ideas of Mao Zedong, which, in the Chinese leadership's opinion, can ensure order and stability in society.

With the aid of administrative and ideological measures, the new Chinese leadership has managed to achieve certain results in normalizing the economy and establishing public order in the country. But many problems of economic and political reorganization remain unsolved, and consequently, the social environment for the emergence of discontent, especially among students, still exists.

The increased monitoring of the attitudes of the intelligentsia and students, and the institution of strict surveillance over people's thought can have only a superficial effect, while in reality they merely foster discontent and cause protest to assume hidden forms. In China's situation, silence today is not a sign of consent, but evidence of dissent, which is building up and growing, with no normal outlet. Hypocrisy and lies are again becoming the devices to which some of the Chinese intelligentsia resort as a proven means of survival.

History shows that universal, consistent introduction of new forms of economic life undermines an existing traditional political system. Nevertheless, this system, while acknowledging in word its weaknesses and flaws, is trying to defend its right to exist and maintaining a tight grip on power, on the right to give orders and make decisions. It is no accident, then, that in its effort to survive, the bureaucracy is hindering further development of economic transformations and resisting implementation of political restructuring. When the transition is made from managing the economy using slogans and political directives to managing it with economic levers, the cumbersome bureaucratic apparatus will become unnecessary. Therefore the CCP will be unable to order the advance of economic reforms aimed at expanding market relations while preserving a certain regulating role for the state, and thus will be unable to successfully accomplish its country's comprehensive modernization and rise to the level of the world's leading countries without political reform aimed at democratization of the existing system.

The present CCP leadership understands that it is impossible to turn back to the old Stalinist-Maoist model of socioeconomic development. Jiang Zemin and other Chinese leaders have repeatedly stated this in their speeches. China has already been drawn into a restructuring process, and it is no longer possible to turn its policies around 180 degrees. At the same time, having encountered difficulties, the Chinese leaders cannot bring themselves to make a dramatic leap forward along the path toward creating a contemporary market economy, because they are afraid of the attendant risk. Nevertheless, the idea of reform itself has not been rejected. It is no accident, therefore, that the slowdown in the reform process is being viewed as a "deepening" of it that is supposed to lead to the creation of stability and order as factors conducive to further progress along the path of reforms, both economic and political.

This process cannot be completed in a short time, since, as experience has shown, the task of dismantling the old system has turned out to be much more complicated and more difficult than anticipated.

Part Two

International Relations in a Changing World

Introduction

One sometimes hears that Soviet political science is at a critical turning point. I think that it would be more accurate to say that political science [*politicheskaya nauka*] has actually now appeared in the Soviet Union. That is true in even a formal sense, since the very term *politologiya* [also equivalent to "political science"—*Trans.*] previously carried the pejorative connotation of "bourgeois pseudo-science," whereas now we actually have an Association of Political Sciences. It is also true in essence, since in place of the ersatz that was previously called the "history of international relations," a full-fledged branch of the social sciences that analyzes political processes in the world, has emerged and gained strength.

Nevertheless, it would be wrong to also say that Soviet political science lacks traditions and a school of its own. Even in the darkest times of totalitarianism and stagnation there were honest and incorruptible scholars who worked and found the courage to speak the truth, rejecting the hypocrisy and dogma of the official ideology. It is enough to recall the martyrdom of Academician Andrey Dmitriyevich Sakharov, who never backed down on his democratic convictions, and refused to bargain with his conscience. Of course, scholars like Sakharov who engaged in a confrontation with the regime were few. However, many political scientists who did not openly oppose the official ideology still did not want to be bound hand and foot by false and mendacious dogmas, and did not join the general chorus directed by official ideologists. These scholars developed a special language of hints, things left unsaid, and circumlocutions—a language that was sometimes vague and diffuse, in which they communicated among themselves in published works and scholarly discussions.

This complication of scholarly language, incomprehensible to the ideological functionaries, became part of the flesh and blood of Soviet political science. Even in the past few years, now that a spade has finally come to be called a spade, this tradition of abstraction, as the American reader may notice, has continued to leave its imprint on Soviet scholars' methods of analysis.

Even now, a sizable cohort of political scientists continues to cling to the old oversimplified notions, seeing their task as finding means of expressing trivial ideas that create the illusion of innovation.

Despite the fact that the final liberation of scholarly thought has not yet occurred, one can speak of revolutionary changes: the Soviet political scientists represented here repudiate ritualistic phrases, oversimplified notions, and stereotypes—in other words, political myths. The purely propagandistic, ideological approach to politics is in its death throes. Stereotyped canons concerning peaceful coexistence as a form of class struggle, the confrontation between socialism and capitalism as the principal contradiction of our era, the intensification of political reactionism in the West, and the innate militarism of Western society have been rejected.

A new understanding of the laws of social development based on the concept of a contradictory but, profoundly integral world has developed. The global problems of humanity that cement the world into a single whole have been recognized. These radical changes are based on a new understanding of the moving forces of history, and a different methodological foundation. Marxist science always considered that history is driven by the unity and struggle of opposites. For several decades, however, specific emphasis was placed on the second part of the formula—the struggle. Qualitative leaps were thought of only as revolutions, breaks, schisms, destabilization and disorganization. An antagonistic formula for the development of human society dominated.

The essence of the intellectual revolution in Soviet political science is the movement to a different model for the development of society—a model that reflects an increase in organization, the development of the system of international relations as an integrated whole, and the transition of that system to a higher level.

The change in ideas about the world is closely tied to the Soviet Union's foreign policy successes. The new system of coordinates in world view has made it possible to end the disgraceful war in Afghanistan, conclude the Soviet-U.S. Treaty on the Elimination of Medium- and Shorter-Range Missiles, make significant progress on strategic arms cuts, normalize relations with China, and in many respects restore trust in the Soviet Union as a peace-loving power.

The articles presented in this section of the collection characterize the most diverse aspects of the development of Soviet political scientists' new views. They do not provide a complete picture, but, it seems to me that the attentive reader will see in them a departure from old patterns of thinking that impeded the development of political science, and will notice the radical changes that the new thinking has introduced. I hope that the reader who is familiar with the first BNA book will appreciate the significant steps forward that Soviet political science has taken in a year, entering a qualitatively new state.

Sergei V. Chugrov

The Concept of Peaceful Coexistence in Light of the New Thinking

In recent years, the theoretical treatment of the problems of peaceful coexistence has been raised to the level of an adequate comprehension of the realities of the modern world and of the objective needs of mankind. A real breakthrough has occurred: from the rigid framework of relations between states belonging to the socialist and capitalist systems, the concept of peaceful coexistence has been extended to encompass the broad scope of universal civilization.

To continue to move forward in this constructive direction, it is useful to examine certain aspects of the concept of peaceful coexistence in their interrelationship.

First, the specific historical conditions that gave rise to a social system-oriented approach to the problems of coexistence in the past, and, at the same time, the limited and internally contradictory nature of that approach.

Second, the universalization of the principle of peaceful coexistence, and its significance for world politics and the components of existing international relations in our time.

Third, the prospects for the development of peaceful coexistence into more advanced forms of international cooperation that will lead to the creation of an integral, civilizationwide world community.

I.

The chief imperative of the international aspect of the historical process of our era is focused in the concept of peaceful coexistence—in this concept, and not in the theory of the world's inevitable split into opposing social systems, and of implacable international class struggle in the name of supplanting capitalism with the new, worldwide

*Corresponding member of the U.S.S.R. Academy of Sciences, Doctor of history, and Deputy Director of the Academy's Institute of World Economy and International Relations. This article appeared in the February 1990 issue of *MEMO*. The translation incorporates minor editorial changes made by the author since its original publication.

socialist socioeconomic formation. In today's contradictory but interdependent and increasingly integral world, the interests of the survival and progress of human civilization have assumed the highest place on the scale of the world community's priorities, a place above all other interests, including class interests.

The internal contradiction between two largely incompatible policies—peaceful coexistence and world revolution—goes back to the beginnings of Soviet foreign policy. Those who brought about the October Revolution saw it as the start of the capitalist system's swift and inevitable collapse, and of the triumphant march of socialism all over the planet. As consistent opponents of man's exploitation by man, aggressive wars, and the subjugation of nations, they viewed liberation from class oppression and from the curse of war as related tasks to be accomplished in a single process of revolutionary world renewal. This vision of historical prospects eliminated the very question of establishing long-term relations with the bourgeois states. In a time of revolutionary romanticism, the zealous urge to straighten the paths of history spawned not only hostility toward the external world in which capitalism continued to hold sway, not only firm belief in the fatal inevitability of its collapse, but also adventuristic schemes that sought to accelerate that collapse by "exporting revolution," up to and including the unleashing of "revolutionary wars" in the name of destroying the worldwide system of violence and oppression and establishing a fraternal union of free peoples.

Reality proved harsher and more complex than anticipated at the outset of the revolutionary path. Progress toward the desired objectives, which had seemed so close, encountered insurmountable obstacles.

The principal forces of the old world, in the form of its major powers, took an openly hostile stand toward the fledgling Soviet state. Class intolerance spurred them toward the violent overthrow of nascent socialism. For this purpose war seemed to them "natural," perfectly acceptable, and even desirable. Indeed, the old order launched a counteroffensive.

Revolutionary events in Europe were only ripening when the young Republic of Soviets found itself facing a very real threat of destruction at the hands of imperialism's superior forces. Soviet Russia had a choice: wage war in the hope that those forces would collapse as a result of revolutionary upheavals whose precise timing remained problematic, or try to establish some sort of peaceful relations with the bourgeois states, to arrive at a kind of modus vivendi with them. As the revolutionary wave subsided in the West and capitalism stabilized, the need to ensure conditions in which the lone socialist state could exist in foreign encirclement became increasingly apparent. The interests of preserving the revolutionary gains in Russia required a sober analysis of the existing situation, no matter how far removed it might be from what one would have liked to see.

Lenin understood this before others. Relying on a careful study of the actual situation, the correlation of forces, and the requirements of social development, he substantiated and proved, on the one hand, the inevitability of the simultaneous existence of states with different social systems for an entire historical period, and on the other hand, the desirability, from the standpoint of nations' interests, and practical possibility of their peaceful coexistence—or, as he put it, "peaceful cohabitation."

However, the Party and the nation did not accept the idea of peaceful coexistence with the capitalist states as a fundamental foreign-policy principle overnight, and not without hesitation. The inertia of oversimplified thinking was too strong, and the new concept seemed too unconventional. Nevertheless, most important was another factor: the exceptional complexity—the uniqueness, one could say—of the historical situation itself.

The Leninist theory of the new social system's foreign policy was shaped, developed, and enriched in the enormously difficult conditions of a bitter civil war, foreign military intervention, economic and diplomatic blockade, and economic devastation. Naturally, the paramount task at the time was to ensure survival of the newborn socialist state. A respite was needed. It was essential to establish at least a truce with those states that were ready to take such a step.

Even so, from the outset the peaceful orientation of Leninist foreign policy was dictated by something more than transitory, tactical considerations. While fully aware that the world had split into two opposing systems, Lenin did not confine himself in his analysis to the class bipolarity of the post-October era. He proceeded from a broad understanding of the dialectics of the world historical process, an understanding that allowed not only for clashing states' interests but also for the possibility that those interests could coincide, regardless of differences in their social systems. Lenin did not oppose social renewal of the world to the development of human civilization as a whole. For him, the class conflict between the new and old formations did not rule out the possibility, even inevitability, of their coexistence on the same planet throughout a historical period. The possibility of peaceful coexistence between states with different social systems as sovereign subjects of international relations is based on some community of interests, common interests that, without affecting the foundations of either system, can arise in both their political relations and, especially, their commercial and economic ties.

The innovative propositions that Lenin formulated simultaneously became the theoretical foundation and long-term practical guidelines for Soviet foreign policy. When Soviet Russia emerged from the difficult and bloody period of armed struggle against internal and external enemies, set about rebuilding, and adopted the New Economic Policy, the Leninist policy of establishing relations with states of the other social system on a permanent, long-term basis of peaceful coexistence began to be translated into practice. The clarity of purpose and consistency of that course paved the way to normalized relations with an increasing number of capitalist states. The question was no longer one of a respite or truce, but of a prolonged period of parallel existence between what was still the world's only socialist state and the states of the other system.

However, the subsequent development of Soviet foreign policy toward the capitalist states was not simple and straightforward: Recognition of the expediency and even inevitability of parallel existence with them was still accompanied by the original objectives of the revolutionary reordering of the world on a common socialist basis. The capitalist system was invariably viewed in an oversimplified way—only as a parasitical, rotting, and dying system on the eve of socialist revolution. Capitalism's capacity for further self-development and its adaptation to the changing conditions of internal and international development were ignored. The all-embracing crisis of a system that was supposed to disappear from the stage of history was seen as meaning that wars and revolutions in the international arena were inevitable and would lead in the foreseeable future to the triumph of socialism throughout the world.

Such conceptual dualism, when translated into practical policy, deepened the class bipolarity of international relations at a time when the capitalist states' governing circles already took a skeptical view of "peaceful cohabitation," and when the most militant rejected it out of hand and were devising plans for the liquidation of nascent socialism by force. They were prompted to do so by class intolerance, reinforced by a sense of economic and military superiority.

Introducing the principles of peaceful coexistence into the practice of mutual relations between states with different social systems was further complicated by the fact that it was a special kind of socialism that found itself in conflict with capitalism—namely, the Stalinist, totalitarian, bureaucratic-command, repressive, anti-democratic model of socialism. That socialism was not inclined toward constructive international intercourse. The besieged-fortress mentality that prevailed in the country, the isolation of a society deprived of democracy, the cultural and intellectual autarky, isolation from other peoples, wariness, and suspicion—all helped those who initiated the "crusades" against socialism to portray us as the enemy. Contacts even with those bourgeois-democratic, liberal Western forces that showed an interest during the interwar period in developing relations with the U.S.S.R. on a basis of peaceful coexistence became significantly more difficult.

The growing threat of war posed by the aggressive bloc of Germany, Japan, and Italy in the early 1930s created an objective predisposition toward establishing a collective security system by the Soviet Union and the Western bourgeois democracies. There was a real chance to embody the chief principle of peaceful coexistence—the prevention of war—in joint practical actions.

In practice, that was not to be. British and French policy leaders at the time chose a path of maneuvering and of appeasing the aggressor. The foreign policy of the U.S.S.R. was by no means consistent in all respects; it exhibited insufficient persistence and flexibility in the search for mutually acceptable solutions. The Soviet-German rapprochement on the basis of secret deals between Stalin and Hitler on the eve and at the outset of World War II can only be termed a gross perversion of the very meaning of peaceful coexistence and a flouting of elementary moral norms of world politics.

Fascist Germany's attack on the Soviet Union was an attempt to settle the historical dispute between the two systems once and for all by military means. That attempt to reverse the course of history was an ignominious failure. The outcome of the war signified a change in the alignment and correlation of forces in the world to the detriment of the imperialist reaction and militarism, and in favor of democracy and socialism.

At the same time, World War II proved convincingly the possibility of cooperation between states with different social systems. It would be difficult to overestimate the experience of the formation and activities of the anti-Hitler coalition, though it can hardly be literally called "peaceful coexistence." Our joint actions with the United States, Britain, and the other allied countries were taken not in peacetime but in war against a common enemy.

In the postwar years, the world changed beyond recognition. The positions of the forces of social and national liberation grew stronger. The world socialist system came into being. The colonial empires collapsed, and a multitude of new sovereign states emerged. The growing activism of the masses and of antiwar movements began to exert an appreciable influence on international relations.

With the appearance of nuclear weapons, the military sphere underwent a veritable revolution. The possibility of using weapons of mass destruction introduced a real threat of the destruction of civilization, a threat that was unprecedented in the history of mankind.

Common sense and the simple instinct for self-preservation dictated a course not of confrontation but of peaceful coexistence. The danger of universal destruction "equalized," so to speak, the opposing socioeconomic systems, states with different social systems, and all— even antagonistic—classes. For the first time in history, an objective universal human interest arose in ensuring global security. The increasing internationalization of economic life in the context of the scientific and technological revolution, and the emergence of global problems created pressures in the same direction.

As a result, the objective content of relations between socialist and capitalist states in the world arena began to take on new features. Apart from the struggle and conflicts stemming from the social natures of the respective states, a growing, if latent, interdependence increasingly made itself felt, as did an incentive to cooperate on the basis of common or coincidental interests, especially the interest of preventing nuclear war. Accordingly, the policy of peaceful coexistence increasingly shifted from serving only the aims of postponing war to become a precondition for eliminating the very possibility of its occurrence. From a condition for the survival of socialism in the system of international relations, that policy objectively became an indispensable condition for survival of a world that, though heterogeneous in its class makeup, was interdependent.

In many respects, however, the practical realization of the favorable new objective preconditions for development of peaceful coexistence depended on a subjective factor: the ability of various social forces—classes, states, parties, governments, and politicians—to soberly assess the changed realities and the fundamentally new situation in international affairs, and to develop foreign-policy strategies accordingly. The history of the early postwar years showed that the traditional thinking prevailed this time too.

The hegemonistic aspirations and imperial pretensions of U.S. ruling circles, reflected specifically in the unleashing of the arms race, in attempts to achieve world domination on the basis of an nuclear monopoly, in the forging of military blocs, and in an unwillingness to take the legitimate interests of the Soviet Union and other socialist countries into account, heightened tension in relations between states belonging to the two systems. The Cold War that broke out between them, accompanied, moreover, by local "hot" wars, left virtually no room for peaceful coexistence.

Stalin's personality cult did enormous damage to the constructive development of the idea of peaceful coexistence. The profound deformations of socialism in the U.S.S.R. undermined the country's international prestige as a peace-loving power. In the eyes of many in the outside world, its image became increasingly somber and threatening.

In the postwar years, the duality of the Soviet Union's approach to the problem of peaceful coexistence persisted and grew even stronger. Profound shifts in the correlation of forces in the world arena were taken as a sign that favorable conditions had emerged for a broad confrontation with imperialism. This relegated peaceful coexistence to a secondary role—as a tactical means of achieving the Stalinist strategic goals of "eliminating the inevitability of war by destroying imperialism." Despite the qualitatively new realities, the proposition concerning the inevitability of wars between capitalist countries to the benefit of socialism continued to be strict dogma. The rise of the democratic and national liberation movement was seen chiefly as undermining the military-strategic positions of imperialism and, once again, strengthening those of socialism. Consequently, the confrontational tendencies of the East's policies, on the one hand, and the West's course of intensifying the struggle and spurring on the arms race, on the other, reacted with each other in a negative, mutually reinforcing way.

Nor was the inconsistency in the theoretical interpretation and practical implementation of the concept of peaceful coexistence fully overcome in the post-Stalin period. Stalin, closing himself off from the outside world behind the Iron Curtain, had predicted the "development of the struggle for peace into a struggle to overthrow capitalism." Although Khrushchev opened up the first breaches in that curtain, he made no secret of his intention to "bury" the capitalist system as one that was historically doomed. Although the truly historical 20th Congress of the CPSU revised the obsolete proposition concerning the fatal inevitability of wars, and proclaimed peaceful coexistence as the general line of Soviet foreign policy, the postulate that, in the event of a new world war, "peoples will no longer tolerate the system that plunges them into devastating wars, and will sweep away and bury imperialism" remained unshaken for another three decades, despite the obvious truth that all mankind, regardless of class distinctions, would be incinerated in the flames of a nuclear conflagration. Negating the essence of peaceful coexistence, the thesis that reduced such coexistence to a "specific form of class struggle in the international arena" also remained an ideological axiom.

By trying to combine the incompatible, we cannot hope to broaden the field in which peaceful coexistence operates and to enhance its effectiveness. The vital force of peaceful coexistence lies in its reliance on the objective community of interests of states with differing social systems. But attempts to subordinate this supraclass community to class interests—or, more precisely, to selfish national interests, or even imperial ambitions—can only harm the cause of peaceful coexistence. Without in any way diminishing the responsibility of the United States and its allies for the confrontation that developed, it is difficult not to admit, at the same time, that we too often acted in a "mirror reflection" of their behavior. This is evident both in our military buildup above and beyond what was needed for defense, even after we attained strategic parity, and in our actions in Eastern Europe, the Caribbean, Africa, and—particularly graphically— Afghanistan.

II.

The path to fully tapping the enormous positive potential of peaceful coexistence was opened only with the initiation of restructuring in our country, and with the development of the new political thinking. In light of the fundamental reassessment of the foundations of our international policy in accordance with the realities of the modern world, party documents, decisions of the Congress of People's Deputies, sessions of the U.S.S.R. Supreme Soviet, and speeches by M.S. Gorbachev and other party and state officials subjected the concept of peaceful coexistence to reconsideration in the context of universal human values.

Above all, the concept was freed of the encrustations of the past that had fettered and deformed it. The thesis regarding the possible destruction of capitalism alone through world nuclear war, and the narrow class-oriented interpretation of the functions of peaceful coexistence in international affairs were dropped as utterly at odds with reality. It was stressed explicitly that a rigid limit to class confrontation in the international arena had emerged in the nuclear age—namely, the threat of universal destruction.

The principle of peaceful coexistence overcame incredible difficulties and obstacles to win widespread acceptance as the only reasonable means of international intercourse in the nuclear age, and it assumed truly universal human significance. From a concept intended to ensure the new social system's survival amid hostile encirclement, peaceful coexistence developed into a concept for the survival of the entire human race in the face of the looming threat of self-annihilation.

The creative development and enrichment of the concept of peaceful coexistence is an important component of the new political thinking and the new approach to solving the burning current problems. Peaceful coexistence, which served from the time of its emergence and for a long historical period as a principle governing the state-to-state relations of socialism and capitalism, is interpreted today as a supreme, universal principle of mutual relations among all the world's states, without exception.

It would be difficult to overestimate the enormous theoretical and practical significance of this fundamental advance in our political thinking. It signifies more than a mere geographical expansion of the sphere in which the principle of peaceful coexistence is applicable—though this in itself is also important for the democratization of international relations—since peaceful coexistence is conceived as a kind of common denominator of the interests not just of socialist and capitalist but also of all other states, including, of course, the states of the Third World.

The primary significance of the universalization of the principle of peaceful coexistence lies in its shift to a fundamentally different set of coordinates—from the sphere of relations between systems to the sphere of civilizationwide relations. Such a transformation has long been an urgent necessity. After all, it is civilizationwide criteria, not criteria based on specific socioeconomic systems, that determine the basic content of relations among states in our time. Of course, there were objective, concrete historical reasons for singling out interstate relations between the socialist and capitalist systems from the global context of all civilizationwide interstate relations. But given the growing interdependence of the modern world, singling out such relations plainly became anachronistic. Moreover, as long as they remained in the spectrum of relations between systems, relations between the socialist and capitalist states in many respects did not fit into the general picture of global relations.

Recognizing the universal nature and primacy of civilizationwide criteria in defining the basic content of the renewed concept of peaceful coexistence essentially amounts to bringing that concept into conformity with the realities of the modern world. In that way, the original internal contradiction of peaceful coexistence, which stemmed from its incompatibility with class struggle in the international arena aimed at replacing the old socioeconomic formation with the new one, is eliminated—or, more precisely, it is factored out of interstate relations.

The fundamental conclusion regarding the civilizationwide nature of relations of peaceful coexistence also raises the question of further developing the general concept of international relations as a whole. If a central, determining link in those relations are interstate relations, and the latter should be based exclusively on the civilizationwide principles of peaceful coexistence, then why have those principles not yet been extended to relations between other subjects of international relations—to various political parties and public movements and organizations? Is there any reason consistent with the current realities to maintain certain preserves for the parties and movements in international life where they can be guided by criteria that are primarily system-based, rather than civilizationwide? More specifically, is the transfer of the categories of class confrontation from the intrasocietal, intrastate sphere to the international sphere consistent with the universal interpretation of the idea of peaceful coexistence?

The answers to these questions can hardly be unequivocal. It is difficult to prove that, in real life, there is no overlap of the intrasystem and civilizationwide spheres of social activity, no overlap of domestic and international development, of ideology and foreign policy. Nevertheless, in the spirit of the new political thinking, the further universalization of the principle of peaceful coexistence and its extension to the whole system of present-day international relations—and not just relations between states—would appear to be quite promising. Indeed, the civilizationwide vision of international development as an integral process of forging, by peaceful, political means, a consensus among diverse and even contradictory interests presumes that all participants in international intercourse should be included in that process, regardless of their system-based differences. And for all of them without exception, the general rule of behavior must be constructive cooperation on the basis of universal human values—not hostile confrontation.

A broadened, civilizationwide understanding of peaceful coexistence also requires that we take a fresh look at it in light of the content and nature of relations among states on less than a global scale. It is also necessary to rethink in new dimensions the extremely important changes in interstate relations within each component of the present structure of international relations.

Among socialist countries. While preserving all the positive elements that accrue from membership in the same system, the socialist countries are substantially expanding the range of their relations and raising them to a higher level. Categories that, for all practical purposes, used to be an attribute chiefly of our relations with the capitalist countries are being introduced into these relations. They include repudiation of the use or threat of force as a means of settling disputes, and the resolution of disputes through negotiation; noninterference in internal affairs, and due regard for one another's legitimate interests; the right of peoples to decide their own destinies; strict respect for sovereignty, territorial integrity, and the inviolability of borders; cooperation on the basis of full equality and mutual benefit; and the scrupulous fulfillment of commitments stemming from the universally recognized principles and norms of international law, and from international treaties.

Some of these principles have previously been professed and implemented in relations among socialist states, but, unfortunately, not always, nor in all respects. The events of 1956 in Hungary and 1968 in Czechoslovakia come to mind. When critical situations arose in relations with the allies, methods based on force often prevailed, in the spirit of the notorious "Brezhnev doctrine." The decisive repudiation of that ugly deformation of Soviet policy—a repudiation stemming directly from the perestroika processes—will make it possible to rid our relations with the socialist states, and other friendly states, of negative aspects that are virtually absent in our relations with capitalist states.

Between socialist and developing countries. In the past, relations of this type came right after fraternal intrasocialist relations in our foreign policy hierarchy, in the "friendly" class. But these relations, too, were sometimes vulnerable as far as our policy was concerned—suffice it to recall the introduction of Soviet troops into Afghanistan. Strict mutual commitment to the principle of peaceful coexistence ensures against a repetition of the grave mistakes of the past, which did enormous damage to our relations with both developing countries and capitalist countries. The extension of the principle of peaceful coexistence to Third World states is also extraordinarily important from the standpoint of recognizing those states' equal rights vis-à-vis all other members of the world community. This extension is intrinsically linked with the principles of Bandung, the nonaligned movement, and the New Delhi Declaration.

Between socialist and capitalist countries. Although no visible change has occurred in the status of these relations, with the globalization of the principle of peaceful coexistence, these ties are put into in a different international context. Their development on the basis of peaceful coexistence can now be evaluated not only within their own framework, but also in connection with all other international relations. In this sense, abandoning the notion that peaceful coexistence is an "exclusive" feature of interstate relations between socialism and capitalism is useful both to those relations themselves and to the entire world community.

Between capitalist and developing countries. Introducing the principle of peaceful coexistence into these relations is a vital necessity now that the period of national liberation struggles and the establishment of newly sovereign states has been fully completed. Peaceful coexistence is called upon to safeguard the liberated states for external encroachments. It contributes to the strengthening of their independence, sovereignty, and national dignity.

Among developing countries. Establishing the principle of peaceful coexistence not only in relations with the socialist and capitalist countries, but also among the developing countries themselves is becoming more important in view of the profound differentiation in the Third World, differentiation fraught with the potential for instability and conflict. Peaceful coexistence is necessary to prevent clashes and promote the political resolution of disputes among the states of this vast part of the world, and to settle regional conflicts and prevent them from escalating to a global level.

Among capitalist states. In reference to this type of relations, the principle of peaceful coexistence sounds unusual, especially if one recalls previous dogmatic predictions of inevitable wars within the capitalist world. Nevertheless, this principle is fully consistent with the essence and nature of interstate relations in today's capitalism. For all capitalism's internal and external contradictions, the interests of interdependence and stability are dominant in relations among virtually all the capitalist states. To apply the concept of "peaceful coexistence" to relations among capitalist states is merely to state the situation that prevails in them.

The intensive improvement of the international atmosphere now under way is contributing to the ubiquitous establishment of the principle of peaceful coexistence as a commonly recognized and universally observed norm of interstate relations. The turning away from confrontation, reduction of the danger of war, development of political dialogue, beginning of real disarmament, strengthening of international security, creation of an atmosphere of trust, political settlement of regional conflicts, and expansion of mutually beneficial cooperation—all this is giving peaceful coexistence a new and rich content and laying a firm foundation for its development into the dominant feature of international relations.

III.

The shift of the concept of peaceful coexistence from the system-based to the civilizationwide phase of its progressive development, a development occasioned by rapid changes and the renewal of political thought, is solving many long-standing theoretical and practical problems; but it is also raising new and fundamental problems. They pertain to the basis of the very idea of peaceful coexistence in its new dimensions, and to its direct and reciprocal relationship to the historical environment. Indeed, how are we to reconcile the new concept of peaceful coexistence with the traditional, long-standing characterization of the present era as a time of transition from capitalism to socialism and communism? Can we expect the civilizationwide model of peaceful coexistence to develop fruitfully if we cling to the postulate that projects a rigidly predetermined replacement of the old system by the new within a certain historical period of time? Will we not again find ourselves in the grip of that old and unresolved contradiction—albeit with an updated concept of peaceful coexistence?

Such apprehension is not without grounds. In the past, the development of the concept of peaceful coexistence was held back by the strictly class-oriented approach that was applied to it. Today, however, the universal human understanding of peaceful coexistence glaringly contradicts the now-classical description of our era as "transitional." If such a description of our era really does correspond to present-day world development, it is hardly possible for states of the old departing system and states of the new system replacing it to interact positively in the world arena.

A reassessment of the nature and content of the present era is a separate theoretical task of colossal scope. And it must be accomplished by all the social sciences working together. There can be no question of somehow "adapting" a new characterization of our era to "fit" the new characterization of peaceful coexistence. It would be more logical, of course, to follow precisely the reverse order of analysis, that is, to deduce the essence of today's international relations from the general laws of world social development. As things happened, however, the conceptual breakthrough came first in the theory and practice of international relations; that is because the renewal of our foreign policy has proceeded at a faster pace than our domestic perestroika. In any event, the new concept of peaceful coexistence is already making a significant contribution to the elaboration of a broader concept of the present era, including the updating of all our notions about the course of development of socialism, capitalism, and "intermediate" or "transitional" systems, and about the principal contradiction of the era.

A kind of "reciprocal effect" of the new interpretation of peaceful coexistence on the definition of the nature and content of the era is helping to reveal both the promise of viewing it from a civilizationwide perspective, and the limitations, and sometimes outright inapplicability, of purely system-based criteria. The civilizationwide concept of peaceful coexistence is also spurring serious adjustment in the rethinking of the essence of all historical development from the standpoint of its global integrity and continuity. Finally, the fact that the updated concept of peaceful coexistence transcends systems is contributing to the forecasting of multidimensional and multivariational social development—in both the foreseeable future, and far beyond the visible historical horizon.

Proceeding from the frontiers that have already been attained in the new international political thinking, we are already deeply penetrating the essence of the developing historical process. An enormously important conclusion has been reached to the effect that mankind is incapable of securing its future in conditions of permanent confrontation, and that the struggle between the two systems can no longer be viewed as the leading tendency of the present era. To a large extent, this resolves the chronic internal contradiction of the concept of peaceful coexistence, removing the question "who shall prevail over whom?" from the confrontational plane. And if our era nonetheless remains a transitional one, in the foreseeable future it will be transitional primarily in civilizationwide, not system-oriented terms.

In light of this prognosis, one of the main features of universal human development in our era appears to be precisely "transition." Transition not from one system to the other on a worldwide scale, or even in the more developed countries, but from a world that is still fragmented and divided into opposing systems to an integral, civilizationwide world community in which socioeconomic and political diversity have been preserved, and even intensified. The introduction into international affairs of the universal principle of peaceful coexistence on the firm basis of common interests not just in human survival but in human progress should serve as a powerful impetus to steady movement in this direction of world development.

At first glance, this proposition might seem paradoxical. Indeed, if humanity is entering a peaceful period of its history, is there any need to continue the policy of peaceful coexistence? What is the point in doing so, if confrontation is receding into the past?

The entire existing world situation and the prospects for that situation's development in the foreseeable future indicate that it is still too early to think about abandoning the principle of peaceful coexistence. Although the principle has for the most part already fulfilled its mission in its original, intersystem interpretation, in its new, universal interpretation it still has a long way to go, and in all likelihood it will have for some time. After all, there is no way the transition to a peaceful period can take place overnight.

Divisive and destabilizing tendencies will long remain a part of the overall picture of international relations. It is not proving easy to overcome the legacy of confrontation; the mutual dismantling of the cumbersome structures of military confrontation is proceeding with difficulty; and international security and trust are only slowly being established. Moreover, the emergence of new differences is highly likely. These differences may stem both from states' conflicting foreign-policy positions (not only along East-West lines, and perhaps even less along such lines than in the manifold variety of international political multipolarity) and from the disparateness and dissimilarity of diverse countries' dynamic internal development. Complications in international affairs can stem from the unreadiness or inability of various countries to promptly "join" the process of creating an integral world community along such lines as democratization, the protection of human rights, openness to the outside world, demilitarization, economic efficiency, scientific and technological progress, and the solution of extremely acute social, environmental, ethnic, and many other problems that used to be considered purely internal. This applies equally to participation in the joint solution of global problems such as environmental protection, the rational use of the planet's resources, and the eradication of famine, disease, illiteracy, and economic backwardness.

All this means that the new model of peaceful coexistence has a dual role to play: to ensure general international stability in a time of dynamic and profound change in today's world, while promoting cooperation among states and peoples in their forward movement along the path to a world of integral civilization.

One could, of course, argue about the very term "peaceful coexistence" and try to demonstrate its suitability or unsuitability with respect to its updated function. From every indication, there is a growing need to search for a new term, although one must not forget the potential negative consequences of rejecting a long-standing positive notion. Without ruling out the future possibility of a more precise term for the new form of peaceful coexistence, it would appear to be more useful at the present stage of its development to concentrate on identifying its real content in all its aspects.

The universal security aspect. The following objectives remain at the core of this aspect: consistent elimination of the threat of war through disarmament, political dialogue, the settlement of international conflicts, normalization of interstate relations, and the establishment of a reliable worldwide legal order. At the same time, the emphasis is shifting from the simple prevention of war to the creation of an all-encompassing set of guarantees that rule out the very possibility of war—either nuclear or conventional war, and on either a global or limited level. In this connection, many interrelated avenues of development of peaceful coexistence immediately open up, including the following:

• the demilitarization of international relations through reduction of arms and armed forces to levels of reasonable sufficiency for defense, rejection of policies relying on force, and further lessening and, eventually, completely eliminating military confrontation;

• the replacement of the system of mutual deterrence and containment that developed during the period of confrontation by global and regional security systems based on a balance of the interests of all sides for the purpose of preventing conflicts and international instability;

• the ensuring of international stability in times of sharp fluctuations in the political climate that resulted from rapid changes in various countries and shifts in relations between states;

• the de-ideologization of interstate relations, or more precisely, the purging of the grim legacy of confrontational ideology and war-oriented mentality, and the creation of conditions for the free competition of ideas in a spirit of mutual tolerance and pluralism, humanism and universal human values;

• the establishment of an international system of emergency mutual aid in the event of natural disasters, industrial and transportation accidents and disasters, and any other situations that pose a mortal danger, as well as joint efforts to combat terrorism;

• the establishment of a legal foundation under relations among states that will guarantee freedom of sociopolitical choice, the sovereignty and independence of every state, and strict observance at the international level of the moral and legal norms that characterize relations among civilized people;

• a strengthening of the role of the U.N. and other international peace-keeping mechanisms, and the provision for their effective interaction with the peacemaking efforts of all states.

The constructive cooperation aspect. This aspect has truly inexhaustible resources for the fruitful development of peaceful coexistence and its growth into something more integrating than present-day international cooperation. In essence, this could eventually entail the peaceful codevelopment of various socioeconomic and political entities, with increasingly closer interaction among them and an interweaving of their constructive international activity with their progressive domestic development. It would be hard to overestimate the role of peaceful coexistence in promoting such an increasingly strong global process. Peaceful coexistence is essential as a catalyst in a whole series of specific areas of international affairs, including the following:

• the joint formation of a truly international, world economy that would promote, on the basis of equality, the stable development of each country, its inclusion in the international division of labor and worldwide economic development, the rational use of its own resources, and mutually beneficial access to the resources of other countries;

• the derivation of mutual benefit from economic, scientific, and technological cooperation, while preserving the diversity of socioeconomic systems and using that diversity to stimulate healthy competition and the intensification of partnership;

• cooperation in solving global problems, beginning with environmental protection and ending with the eradication of famine, disease, and drug abuse;

- mutual assistance in the event of domestic socioeconomic difficulties and crises in the world economy that could complicate the overall world situation, and joint efforts to overcome economic backwardness;
- the creation of favorable international conditions for the synthesis of everything positive generated by the various systems, in the interests of the common welfare;
- the broad and free exchange of cultural achievements and spiritual values, and the creation of an atmosphere of universal human solidarity;
- cooperation among countries and peoples in ensuring and safeguarding human rights in all their fullness and variety throughout the planet and the imparting of the most important element—humanistic content—to the idea of peaceful coexistence, cooperation, and codevelopment.

Looking into the not-too-distant future, one can assume with a high degree of probability that the model of peaceful coexistence now taking shape, a model whose mission is to support the transition to an integral world community, will undergo substantial further evolution. The vigorous interaction and comprehensive mutual enrichment of two global tendencies—the strengthening of security and the expansion of cooperation—can give rise to a qualitatively new pattern of world development. This pattern organically combines the establishment of a universal code of civilized behavior in the international arena with the interweaving of domestic social processes and civilization-wide world processes. A peaceful and constructive era of human history will lead the way to the dialectical unity of the world's diversity.

It is quite appropriate to ask whether all the states that maintain relations of peaceful coexistence among themselves today are prepared to work jointly toward a goal that is so alluring but difficult to achieve. Although the objective preconditions for universal human progress are present, is it not possible that those who are dominated by the burdensome legacy of the confrontational way of thinking and acting could prevent the historical opportunity from being seized? Will not inertia-bound domestic and international structures and deeply entrenched selfish interests stand in the way?

It is tempting to brush aside these doubts. But the dynamics of world development cannot be foreseen from a perspective that is rigidly determined by objective factors alone. The role of subjective factors is too great. Although they may not be able to completely block the effect of objective factors, these subjective factors can make significant and long-lasting adjustments in the course of events in the international arena.

Nevertheless, the overall, long-term prognosis inspires hope for the ultimate success of the policy of radically reconstructing international relations on a civilizationwide basis and integrating them in the common historical process. We are already living in a world that is fundamentally different from what it was just a half-century ago. Societies and states that only recently seemed completely incompatible and doomed to endless confrontation have changed or are changing. And for all the dissimilarity of the changes taking place, they have a common civilizationwide orientation that is consonant with the main tendency of overall world development in our era. Despite all the difficulties and barriers, that is what foreordains mankind's insurmountable advance into a peaceful and creative future.

The Warsaw Treaty Organization: Past, Present, and Future*

The Second Congress of People's Deputies opened shortly after the democratic changes that rapidly unfolded along a broad front in the German Democratic Republic, Czechoslovakia, and Bulgaria. As the congress drew to a close, the situation remained tense in Romania, where patriotic forces had overthrown the Ceausescu dictatorship. Life itself had placed on the agenda the state of affairs in the Warsaw Treaty Organization and its future. The question was being actively discussed within the Warsaw Pact itself, at sessions of its various agencies.

*During the Congress, our correspondent G. Sturua asked People's Deputies Marshal V.G. Kulikov; historian R.A. Medvedev; economist N.P. Shmelev; and V.M. Falin, a senior staff official of the Central Committee of the Communist Party of the Soviet Union,** to share their views on the Warsaw Pact's past, present, and future.*

V. G. Kulikov: From a Military-Political to a Political-Military Alliance

Sturua: What stages could you distinguish in the Warsaw Treaty development?

Kulikov: I would distinguish three major stages, though such a division is arbitrary, in my opinion.

In the first stage, prior to 1975, the basic efforts of the Warsaw Treaty countries were aimed at strengthening the alliance's defense capability. While seeking to attain strategic parity between the Warsaw Treaty and NATO, the allied countries simultaneously waged an active struggle for peace, for a turning from the Cold War to a relaxation of international tensions, and for a stable and secure Europe within its postwar borders.

However, the following decade (the second stage in the Warsaw Treaty development) could be called a time of missed opportunities. While noting the destabilizing actions of the West during this period, at the same time we must admit that the responses of the Warsaw Treaty states to the militaristic challenges of the United States and NATO were not always appropriate. And this by no means helped to improve the planet's political climate.

---

*This article appeared in the March 1990 issue of *MEMO*.
**In July 1990 V.M. Falin became the secretary of the CPSU Central Committee.

In the 1970s and early 1980s, priority was given to the military aspects of ensuring security at the expense of the political aspects. We found ourselves drawn into an arms race, which hurt the socialist countries' domestic and international situations.

The present stage of the Warsaw Treaty's development, I think, began in 1985. The shift to the positions of the new political thinking in international affairs, the major perestroika processes in the allied socialist countries, the adoption in 1989 of the document concerning the strictly defensive orientation of the Warsaw Treaty's military doctrine, and the socialist countries' unilateral steps to reduce their armed forces and weaponry have resulted in a substantial improvement in the international climate. It is impossible not to see that, in connection with the emergence of positive trends engendered by the efforts of both East and West, a certain reduction in tensions in the world arena has been achieved. However, the trend toward disarmament, a substantial reduction in the level of military confrontation, and the total exclusion of the use of military force, or threat of force, from the practice of international relations has not yet become irreversible.

Sturua: How do you characterize the contribution that the Warsaw Treaty's other members, apart from the U.S.S.R., are making to its joint military efforts? How important is this contribution from the standpoint of ensuring the U.S.S.R.'s defense capability?

Kulikov: I wouldn't specifically single out the interests of the U.S.S.R's defense capability from the standpoint of the use of the allied countries' potential. We are strong by virtue of the alliance and unity of all the commonwealth's states. One characteristic feature of the socialist countries' cooperation has always been their full equality in the Warsaw Treaty. This principle is realized in the activities of all the agencies of the socialist defense and political alliance, including its military agencies. A decision or recommendation takes effect only with the consent of all the parties concerned, which have equal rights in the resolution of any given issue.

Take, for example, the Warsaw Treaty member states' Combined Armed Forces. Each allied country has contributed well-trained troop contingents to the Combined Armed Forces. Their number and composition, as well as their organization, weaponry, and equipment, are determined by the government of each state with due regard for the recommendations of the Warsaw Treaty Political Consultative Committee, the Committee of Defense Ministers, and the Joint Command of the Armed Forces, depending on a given country's economic and military capabilities, and proceeding from the tasks of ensuring the defense capability of each individual country and of the commonwealth as a whole.

Sturua: Today we admit that crisis processes have accumulated in both the domestic and foreign policies of the socialist commonwealth's members. In your opinion, have these processes affected the Warsaw Pact's activities, and if so, in what way?

Kulikov: Yes, to fail to mention this would be to fail to tell the whole truth about the Warsaw Treaty Organization. Crisis phenomena in the economy, public life, and the development of the communist and workers' parties in a number of our alliance's countries have led, during a certain period, to a reduction in the effectiveness of Warsaw Pact members' efforts to achieve their proclaimed objectives.

Thus, in the late 1970s and early 1980s, the element of force began assuming more and more significance in the Warsaw Pact's foreign-policy activities. The accomplishments and experience of the détente of the early 1970s gradually gave way to stereotypes from the times of the Stalin personality cult. As in former times, the world, which was becoming increasingly interdependent and interlocking, was divided into "ours" and "theirs." Numerous initiatives were never supported by actual deeds that the world community at large could understand.

I want to stress once more that for these and other reasons, by 1985 the Warsaw Treaty authority in the world arena had declined. However, today as never before, the activities of our alliance are attracting great attention all over the world. The perestroika processes that have encompassed most of the socialist commonwealth's countries have extended to both the foreign-policy and military realms of the Warsaw Treaty, and in those realms profound breakthroughs have been made in the most important, fundamental areas of the struggle for a peaceful future for mankind. I will be so bold as to assert that there will be no relapses to the past.

Sturua: In your view, is there a need for the Warsaw Treaty's continued existence in light of the changes taking place in the world and in the socialist countries? If yes, do you not believe that the Warsaw Treaty, at the same time, is in need of reforms?

Kulikov: Under present conditions, the Warsaw Treaty Organization's role in ensuring stability and security in Europe is growing more and more. Cooperation among its members in creating a common European home, promoting disarmament, and building confidence is a sure guarantee that the consequences of the Cold War will be overcome, the processes of détente will be strengthened, and ultimately, peace on the European continent will be maintained.

At the same time, I should point out that the existence, alongside the Warsaw Treaty, of the NATO bloc is a political reality for us. I believe that a time will come when both these alliances will be disbanded. Their simultaneous dissolution could occur as progress is made in disarmament, confidence building, and the development of cooperation in Europe.

Understandably, the path to this goal is not an easy one. It entails profound changes in relations between NATO and the Warsaw Treaty, and a change in the very nature of these organizations. In other words, what is at issue is their transformation from military-political to political-military alliances, something which, unquestionably, is impossible without reforms. Thus, we can already speak of the priority development of civilian areas of activity, and of a reduction in the military elements.

The Bucharest meeting (1989) of the Political Consultative Committee can serve as an example of this. For the first time, ministers of foreign trade and officials of the allied states' foreign economic departments took part.

Thus, the socialist countries' continued cohesiveness, and changes in the nature of the Warsaw Treaty's activities, are seen as a reliable guarantee that the allied states' internal problems will be overcome, and that the Warsaw Treaty will accomplish its objectives and tasks.

R. A. Medvedev: Dissolution of the Warsaw Treaty Will Not Lead to Instability

Sturua: The East European socialist countries have entered a new era. The time has come for a more thorough and objective analysis of the past. How would you characterize the phenomenon of the East European socialist countries in general?

Medvedev: The processes currently taking place in these countries were, of course, inevitable. The fact is that postwar East European socialism followed the worst authoritarian model. In almost all the East European countries, it was not without the help of the Soviet Army, to say the least, that that model was implanted. In other words, it was in many respects a case of exporting revolution, something which we condemn in principle and theory, but which Stalin in fact did in the late 1940s. That can be proven by looking at the situation that prevailed in the East European countries' communist parties in the mid-1940s. Romania and Hungary had small communist parties that wielded relatively little influence. In Poland, the Communist Party had been disbanded by the Communist International in 1937. New, underground party groups that arose in Poland during the war exerted no great influence on Polish society. Czechoslovakia had a rather strong Communist Party, and for this reason a relatively democratic regime was established in that country in 1945; by 1948 it had evolved into an authoritarian regime.

Yugoslavia was an exception. There the revolution was directed by internal forces. The movement in Yugoslavia developed as a popular revolution. Moreover, the Yugoslav people, for the most part, liberated their country from the German occupation forces on their own, although they had some help from the Soviet Army. That is why, despite an extremely grave economic situation, socialism is not being questioned in a political sense in Yugoslavia today.

The East European states, which were called socialist (significant elements of socialism actually were present in them), were essentially authoritarian states with various restrictions on democracy, and as we are seeing today, they did not enjoy the support of the majority of the people. To a significant extent, their regimes were maintained by force, including the force of the Soviet Army, units of which were stationed in a number of East European countries.

Sooner or later these props based on force were bound to collapse.

Discontent with the ruling regimes mounted. A democratic movement unfolded in the East European countries, although it is true that it did not always find a direct and clear expression. The democratic perestroika that began in the U.S.S.R. five years ago exerted a profound influence on the East European peoples' public awareness. As it deepened, it inevitably had to lead to the collapse of their authoritarian regimes. Of course, all these processes proceeded differently in different countries—I am speaking here only of the general trend.

Sturua: To what extent did the deformations of socialism and the establishment of the administrative-command system in the Warsaw Treaty member states affect the alliance's activities and the international situation?

Medvedev: Even if we had not had the administrative-command system, I still do not think we would have managed to avoid the Cold War. I am not sure the Western countries would have been content with a "good," democratic socialism, and would not have created military alliances directed against our country. We would still have had to organize our own military-political alliance. However, it seems to me that the overall situation would have had a different, less confrontational character. There would have been greater opportunities for the use of political means to resolving disputes and conflicts, and for cultural and economic cooperation.

Sturua: The leaders of the five countries whose troops were sent into Czechoslovakia in 1968 have officially condemned that action as intervention in the internal affairs of a sovereign state. At the same time, you have doubtless encountered other assessments of that event, such as this one: Given the harsh confrontation between East and West, the "Prague Spring," regardless of how it is interpreted, had the objective effect of destabilizing the international situation. A political solution of the crisis was hardly possible, for it would have presupposed, at a minimum, an unthinkable degree of flexibility on the part of the Brezhnev regime. For its part, the West, in contrast to what we see today, was obviously unprepared to react to the situation that was developing with regard to Czechoslovakia in a balanced and reasonable manner. Meanwhile, the prompt "crisis resolution" did not derail the process of establishing détente. Moreover, it apparently gave Moscow confidence in building bridges to the West. What would you say about this view?

Medvedev: As a historian, I do not agree with that. The year 1968 was only the start of the conservative turnaround that the Brezhnev regime carried out following the period of the Khrushchev reforms. Those reforms were not always successful, but it was nevertheless a time of relative progress for our country. After coming to power, Brezhnev also followed a reformist course to some extent until early 1968. The policy of combating Stalinism—for example, its manifestations in science (medicine and biology)—continued, if only in part. The condemnation of voluntarism and subjectivism were pushing Brezhnev toward political actions that could have enjoyed public support. In other words, in 1965 to 1967, the question of which path the Soviet Union would take was still unresolved. The 1960s was a time of struggle between progressive and reactionary forces in society. Some tried to defend the values that entered our life with the era of the 20th Party Congress, while others pushed in the direction of what we now call stagnation or even conservative reaction.

Under these circumstances, the entire progressive Soviet intelligentsia viewed the Czechoslovak events as an enormous boost to its efforts to block the country's reversion toward Stalinism. We welcomed the Czechoslovak spring as a step in the right direction and an example for the Soviet Union. Had democracy triumphed in Czechoslovakia, it would have become a catalyst for democratic changes throughout all of Eastern Europe, including the Soviet Union. That is what the conservative forces feared, and that is why they resorted to armed intervention.

Sturua: Some people claim that the transformations in Eastern Europe are connected with tapping socialism's true potential, while others speak of the restoration of capitalist principles in these countries. What is your view of this?

Medvedev: If these processes had begun in the late 1960s and early 1970s and followed the Czechoslovak example, their socialist orientation would be beyond doubt. Today, however, after a 20-year period of stagnation, nonsocialist forces have gained a significant opportunity in the East European countries. The potential that these countries will take the socialist path has diminished. At the same time, the realization of this potential ultimately depends on our tact, tolerance, and goodwill.

Sturua: How do you see the Warsaw Treaty's future in the context of the struggle between socialist and nonsocialist principles in Eastern Europe?

Medvedev: I think that the Warsaw Treaty Organization will be preserved, but only nominally. We will maintain good relations with the East European countries, but neither the new Czechoslovakia, the new G.D.R., nor the new Poland will, as I see it, maintain allied military ties with us in their previous form. Already, the Warsaw Treaty and its Joint Command are largely a formality. For example, only with reservations can the Polish and Hungarian armies be considered a part of the Warsaw Treaty's armed forces.

In my view, the unilateral dissolution of the Warsaw Treaty would not lead to instability. On the contrary, it would severely weaken the political and military foundations of the NATO alliance. The ability of peace-loving forces in the West to demand the breakup of NATO would increase. The Warsaw Pact's calm and gradual abolition as the result of a spontaneous democratic process would undermine the political basis of the Western military alliance's continued existence.

N. P. Shmelev: I Would Not Rush Events

Sturua: The opinion exists that military-political alliances are economically burdensome for their leaders. Is that true of the Warsaw Treaty?

Shmelev: In my opinion, the question contains its answer: all military alliances are burdensome. I see in the realization of our dream—the withdrawal of Soviet troops from the European countries—not just political and military pluses, but also considerable economic benefits. I think our Warsaw Pact partners also find the military alliance costly.

Sturua: What do you see as the differences and similarities between our economic perestroika and the processes taking place in the East European countries' economies?

Shmelev: I think that, with the exception of a few islands of the old directive system, or of barracks socialism, as I would call it, identical processes are taking place everywhere—in the political, cultural and intellectual, and economic realms. We are all moving toward democratic, humane, market socialism. I don't believe in the effectiveness of any other type of socialism. We are all returning to ordinary common sense, and armchair theories that have proved unviable are being scrapped. The speed of this process is different everywhere. Unfortunately, although perestroika in the Soviet Union provided a powerful impetus for the transformations in Eastern Europe, today, I think, we are nonetheless starting to lag behind our East European friends.

Sturua: What role do you assign to the expansion and deepening of economic ties between Eastern and Western Europe?

Shmelev: I see this as a very serious factor in the success of progressive processes throughout Eastern Europe and the Soviet Union. I think that even our country has let lapse the time when it could have solved its problems using internal resources alone. I fear that without external assistance, the processes of our economic perestroika will be terribly drawn out. I am not even sure that we will be able to cope with the problem of promptly putting our economic and financial situation on a sound footing without enlisting external resources. Eastern Europe needs such assistance all the more. I can only welcome the fact that plans for such assistance are now being formulated.

Sturua: How could economic cooperation between the Soviet Union and the East European countries develop in the future? Some think that dissolution of the Warsaw Pact would result in the practically automatic reorientation of those countries toward the Western economy.

Shmelev: One point of the Ryzhkov program unveiled at the Congress—a point that has my unconditional backing—calls for a transition in our economic cooperation with Eastern Europe to world prices, and for a move to a common market of the CMEA countries and convertibility of their currencies. I think that if we achieve this, our cooperation will no longer be founded on a distorted basis, whereby we subsidize someone and someone else subsidizes us, and all this is done in a veiled form, and whereby our cooperation is organized primarily through pressure, directives, and commands. Only then will we finally attain the possibility of the free movement of goods, labor, capital, and scientific and technological knowledge across our borders; in other words, only then will we put our cooperation on a normal economic basis. If we succeed in this, there are a great many compelling economic motives by which the socialist countries' integration, rather than developing under political prodding, will proceed from natural requirements. For example, objectively the Soviet Union's market is a magnet for the most diverse countries. If we permit our East European partners unimpeded access to it, that will become a natural incentive for integration.

Moreover, most East European countries' industry is not competitive by world criteria. Their reorientation from the growing Soviet market to the West is physically impossible in the near future. And later on, when all-European processes reach a new stage of development, it seems to me that a certain equilibrium will be established—in principle, the alternative of orientation toward the West or toward the East will not be an issue. The sole criterion will simply be the existence of demand. Additional, coercive measures to bring countries together will become irrelevant.

What role the dissolution of the Warsaw Treaty will play in this is hard to say just now. I wouldn't rush events. For the time being, after all, we are talking about doing away with the military organizations within the alliances, and about giving those alliances a more pronounced political character. It is hard to say what the situation will be 10 years from now. The tasks we have discussed will be hard enough to accomplish in the coming decade.

V. M. Falin: We Are Seeking to Modernize the Warsaw Treaty

Sturua: What do you see as the differences and similarities between NATO and the Warsaw Treaty?

Falin: The similarity is mainly historical. Both alliances were born of the Cold War. The military-political groupings were created in the belief that the factor of force was decisive, and that politics, diplomacy, and the like were merely certain applied elements of force. In other words, politics had come to serve military strategy, rather than the other way around. And quite a few stereotypes and deformations will have to be overcome before we all start thinking in a manner commensurate with the time and its requirements.

I would like to single out one point on which the two alliances' attitudes separate them—it is, first, the acceptance (or nonacceptance) of the possibility of a comparatively rapid simultaneous dissolution of these organizations. The Warsaw Treaty's proposal for dismantling the military alliances in Europe remains on the agenda. NATO has yet to make a positive response to this proposal.

Sturua: Do you believe that the preconditions for dismantling NATO and the Warsaw Treaty are now ripe? In your view, is the military alliances' simultaneous dissolution the thing we should be talking about?

Falin: The notion of synchronicity, of course, is relative, but the need for the military alliances' parallel dismantling is beyond doubt. Are the conditions for their dissolution ripe or not? I can say that the preconditions at least exist for NATO and the Warsaw Treaty to be transformed from alliances that are primarily military into organizations that are chiefly political, and from organizations that divide Europe, and even certain states, into hostile camps, into entities that could unite the parts of a vast region—for example, by devising common doctrines and creating joint security structures that would reflect the interests of all sides. At some point, the simple truth that Europe fought its last wars a long time ago must find both verbal recognition and material expression on not only the political but also the military level. No wars are admissible here—be they nuclear, chemical, or conventional. If Europe has a future, it can only be a peaceful one. In that sense, the common European home is not a beautiful dream, but the only reasonable alternative. The contours of that alternative, incidentally, were outlined long before World War II, but ignoring the realities led to the greatest tragedy in the history of mankind.

Sturua: How do you envision the process of eliminating military confrontation in Europe? Is the building of a common European home the "final stop" in that process?

Falin: There are no final stations in the process of development. And naturally, the common European home is no exception. We are dealing with parallel processes that must develop, it seems, in an interrelated fashion. As we look toward a different kind of future, it would appear that we should give up the habit of looking to past experience for answers. Experience can prevent us from repeating mistakes, but it does not contain the knowledge of how to solve problems constructively that were unknown in the past. After all, a new stage of civilization is opening up before us.

How will the process of overcoming the division of Europe proceed in reality, and what sort of correlation will there be among military, political, economic, and cultural components? If we overemphasize one element somewhere, we will once again upset the internal, structural balance. Obviously, we must proceed in all areas in a coordinated fashion. We will have to make serious efforts to establish economic cooperation and to eliminate any sort of discrimination and barriers. Otherwise, even if the political and military division in Europe is overcome, Europe may find itself divided into economic zones, and we will begin to stumble on them, and consequently the very institutions that states are now prepared to abandon will begin to reemerge.

The most important task, however, is to instill the habits of a new political culture in people. To teach them to treat one another with tolerance; to see, as an Arab proverb puts it, the person walking toward one not as a potential enemy but as a likely teacher.

Sturua: In analyzing the prospects for overcoming confrontation in Europe, we cannot overlook the so-called German problem. The possibility of German reunification continues to elicit extremely complex feelings in Europe and the United States. What accounts for these feelings, and are they justified?

Falin: First of all, we must clarify just what the "German problem" is, and what meaning has been invested in this notion before, during, and since the war. Remember the watchword with which

Hitler started the war? It was the slogan of "uniting all Germans in a single German reich." And it is probably fitting that the essence of the Teheran, Yalta, and Potsdam decisions was the creation of a situation in which a threat to peace could never again emanate from German soil. At the time, the British and Americans took the view that Europeans would cease to be hostages to German militarism and imperialism if Germany were divided into several states.

Let us also recall that, in the thinking of certain Americans who pondered the postwar world order from 1943 to 1945, the preservation or emergence in Europe of a power that would be capable of determining the character of development on the continent without the United States was tantamount to Washington's having lost World War II. If putting Germany under direct American control was impossible, then better to divide it. Such was the logic that has defined much in Europe and beyond.

The "German problem" in its present interpretation arose in the West at the height of the Cold War, when talk of future unity was intended to justify the separation of the Western occupation zones into an individual state entity, and the militarization of that state. We discover in American government documents that the intention to exploit West Germany's anticommunist, military, and human potential, and its territory in the hegemonistic U.S. policy of that time was the primary and decisive consideration.

Of course, much has changed since then. Parents give life to their children, but they are not at liberty to lead them by the hand through the labyrinths of fate. In some respects, this is also true of politics.

I have often had occasion to state the view that the time has come, without upsetting existing European structures and territorial realities, to ensure that the vestiges of the war do not burden relations between Germans in the East and the West. We can do this if, in proposing various plans and working for various solutions, we do not look for confirmation of the favorite Cold War dogmas. Otherwise, the door to the future will be closed once again.

Sturua: We are accustomed to assessing the relationship between centrifugal and centripetal tendencies with respect to NATO, but what is that relationship within the Warsaw Treaty? Don't events in Eastern Europe offer grounds for thinking that centrifugal tendencies will prevail, at least in the near future?

Falin: Centrifugal phenomena are pronounced in our alliance today. But I would state that with one amendment: They are based on a desire not so much to dismantle as to modernize the Warsaw Treaty, which we ourselves have been trying to accomplish. The Soviet Union was one of the first to propose the politicization of the Warsaw Treaty.

I attach considerable importance to a view that is being formulated in the West with greater emphasis than in our country—namely, the role of NATO and the Warsaw Treaty as factors for stability in Europe. A better Europe will arise not through the mechanical destruction of the old, but through the sort of modification of what exists that will allow a balance of national interests to find its optimal expression.

In the sense of consolidating the new political thinking, we are just setting out on the path. We are creating a good deal without having yet received proper reciprocal understanding on the part of NATO. In essence, we are following a policy of setting a good example. In my opinion, such actions and policy adjustments have not yet exhausted their usefulness. However difficult and, in some respects, dangerous such a policy may sometimes be, I am convinced that it will bear fruit and accelerate the development of new political thinking in the West, too. Yet something else is also clear: there are certain limits to the initiatives that one state or group of states can take, for interdependence is an objective fact.

Are Negotiations on Tactical Nuclear Weapons Possible?

SERGEY VADIMOVICH KORTUNOV*

Why the West Is Not Eager to Enter Into Negotiations

What, one wonders, could be bad about negotiations? After all, the sides taking part in negotiations work out compromises. Neither side—assuming, of course, one is speaking of equal partners—can force the other to accept solutions that damage its security. Negotiations represent a search for compromises and the removal of mutual concerns. Why, then, were the NATO countries so stubborn when it came to negotiations on Tactical Nuclear Weapons (TNWs)? After all, if anyone has a concern about that problem, it is the Soviet Union: The Warsaw Treaty countries have a tremendous superiority in tactical nuclear missiles. Moreover, by every conceivable estimate, in the event of a nuclear war in the European theater, the western part of the continent, by virtue of its dense population, high concentration of industry, and simply its material wealth, would suffer far more than the eastern part.

Why, then, has the West refused for so long a time to agree to begin even preliminary consultations on this issue? The reason must evidently be sought beyond the limits of purely military problems, although military considerations also unquestionably play a role here. The problem of TNWs represents a tight knot of the most diverse European and world problems—military, political, economic, and even moral and psychological—which are bound up with overcoming deeply rooted stereotypes of thought and various emotional encrustations built up during the years of the Cold War.

The essence of the problem, I dare say, is that tactical nuclear arms are an inseparable element of the political structure established in Europe during the postwar period. Removing this element from it presupposes that structure's profound transformation, if not fundamental breakup. What am I referring to?

---

*Candidate of history, adviser with the U.S.S.R. Ministry of Foreign Affairs' Administration for the Problems of Arms Limitation and Disarmament. This article appeared in the February 1990 issue of *MEMO*. Some revisions to this article were made for this collection.

Europe's politico-military relations during the past few decades have been characterized by significant military confrontation, mutual suspicion and mistrust, with a strong admixture of ideological dogmas and militaristic thinking. For a long time the states of East and West were hostages to inaccurate, caricatural images of each other that stimulated the buildup of armaments. Consequently, a monstrous concentration of military might developed in the center of Europe that greatly exceeded every conceivable criterion for defensive capability.

There is evidently little to be gained now from trying to determine who bears most of the blame for the existing situation—East or West. That would hardly bring us closer to making the transition from overarmament to reasonable defense sufficiency.

But it is obvious that the excessive trust in the quantitative side of military power expressed in the plainly excessive military potential of Soviet tanks, armored vehicles, artillery, and tactical missiles was perceived in the West as material proof of the Soviet Union's aggressive intentions and aroused concern for the West's own security. In that context, the tactical weapons deployed in Europe were intended, as West European circles saw them, to become, on the one hand, a shield in the event of an invasion of Soviet "tank armadas," and on the other, a key component of so-called U.S. nuclear guarantees, which provided a "transatlantic coupling" with U.S. strategic nuclear forces.

For their part, the Americans started to regard TNWs as a powerful means of pressuring their allies to comply with a rigid framework of Atlantic discipline. Therefore, in emphasizing "superior Soviet military power," they had a stake in preserving an "image of the enemy" in their allies' eyes, orienting them toward the worst-case possibility for the development of events. And for that reason even the "overarmament" of the U.S.S.R. and the other Warsaw Treaty states, which objectively served to promote that image, actually played into Washington's hands.

The powerful infrastructure that the Soviet Union built for a "limited nuclear war" in Europe also served the U.S. interests in this connection. While publicly denying the possibility of such a war and refusing to admit that plans existed for preventing one from turning into a full-scale nuclear conflict, the U.S.S.R. created there an extremely impressive potential of "Eurostrategic" weapons and means of their delivery (RSD-10, R-12, and R-14 missiles; and Tu-22, Tu-22M, and Tu-16 medium-range nuclear bombers), operational-tactical missiles (OTR-22 and OTR-23), and tactical weapons (Luna [Moon] and Tochka [Pinpoint] missiles; 152-mm., 155-mm., 203-mm., and 240-mm. nuclear artillery; and Su-7, Su-17, Su-24, MiG-21, MiG-23, and MiG-27 tactical aircraft). In terms of their missile component, all these weapons exceeded corresponding NATO weapons several times over. The West quite justifiably interpreted such actions as a sign of the U.S.S.R. approaching the American concept of a "limited nuclear war"—contrary to the officially declared principles of Soviet military doctrine.

For all intents and purposes, all this contributed to preserving the model for maintaining security in Europe through military force based on nuclear deterrence [*sderzhivaniye*], that is, on the sides' creating and maintaining equal danger for one another. Under these conditions, tactical nuclear weapons became a kind of "sacred cow" in the West, since they came to be regarded as a kind of symbol of security that cemented the "Atlantic partnership."

And for this reason, too, our appeals for a "third zero,"* that is the complete elimination of TNWs in Europe, appeals dictated, of course, by the noblest of motives, were always perceived in the West as an "assault" on that partnership and an effort to "drive a wedge" into relations between the United States and Europe and deprive NATO of the "nuclear shield" that had been created as a counterweight to the Soviet superiority in conventional armed forces on the continent. From the West's standpoint, elimination of TNWs would inevitably lead to a crisis in NATO that might ultimately lead to the collapse of that organization, since its automatic consequence would be the Americans' "withdrawal" from Europe and, consequently, the refusal of the United States to provide any sort of "nuclear guarantees" for its allies.

These circumstances, it seems, explain rather persuasively why the very phrase "third zero" evokes an extremely distressed Western reaction and, for all intents and purposes, helps proponents of continued inviolability of tactical nuclear weapons in Europe. It is characteristic that for all the disagreements among NATO countries over TNWs, they all agree on the unacceptability of the concept of completely eliminating them in Europe.

Taking that into account, the Soviet position on TNWs was modified. In particular, it was stated at the highest level that the Soviet Union regarded elimination of these weapons as a process that should occur in stages. It follows that the progress toward complete destruction of nuclear weapons could be ensured by Europeans together, without giving up their respective positions: the U.S.S.R. remaining faithful to its nuclear-free ideals, and the West remaining faithful to the concept of "minimal deterrence." In that connection, it is necessary to clarify what the concept of "minimal deterrence" represents, and

---

*[The 1987 treaty on the Elimination of Medium- and Shorter-Range Missiles had accomplished a "double zero" by eliminating missiles in two categories: medium-range and shorter-range or "operational-tactical" in the Soviet terminology.—*Trans.*]

assess the limit beyond which the potential for defensive nuclear retaliation turns into offensive capability. The Soviet Union proposed that experts from the U.S.S.R., the United States, Great Britain, and France, as well as the states where nuclear weapons were deployed, hold a thorough discussion of these questions.[1]

That way of posing the problem is unquestionably more acceptable to the West. At the same time, it needs to be elaborated in more detail. Some European circles continue to fear that the U.S.S.R. is trying to lure the NATO countries into a trap: to achieve large reductions and then propose a "zero" that will be hard to refuse without serious political losses.

Federal Republic of Germany's Foreign Minister H.D. Genscher has pointed out the groundlessness of such apprehensions: "The United States is conducting negotiations with the U.S.S.R. on a 50-percent reduction in strategic offensive arms, but we are not trying to dissuade it from doing so on the pretext that it could result in the complete elimination of strategic offensive arms." He also made the following argument in favor of negotiations: "Only through negotiations will we be able to achieve results that are acceptable to both sides—results, moreover, that are binding and, therefore, irreversible. Unilateral reductions are better than nothing, but they are worse than treaties, since the former can be annulled."

On the Modernization of Weapons and Inertia in Thinking

One of the most sensitive problems in the area of of TNWs is the question of modernizing tactical nuclear weapons. Just what is at issue here? After all, if a weapon exists, its modernization is a perfectly natural process. The removal from service of obsolete military equipment and equipment that has outlasted its projected lifetime is done in every army of the world. As for TNWs, both the Warsaw Treaty states and NATO have consistently updated their tactical nuclear missiles, as well as their aircraft and artillery capable of delivering nuclear weapons. Until recently no one particularly emphasized that fact. What, then, has occurred recently?

Let us first look at the facts. Under the current balance of tactical nuclear forces between the Warsaw Treaty Organization (WTO) and NATO, the WTO holds approximately 12-fold superiority in launchers of tactical nuclear missiles with a range of up to 500 km. (1,608:136), while NATO exceeds WTO in terms of tactical strike aircraft with a range of up to 1,000 km. that are capable of delivering nuclear weapons (4,075:2,783). In heavy artillery with a range up to 30 km. that is

---

[1]See *Pravda*, July 7, 1989.

capable of delivering nuclear shells, there is approximate equality (more than 6,000 on each side). [Some of the figures in this article may vary from accepted Western figures.—*MEMO* eds.]

The overall balance of forces in tactical nuclear weapons cannot be precisely defined at this time, since the Soviet Union has not yet published the relevant figures. That has allowed the West to claim what, in all probability, is a blatantly exaggerated figure—up to 10,000 units for the U.S.S.R., as opposed to 4,000 units for NATO.

In the missile component of TNWs, NATO Lance missiles (with a range of up to 120 km.) deployed in the F.R.G., Great Britain, Belgium, the Netherlands, and Italy, and French Pluton missiles (up to 120 km.) are countered by R-17 or Skud-B missiles (300 km.), Tochka or SS-21 missiles (70 km.), and Luna or Frog-7 missiles (70 km.) deployed in the Warsaw Pact states.

Of course, taking into account the operational relationship between TNWs and central strategic nuclear systems, parity in that area between NATO and the Warsaw Treaty Organization is of no fundamental military significance. At the same time, it is not irrelevant how many and what sort of nuclear systems are aimed at targets located within their national territories.

So far as the problem of modernization is concerned, it must be noted that replacement of obsolete missile complexes with more modern ones took place in the Warsaw Pact's forces in the 1980s. In particular, the Luna missile complexes (deployed in 1964) were replaced with Tochka missile complexes (deployed starting in 1975).

It is important to note that the Luna complexes that were being replaced and the Tochka missile complexes that replaced them have approximately the same range—up to 70 km. As for R-17 tactical missiles (deployed in 1962), they were partially replaced by Oka (SS-23) operational-tactical missiles, which, however, were eliminated in accordance with the Treaty on the Elimination of Medium- and Shorter-Range Missiles. The other components of TNWs—aircraft and artillery—have been updated in accordance with existing plans, the data on which have not yet been made public, either.

The decision in principle on the need to "modernize" TNWs in NATO made at the session of its Nuclear Planning Group in 1983 in Montebello (Canada) was based on the argument of Warsaw Pact superiority in those types of weapon systems. At the same time, a decision was made to withdraw 1,400 nuclear weapons (land mines, antiaircraft missiles, and Honest John missiles) from Western Europe by the end of 1988, over and above the 1,000 units that had been withdrawn before 1980. Thus the "Montebello Plan" envisaged the removal of certain obsolete types of TNWs from service, along with the deployment of weapons that were more effective from the standpoint of power, accuracy, and increased range.

According to a definition given in the *Soviet Military Encyclopedia* [*Sovetskaya voyennaya entsiklopediya*], "modernization of military equipment" is "the updating of obsolescent models of military equipment by changing their design, materials or manufacturing technology in order to substantially improve their characteristics and the effectiveness of their use."

Let us look at the NATO countries' activities in the area of TNWs from this standpoint.

In the United States, a Lance-2 missile with a range of up to 480 km. has been under development to replace the Lance missile since November 1988; its deployment is projected for the mid-1990s. [In 1990 it was decided to abandon this program.—*MEMO* eds.] Production of a total of 1,000 missiles is planned.[2] At the same time, the SRAM-T guided air-to-ground missile,[3] with a range of up to 500 km., is under full-scale development with the intention to equip practically all U.S. and allied tactical aircraft in Europe with it as replacements for gravity bombs. In addition, obsolete B-28 and B-43 bombs have already been replaced by new B-61s. Nuclear artillery were recently reequipped with new W-79 shells for 203.2-mm. mortars (to replace W-3 shells). Production of new 203.2-mm. neutron shells began in 1988. At the end of 1989, W-48 155-mm. shells were replaced with W-82 shells of the same caliber. According to some figures, despite a reduction in the number of weapons, their total explosive force has increased as a result of these steps.

In France an Hadès missile (with a range of up to 350 km.) with a conventional and neutron warhead is being developed to replace the Pluton missile (its deployment is expected in 1992). Altogether, plans call for the production of 90 missile complexes. Since late 1988, the French air force Jaguar and Mirage-III E aircraft have been replaced by Mirage-2000Ns equipped with ASMP air-to-surface missiles (with a range of up to 300 km.)

In addition, NATO is now planning to deploy an additional number of F-111 fighter bombers and FB-111 bombers, which it proposes to outfit with the SRAM-T air-to-surface missiles, placing them under the tactical air command and NATO's Supreme Allied Command in Europe. On the whole, "modernization" will more than double the number of British and French nuclear warheads capable of reaching the U.S.S.R.'s territory.[4]

---

[2]These missiles are designated by the term FOTL (Follow-on-to-Lance), as well as by the term ATACMS (Army Tactical Missile System); it is planned to deploy them on salvo-fired rocket launchers (two missiles per launcher), which all the NATO countries have in use. The Pentagon is planning to equip them with warheads from the medium- and shorter-range missiles that are being dismantled.

[3]The TASM (Tactical Air-to-Surface Missile) program.

[4]See *Survival*, March/April 1989, p. 148.

From this list of projects alone it is evident that a series of measures being carried out by NATO "without too much noise," so to speak, is aimed at "compensating" for the elimination of U.S. medium- and shorter-range missiles under the Treaty on Medium- and Shorter-Range Missiles. West German Admiral Schmelling has compared such "modernization" to trading in an old heap for a Mercedes, plus a BMW, plus a Porsche.

The most typical example is the Lance-2, which was to replace the U.S. Lance missile complexes deployed in a number of West European countries and whose normal operating life ends in 1995. The Lance-2 was not simply an updated version, but a fundamentally different class of missile with a range that approaches that of operational-tactical missiles (or, as they are also called, shorter-range missiles), including the Soviet Oka missile that is to be dismantled under the Treaty on Medium- and Shorter-Range Missiles. In this connection, there was every reason to consider U.S. work on developing the Lance-2 missile to be, if not an outright violation of that extremely important accord, at least an attempt to circumvent it.

Although the Lance-2 program carried the greatest political weight and was until recently at the center of European debates, in terms of military technology the key element in modernization has been, from the very beginning, the improvement of air-launched systems. This is evident not only from the substantially higher potential deployment of air-launched and ground-based missiles, but also from actual plans for the deployment of additional aircraft-based U.S. missiles in Europe.

In combination with the high accuracy of their guidance systems, the range of these missiles provides for the guaranteed delivery of weapons to targets without the need for the aircraft carrying the missiles to come within range of the enemy's antiaircraft systems. Obviously, in that case the anticipated loss rate of one's own planes is substantially reduced, and the Warsaw Pact's superiority in fighter-interceptors is largely negated.

Thus, on the issue of the modernization of TNWs, the following preliminary conclusions can be made. In the past few years both the Warsaw Pact and NATO have updated their weapons systems. However, whereas the principal characteristics of the updated Warsaw Pact systems, including their range, are comparable with the characteristics of the systems that they replaced, and the replacement of tactical nuclear missiles has been halted at the present time, NATO intends to rearm its air-launched tactical missile arsenal with systems that closely approach shorter-range missiles in terms of their characteristics. Thus, a material base is being placed under the new U.S. doctrine of Air/Land Battle, envisioning tactical nuclear weapons strikes against the second and third echelons of the Warsaw Pact's forces.

According to the interpretation of the "Montebello decision" by former U.S. Assistant Secretary of Defense R. Wagner, it presupposed "getting away from relying on short-range systems, and a shift in favor of longer-range systems as being more useful from the political stand-point and, to the extent that they increase the potential for striking targets in the depth of the defense, thereby enhancing . . . military potential."[5]

Thus, on the issue of TNW modernization, NATO is still clearly affected by the inertia of Cold War politico-military thinking. That is understandable, since the Montebello decisions were made in 1983 when dialogue between East and West on disarmament problems was essentially frozen. It was the time when negotiations on limiting nuclear arms in Europe and limiting and reducing strategic arms had been broken off.

Now the situation is different. The Treaty on the Elimination of Medium- and Shorter-Range Missiles has been concluded and is being successfully implemented. Talks on reducing conventional armed forces in Europe have begun, and here the prospect exists that agree-ments could be reached as early as this year. The Soviet Union is carrying out major unilateral reductions of its arms and armed forces, as well as the reduction of a certain number of its tactical nuclear weapons, in Europe: In 1989, for example, 500 nuclear weapons (166 bombs, 50 artillery shells, and 284 missiles) were withdrawn from its allies' territory; TNW delivery systems are also being reduced, includ-ing 24 tactical nuclear missile launchers.

Against this background, TNW modernization in Europe clearly strikes a dissonant chord. The arsenal of weapons that modernization advocates would like to have by the mid-1990s does not fit in with the current dynamics of the development of East-West relations. Evi-dently the time has come for serious discussion of the question of TNW modernization.

Of course, it should be clear to every serious specialist in disarma-ment that it would be unrealistic, under today's conditions, to argue for the rejection of modernization in general, especially since all tactical nuclear weapons—missiles, planes and artillery—are, in essence, dual-purpose systems. And as long as weapons exist, they need to be updated. In the process, of course, they are improved.

In that connection, the goal should probably be not the mutual renunciation of modernization, but an agreement to strictly regulate it. Such an agreement would presuppose, for example, bans on increasing the number of tactical weapons capable of delivering nuclear

---

[5]*Hearings Before the Committee on Armed Services, U.S. Senate*, Washington, 1984, p. 3636.

explosives, on increasing the range of ground-based and air-launched missiles, on developing new types of nuclear weapons, and on increasing the number of missiles and bombs that various types of aircraft are equipped to carry. That, in turn, would help define the limits of "minimal deterrence" for Europe. It is important to break out of the vicious circle of "modernization as a response to modernization," which is the engine of the arms race.

Are the Sides' Positions So Very Far Apart?

At present serious disagreements remain on the question of beginning negotiations on TNWs between the NATO and Warsaw Pact countries. In all fairness, though, it should be noted that lately those disagreements have become less profound.

On the one hand, the NATO countries no longer categorically reject the idea of negotiations. They have in fact essentially expressed a willingness to enter into such negotiations, albeit on certain conditions. On the other hand, the Warsaw Pact countries no longer so categorically insist on the immediate elimination of TNWs in Europe, emphasizing instead their asymmetrical reduction to equal quantitative levels.

The sides have clearly moved closer together, which should be welcomed. What, then, are the remaining differences?

First, the Warsaw Pact countries are proposing to begin TNW negotiations in the near future, and without linkage to the solution of other disarmament problems. The NATO countries' linked negotiations to the implementation of agreements on reducing conventional armed forces in Europe have begun.

Second, the Warsaw Pact favors participation in the negotiations by all the Warsaw Pact and NATO nuclear powers and all other interested members of the two alliances, particularly those that possess tactical weapons capable of delivering nuclear explosives, and those on whose territories TNWs are deployed. As is known, the NATO countries have expressed a willingness for negotiations between the U.S.S.R. and the United States—granted, "with consultations with interested allies."

Third, the Warsaw Pact position envisages negotiations on, and consequently, the reductions of, all categories of TNWs—ground-based missile complexes with a range of up to 500 km., front-line (tactical) aircraft and artillery capable of delivering nuclear explosives, the nuclear components of those systems, and nuclear land mines. The NATO countries are prepared to conduct negotiations only for the purpose of reduction of American and Soviet ground-based, short-range nuclear-missile forces to equal and verifiable levels.

As we can see, differences in positions remain, and rather significant differences, at that. At the same time, the Warsaw Pact countries at the April 1989 meeting of the alliance's Foreign Ministers' Committee adopted a statement that they are "prepared to consider any other possible proposals and measures aimed at reducing and eliminating tactical nuclear arms in Europe, and contributing to increased stability on the continent at an increasingly lower level of military capabilities, while observing the principles of equality and equal security, and ensuring effective verification of the fulfillment of agreements." Moreover, the same document notes that "attainment of the goals of reducing and eliminating tactical nuclear missiles could also be advanced by other multilateral and unilateral reciprocal measures." Speaking in Strasbourg in June 1989, M.S. Gorbachev declared the Soviet Union's intention, on the threshold of negotiations on TNWs, to undertake further unilateral reductions of tactical nuclear missiles in Europe.

Thus, the Warsaw Pact position is fairly flexible and does not rule out various alternatives for solving the problem of TNWs. However, the interests of strengthening stability in Europe and ensuring the sides' equal security place limits on that flexibility.

In any event, the very fact that the Warsaw Pact and NATO have publicly set forth their positions on the problem of TNW negotiations indicates that that issue is becoming firmly established on the international agenda, even though it has not yet become the subject of direct East–West dialogue. In any case, the NATO countries have come to understand that they cannot avoid negotiations on TNWs and, at a certain stage, will have to begin them. What those negotiations produce—elimination of TNWs, preservation of a certain number, or possibly, a decision to provide a legal framework for their modernization—is another question.

In principle, this amounts to a fundamental change in the situation concerning TNWs. The reason for this change must be sought, first, in the rapidly changing situation in Europe as a whole, the NATO countries' reassessment of the level and nature of the Warsaw Pact military threat, and—most important, the seriousness of those countries' assessment of the breakthrough that was accomplished in the Vienna talks.

In this context, the TNW issue surfaces in debates on the future of Europe. In the final analysis, disarmament is not an end in itself, but only one means for reaching a new kind of peace based not on a guaranteed threat of military force, but on the guaranteed absence of such a threat.

This is the view from which one must regard the progress in European disarmament. The Warsaw Pact is prepared, as it has repeatedly declared, to eliminate all existing imbalances and asymmetries, but that should be only the first step toward realizing the main objective, which is to create conditions that would eliminate the possibility of offensive operations, and thus would eliminate the possibility of the outbreak of war. The main objective, following elimination of imbalances, should probably be a stage of reductions (it could provisionally be called "Vienna-2") that thus result in restricting Warsaw Pact and NATO military capabilities to highly defensive structures that would satisfy each side's concern for its security.

Consequently, the objective of negotiations consists of not just reducing the level of confrontation in Europe, but through that reduction and a reorganization of the armed forces and structures of the NATO and Warsaw Pact military organizations, of gradually attaining a state in which the military confrontation between the alliances would be eliminated. That would create the prerequisites for eliminating the bloc approach to European security.

Naturally, the talks of "the 23" and of "the 35" that have begun do not fully exhaust all the problems that arise in this connection. Here we have in mind attaining genuine stability and security in Europe's military situation; we also must consider the effect on it of arms that are not part of the mandate for the talks of "the 23." That includes tactical nuclear weapons.

Of course, the connection between the reduction of conventional armed forces and the reduction of tactical nuclear weapons is not direct and rigid. On the contrary, a certain degree of flexibility can be permitted in defining the sequence in which specific issues are taken up, which is why the Warsaw Pact agreed not to include TNWs in the mandate for the Vienna talks. At the same time they must not be left entirely outside the arms reduction process. To do so would not accord with the objective jointly set by the Warsaw Pact and NATO to give a purely defensive posture to their military forces. In fact, that is the main reason for the Warsaw Pact states' insistent appeals to begin negotiations on reducing tactical nuclear arms in Europe.

While no one is now seeking to tie the issues of conventional armed forces and of tactical nuclear arms together in a single knot, it is impossible not to see a certain objective connection between them. The point, in part, is this: As is known, tactical nuclear weapons and conventional weapons are closely interwoven, especially in operational and organizational respects. Therefore, the reduction of conventional armed forces in Europe, including dual-purpose systems, will inevitably result in a reduction of each side's systems for the delivery of tactical nuclear weapons. Incidentally, this connection is demonstrated practically in the fact that the measures being taken by the Soviet Union to unilaterally reduce its troops and weapons in Europe also include the reduction of tactical nuclear weapons.

On the other hand, achieving positive results in the multilateral talks in Vienna on deep cuts in conventional armed forces in Europe, and withdrawing the most destabilizing types of conventional arms from state arsenals will substantially reduce, and eventually eliminate entirely, the mutual threat of surprise attack and the launching of broad-scale offensive operations using conventional weapons. All grounds for preserving tactical nuclear weapons in Europe's military arsenals—at least in their present numbers and with their present characteristics—will thereby be eliminated. Incidentally, many Western specialists admit this. Thus, H. Binnendijk, director of studies of the International Institute for Strategic Studies in London, states that if the imbalances and asymmetries in conventional forces were eliminated, NATO would require substantially fewer TNWs for "adequate deterrence."[6]

The converse relationship is also obvious. The lack of a solution to the TNW problem could, in the not-too-distant future, become a brake on progress in talks on deep cuts in conventional armed forces in Europe. It is obvious that, if other arms are cut, the uncontrolled modernization, not to mention further buildup, of that type of weapon that possesses huge destructive potential and first-strike capability, will have an increasingly destabilizing influence on the politico-military situation in Europe.

Therefore, an effort should be made to have practical measures for reducing conventional arms and tactical nuclear systems that complement and reinforce one another in strengthening stability on the continent and supporting the process of reducing the two alliances' military confrontation, especially if the goal of ending that confrontation is to be seriously pursued. In that context, a first stage in tactical nuclear arms reductions that would be in keeping with the nature of the original agreement in Vienna on the elimination of imbalances and asymmetries might include reduction of tactical nuclear arms in all their principal categories to equal quantitative levels that are substantially lower than either side's current levels within a zone of agreed-upon breadth, for example, within the zone of the first strategic echelons of the Warsaw Pact and NATO. Subsequently, additional deep cuts of tactical nuclear weapons would be made throughout the zone from the Atlantic to the Urals.

Other approaches to the problem of TNWs are also possible. For example, talks might aim first at a substantial reduction of tactical missiles and nuclear artillery. "Minimal deterrence" might eventually be maintained by a certain agreed-upon number of aircraft carrying

---

[6]See *Survival*, March/April 1989, p. 152.

nuclear bombs and air-to-surface missiles.[7] In that context it would be necessary to agree on permissible limits for the modernization of those components, including limitation of missiles' range.

From the outset, one of the potential difficulties in the way of talks has been what to do with the nuclear components of dual-purpose systems. Agreement to eliminate them would entail resolution of extremely complex issues of monitoring both the elimination itself and, possibly, the production of fissionable materials. So far there has been no discussion of these issues in nuclear disarmament talks. It might be necessary for each side to limit itself in the first stage to reducing the number of delivery systems, while postponing the question of nuclear munitions until a later stage. Even the limitation of delivery systems, however, represents a complex problem, since some (aircraft and artillery) dual-purpose systems are already being discussed in the Vienna talks. Here it will evidently be necessary to set limits on systems that are capable of delivering nuclear weapons, and to agree on external and functionally based identifying features for them.

Finally, at present it will probably be difficult to involve France in the negotiations. It is well-known that France regards its short-range nuclear weapons not as tactical weapons but as "prestrategic" weapons. In that connection, and also because France is not a member of NATO's military organization, Paris has emphasized in every way possible that the problem of TNWs does not concern it. In contrast to the Americans and the British, the French make it clear that their existing "prestrategic weapons" (Pluton missiles and Jaguar A and Mirage-IIIE aircraft) are intended for purposes other than "compensation for the Warsaw Pact's superiority in conventional arms." Therefore, according to their logic, even after the imbalances and asymmetries between the Warsaw Pact and NATO are eliminated in the area of conventional arms, France will still need "prestrategic weapons."

Taking that position into account, the first stage of negotiations might be bilateral Soviet-American negotiations. The other NATO nuclear powers could join them later, in the context of further progress in the Vienna talks and improvement of the overall political situation on the continent. At the same time, once TNW talks begin, those states should naturally show restraint with regard to their nuclear weapons. As a report by the Peace Research Institute Frankfurt right-

---

[7]The Peace Research Institute Frankfurt proposes, as one option, leaving no more than 300-400 units of nuclear weapons on aircraft.

fully points out, "it is impermissible, while the United States and the U.S.S.R. are reducing their tactical nuclear arsenals, for Great Britain and France to continue to increase theirs."[8]

Thus, the level of "minimal deterrence" for Europe cannot be regarded as some sort of constant. It will evidently change in relation to the evolution of East-West relations as a whole. The objective of completely overcoming "deterrence" can be posed in a situation in which even deeper cuts are made in conventional armed forces, and naval forces and naval arms are limited, when the objective preconditions are created for comprehensively solving the problem of ensuring European security.

* * *

In the general context of the rapid evolution of East-West relations, the discussion of the issue of TNWs is, in essence, a discussion of the role of nuclear arms in general and, in a broader sense, of what peaceful coexistence should be like as a realistic ideal.

In that sense, the TNW question is a kind of litmus test of changes taking place. Therefore, the moment when the Warsaw Pact and NATO begin negotiations on this problem can evidently be considered, in a certain sense, a turning point for Europe and the world as a whole. It will probably also indicate a fundamental change in the West's attitude toward what is going on in the Soviet Union.

Without a doubt, the gradual removal of the nuclear component from the European military equation will be yet another sign of the dismantling of the security model that has been based on military force, and the start of the building of a new world based on normal civilized relations between East and West.

---

[8]*PRIF Reports*, Nos. 6-7, 1989, p. vi.

Old and New Elements in the Middle East Conflict

NIKOLAY NIKOLAYEVICH SPASOV*

And he said to them, "Therefore every scribe who has been trained for the kingdom of heaven is like a householder, who brings out of his treasure what is new and what is old." (The Gospel According to St. Matthew 13:52)

Facets of Ideologization

The first thing that distinguishes the Middle East conflict is its longevity, so to speak. One could say that it is the same age as the contemporary system of international relations that took shape in the first postwar years. Other regional conflicts are much younger.

Faced with such a striking example of long-standing enmity and suspicion on the scale of an entire region, one naturally wonders: What are the sources of the conflict, and what are its causes? If one scrapes away the surface layers, the driving contradiction can probably be identified as the problem of implementing a modus vivendi for two peoples—Jews and Palestinian Arabs—that would create the conditions for their stable reconciliation and peaceful coexistence in their common historical homeland.

It would be senseless to try to sort out which of the two peoples has greater historical rights to the territory that the Romans called Palestine. That approach will inevitably lead to the vicious circle of the age-old argument about the geographic boundaries of the land that the Lord, according to the Old Testament, gave to Abraham and his descendants (First Book of Moses, Genesis 12:5-7). And therefore one hardly needs to delve into the chronicle of the turbulent vagaries of fate in the historical process in the Middle East to be convinced of the futility of attempts to substantiate any preferential historical rights of one nation over another to certain territories. One needs only to recall the debates surrounding Nagorno Karabakh.

*"N. Spasov" is the pen name of Candidate of History Nikolai Nikolaevich Spasski, a political scientist and researcher on the staff of the U.S.S.R. Ministry of Foreign Affairs. This article reflects the personal views of the author. It appeared in the March 1990 issue of *MEMO* and includes brief additions made by the author for this volume.

Furthermore, let us not forget the universal maxim of civilized international relations, a maxim on whose affirmation hinge all hopes that some day the primacy of law will triumph in these relations. An injustice committed against one nation in the past cannot justify committing a reciprocal, "compensatory" injustice against the "offending" nation in the present or future. In analyzing any ethnic conflict and working out scenarios for its settlement, one should proceed from current political realities.

From the moment that the U.N. General Assembly, on November 29, 1947, passed Resolution 181(2), calling for the partition of Palestine, then under the mandate of Great Britain, into two independent states—Arab and Jewish (incidentally, both the U.S.S.R. and the United States voted in favor), the Middle East problem took on clearly defined outlines. It was necessary to ensure not only the creation, but also the peaceful coexistence of two states; to introduce into their relations with each other, and with their neighbors, the basic principle of the impermissibility of acquiring territory through military force. But whereas, after declaring the establishment of the State of Israel on May 14, 1948, the Jewish population was able to exercise the right that had been granted to it, the Palestinian Arabs did not succeed in doing so. And Israel was not alone to blame for this.

As a result of a sequence of military conflicts, the territories that the General Assembly had set aside for an Arab Palestinian state ended up under Israeli occupation. Initially, however, even the Jews themselves hardly regarded the realization of their national aspirations as something irreversible. The Arab countries, as we know, did not recognize Resolution 181 and Israel's right to exist, and until relatively recently the majority of them held the position that Israel should be liquidated as a "national home for Jews," and that one state—predominantly Arab in nature—should exist in Palestine.

It is not surprising that this sort of situation led to the development among the Israeli population of durable stereotypes of a "siege mentality," stereotypes which subsequently proved ideally suited to self-perpetuation. Even today, when Israel's right to exist is not in question in the Arab community (with one or two exceptions that are, to all appearances, most likely due to the force of inertia, or are purely rhetorical in nature), when the Palestine Liberation Organization has finally recognized this right—these stereotypes of distrust and suspicion are instilled in Israelis' minds literally from infancy. Without, of course, accepting such exaggerated concern for one's own security at the expense of others' security, one can nonetheless understand it. We are dealing here with complexes that are the result both of centuries of persecution and the shock of Nazi genocide. The anxieties of the first decades of the Israeli state's independent existence have also left their mark.

Emotions are emotions, however, and facts are facts. Whereas the Israeli people were able to exercise the right to create their own state that was granted to them by Resolution 181, the Arab people of Palestine, we repeat, were unable to do so. Consequently, in order to solve the key problem in the Middle East conflict, the Palestinians' right to self-determination must be ensured in actual practice: they must be given the opportunity to create an independent state. And then they themselves can figure out in what form that opportunity should be realized.

Of course, the facts cited here, taken alone, do not explain either the acute and chronic nature of the Middle East conflict, or the place it occupies in the forefront of world politics. An attempt to expand the limits of the conflict, that is, to understand it not as a conflict between two relatively small national social units—the Jewish and Arab populations of Palestine—but as a confrontation between all the world's Arabs, on the one hand, and all Jews, on the other (according to some American estimates, they number 250 million and 13 million people, respectively),[1] hardly sheds additional light on the problem. One can assume that the unique nature of the Middle East conflict, which distinguishes it from all other conflicts and makes it so resistant to efforts to settle it, is due, to a critical extent, to the fact that it has been completely permeated by ideology.

But this is only part of the picture. It is common knowledge that the bitterness of ethnic conflicts increases by whole orders of magnitude when the contradictions between nations take on a specific, religious, form of ideological disagreement. Religion is the most ancient and probably the most powerful instrument of ideological motivation for people's actions (in their extreme manifestations—actions that are predominantly not constructive, but destructive in orientation).

Let us recall in this connection that from time dating to the Crusades for recovery of the Holy Sepulcher Middle East conflicts have been painted in heavily religious colors. And if we turn now to the fundamental conflict in the Middle East—the Arab-Israeli conflict—we immediately see the religious component, which is underscored many times over by the fact that at the center of the conflict is a dispute over control of a city—Jerusalem—that is held sacred by three world religions.

Let us also recall that, although the Arab-Israeli confrontation sometimes overshadows everything else that is happening in the Middle East in terms of scale and intensity, it by no means exhausts the gamut of contradictions in that region. Moreover, practically all of the

---

[1]See *The New Republic*, May 22, 1989, p. 24.

conflicts in and around the Middle East also have religious overtones. Suffice it to list the major conflicts: the Iran-Iraq war—a military clash between theocratic Shiite Iran and predominantly Sunni, Baathist secular Iraq; Ethiopia—a conflict between the central regime, which is supported primarily by the Christian Amharic population, and Eritrean separatists, representing Somali Muslims; Sudan—a struggle between the Moslem North and Christian South; and finally, Lebanon—a classic example of civil war with religious origins, where everyone is against everyone else—the Christians (Maronites, Eastern Orthodox, Catholics), the Moslems (Sunnis and Shiites), and the Druze; and let us not forget Cyprus, where the demarcation between nationalities also has a religious component, although one that has faded.

In addition, the outbreak of the Middle East conflict came at a time when not only were the Jews acquiring national statehood, but the Arabs, too, were forming their contemporary national states. During such periods, when nationalism is on the rise, its advocates are particularly inclined to turn to religion for motivational support. Thus, religious orthodoxy, with the sanction of the powers that be, receives a powerful impetus, which makes it possible for it to seek consideration of its canonical priorities even in cases when they are in direct conflict with national interests in their current interpretation.

Equally important is that the circumstances we have mentioned constitute what might be called the surface layer of the ideological dimension of the Middle East situation. The Middle East conflict would be no different from all the other knots of regional strife in world politics if one of the sides were not Jews. It is this aspect that determines a phenomenon that has no parallel, which is that a significant share of the earth's population is concerned to one degree or another with the Middle East conflict. The point here is not solely, or even primarily, that the Jewish diaspora is represented and fairly influential in many countries of the world. Rather, the primary cause for the heightened interest in the Arab-Israeli conflict lies in the very nature of the ambiguous, contradictory, and painful legacy of relations between the Jewish communities that are scattered around the world and their immediate surroundings.

After World War II a guilt complex, often an unconscious one, over the Jews developed in the West. And it was not so much a desire to atone for centuries of persecution, as it was a reaction to the monstrous deeds of the fascist holocaust. These feelings were particularly strong among intellectuals. To fail to take into account Israel's great moral authority in the eyes of the Western public, an authority paid for by the millions of victims of Hitler's genocide, would be to leave out one of the fundamental factors influencing the evolution of the Middle East situation.

This does not mean, however, that the establishment of a "new" attitude toward Jews after the World War II occurred painlessly. In the Western countries anti-Semitism really was pushed out to the periphery of political life. Not only in policy-making circles and among intellectuals, but across the entire social spectrum it became the norm to view anti-Semitism as something indecent. At the same time, however, Jews' acquisition of not just moral equality but even, in a certain sense, moral superiority as victims of monstrous crimes, and their obtaining their own national homeland and, finally, virtually unimpeded opportunities for integration into their surrounding societies—was all looked on with a good deal of ambivalence, and it sometimes resulted in outbursts of anti-Semitism.

In addition, in a number of countries during certain periods of history, Jews were associated with negative, nihilistic excesses of the revolutionary movement. For example, "concepts" attributing such excesses to a "Zionist-Masonic conspiracy" enjoyed wide currency.

No particular emotional attachment to the new state of Israel developed among the non-Jewish population of the Soviet Union. This was true despite the fact that Israel's very establishment was in many respects made possible because of the U.S.S.R.'s consistent position, and that our country was the first to recognize it *de jure*. The roots of this anomaly must once again be sought in history.

In the second half of the 19th century and in the 20th century, relations between the peoples populating the present Soviet Union, particularly the Slavic peoples, and the Jewish diaspora developed rather painfully. Tsarist Russia "enriched" the international political lexicon with the word "pogrom." It does not require any particular sagacity to hypothesize that the anti-Semitic views of A. Rozenberg (who was born and taught school in Revel [Tallinn], from which he moved to Munich in 1919), who became one of the leading architects of the racial theory of National Socialism, did not develop in isolation from the ideas of the Black Hundreds. The final period of Stalin's life was marked by a noticeable whipping up of anti-Semitism. It would be no great exaggeration to suppose that but for his death, we would have been fated to become witnesses to yet another example of the repression of an entire people.

It is no surprise that, given a fairly developed tradition of anti-Semitism in this country, recurrences of it could be felt right up to the relatively recent past, and not just in the ordinary attitudes of the masses. Of course, it would be frivolous to exaggerate the extent of these views and to attribute to them some sort of influence on the formation of the state's foreign policy. The digression we have made has just one purpose—to outline, at least in sketchy form, the fragments of an internal political background that usually receives little attention in published works, a background that is part of the total context in which the official approach to the Middle East problem is developed and implemented.

If one considers the plane on which policy is actually developed, the growing preference that our country gave to the Arab side in the Arab-Israeli conflict from the 1950s on was in many respects because it became customary, especially after the three-country aggression of 1956, to identify Israel with the classic colonial powers. Looking back today, one concludes that this analogy was probably not entirely correct. Yet because of it the entire definition of the conflict changed in a fundamental way: It was shifted to our familiar, two-axis system of coordinates—"imperialist aggression" versus the "national liberation movement," a system that allowed no room for options in choosing sides. But that is still not all.

Through the Looking Glass of Global Confrontation

As already noted, the autonomous dynamics of the Middle East conflict received an additional impetus from the fact that, starting in the 1950s, the dividing lines in the Middle East coincided with the dividing lines in the global confrontation between the two world systems. In both Moscow and Washington it became standard to view this problem through the prism of the strategic struggle between them. Formation of such approaches took place at the height of the Cold War, in the years when a black-and-white view of the world predominated. Both sides were concerned with recruiting the young Middle East states that had escaped the guardianship of the waning colonial powers into the camp of their potential allies.

Both sides viewed the mechanism for such recruitment in pretty much the same way. Primary emphasis was placed on supplying arms and sending in specialists. And since many Middle Eastern states were involved in internecine conflicts, according to the logic of confrontation it was quite naturally taken as a given that your ally's enemy is your enemy too. So a great power with global commitments found itself drawn into local strife. Moreover, a party to a local conflict that suddenly saw its local opponent calling on one of the superpowers for protection, really had no alternative but to appeal, in turn, to the other superpower for help.

Add to this the petroleum factor, which also reached its full power in the 1950s. The Americans openly justified their interests in the Middle East by citing the need to ensure an uninterrupted supply of oil.

The great powers' involvement in local Middle East problems had a series of negative consequences. Principally, not only did it not contribute to the settlement of conflicts, to the contrary, it led to their continuation and, in a number of cases, to both their vertical escalation—by building up the direct participants' military potentials—and horizontal escalation—by drawing more and more countries into the conflicts. Objectively speaking, under the confrontational rules of the game that were in force at the time, the great powers' involvement in any given regional problem effectively blocked the possibility of its being solved, and it is clear why.

First, a military solution was essentially ruled out, since the patron state always had the resources to raise the stakes by providing additional military assistance (up to and including dispatching its own troops) in the event that its client party to the conflict should find itself in a difficult position. Incidentally, it seems that in November 1956 it was not so much the threat of Moscow's missiles, as it was the real prospect that Soviet volunteers would appear at Suez and Port Said (taken together, of course, with Washington's strongly voiced disapproval of the three-country action) that provided the argument that forced both London and Paris to retreat. In any case, the Soviet government's warning: "We are fully resolved to use force to destroy the aggressors and restore peace in the East"[2]—left no room for ambiguity.

Second, a political solution with the involvement of the two superpowers was virtually impossible, since during the years of the Cold War neither the Soviet Union nor the United States was prepared to encourage its regional clients to seek compromise solutions based on a mutually acceptable balance of interests.

The involvement of the two superpowers in Middle East conflicts led directly to an intensification of the arms race in the region. This primarily took the form of a buildup of their direct military presence, chiefly through acquisition of military bases, establishment of military depots, maintenance of naval fleets, execution of military maneuvers, and dispatching of military advisers (here one must make an adjustment, of course, for the highly unequal capabilities that they had at their disposal; those of the United States were significantly greater than those of the Soviet Union). The regional arms race also intensified through massive injections of arms for the local regimes. What is very significant here is that, while being integrated, willy-nilly, to the extent that it received military aid, into the global system of military preparations under the aegis of a friendly superpower, the receiving country not only did not forget the priorities of its own strategy in the given region, but generally gave them paramount importance. Accordingly, its local opponent had no choice but to take countermeasures.

---

[2]See *The USSR and Arab Countries: 1917-1960. Documents and Materials*, [*SSSR i arabskiye strany. 1917-1960 gg. Dokumenty i materialy*], Moscow, 1961, p. 259.

Thus, an arms race having its own dynamics and duplicating, on a smaller scale, the military competition between the great powers and their military allies was reproduced on the regional level. So there is nothing surprising about the fact that today the Middle East is third in the world, after NATO and the Warsaw Pact, in terms of military expenditures.

The combination of the total and multilayered ideologization of the Middle East problem with the steadily progressing militarization of the region has meant that practically every military clash there has created the real danger of a major war involving the U.S.S.R. and the United States. And that is notwithstanding the great powers' own recognition of their stake in not allowing the Middle East conflict to reach a global level.

To illustrate this aspect of the problem, let us take a look at how far the Soviet Union and the West were prepared to go to support their friends in the Middle East in every successive outbreak of military confrontation in the region, tracing the changes in their reactions along these lines.

Let us take, for example, the Suez crisis of 1956. It has not taken root in the Soviet people's historical memory the way many others have. Perhaps that is due to a belief in the reassuring and comforting maxim: "All's well that ends well." Or perhaps there is a more obvious reason: During those fall days our attention was absorbed by the events in Hungary. Nevertheless, from an impartial and conscientious analysis of this crisis one can draw many instructive lessons for today, when we are trying to devise a mechanism that will provide a reliable guarantee against any repetition of adventures such as that in Afghanistan. After all, it was in the course of the Suez crisis that the seeds were sown that sprouted later in the 1962 Cuban crisis. One can assume that N.S. Khrushchev and his circle perceived the Suez crisis as a dress rehearsal for future, more decisive steps in support of the national liberation movement—steps up to and including the appeal to the nuclear missile argument.

It is interesting to reproduce the most intimidating passage from a message sent by N.A. Bulganin, Chairman of the U.S.S.R. Council of Ministers, to British Prime Minister A. Eden on November 5, 1956. By way of explanation, it should be noted that the Soviet leadership of that time had a particular attachment to missile technology. We had barely (since 1955) started to arm ourselves with the first medium-range SS-3 missiles, and we were on the threshold of testing the first SS-6 intercontinental ballistic missile (a test that was conducted successfully in August 1957). One can understand the desire to try out the newly acquired missiles at the first convenient opportunity. Not in practice, only in politics. The sense of pride in the Soviet Union's achievements in missile development shows through in practically every phrase in the letter from the Chairman of the Council of Ministers: "In what position would England find itself if it were attacked by stronger states possessing all sorts of modern destructive weapons? After all, today these countries might not even send naval or air-force fleets to England's shores, but use other means, such as missile technology."[3] From every indication, the Kremlin at that time was aware that this was not something to joke about. It is difficult to interpret the following warning in any other way: "A war in Egypt could spread to other countries and grow into a third world war."[4]

The fact that this act of self-assertion through force was carried out with impunity inevitably meant that a confrontation on a regional stage involving nuclear missiles was unavoidable in the very near future. And no one doubts that the Soviet Union supported the right side in the conflict—the victim of aggression. But that is not the issue: the fate of the Suez Canal and the fate of humanity are nonetheless, quite likely, incomparable, so that the latter cannot be put at stake for the sake of the former.

Unlike the Suez crisis, the Caribbean crisis did not develop according to the scenario that Moscow apparently had counted on. One has to think that October 1962 dissuaded our leadership of the effectiveness of the tenet, which had nearly been proven in November 1956, that a noble end (including support of the world revolutionary process) justifies if not all, then very, very many means.

Later on, having learned from bitter experience, the U.S.S.R. and United States took a different approach to the Six-Day Arab-Israeli War that broke out on June 5, 1967. Despite the fact that the sympathies of Moscow and Washington were clearly aligned with the opposing sides in the conflict, the two powers shared a common interest in one main goal: to prevent an escalation of the conflict, and to facilitate the rapid termination of hostilities. In essence, we have here the first limited experience of constructive Soviet-American cooperation in the interest of settling a regional conflict. Ways of settling the conflict between Israel and the Arabs were thoroughly discussed during the talks between A.N. Kosygin and Lyndon Johnson in Glassboro (New Jersey) on June 23 and 25, 1967. It was during those meetings that a general agreement was reached on the fundamental principle of "land in exchange for peace,"[5] which formed the basis of the Security Council's Resolution 242 of November 22, 1967—the basis for a Middle East

---

[3]*Ibid.*, p. 258.
[4]*Ibid.*
[5]See L. Johnson, *The Vantage Point: Perspectives of the Presidency, 1963-1969*, New York, 1971, pp. 298, 483-484.

settlement. (Granted, for the sake of objectivity, one must mention that at this stage we made a special effort not to advertise our approval of this principle.)

The crisis of October 1973 did not cause any cooling in Soviet-American relations that was visible to the untrained eye, either. At the same time, the very fact that on October 24, in connection with different understandings concerning the implementation of the second cease-fire, the United States took the step of placing all of its nuclear and conventional forces on combat alert indicates how high the stakes had been raised.[6]

The examples cited here far from exhaust the list of episodes in which the Middle East conflict has played the role of an irritant in Soviet-American relations. As a result of the integration of the Middle East conflict into the global context of relations between the two superpowers, everyone loses. On the one hand, in their efforts to untangle the knot of conflict within a local framework, the region's countries in many ways find themselves hostages of the current state of Soviet-American relations. These relations, in turn, can hinge on various unpredictable events in the development of the Middle East situation that are determined by strictly local factors.

New Winds

The new winds in the international climate that started in 1985 have not bypassed the Middle East. The change that took place in the model of relations between the U.S.S.R. and the United States in regional affairs was of special significance for the region's states, as it was for countries located in other conflict-torn parts of the world. This process is still just in the initial phase. At the same time, the general trend in the movement can be discerned fairly clearly: from confrontation through dialogue, the purpose of which is to identify and expand areas where interests coincide, to mutual understanding and, when possible, to cooperation dealing initially with at least certain aspects of a regional settlement.

The new developments emerging today between Moscow and Washington in dealing with regional matters are affecting in the most direct way possible the concepts of national security, the priorities of domestic development, and the stereotypes of behavior in relations with the surrounding world that parties to regional conflicts developed throughout the post-war decades with an eye to relations between the world's mighty powers. Until just recently they carried out military development and planned their foreign policy actions in accordance

---

[6]See *The Memoirs of Richard Nixon*, New York, 1978, pp. 937-940.

with the thesis that there was a clash of interests between the U.S.S.R. and the United States in their particular region. Now these countries are beginning to discover for themselves—and not all of them feel comfortable with this—how much more far-sighted and beneficial it is to pursue a policy in regional and world affairs that assumes cooperation, rather than competition, between the two superpowers.

Finally, the state of affairs in other regions of the world where there are conflicts cannot help but affect the development of events in the Middle East. Although the development of these processes is painful and uneven and accompanied by slowdowns and setbacks, there is reason to claim real progress toward settling such dissimilar conflicts as those in Namibia and Angola, Central America, and Cambodia. With regard to the Middle East conflict, it is still early to talk about any significant movement toward a settlement; it would be more appropriate to note the ripening of prerequisites for a future breakthrough.

Among these prerequisites one should include shifts in the approaches taken by the Soviet Union and the United States to regional problems, as a whole, and the Middle East conflict, in particular.

Let us start with the Soviet Union. The most important thing here is that we have finally started learning to formulate our national interests on the basis not of a false notion of prestige, but of the people's real interests, oriented toward a peaceful future—both their interests in relations with the external world as a whole, and their interests with respect to that world's various regional segments, including, of course, the Middle East.

Until recently it was considered a given that, whereas in global affairs our Third World friends almost automatically copied the Soviet Union's position, in regional affairs we aligned ourselves with the positions of our friends in those regions, without really giving it much thought. Yet it is essentially just as abnormal for a great power to uncritically accept the position of a friendly country that is a party to some conflict or other as it is for a small developing state to blindly follow the zigzags of its patron state's policies. Both have their specific national interests. Today we are coming to an understanding of this and are implementing it in our practical policies. Although, of course, perestroika in international relations, unlike domestic reforms, is an area where not everything depends on us alone, where not everything can be achieved through unilateral actions, and where painstaking work with one's partners—the work of persuasion—is required.

Another fundamental change, which has taken place within the context of the new political thinking, is that a basic conclusion has been drawn as to the unacceptability of using force and the threat of force to achieve political, economic, or other goals. Our adherence to this fundamental principle was proven by the withdrawal of Soviet troops from Afghanistan. Incidentally, in the context of the Middle East that action has produced quite tangible positive benefits for us by removing a serious obstacle that had been hindering relations between the Soviet Union and many Moslem countries.

The principle of de-ideologizing international relations literally liberated Soviet diplomacy, including diplomacy with regard to regional matters. Taboos were lifted on contacts with parties that we found ideologically disagreeable, taboos that were in keeping neither with the Soviet state interests, nor with the interests of reaching regional settlements. It is now becoming the practice to maintain a dialogue with all political forces that enjoy real influence, regardless of their ideological coloring. As for the Middle East, that region has never before seen such a high level of activity in Soviet diplomacy. A landmark was set by the U.S.S.R. Foreign Minister's February 1989 trip to five Middle Eastern countries (Syria, Jordan, Egypt, Iraq, and Iran), the central event of which was the set of talks E.A. Shevardnadze held in Cairo with the Egyptian leadership, PLO Executive Committee Chairman Y. Arafat, and Israeli Foreign Minister M. Arens.

New flexibility can also be seen in the Soviet approach to the very essence of a settlement. It is ready to support any steps if they are productive and will lead to a comprehensive solution. As for the settlement mechanism, the Soviet Union adheres firmly to the following position: the optimal formula for achieving a comprehensive settlement of the Arab-Israeli conflict and its key problem—the Palestinian issue—is an international conference, which is seen as a combined, multilevel process. The U.S.S.R. favors exploring various approaches in preparing and holding such a conference, and favors combining bilateral, trilateral, and multilateral activities within the framework.

Today it would be ridiculous to deny the need to use bilateral channels. The Camp David peace process, which resulted in the normalization of relations between Israel and the Arab world's largest country—Egypt—evidently attests to the possibilities inherent in bilateral channels. But bilateral instruments are not all-powerful, since a solution of the problem of self-determination for the Palestinian people cannot be achieved in the context of improved bilateral relations between Israel and any other single Arab state alone. By virtue of its genesis and current status, the Palestinian problem is a regionwide, international problem. Moreover, there is the matter of guarantees of future agreements. Therefore, just as a conference is not an alternative to direct bilateral negotiations, neither can the latter take the place of an international mechanism. It seems to me that a solution needs to be sought not in pitting these two approaches against one another, but in organically synthesizing them.

In this connection it makes sense to touch on the question of diplomatic relations with Israel. There is no denying that if this problem is considered in abstract terms, one must admit that ideally we should strive to have diplomatic relations with all the world's countries, regardless of any differences of opinion that may exist on specific problems. But we have paid too dearly for dogmatism and refusal to compromise in politics. Still, we should be guided by the main goal in the Middle East—to help establish a lasting, just peace in the region, based on a balance of interests; to extinguish a permanent hotbed of military danger located in direct proximity to our homeland's southwestern borders; and to remove this problem, which has diverted our attention from the objectives of establishing and developing peaceful cooperation with the surrounding world, including all the Middle Eastern states, from the foreign policy agenda. I think that there is nothing wrong with our being a little pragmatic in pursuing this goal. But today the prospects for a Middle East settlement depend primarily on Israel, or more precisely, on the current leaders of the Likud bloc, who do not accept the principle of "land for peace," reject the idea of convening an international conference, do not recognize the Palestinians' right to self-determination and the establishment of their own state, and refuse to recognize the PLO and enter into a dialogue with it.

One wonders what sort of political meaning would an agreement by us—taking into account current realities—to restore diplomatic relations with Israel carry? Regular dialogue is already maintained between our countries, including dialogue at a high level, consular groups are functioning, and the problem of Jewish emigration from the U.S.S.R., which used to be a stumbling block, has essentially been eliminated in light of the Vienna Final Document [signed in January 1989 at the conclusion of the Vienna follow-up meeting of participants in the Conference on Security and Cooperation in Europe]. So it is perfectly reasonable to return to the question of diplomatic relations with Israel in the context of the beginning of the peace process in the Middle East. It is no secret that Israel has an interest in restoring diplomatic relations with us. So let that interest be an additional factor encouraging it to modify its position.

In recent years there have also been changes in the United States with regard to the Middle East conflict and its players, although they are far from equivalent to those that have taken place in Soviet politics.

First and foremost, one should mention a change in the attitude toward Israel. For many years, in any collisions in the Middle East the American public as a whole sided with Israel. In some ways this rule is still in effect today. But fundamental changes have also taken place. Israel has lost its martyr's halo of moral infallibility. The Israeli invasion of Lebanon in the summer of 1982, which led to the tragedy of the Sabra and Shatila Palestinian refugee camps, can be taken as the symbolic turning point in this long and circuitous process of the transformation of Israel's image in Americans' eyes.

Furthermore, the American Jewish community is demonstrating increasing independence in its thinking and behavior. There is a growing understanding within it that the interests of American Jewry—an influential religious-ethnic group within the United States—are by no means identical to the interests of Israel, which is following a course of its own. At the same time, one can see a relative narrowing of the American Jewish community's potential for influencing official Washington. Accordingly, since that community has served and continues to serve as the main voice for Israel's "concerns" in the United States, the Israelis are finding it considerably more difficult to get the United States to take their position in each new case.

We should point out that the liberation of American Middle East policy from an a priori orientation toward Israel can be felt even within the Democratic Party, which has traditionally been a defender of Israel. This process can be seen even more vividly in the Republican wing of American political life. From every indication, President Bush is significantly less dependent on the pro-Israel lobby than his predecessors, and consequently is less subject to its influence. He is little indebted to these circles for his election as president. A number of leading members of the Bush administration have considerable business interests in the Arab world. Finally, the Arab community in the United States, which, incidentally, has been noticeably gaining influence in recent years, is represented among Bush's aides at a fairly high level by J. Sununu, White House chief of staff. It is revealing that in 1986, as governor of New Hampshire, Sununu refused to join with the governors of the other 49 states in signing a proclamation condemning the well-known 1975 U.N. resolution that recognized Zionism as a form of racism.[7] One can say with confidence that in the not-so-distant past such a challenge would quite certainly have cost a person his political career. Sununu's appointment to such an important post despite the unambiguous dissatisfaction expressed by Zionist circles is further evidence of the decline of the Israeli factor's importance in the United States' domestic political arena. In short, Israel no longer has the right to veto any steps the United States might take in the Middle East.

The process that has taken form—even if only in sketchy outline so far—of the distancing of U.S. Middle East policy from Israel is really quite natural. Whereas in our country the formation of a concept of

[7]See *Time*, Nov. 28, 1988, p. 25.

national interests was in the most rudimentary stage until just recently, in the United States, on the contrary, it was quite thoroughly developed. Despite that fact, in Middle Eastern affairs Washington often pursued a course that diverged from U.S. national interests in even their most traditional interpretation. All one needs to do is look at the Arab world with its geostrategic importance, immense human resources, and natural wealth, project its role into the 21st century, and compare it with corresponding characteristics of Israel. It would seem that the Arab states should be of considerably greater interest to the United States than Israel, including interest from the standpoint of global competition between the two systems. This is not what happened, however.

A great number of people in the American establishment continue to think of a solution of the Middle East problem solely in terms of unilateral concessions by the Arabs. The following maxim from the journal *Commentary*, published by the American Jewish Committee, is quite typical in this respect: "People who yearn for a settlement should plead for a change of course from the Arabs, not the Israelis."[8] Or we can cite the journal *The New Republic*, which reflects a point of view that is widely held in the United States: "The Arabs, who have conquered more civilizations than any other people in history, do not accept the inevitability of national coexistence."[9]

Even within such a limited framework, however, a marked increase in the activity of American diplomacy with regard to a Middle East settlement has proved possible. After all, for all intents and purposes, from the time that Ronald Reagan put forward his plan of September 1, 1982, right up until the end of his presidency, the problems of the key conflict in the Middle East—the Arab-Israeli conflict, as opposed to the Iran-Iraq and Lebanese conflicts—were not on the list of the Washington administration's foreign-policy priorities. But then came 1988. At the very beginning of that year Secretary of State G. Shultz came out with a rather complicated, if not to say intricate, settlement plan, which represented an attempt to combine a comprehensive approach with "intermediate measures" and "small steps," which the Americans have traditionally preferred. The motives for proposing such a plan are understandable, of course. The United States simply could not allow itself not to react to the qualitative change in the Middle East situation, to the shifts that were emerging in the positions of the parties involved, and to the increase in Soviet diplomatic activity in the region. One cannot rule out the possibility that in developing the "Shultz plan" the State Department understood

---

[8]*Commentary*, Oct. 1988, p. 42.
[9]*The New Republic*, May 22, 1989, p. 24.

that it had no chance of being implemented—it would have been naive to expect success in such an extremely complicated matter in an election year in both the United States itself and in Israel. It is more likely that the Reagan administration's last-minute activity in Middle Eastern affairs (including its December 14, 1988, decision to enter into direct dialogue with the PLO) was viewed as a springboard for the next administration's Middle East policies. At the same time, Washington signaled, in effect, its renewed interest in Middle Eastern affairs.

At the same time—and this is very revealing—the fiasco (which was to a great extent planned) of the Shultz plan was used as evidence that a comprehensive approach to a Middle East settlement "would not work." Today the Bush administration's platform, to a very significant extent, comes down to encouraging establishment of a dialogue between Israel and the Palestinians under conditions that are acceptable to the Israelis. So, in some seven years American diplomacy has moved from an attempt to formulate its own scenario for a comprehensive settlement—the "Reagan plan"—through the compromise Shultz plan with its idea of "wedding" different approaches, to an orientation toward supporting intermediate measures, with no other alternatives.

The renewal of U.S. interest in a Middle East settlement manifested itself in two serious shifts in the American position. One of them has already been mentioned—the reconsideration of its attitude toward a direct dialogue with the PLO. As one might have expected, the Likud reacted to Washington's decision with unconcealed irritation. The other shift is the American leadership's gradual adoption of a more realistic view of the Soviet Union's role in the Middle East. Official statements present a thesis from which it follows that the United States has been able to make certain adjustments in its attitude toward the U.S.S.R.'s role in Middle Eastern affairs solely because the Soviet Union's own policy in the region has changed. This underestimates the reciprocal connection that absolutely must exist between the two powers' Middle East policies.

As in the past, official U.S. documents invariably stress that one of the main goals of U.S. strategy in the Middle East is to contain the Soviet influence.[10] At the same time, one gets the impression that a fundamental tenet of early Reaganism, according to which removing the U.S.S.R. from the Middle East was viewed as a necessary condition for settling the conflict, is becoming a thing of the past. In this respect the statements made by Bush himself at the joint press con-

---

[10]See, for example, "National Security Strategy of the United States. Report of the President to the Congress" (*Department of State Bulletin*, Vol. 88, No. 2133, April 1988, p. 22); and *Building for Peace. An American Strategy for the Middle East*, Washington, D.C., 1988, p. 4.

ference held at the end of the Soviet-American summit in Malta are very indicative. He admitted, "that may not always have been the way the United States looked at it as to whether—how constructive the role the Soviets might play [in the Middle East—N.S.]."

Today, it is being acknowledged more and more widely, albeit without enthusiasm, that without the Soviet Union's participation—in one form or another, at one stage or another—a Middle East settlement will be impossible. In this connection, there is often talk of only "selective cooperation" with Moscow, the goal of which would be not so much a final settlement of the conflict, as a "regulation" of its forms. One also hears the familiar theme of testing "Soviet intentions."[11] Nevertheless, the new accents in U.S. Middle East policy open up opportunities for the intensification of a nonconfrontational, substantive discussion between the Soviet Union and the United States on the Middle East. In the context of such an exchange of views, one cannot rule out further constructive evolution of the American approach.

In summing up what has been said about the new aspects of that approach, let us point out in advance, to avoid any misunderstanding, that they have not yet affected the central priorities of the U.S. policy regarding a Middle East settlement. Let us list those priorities.

1. The maximum strengthening of relations with Israel continues to be of paramount importance. Let us cite a program document prepared in 1988 with a new administration in mind by a bipartisan group co-chaired by former Democratic presidential candidate W. Mondale and L. Eagleburger, who was subsequently appointed by Bush to the post of deputy secretary of state. The authors of the report believe that one of the future president's first tasks should be to affirm "this relationship of trust based on strong relations, close consultations, and an ironclad commitment to Israel's security."[12] This is echoed by R. Hunter, an authoritative American specialist on the Middle East: "the U.S. commitment to Israel's survival and security must be unquestioned."[13]

2. Along with real concern over the scale of the arms race in the Middle East, the main emphasis is still being placed not on measures to limit it, but on strengthening Israel's military potential. "Preserving Israel's military superiority is the only way to ensure Israel's security and discredit the Arab war military option."[14]

3. Looking to Israel, Washington is still unprepared to recognize the Palestinians' right to self-determination, up to and including the formation of an independent state. Washington goes no further than acknowledging Palestinians' "legitimate rights."

---

[11]See *Building for Peace* . . . , p. xxi.
[12]*Building for Peace* . . . , p. xv.
[13]*Foreign Policy*, Winter 1988/89, p. 17.
[14]*Building for Peace* . . . , p. xvii.

Between Alarm and Hope

Let us take a quick look at what happened in the second half of the 1980s in the Middle East itself, and at what sort of changes took place there in the alignment of forces and opinions that made innovations in the great powers' approaches possible. The most important thing seems to be that throughout the Middle East region, in circles covering a very wide spectrum of political, ideological, and religious orientations, the conviction has crystallized that the Arab-Israeli conflict is ripe for a settlement, and that preservation of the status quo is fraught with the potential for an explosion that would almost certainly spill over the region's borders. The intifada—the nonviolent uprising by Palestinians living in the occupied territories that has been going on since December 1987, which in essence is a form of civil disobedience, reminiscent in some ways of the well-known campaigns in India in the 1920s and 1930s that are associated with the name of Mahatma Gandhi—has played and is continuing to play a definite role in the spread of these views. The intifada has clearly illuminated for all the parties involved in the conflict the fact that there is no possibility of returning to the previous situation. Israel's leaders have realized that they can no longer govern as they have in the past. An understanding of the urgent need to take some sort of practical steps toward removing the deadlock is having an increasing effect on the behavior of all the parties to the conflict, albeit in different ways.

During these same years, a number of destructive factors that argue in favor of taking urgent, collective measures to solve the conflict have become apparent. For example, the arms race in the region has been picking up speed and assuming qualitatively new dimensions. A whole group of countries in the Middle East have medium-range surface-to-surface ballistic missiles (according to American data, 10 countries in the region now have such missiles). A number of states have acquired the ability to wage chemical warfare. American military experts believe that at least two states with medium-range missiles have developed chemical warheads for them. The proliferation of high-precision medium-range missiles means that all parties to the conflict face the temptation to carry out a first strike. And where the danger of a first strike exists, there is also the temptation to carry out a preemptive strike.

The creeping spread of arms through the Middle East is taking place at the same time that the U.S.S.R. and the United States, in accordance with the Treaty on the Elimination of Medium- and Shorter-Range Missiles, are destroying their missile systems of this sort. For the Soviet Union this problem is of much more than abstract interest—missiles deployed in the Middle East are perfectly capable of reaching its southern regions. It is no coincidence, therefore, that the U.S.S.R. and the United States, by mutual agreement, have placed the problem of preventing the proliferation of missiles and missile technology on the agenda for bilateral exchanges of views.

It should also be mentioned that the cessation of fighting on the Iran-Iraq front in August 1988, which freed the energy of two major regional powers with their own interests and ambitions, may also have a complicated effect on the Middle East peace process. One can assume that the realignment of political forces in the region accompanying this event will for some time place an additional burden on the fragile framework supporting regional stability.

The fact that the tendency for the Middle East's policy-shaping circles to turn toward pragmatism is taking place against the backdrop of a polarization of forces in both the Arab world and in Israel, and a radicalization of both the left and right wings, is causing serious worry both in the region and beyond its borders. For example, Arafat and his supporters are having some difficulty restraining extremist inclinations among Palestinian young people. Quite a few of them are dissatisfied and believe that he unjustifiably made major concessions without receiving anything in return. The influence of Islamic fundamentalism can be felt among Palestinians. At the same time, in Israel, too, one can see an attraction to simple solutions (that is, predominantly those based on military force). Adherents of orthodox Zionism are active. It is self-evident that if supporters of the hard line on both sides should reach the helm of power, a military confrontation would be inevitable.

A chronic factor that keeps the Middle East in turmoil is terrorism, which manifests itself, in part, in political assassination and the seizure of hostages. Extremist actions in the region further destabilize the situation, make its development unpredictable, undermine the authority of the responsible forces calling for dialogue, and put trump cards in the radicals' hands. What is more, terrorism stirs up public opinion. As a result, a U.S. president, in developing the United States' strategic policy on a Middle East settlement, is forced to bear the problem of American hostages in Lebanon constantly in mind.

For all their fragmentary nature, the points cited here confirm that the situation in the Middle East is developing in such a way that movement toward a comprehensive settlement of the conflict needs to be started immediately.

The central event of the past few years was the November 15, 1988, proclamation, at an extraordinary session of the Palestine National Council, of the creation of an independent State of Palestine. At the same time, the PLO recognized Security Council Resolutions 242 and 338, recognized Israel's right to exist, and rejected terrorism. The PLO's position on this score was to a great extent cleared of ambiguities in a number of statements made by Arafat after the session. Thus, obstacles were removed that the United States and Israel had used as pretexts to justify their tactic of boycotting the PLO. Another important event was the completion of Egypt's reintegration into the Arab world. Taken together, these new factors provided a powerful impetus to political and diplomatic activity in the Middle East.

In April 1989 Israeli Prime Minister Y. Shamir, the leader of the Likud bloc, presented the idea of holding elections among the Palestinian population of the West Bank of the Jordan River and the Gaza Strip. Under his plan, election results would be used to form a delegation of Palestinian representatives that would discuss with Israel the question of granting autonomy to the West Bank and Gaza for a transitional period. After that, the plan calls for negotiations on the ultimate status of these territories. Israel's willingness to hold elections is tied to the Palestinians' acceptance of a series of conditions. Measured in absolute terms, this proposal definitely only goes part of the way. But for the Israeli leadership it was an almost revolutionary step forward, since until then not a single Israeli government had agreed to any negotiations even with "appointed" Palestinian representatives. The maximum that Israel was prepared to do was to include Palestinians in delegations from Egypt or Jordan. Essentially, the Shamir plan meant recognition by Israel's ruling circles of the indisputable fact that no one is capable of replacing Palestinians at the negotiating table.

The PLO leadership, of course, could not accept the "Shamir plan" in the form in which it was presented. At the same time, does not reject the idea of elections as such. But in order to sanction the idea of elections, the PLO needs certain guarantees. It is fundamentally important to the PLO that elections be included in the context of a comprehensive peace process that would lead to the Palestinian people's exercise of their right to self-determination and creation of an independent state. As far as elections themselves are concerned, the Palestinians are proposing that they be held under the aegis of the U.N. and in the presence of U.N. forces.

The 10-point peace plan put forward by Egyptian President H. Mubarak on September 11, 1989, was intended to reconcile the approaches of Shamir and the PLO. The key idea of this plan was to bring the Israelis and Palestinians together and help them begin a substantive discussion about organizing elections in the occupied territories. The plan took into consideration all of Israel's main concerns; nonetheless, progress was once again blocked by the Likud leadership's negative position: Shamir called the discussions proposed by Mubarak "talk of surrender."

Subsequently, however, when the Americans entered the game, proposing their own interpretation of the framework for a Palestinian-Israeli dialogue (the "Baker plan"), an interpretation that turned out to be practically identical to that of the Israelis, Israel gave the go-ahead for talks with Palestinian representatives on the question of holding elections. True, its consent was given in such a form that one has to wonder whether this step forward will not be followed by two steps backward, as has repeatedly happened in the past.

History knows many examples in which the escalation of conflicts over the question of approaches to the search for peace, and the incorporation of those conflicts into the domestic political fabrics of states balancing on the brink of war have ultimately resulted in the devaluation of the idea of peace as such. Polarization over problem, which has been long-standing for the Israelis, of peace under conditions of security, has become so volatile that in March 1990, it resulted in a vote of no-confidence in the government for the first time in Israel's entire 42-year history. Moreover, the no-confidence vote was tied directly to disagreements between the Likud bloc and the Labor Party in connection with an American proposal for an Israeli-Palestinian meeting in Cairo. The coalition government that had existed since the fall of 1988 was dissolved. As might have been expected, the new round of political internecine quarrels that subsequently gripped the country did not benefit the timid beginnings of attitudes disposed to compromise that had emerged.

In view of the profound over-ideologization of the Middle East conflict, a genuinely lasting Middle East peace reflecting a carefully weighed balance of the interests of all the parties involved is possible only through the development of nationwide consensus in Israel and the nations of the principal Arab participants. It goes without saying that in order to have any chance of implementation, the idea of peace must be established in the political life of the region's countries as a leading value in its own right. Yet just the opposite has been happening. The fact that this idea has been turned into the object of domestic political dispute is resulting in its being perceived in rival party circles as an end that has subordinate, secondary importance—as a means that can be put into play for the sake of attaining what those circles see as a higher end, in their struggle for power. That is an extremely alarming symptom.

For example, who could have imagined that gradual shifts in the area of regularizing relations between the U.S.S.R. and Israel, and the rise in Jewish emigration from the Soviet Union would lead to an outburst of harsh mutual incriminations among the circle of immediate participants in the Arab-Israeli conflict and the parties involved in it indirectly. Yet that is exactly what happened. With the virtual removal of limits on emigration from the U.S.S.R. on the basis of nationality, a flood of Soviet Jews poured into Israel (in 1989, according to preliminary data from the Ministry of Internal Affairs, more than 102,000 people left, which is 3.4 times as many as in 1988). It can be assumed that maintaining this high level of emigration from the U.S.S.R. to Israel over the next few years would cause a certain transformation of the region's demographic situation. Naturally, this forecast has stirred up radicals on both sides of the Arab-Israeli dividing line. Passions have started heating up. Israeli political figures, including the head of the government, have started talking about the need to hold on to the occupied lands in order to settle the new immigrants on them. Once again, the specter of a "greater Israel" has been resurrected. It is understandable that such a turn of events is arousing stormy opposition among Arabs, and that feelings of dissatisfaction with and even ill will toward the Soviet Union are spreading among them.

Nevertheless, an unprecedented historical opportunity exists to begin moving toward a comprehensive settlement of the Middle East problem. A. Lewis, a well-known American columnist, writes: "The two sides have never been so close, so tantalizingly close, to a face-to-face negotiation."[15] This opportunity should not be lost.

A natural question arises: What can the U.S.S.R. and United States do to help prevent this opportunity from slipping by? Today the time has probably come when they could, leaving behind their own political and ideological ambitions—leaving behind, if you will, their own identities—support with the full force of their authority any steps aimed at promoting the process of a comprehensive political settlement in the Middle East, including steps taken locally.

Granted, extremely fundamental differences really do remain between the parties to the Middle East conflict. Recently, however, one basic zone in which their priorities coincide has emerged in their policies. Whereas the participants in the conflict generally used to think in terms of ensuring their security and solving the Middle East problem through the use of predominantly, if not exclusively, military means, today they increasingly see the guaranteeing of security as a political process. It is in the interests of the world community to support this trend and to contribute to its consolidation.

---

[15]*International Herald Tribune*, Oct. 2, 1989.

The Political Reefs of the Caribbean Crisis

SERGEI VLADISLAVOVICH CHUGROV*

In the last days of January this year the Trilateral Symposium on Problems of the Caribbean Crisis** was held in one of the old mansions on Moscow's Lenin Prospect. It was organized by the U.S.S.R. Academy of Sciences' Institute of World Economy and International Relations and the Soviet Political Science Association, with the support of the Soviet Peace Fund, for the purpose of continuing the exchange of views on this topic between Soviet and American delegations that began last year at Harvard. For the first time the meeting in Moscow brought together at a round table delegations from the three sides that were drawn into the tumultuous vortex of events in the "hot October" of 1962. We are publishing an article analyzing the basic directions and key points of the discussion that unfolded at the symposium.

You get a strange sensation when something is being discussed that almost happened, but did not. Although more than 26 years have passed, our ignorance or half-knowledge, and deliberate or unconscious distortions of history are forcing us to return to the events of 1962. At that time the course of political development, running up against the Caribbean political reefs, took a sharp turn to one side. This forces political scientists—this time, fortunately, only mentally—to sketch out various possibilities of what might have happened.

It is just as important, in my opinion, to understand now—from the vantage point of our new capacity for self-analysis—those currents and hidden political eddies, chance occurrences, and obvious absurdities that were inexorably leading the world toward disaster. How unique is this intertwining of the objective and the subjective? Can one speak of a "Caribbean model" of the development of a crisis? Could there ever conceivably be another convergence of political vectors that could lead to such a situation?

---

*Candidate of history, deputy editor in chief of *MEMO*. This is a slightly abridged version of the article that appeared in the May 1989 issue of *MEMO*.
**[The "Caribbean crisis" is the Soviet term for what is referred to in the United States as the Cuban missile crisis.—*Trans.*]

One can hardly accuse political science of lacking interest in these questions over the course of two-and-a-half decades. But only now, it seems, has a new level of candor and analysis become possible. Why? In the first place, the very passage of time is eroding the barriers of secrecy. But more important, humanity is thinking in new directions, and our glasnost is making it possible to go beyond the pernicious tradition of "we don't talk about that," beyond the political prohibitions and biases of past decades. And finally, that same inexorable passage of time is forcing us to hurry: Although the two co-directors of the momentous events—Khrushchev and Kennedy—will never be able to sit down at the same table, there are many other members of the teams who, with no cause to complain of failing memory or illness, are capable—to their mutual satisfaction—of putting together a jigsaw puzzle from scattered and sometimes strange pieces.

I will say right off that the way in which the contours of these pieces fit together was far from ideal. Actually, until now there have been three outlines—the Soviet, the American, and the Cuban, each with its own style, temperament, and coloring. But now a portrait of the events is being compiled, albeit an incomplete one, in which the differences in style are no longer so glaring.

Over the course of two days I had the opportunity to enter into and emerge from the crisis together with its participants, witnesses, and "biographers." You can see how the political epicenter of the crisis in the fall of 1962 was represented at the meeting from the list of delegates and their official positions at that time: A.A. Gromyko, U.S.S.R. minister of foreign affairs; A.F. Dobrynin, Soviet ambassador in Washington; and A.I. Alekseyev, U.S.S.R. ambassador in Havana. Serving in the role of witnesses who were involved in the development of events in the inner sanctum of Soviet politics in those years were S.N. Khrushchev and S.A. Mikoyan, the sons of leaders at that time. The sons, of course, did not have their fingers "on the button," but they were attentive and interested observers. The American participants in and witnesses to those events included (once again I will note the posts they held then) Defense Secretary Robert McNamara; McGeorge Bundy, the president's national security adviser; Theodore Sorensen, special counsel to the president; Gen. William Smith, deputy chairman of the Joint Chiefs of Staff; and Pierre Salinger, the White House press secretary.

Speaking of the Cuban delegation, one should name first of all the head of the delegation, Jorge Risquet Valdez, member of the Politburo of the Cuban Communist Party Central Committee; Rafael Hernandez, who was then Cuban Chief of the General Staff; and Sergio del Valle Jimenez, one of Fidel's closest comrades in arms and who was involved in the very beginning of the Cuban revolution.

The symposium's "brain trust" consisted of leading historians and political scientists. They included G. Kh. Shakhnazarov, Ye. M. Primakov, G.A. Arbatov, V.V. Zhurkin, O.N. Bykov, A.K. Kislov, D.A. Volkogonov, F.M. Burlatskiy, and other scholars. The American intellectual potential was represented by such names as Raymond Garthoff, Joseph Nye, Graham Allison, James Blythe, Jr., and others.

So, for the first time all three sides sat down at one table to discuss the harsh confrontation that took shape in the fall of 1962. No matter what seating arrangement was chosen, the delegations inevitably ended up side by side at the conference table. Perhaps that is symbolic: There would be no insane balancing on the brink of war if the most hotly disputed questions were resolved in this manner.

To ensure that the discussion be as candid as possible, the participants agreed to bar the biased and vigilant "supervision" of the press. One can hardly say that everyone was totally candid—prejudices are still too strong, and the caution with which everyone is familiar is too deeply rooted. But the level of amicable trust and the relaxed atmosphere that were achieved at the meeting nonetheless make it possible to speak about a fundamentally new state both of political consciousness and of our new knowledge about the Caribbean crisis. Respecting the desire of the participants in this "sentimental journey" into the past to preserve relaxed thinking and complete freedom of self-expression, we have to remove the quotation marks from quoted statements and, in a number of cases, keep comments anonymous. We do so at least as far as this reflects the desire of the discussion's participants themselves, and until a verbatim report of the symposium is prepared for publication.

Genesis of the Crisis

There is no question that the roots of the crisis go back to a mutual lack of understanding and an erroneous interpretation of each other's intentions. No matter how often the Americans repeated, their hands on the Bible, that they had no intention of carrying out a mass invasion of Cuba, their actual deeds said just the opposite. What were these actions?

Primarily they were the events that took place on April 17 to 19, 1961, as a result of the landing of counterrevolutionary mercenaries near the town of Playa Jiron on the Bahia de los Cochinos (Bay of Pigs). The operation was carried out under cover provided by U.S. armed forces. Finally, certain Congressmen made open threats against Cuba.

Here we should stop and think—after all, all these points have served for a long time as the basis of Soviet justification for the deployment of Soviet missiles in Cuba. True, but the paradoxical nature of the current situation is that today an American participant in the events is listing these facts. And drawing the conclusion that if he had been the Cuban leader, he himself would have expected an American invasion.

So that is how time sets everything straight. But does it really take almost three decades to learn to put oneself in another's place? The essence of the situation, however, lies elsewhere: One would like very much to believe the Americans who were at the peak of the power pyramid in 1962 and who say that at that time the leaders of the United States had "no intention whatsoever" of attacking Cuba. (It is understood, of course, that there was a "gentleman's set" of operational plans drawn up by military men.) And if the people on the Potomac had somehow managed to indicate their lack of aggressive intentions, maybe history would have turned out differently. Or maybe not; the level of mutual suspicion and mistrust was so high.

As for the situation that developed around Cuba in the early 1960s, the list of manifestations of hostility toward the Cuban people's choice might also include the diplomatic isolation of Cuba on the continent, its exclusion from the Organization of American States, and the United States' establishment of an economic blockade. Cuba also adds to this list the continuing recruitment of soldiers of Cuban origin in the United States, naval maneuvers along the island's coast, and the practicing of landing operations (the Americans rehearsed such operations in Puerto Rico). We did not know where and when the invasion would be, stressed a member of the Cuban delegation, but we were absolutely sure that there would be one.

So, it would seem that there is already an answer to the question "why?" But this is only part of the explanation of why Soviet missiles appeared in Cuba.

Quite possibly, the missile crisis can be understood only in a strategic context. The United States had a great advantage over the Soviet Union in terms of nuclear weapons. According to the fairly well-known testimony of R. McNamara, which was heard once again at the symposium, the ratio was 17 to 1 (the United States had approximately 5,000 weapons, and the U.S.S.R. about 300). But for all this, as the former defense secretary claims, the Kennedy administration did not consider the possibility of a first nuclear strike. Fortunately, whether this is true is not of vital importance today. What is important is the admission by the Americans that the Soviet Union had grounds to believe (even though they were mistaken grounds—risk is unacceptable in such matters) that Washington was prepared to strike.

Our country's nuclear missile power was so negligible that we simply were not considered a factor. In any case, that is how the situation was perceived in Moscow, and that is the only way it could have been perceived. Hence, in my opinion, a desire to equalize the balance appeared perfectly obvious. And if in 1962 the balance of forces in terms of nuclear warheads was 17 to 1 in favor of the United States, one should recall that several years earlier it could have been described as "infinity to zero." Only in 1962, according to testimony from experts, did we acquire our first missiles that were capable of reaching U.S. territory.

Thus, it seems to me, the psychological underpinnings of the situation become clear: A sense of inferiority played a role, as did a temptation to let the United States feel the vulnerability of its territory, and to demonstrate the new Soviet capabilities (in other words, to use the expression attributed to Khrushchev himself, "let a hedgehog loose in the pants" of the Americans).

This was the aim with which R-12 missiles with a range of up to 2,000 kilometers were delivered to Cuba, and R-14 missiles with a range of over 4,000 kilometers were on the way. It is very important to emphasize that at the moment of the culmination of the crisis, when literally everything was hanging by a thread, *not a single missile had been fitted with a warhead.*

How did the idea of deploying Soviet missiles in Cuba first arise? There are three versions. According to the first one, Khrushchev first discussed the possibility of deploying missiles off the coast of America tête-à-tête with A.I. Mikoyan in late April or early May 1962.

According to another version, the idea arose in May or April during a stroll taken by Khrushchev, who was on vacation, and Marshal R. Ya. Malinovskiy, along the Crimean shore. The defense minister, pointing to the horizon, spoke at the time about the deployment of medium-range American missiles in Turkey. Did the idea of the missiles arise amid the sound of the breaking waves?

According to the book *Khrushchev Remembers*, which contains a wealth of information, the Soviet leader was preoccupied with the idea of attaining strategic parity with the United States. If one can trust the accuracy of these memoirs, the "Cuban option" arose during a visit to Bulgaria in May 1962, and Khrushchev shared his ideas with other Soviet leaders who appeared to hold similar views.[1]

Regardless of the details, it seems to me that all the versions come down to the fact that the idea emerged in April or May of 1962 and was initially considered within a narrow circle of people. According to one of the symposium's participants, among those with whom Khrushchev discussed the plan were A.I. Mikoyan and F.R. Kozlov, members of the Presidium of the CPSU Central Committee, as well as A.A.

---

[1]Nikita Khrushchev, *Khrushchev Remembers*, ed. and trans. by Strobe Talbott, Boston, 1970, Vol. I, p. 494.

Gromyko, R. Ya. Malinovskiy, and Marshal S.S. Biryuzov, who had only recently been appointed commander in chief of Strategic Rocket Forces. Somewhat later A.I. Alekseyev, who had been appointed Ambassador to Cuba, was also included in the discussion.

Evidently, the question was submitted to the Presidium of the Central Committee in the first half of May. After lengthy meetings in the Kremlin, as eyewitnesses report, many members of the Presidium would go to Khrushchev's home and, locking themselves behind closed doors, debate to the point of exhaustion.

From every indication, the decision to deploy missiles in Cuba was not arrived at easily. The circumstances were weighed and analyzed from various angles. The purpose of deploying the missiles was to deter aggression against Cuba, but, naturally, the Soviet leadership could not ignore the possibility of a change in the strategic situation.

Decision making by the Soviet leadership was usually a collective effort, but certain of Khrushchev's personal traits inevitably left their imprint on the discussion—in particular, a certain authoritarian manner and tendency to be peremptory in his opinions. As noted at the symposium, many members of the leadership preferred to keep any objections to themselves. Khrushchev knew how to insist on having his way, which had its pluses and minuses. If one judges the Caribbean crisis on the basis of its consequences, the minuses of this style showed themselves while the crisis was brewing, when the decision to secretly deploy "nonoffensive weapons" was made, and the pluses were evident at the point of the decisive withdrawal from the state of confrontation.

During the course of the debates on those days in May 1962, O.V. Kuusinen, after some hesitation, supported the plan. Later, other members of the Presidium also voiced their support. Judging from one of the accounts, A.I. Mikoyan expressed two reservations. He expressed doubt, first of all, that Castro would agree to accept the missiles, and second, that it would be possible to keep their deployment secret from the United States. Khrushchev then proposed sending S.S. Biryuzov to Cuba to clarify the situation.

The delegation, which was headed by Sh. R. Rashidov, candidate member of the Presidium of the CPSU Central Committee, and comprised mainly of agricultural specialists, arrived in Cuba. The inclusion in the delegation of the quiet "engineer Petrov" gave the whole situation the aura of a thriller. A.I. Alekseyev, who had been appointed Ambassador but had not yet had time to receive formal acceptance by the Cubans, asked Raul Castro to present the "engineer" to the Cuban leadership. Raul Castro understood everything, and Marshal S.S. Biryuzov was received.

Despite Mikoyan's fears, F. Castro, judging from eyewitness accounts, did not dismiss the idea of missile deployment out of hand, but instead received it favorably and promised to think it over.

After the Soviet proposal had been made, Castro brought together the six leaders who made up the Secretariat of the party Central Committee and outlined the situation. According to testimony by Cubans, the proposal received unanimous approval. It was immediately perceived as a way to change the balance of forces between socialism and capitalism. Returning to Moscow, Biryuzov supposedly informed Khrushchev not only of Havana's consent, but also that the missiles could be deployed secretly. But an opposite version was also presented at the symposium—in defense of the late S.S. Biryuzov's honor—that his report said nothing about secrecy. It was Khrushchev himself who was carried away with that idea.

The Cuban leadership proposed that the agreement that had been reached be widely announced. But during a visit to Moscow by Raul Castro in July 1962, the Soviet leader said no. Cuba did not insist, recognizing that the Soviet side was better informed and could therefore make a more carefully weighed decision.

The crisis was moving inexorably forward.

The Development and Culmination of the Crisis

The step-up in military activity in Cuba was noted both in speeches on Capitol Hill and in the American press. But on October 14, a U-2 reconnaissance plane took photographs of the missile bases in Cuba that opened the Americans' eyes to the true nature of what was happening. Until those photographs were obtained, the CIA had thought that "the Soviets were installing antiaircraft missiles with a range of 25 miles." On October 16 the photographic evidence was turned over to President Kennedy.

On October 18, 1962, the President received A.A. Gromyko in the Oval Office. During the discussion, after a number of barbed comments, the President offered assurances that the United States had no intention of invading Cuba. He stated outright that the landing at the Bay of Pigs had been a mistake. But the question of the Soviet missiles, apparently weighing on the minds of both men, never came up. Neither could bring himself to touch this sore spot. Why? After all, the photographs of the missile installations were in the President's desk drawer.

A.A. Gromyko explained at the symposium that Kennedy did not ask a direct question about the missiles, and that if the question had been raised, the President would have received a "proper answer."

We are dealing here with probably one of the most complicated psychological stratagems of the entire political situation at that time, which indicates what a long road has been travelled from distrust and total secrecy to the mutual inspections of military installations today.

As noted at the Moscow symposium, the fact of the deployment of Soviet missiles right next door to the United States elicited something like shock among certain members of the U.S. administration. As R. McNamara acknowledged, in attempting to estimate in 1961 what Soviet armed forces would be like in seven years (in 1968), American strategists focused on the "Soviets' capabilities," and not on their intentions. But it never occurred to anyone to analyze the chances that Soviet missiles would appear off the coast of America.

As we well know from the numerous accounts of the development of the crisis, the chronological chain of events took shape as follows. On October 22 President Kennedy spoke on radio, stunning Americans with a report on the presence of Soviet missiles in Cuba. American naval forces were given the order to establish a "quarantine" (the diplomatic euphemism for a blockade) around Cuba, so that no transport ships with offensive weapons could pass through. As Soviet sources confirm, the initial impulsive response to the blockade of Cuba's coastline was a decision to ignore it and lay the blame for any possible use of force on the United States. Soon, however, this decision, which was fraught with the potential for the most unpredictable consequences, was rescinded.

What was the main reason for the harsh White House reaction in the form of an ultimatum, which left so few options for diplomatic maneuvering? First and foremost, Americans claim, the extremely strong tradition of resisting any placement of non-American weapons in the Western Hemisphere, which goes back to the roots of national notions of security. They believe that public opinion in the country would never have accepted foreign missiles in Cuba.

Washington's tempestuous reaction to the Soviet missiles is also attributed to the fact that their deployment was carried out under cloak of the strictest secrecy. It is surprising, but it seemed to me that when McNamara, Bundy, Gen. Smith, and other Americans raised this delicate subject, in addition to the confident accusatory tone in their voices, one could also hear hints of bewilderment and confusion, such as one might hear from someone who has been insulted but does not know why. True, the American plans regarding the missiles deployed in Turkey and Italy were entirely open and public. The Soviet Union, however, had shipped and installed its missiles secretly and clandestinely. It was not a feeling of fear, but a sense of having been deceived, it seems, that did the most to "knock the Americans out of their saddle." At the symposium, the Americans came up with a highly original and at first glance paradoxical method for solving the secrecy problem: You could have brought the weapons in secretly, but informed Kennedy about it. There is only the appearance of a paradox here. Unfortunately, only familiarity with the norms of the new thinking shows that openness is beneficial, while secrecy and deception sometimes lead to unthinkable costs.

So why, then, the veil of secrecy over the missiles? A rational explanation that I heard from our side was that this action could not have been carried out openly at all, and the political benefits would have been lost. Another reason for the secrecy and silence was the specific nature of the domestic political situation in the United States: The country was on the threshold of off-year elections. Naturally, the Soviet leaders, as noted at the symposium, could not help but foresee that a negative reaction by the White House and Congress to the deployment of the missiles would be multiplied by the heat of preelection passions, and therefore they tried to drag out the "latent period" of the preparations. According to G.N. Bolshakov, a participant in the symposium who had been a staff member of the Soviet Embassy in Washington and editor in chief of the magazine *Soviet Life*, one of Khrushchev's oral messages to President Kennedy, transmitted on the eve of the crisis, stated that "the Soviet leaders well understand President Kennedy's position; they will not take any actions with respect to the United States before the 1962 Congressional elections, and hope that once the elections are over we will move toward a new round of active negotiations."

Thus, the secret was temporary and certainly could not have been kept for long. And anyway, no matter what the approach—secret or open—the Americans' reaction to the deployment of the missiles would have been essentially the same. All we can talk about is variations in the emotional coloring and the "temperature" of the reaction. Again, the Soviet leadership was certain that an invasion of Cuba was going to take place. And what awaited the Cubans, then, if the deterrent factor was absent, and an invasion began?

All this is true. In my opinion, however, the analysis of the Caribbean crisis conducted at the symposium from the vantage point of our current knowledge and experience indicates that the negative consequences of keeping the operation secret immeasurably outweighed the positive results obtained. I am sure that the attempt to keep the missiles' deployment secret was not only politically dangerous, but doomed to failure. Naturally, the Americans would certainly be put on guard by the increase in the number of transport ships crossing the ocean. Khrushchev and many others believed that the sharp increase in the number of transport convoys was the reason that the secret plan had been discovered. But I do not think that was the main reason. According to the information of the American scholar R. Garthoff, at the time the "quarantine" was imposed, 16 Soviet ships were on their way to Cuba, and only seven of them carried missile components and equipment for their installation. From every indication, what attracted the attention of American intelligence, was primarily the construction work that was under way on the island.

Granted, despite all its sophisticated intelligence-gathering equipment, Washington seriously underestimated the size of the Soviet presence in Cuba. According to an official estimate by American intelligence, the number of Soviet military personnel there grew from 4,500 as of October 3, to 8,000-10,000 as of October 22, and to 12,000-16,000 as of November 19, 1962. According to retrospective estimates made in early 1963, at the culmination of the crisis, there were 22,000 Soviet military personnel in Cuba. These figures are surprisingly far from the actual numbers. At the time there were 40,000-42,000 Soviet soldiers and officers on the island.

How could such a huge mistake be made in the estimates? This was partly explained by the answer to a question asked at the symposium by the Americans, who wondered what sort of "skirmish" had occurred between Soviet and Cuban troops at the most heated moment of the crisis. American intelligence reported on October 27 that in the area where the Soviet installations were being placed, a concentration of Cuban troops and some sort of disarray, which was interpreted as a clash, had been observed. In fact, as one of the Soviet participants in the meeting related, through the fault of two soldiers, a compartment of an ammunition warehouse had exploded. Troops had to be brought up immediately to deal with the consequences of the explosion. Some of the Soviet soldiers were dressed in Cuban uniforms. Naturally, there were no skirmishes. But the story of this incident explains, to a significant extent, why the Americans erred in estimating the size of the Soviet contingent.

Miscalculations, incorrect estimates, and erroneous interpretations of the intentions of the parties involved, multiplied by the factors of fear and a shortage of time, led to a situation in which the crisis took on irrational characteristics and threatened to get entirely out of control. Despite the fact that daily contacts and consultations between the sides reached the highest level on Friday, October 26, it is generally agreed that on Saturday the crisis peaked. A report reached Washington that the tanker Groznyy was moving toward the blockade line. And that report was followed by even more threatening news: a U-2 reconnaissance plane had been shot down over Cuba.

How did this happen? (Here, by the way, is an interesting detail: the Soviet ambassador to Cuba at that time only found out the details of the incident 15 years later.) According to participants in the events,

Fidel Castro gave the order to shoot down without warning all military planes appearing over the island's territory. The order was clearly meant to refer to low-flying aircraft; moreover, it could not apply to Soviet units, of course. Nevertheless, the appearance of a U-2 plane in the sky caught our command by surprise. It was flying along, and in two minutes it would be within range—should it be shot down or not? The telephone did not help solve the problem; General I. Pliyev could not be reached at the critical moment, and a decision had to be made with lightning speed. Two missiles were launched. The first missile downed the plane. On the morning of October 28 a telegram arrived from Marshal Malinovskiy. The essence of it was that the plane had been shot down in haste, and that a peaceful solution would have been possible. It is also known that Khrushchev was upset by the incident and considered it a mistake.

Why was so much attention given to this episode in the debates and discussions? First, it was possibly one of the most dangerous moments of the crisis. And secondly, many conjectures and myths have grown up around the incident. In particular, there was a widespread belief that the plane had been shot down by the Cubans. This version went on to acquire utterly grotesque features. Assertions that "Fidel himself had pushed the button" appeared and were quoted repeatedly by the press. Although the Cuban leader does know how to handle weapons fairly well, he physically had no opportunity to do so. According to testimony by Cuban participants in the events, he was in Havana, while the plane was shot down in the eastern part of the country. In general, this version is unfounded because the Cubans had no missiles of this sort. On the other hand, according to unanimous reports, Fidel Castro's reaction was positive.

Some of the Americans' comments about their state of mind at the moment of the crisis's culmination portray a disturbing escalation of emotions. The general mood was that war was about to break out.

The rumor that documents were being burned at the Soviet Embassy in the United States fanned the flames. Did that really happen? A.F. Dobrynin authoritatively denied it: No, there was no burning of documents. But preparations were made for the unexpected, working meetings were held, and precautionary measures were discussed.

On the whole, naturally, neither side expected that nuclear war would be started through a premeditated action. But, in the first place, it was absolutely unclear where an escalation of the crisis could lead. Furthermore, it was impossible to rule out an accident (according to the "principle," as one of discussion's participants put it, that "there's always some idiot who hasn't been warned"). The acute sense of alarm in Moscow stemmed from the expectation that the United States could invade Cuba within hours. This was confirmed both by information from Havana and intelligence data. Indeed, as it became known much later, on the morning of October 27 the President gave instructions to prepare for a possible strike against Cuba by October 30 in the event that diplomatic efforts failed.[2]

As a former member of the top echelon of the American command said at the symposium, preparations at the time were being made along two lines. First, combat aircraft were being massed for a possible bombing of the Soviet missile launching sites, that is, preparations were being made for a sort of preemptive strike. Second, a number of units of the U.S. Army were being deployed to the south, that is, the possibility was being entertained of an invasion by several divisions with air support. Naturally, there were debates in the military establishment involving "hawks" and "doves" over which option to choose. There was even a suggestion that an invasion force be given tactical nuclear weapons. (Fitting the Honest John with warheads was out of the question, McNamara said, stressing that he never would have agreed to that.)

And just what was happening in Cuba at the moment of the culmination of events? According to comrades in arms of Fidel Castro, stepped-up preparations were made for repulsing an attack, 270,000 men were mobilized, positions were taken up, and the terrain was prepared—Cuba was ready to resist "not for three days and not for three months, but to the last soldier." Possible losses might be on the order of 100,000 men. Members of the Cuban delegation stressed that Soviet soldiers were also prepared to die with weapons in their hands. After the decision to remove the missiles was announced, they said, Soviet and Cuban soldiers embraced each other and wept.

As already noted, the rapid rise in the urgency of the crisis coincided with the peak in the sides' efforts to settle it. Three types of communication were employed. First, there were telegrams signed by Kennedy and Khrushchev (they were duplicated through both embassies); second, there were unsigned messages that were transmitted orally; and third, there were various sorts of commentaries. Today the antediluvian method that was used by our Embassy to communicate with Moscow at that time draws a bitter smile: When a coded cable was ready, a phone call would be made to Western Union, a messenger on a bicycle would arrive, and he would be handed a package that nearly tipped him over as he rode back to the telegraph office. All in all, it was a strain on the nerves. One cannot help recalling in this connection that eight months before the crisis a suggestion had been made to set up a "hot line"!

---

[2]See R. L. Garthoff, "Cuban Missile Crisis: the Soviet Story" (*Foreign Policy*, Fall 1988, p. 76).

Personal contacts between the Soviet ambassador and Robert Kennedy played an important positive role. Confidential oral messages were conveyed through this channel. Starting on October 23 such meetings were held practically every day—both at the embassy and in Kennedy's office in the Justice Department. They sometimes lasted until 1 or 2 a.m., and morning meetings were also held. Personal contacts between embassy staff and American political figures and journalists were used simultaneously.

On October 26 a message from Khrushchev addressed to the president was received in Washington. It arrived in parts between 6 and 9 p.m. It said that he would agree to remove the missiles in Cuba in exchange for a guaranteed pledge by the United States to abandon any plans for invading Cuba in the future. The Americans reported that everyone in the White House heaved a sigh of relief, realizing that a basis had been found for extricating themselves from the quagmire of the crisis. But on the morning of Saturday, October 27, when a positive response to Moscow was being drafted, a second "letter from Khrushchev" was received, in which the question of American missiles deployed in Turkey was raised. There was a striking difference in tone between the two messages: The first was emotional and agitated, while the second was carefully weighed and firmer in tone.

According to assertions by American participants in the events of October 1962, the demand to include the question of removing the "Turkish missiles" in the package of conditions for settling the crisis put the White House in an awkward position. As noted at the symposium, the U.S. administration believed that the missiles in Turkey (and Italy) represented a source of crises, and in any case had been planning to remove them. However, the president did not believe that he could decide this matter alone, without consulting U.S. allies. Therefore, a promise was made (through Robert Kennedy) to remove the missiles from Turkey over the course of several months after the crisis had been settled, but to do so outside the official package of accords. Evidently, this solution satisfied both sides. The problem of the "Turkish missiles" did not become a stumbling block, and it was not even a central issue in the settlement. An American participant in the crisis stated outright that this issue had been resolved separately, and not as part of the negotiations on the Cuban crisis. However, the tactical linkage of the questions involving missiles in Cuba and in Turkey subsequently gave rise to speculation that the Soviet Union had deployed its missiles close to the United States in order to "exchange" them later for American missiles. As we see, such speculation is groundless.

Why was it that Cuba did not participate in the blitz-negotiations to reach a settlement? Today, sitting back in comfortable armchairs, we can take our time weighing and comparing the facts. At that time, however, when both Havana and Moscow expected a possible invasion in a matter of hours, all that was needed was rapid and unambiguous steps in the direction of a resolution ("escape the crisis!"). The White House, for its part, ruled out the possibility of direct negotiations with Havana, since the "missiles were controlled by the Soviets, and not the Cubans." As one American participant in the events explained, the United States conducted the negotiations without its allies, and it expected the same from Moscow.

But from every indication, the Cubans still feel a lingering bitterness over the fact that they were not invited to take part in the settlement. Granted, Cuba could have gained the opportunity to have its demands met more fully—for example, to have U.S. military cutters removed from Puerto Rico, to have the U.S. economic blockade lifted, and to have Guantanamo returned. This probably could have happened if all the parties involved in the conflict had had time on their side. But unfortunately, they did not.

On that "black Saturday" of October 27, no one in Washington or Moscow knew how subsequent events might develop. While the White House was awaiting a response from Khrushchev, preparations were continuing for a strike against Cuba. And during those tortuous hours of waiting, Kennedy, the American sources say, had still not decided whether to start an invasion if Moscow refused to accept the American compromise. It only became known fairly recently that the President was considering the possibility of a further concession on the issue of missiles in Turkey in the course of diplomatic negotiations.[3]

Khrushchev's response was made public literally a few hours later, together with an announcement of the order to dismantle the launching sites in Cuba. The peace had been preserved. The Caribbean crisis was over, and an escalation into armed conflict had been avoided.

Lessons From the Crisis

All the stages of the Caribbean crisis—its origin, development, culmination and resolution—are extremely instructive from the perspective of the present day. In his message to the symposium's participants, M.S. Gorbachev noted that "studying the mechanisms whereby crisis situations of this sort emerge, as well as the ways to resolve them politically and diplomatically, has not lost its relevance, particularly in a situation in which the new political thinking is receiving an increasingly broad response and practical application in world

---

[3]*Ibid.*, pp. 72-73.

affairs." In a certain sense, the new thinking itself is the product of the search for a system of relations among states that would prevent the development of crisis situations.

To draw real lessons from the Caribbean crisis, one must understand first and foremost how close humanity came then to the nuclear abyss.

The symposium's participants differed in their views of how realistic the possibility of a nuclear disaster had been. Even among the Soviet delegation there was a whole spectrum of assessments—from a complete denial of the risk of nuclear war to a categorical admission that the world had stood on the brink of such a conflict.

As noted during the discussion, at that time Khrushchev was engaged in bluffing: He said, "We are cranking out missiles like sausages." The enormously powerful nuclear test explosion at Novaya Zemlya was one of a series of such actions carried out for effect. Carried away with the opportunities that had opened up, the country—possibly against its will—was being drawn into the vicious circle of the power game, noted Academician G.A. Arbatov.

One should remember that the level of political analysis was very low at that time. Few people realized how high the stakes were in that game. How would events have turned out if a Soviet missile had destroyed a ship, rather than shooting down a reconnaissance plane? And what if the tragedy that befell President Kennedy had occurred a year earlier? If Khrushchev had retired for his "well-deserved rest" in October 1962 rather than in October 1964? There are so many "ifs" that could be added to this list. The essence of this view is that: "We must not stop a step short of catastrophe, but run as far away from it as possible."

Another opinion is that it is inappropriate to ask the question of whether it was right or wrong to deploy the missiles. It is unlikely that there is anyone capable of answering this question, as in most cases involving predictions about the past. If the United States was known not to be harboring any plan to invade Cuba, then the deployment of the missiles could definitely be classified as a mistake. But who at that time was able to interpret unequivocally the intentions of the other side? That's the first point.

The second point is that actions are always judged by their results. The resolution of the Caribbean crisis was accompanied, on the whole, by positive results. I will sum them up as simply as possible: After withdrawal of the Soviet missiles, Cuba received a guarantee of security, and American nuclear missiles were removed from Turkey. But I do not think that is even the main point. As noted at the symposium, there is every reason to believe that if the Caribbean crisis had not occurred, the danger of nuclear war in the subsequent period would have been greater. Thus, the Caribbean crisis can be perceived as a sort of vaccination, an inoculation against nuclear confrontation. The stern warning is still having an effect to this day.

The majority of participants in the discussion, it seems, approved of the figurative comparison to a vaccination. But they suggested another, equally metaphorical comparison: Does it make sense to perform the inoculation using a dirty needle with the risk of AIDS infection?

The conclusion is still unambiguous: Playing with fire is unquestionably a dangerous business, and it would have been better for everyone if the crisis had not become so acute and assumed such threatening dimensions. But, as the discussion's participants noted, in 1962 nuclear conflict did not threaten the existence of humanity. A different situation developed in the 1970s and 1980s, when whole palisades of nuclear missiles appeared on the planet. Therefore, there are grounds for the claims that the Caribbean crisis taught us caution and prudence in dealing with such a delicate political reality as the balance of interests.

Even right after the Caribbean crisis, however, when the shock from the danger had not yet worn off, not all American political figures realized that humanity found itself in a new situation. Most Americans, unquestionably, felt a huge sense of relief and hailed the wisdom of both powers' leaders. There was a group of critics on the left (they were given the name "revisionist historians") who asserted that the president should bear responsibility for the crisis and for the risk to which the nation had been subjected. They accused Kennedy of not having worked actively enough to seek a political solution. A group of critics on the right, consisting mainly of figures from the previous administration, called the Soviet-American accords a "sell-out," heaping anger on Kennedy for not having permitted an invasion of Cuba. These "hawks" were opposed to a peaceful settlement then, and they have still not reconciled themselves to the existence of a socialist Cuba today. Although there have not been any situations since 1962 that reached such a critical point, the blackmail by force to which Washington has resorted over the past quarter-century, the aggression against Grenada, provocations against Libya, confrontational actions in the Middle East, and many other examples confirm that there is no guarantee against a repetition of the 1962 situation.

The Soviet Union has also traveled a difficult path toward recognizing the mechanisms of political equilibrium in the nuclear missile age. The excessive ideological baggage that burdened international relations, and the less than tactful handling of the subtle mechanics of regional politics, which resulted, for example, in the ill-considered decision to opt for military force in dealing with the complex Afghan situation—these are evidence of an insufficiently responsible understanding of the interconnected nature of regional and global stability. That is evidently why it is so important now to sum up the lessons of the events of 1962, which serve today as a canonical example—yet one that has been far from thoroughly studied—of the rapid escalation of a regional crisis into a global one.

The main lessons of the Caribbean crisis, interpreted from the standpoint of the present world situation, were formulated by Academician Ye. M. Primakov, who chaired the discussion of this topic. In thesis form, they can be reduced to the following six points:

• given today's existing level of arms, states should not count on achieving military superiority;

• political pressure and the display of force cannot be viewed as methods by which states can achieve their goals;

• the desire to gain "a monopoly on action," in other words, denial of the other side's right to make an appropriate response is fraught today with potentially dangerous consequences for the world;

• an attempt to view regional situations through the prism of global confrontation not only destabilizes the world situation, but also rules out the possibility of settling regional conflicts;

• relations between states must be de-ideologized, since ideological or political hostility that becomes a dominant factor in such relations turns into a threat to peace; and

• the danger of confrontation grows significantly in the absence of normal contacts between countries and peoples.

On the whole, the quintessence of these conclusions is this: A reliable guarantee of security can be provided today only through political means, and by rejecting reliance on methods based on military force.

A considerable part of the discussion was taken up by the analysis of many more specific lessons. They included, for example, the role of chance, of the incorrect interpretation of the other side's intentions, of disinformation, and of irrational factors that cannot be evaluated and analyzed properly when there is a severe shortage of time as a crisis escalates. As an example, one can mention the notorious O. Penkovsky, who is frequently called possibly the most successful Western secret agent working in the Soviet Union.[4] The information he handed over to the West was considered extremely valuable there in analyzing the data supplied in photographs of Soviet missile installations. Nevertheless, in the opinion of McGeorge Bundy, "the Penkovsky factor" did not play any appreciable, much less strategic, role in the Caribbean

---

[4]Ch. E. Bohlen, *Witness to History (1929-1969)*, New York, 1973, p. 489.

crisis. But one detail does give one food for thought: Just before his arrest he managed to transmit a visual signal from his apartment. However, as the American political scientist R. Garthoff reported at the symposium, Penkovsky got mixed up and, instead of sending a signal indicating his exposure, in his panic he gave a signal indicating that the Soviet Union was ready to attack the United States. Fortunately, the Americans regarded that signal as false, and it was not even reported to the director of the CIA. But we have here a fateful role for humanity, and it forces one to reflect on the possibility of a tragic chain of chance or coincidence. Just imagine a convergence of circumstances in which the exposure and arrest of Penkovsky had coincided with the culmination of the crisis. The interpretation of the signal could have turned out to be quite different.

An analysis of the Caribbean crisis also leads one to reflect on the personal traits of political leaders. In the opinion of a number of the discussion's participants, Khrushchev and Kennedy played unique roles in resolving the crisis. How would the crisis have ended, if there had been individuals in their places who were inclined to reflection and were less decisive? Or just the opposite—"decisive" enough to be capable of impulsive actions that went beyond the limits of prudence and responsibility? Over the many centuries of the history of conflicts, those politicians who were most apt in getting into crises and who emerged from them with the maximum benefits for their own countries have always received the highest marks. In this connection, the idea suggested by one of the symposium's Soviet participants, Professor A.O. Chubaryan, is of special interest: Considering the imperatives of the nuclear-missile age, we should study first the experience of those leaders who have been most skillful in avoiding crises.

Assessing the lessons of 1962, O.N. Bykov spoke of the importance of regular personal contacts between the powers' leaders. In his opinion it is significant that the leaders of the U.S.S.R. and the United States, who sent the symposium their greetings, spoke by telephone a few days before the meeting opened. As we know, there was a telephone line between the U.S.S.R. and the United States in 1962, but the Cold War atmosphere and the lack of a tradition of regular contact ruled out the possibility of resorting to direct conversation in a crisis situation, which forced the sides to use traditional diplomatic channels.

In times of crisis, A.K. Kislov noted, sometimes what is important is not even so much the sides' intentions as the correct interpretation of those intentions. To achieve this we need to expand our communication and mutual contacts.

Communication should not be developed only between the great powers. Peace on the planet is important not just to them, but to small countries as well, G. Kh. Shakhnazarov stressed during the discussion.

The great powers now understand that for small countries so-called "low-intensity conflicts" are in essence high-intensity conflicts. He also reminded those present that any violation of the sovereign rights and interests of small countries can lead to sad consequences for all.

Izvestia political commentator S.N. Kondrashov directed the symposium participants' attention to the need for broader glasnost and openness in politics. Analyzing the lessons of the Caribbean crisis, one is struck by the fact that the Soviet people did not become frightened over the development of events until after the crisis had ended—after the fact. The tradition of keeping secrets from one's own people even after others have revealed them is not only immoral, but harmful.

V.G. Komplektov spoke about the political costs of maintaining secrecy in a certain category of military matters. Attempts to secretly achieve some sort of advantage over the opposing side are often fraught with complications. We are familiar with the proposition that the opposing side is supposed to know both about the existence of weapons and about how they can be used.

I would also like to say something about one personal impression. In the discussions among the three delegations at the round table, in the conversations and emotional responses, an informal feeling emerged of having lived through something together. Questions such as "what did you think then"; "when did you find out"; and "how did things seem to you at the time" made it possible to understand the overt and hidden motives and the psychological backdrop against which decisions were made then, and to destroy, step by step, the barriers of misunderstanding that had endured for decades. I think that when a feeling of having survived something together emerges, when one becomes able to put oneself in the other person's position, there is no place for the "image of the enemy," or for the excruciating, blind sensation of fear in the face of disaster.

Do the results of the symposium mean that we can close the book on the history of the Caribbean crisis? Obviously not. This can be done only when all the secret materials from that period are published and analyzed. The next step should be taken at the next symposium, which is being planned to be held in Cuba.

Part Three

The U.S.S.R. in the World Economy

Introduction

In the very first years of perestroika the Soviet political leaders set out to integrate the country into the system of modern world economy. Setting such a goal might have seemed as natural to the uninitiated as it seemed unexpected to the expert in Soviet economic theory and practice. It was unexpected because it contradicted the entire system of established ideology which viewed the world as divided into two incompatible and hostile camps.

Granted, it was in keeping with world experience and common sense. But such arguments could not be taken seriously, and they only exposed the "political immaturity" of the person who presented them. The only guiding logic that was permissible was the logic of the self-development of "real socialism." Therefore, for many people the idea of integrating with the "imperialists" may have seemed incomprehensible and even blasphemous. On the other hand, for those who believed in the rebirth of common sense, it evoked an aching sense of hope that perestroika was really serious.

Now, from the perspective of 1990, many of the realities of three to five years ago seem remote and implausible. A number of radical changes have occurred in the minds of both scholars and the public at large. At present in books on the Western countries, the terms "imperialism" and "general crisis of capitalism" are increasingly rare. Convergence has turned from a pejorative word into the subject of constructive discussions. The extremely popular MacDonald's restaurant on Pushkin Square serves as a constant, hourly advertisement for joint ventures and foreign capital investment in the country.

Thus, difficulties caused by ideology are gradually being overcome at both the top and the foundation of Soviet society. However, that has proved to be only the beginning of our return to the world. Overcoming the deformations of the country's economic system, creating effective incentives for productive labor, and reforming the foreign economic activity have proved to be a much more difficult matter.

Here the serious problems still outnumber the real accomplishments. Should we endeavor to increase the Soviet share of world trade, if the bulk of exports consists of fuel and raw materials, while the bulk of imports consists of grain, food products, and inefficiently used equipment? Should we take out external loans to solve internal problems, or first solve the problems, and only then take out loans? Will participation in international economic organizations result in encroachments on Soviet sovereignty, and if not, when and how should we attempt to join them?

These are just a few of the highly practical questions that the authors of the articles in the final section examine. The articles were written for the Soviet reader brought up on textbooks in Marxist political economy and relatively unfamiliar with world economic practice. Therefore, in some cases you may encounter the exposition of elementary truths. Skip them. But nearby there will be information about certain aspects of Soviet economic life, and recommendations for practical actions. That may prove interesting. The articles that are included contain a great deal of criticism of our previous development, and they are suffused with pain and anxiety for the country's fate. "Airing one's dirty linen" is not in the tradition of the Russian people. But glasnost is glasnost, and there cannot be one truth for internal consumption and another for export.

Valery A. Slavinsky

Perestroika and the Soviet Economy's Need for External Financing

Vladimir Viktorovich Popov*

Expanded borrowing on the international credit market to finance urgent economic needs that have evolved in the course of perestroika has resolute proponents and equally resolute opponents. Some economists, such as N. Shmelev, believe that external loans should be used to increase imports of common consumer goods in order to relieve the threatening growth of tension on the consumer-goods market.[1] Others, such as S. Shatalin, hold that foreign credits should be used to import equipment for the production of common consumer goods—in which case it would be easier to pay off the creditors.[2]

The opponents of expanded foreign borrowing point out that it is dangerous to live on loans, that the U.S.S.R.'s international indebtedness is already great, and that increasing it further could create a creditworthiness crisis. Therefore, they say, efforts to expand the supply of consumer goods should rely not on increasing imports on credit but on changing the structure of national income (increasing consumption at the expense of investment) and the mix of imports (expanding imports of consumer goods at the expense of producer goods). It is interesting that those who oppose increased borrowing abroad include both promarket economists who are proponents of radical economic reform, such as L. Abalkin, A. Aganbegyan, O. Lacis,[3] and their critics, such as M. Antonov, R. Kosolapov.[4]

In fact, the government itself was until recently against seeking major new credits abroad. Its program for restoring economic soundness is still based on plans for structuring domestic resources—reducing both military expenditures and investment in the construction of production facilities, in favor of increased spending on consumption.

*Doctor of economics, senior research associate at the U.S.S.R. Academy of Sciences' Institute for the United States and Canada. This article appeared in the March 1990 issue of *MEMO* and was updated for this collection.
    [1]See *Izvestia*, June 9, 1989.
    [2]See *Pravda*, May 4, 1989.
    [3]See *Moskovskiye novosti* [*Moscow News*], No. 6, 1989, p. 12; and *Izvestia*, Aug. 1 and May 10, 1989.
    [4]See *Nash Sovremennik* [*Our Contemporary*], No. 8, 1989, pp. 71–110; and *Ekonomicheskiye nauki* [*Economics*], No. 8, 1989, pp. 69-79.

The very same differences on the issue of financing Soviet economic expansion from external sources can be found among Western specialists, as well. A great many economists favor the large-scale use of credits (J. Vanous, P. Desai, W. Leontieff, E. Hewett). Others, on the contrary, are not in sympathy with that idea—granted, for reasons different from those of our economists. In particular, both the economists and the politicians express concern that the extension of Western credit to the U.S.S.R. would weaken incentives for internal restructuring and would enable Soviet leadership to postpone radical economic reform and, possibly, the planned reduction in defense spending.[5]

It is also maintained that an influx of foreign capital into the U.S.S.R. could weaken and render ineffective the financial limitations that are currently so necessary for Soviet enterprises and for the Soviet government, and that the importation of consumer goods financed by an influx of capital could confront Soviet producers with fierce competition, which apart from its other effects, could undermine the position of potential Soviet exporters.[6]

In short, the issue of expanding external indebtedness is one that attracts universal attention, and it would not be an exaggeration to say that the scope and intensity of the controversy over this matter reflect the importance and urgency of the problem.

So, do we need major new loans abroad or not? Before giving a definite answer, let us attempt an approximate assessment of our economy's need for capital investment and expenditures on other urgent needs connected with perestroika.

How Much Investment Do We Need?

Compared to other countries, the U.S.S.R. invests a great deal. In the United States, for example, the share of net investments (total investments less depreciation) amounted to approximately 6 to 7 percent of national income in the 1980s. The corresponding Soviet indicator—the accumulation fund as a share of national income (25 percent)—is not entirely comparable to the American figure, since national income in the U.S.S.R. is calculated without the service sector. However, even calculating Soviet national income by the Western method, the share of accumulation in National income is still excessively high—about 20 percent, as against 6 to 7 percent in the United States.

---

[5]See *The New York Times*, July 31, 1989.
[6]See R.I. McKinnon, *The Order of Liberalization for Opening the Soviet Economy*, Stanford University, 1989.

The indicators for rates of investment/GNP ratio in our country also differ from those in other countries. From 1980 to 1985 the ratio of gross investments to gross domestic product averaged 15 percent in the United States; 18 to 21 percent in Great Britain, the Federal Republic of Germany, and France; and 30 percent in Japan, while in the second half of the 1980s it was over 30 percent in the U.S.S.R. On the other hand, when housing construction is taken out of gross investment, the ratio to gross domestic product was 11 percent in the United States, 14 to 16 percent in the major West European countries, 25 percent in Japan, and over 25 percent in the U.S.S.R.[7]

In addition, some Soviet economists believe that defects in official statistics (for example, the counting of the turnover tax, the artificially low prices for raw materials and other materials, and the artificially high prices for finished goods) cause the understatement of gross and net investments. The real ratio of the accumulation fund to overall national income, they point out, is on the order of 40 percent—in other words, approximately 30 percent when calculated by the Western method.[8]

It is also worth noting that CIA statistics yield similar results. At present, incidentally, they offer the only such evaluation of the dynamics of postwar Soviet GNP by individual components. According to the CIA data, the rate of accumulation in the 1970s and 1980s generally exceeded 30 percent.[9]

Calculating the share of personal and social consumption in national income, and assessing the extent of accumulation as a remainder yields similar results. Indeed, the sum of basic monetary incomes (wages and salaries, collective farmers' incomes, stipends and other transfer payments) amounted in 1987, after adjustments,[10] to about 400 billion rubles, in other words, about half the national income, as calculated by the Western method.[11]

In other words, if military expenditures amounted to 77 billion rubles, as was recently announced,[12] or about 10 percent of the national income originating in all branches of the economy, including the service sector, then net investments possibly swallow as much as

[7]*Argumenty i Fakty* [*Arguments and Facts*], No. 13, 1990.

[8]See V. Selyunin, "Growth Rates on the Scales of Consumption," *Sotsialisticheskaya industriya* [*Socialist Industry*], Jan. 5, 1988.

[9]See *U.S.S.R.: Measures of Ecnomic Growth and Development, 1950-80*, Washington, 1982, pp. 76-78; *Gorbachev's Economic Plans*, Vol. I, Washington, 1987. p. 16; and *The Soviet Economy in 1988: Gorbachev Changes Course*, 1989, pp. 38-40.

[10]Net of taxes, increases in savings-account deposits, and the value of government bonds sold to the public; plus nonmonetary benefits from social consumption funds (cost-free education and health care, state subsidies for the maintenance of housing stock); plus government subsidies on consumer goods, net of turnover taxes on those same goods.

[11]See *Moskovskiye novosti*, No. 34, 1988, p. 12.

[12]See *Pravda*, June 11, 1989.

40 percent of national income. Many economists believe, however, that real defense expenditures come to about 20 percent of national income (this accords with the CIA estimate of 15 to 17 percent of GNP), while about 30 percent goes for investments.

One way or another, it turns out that our expenditures on investment account for a very large share of national income and GNP—at least as large as that of Japan, and possibly even larger. But the effectiveness of these investments—their return as measured by the rate of growth of real consumption—is significantly lower than in other Western countries.

Why is the share of investments so high, and why do we spend just slightly more than 50 kopeks out of every ruble of national income on consumption, when that ratio is much higher in other countries (85:100 in the United States, for example)? The short answer to that question is the extremely ineffective and wasteful system of all-encompassing directive planning that still prevails in our economy. With absolute inevitability, this system gives rise to a multitude of disproportions, since it is simply a literal impossibility to foresee, take into account, and plan everything from above—to balance, in a planned fashion, the supply and demand for millions of different articles in such a way that the needed products are produced and delivered to the needed place at the right time.

Because of this desire to embrace the unembraceable, to regulate the living economic organism down to the last little nut or bolt, and to force it into the Procrustean bed of rigid plan prescriptions, the use of production capacity is extremely low, since there is first a "shortage" of raw materials, then of fuel, then of manpower, and then of needed equipment. According to official statistics, our industrial sector operates at close to 90 percent of capacity, but alternative evaluations put the indicator significantly lower—we would be doing well if we operated at least at 70 percent of capacity, on average.

There are also immense losses in the form of excessive inventories of goods and materials. The system of rationed supply is able to provide more or less on-time deliveries to ensure uninterrupted production only if inventories of raw materials and supplies are maintained at levels several times higher with respect to output volume than in a market economy. Thus, in 1985 the ratio of inventories to monthly sales volumes was 2.4:1 in Soviet industry, and 3.6:1 in the trade network, while in the United States the comparable figures have never exceeded 1.9:1 and 1.7:1, even during the deepest recessions, which are accompanied by a rapid buildup of inventories. In the first half of the 1980s, investments in inventories of materials, supplies, and finished goods amounted to 6 percent of national income in the U.S.S.R., and less than 1 percent in the United States.[13]

---

[13]See N. Schmelev and V. Popov, *The Turning Point: Revitalizing the Soviet Economy*, New York, Doubleday, 1989, pp. 128-154, 183-184.

The fact that our economy's accumulation fund is bloated beyond all normal limits attests, of course, to the economic mechanism's extremely low efficiency. Despite the phrase, repeatedly voiced by highly placed speakers, that "we live no worse than we work," the excessively high share of investments attests precisely to the fact that we do live considerably worse than we work, that we are unable to make sensible use even of what we do produce, that we still have an economy that works primarily for itself and not for the consumer, and finally, that our economic mechanism (as G. Popov put it at the Congress of Peoples' Deputies) is like an automobile that burns gas but does not go anywhere.[14] This view is also confirmed by the fact that comparisons to other countries in terms of output and productivity are invariably more favorable to us than are comparisons in terms of consumption levels.

At the same time, the excessive investments, which today consume the lion's share of national income, can and must be regarded not only as losses attesting to the depressing inefficiency of the existing economic mechanism, but also as an immense reserve—an untapped potential lying literally on the surface—for increasing real incomes and real economic growth rates. If we succeed in shifting our economy to a market track and in cutting our losses, accordingly, to the level of average market economy, we will be able to increase our consumption fund by almost half without any additional investment—with the same fixed assets, and the same technology and work force that we now have. How? Simply by reorganizing, reallocating resources, cutting losses, making more efficient use of what we do create.

In other words, if economic restructuring is crowned with success, we will not need the immense accumulation fund that we now have, since it will be possible to achieve the same results, the same and even higher levels and rates of growth in real consumption, with smaller capital investment. This does not mean that the need for financial resources will decline with the progress of restructuring, however, since there is an acute need to expand capital expenditure and current expenditure in various areas of the economy.

Where Money Needs to Be Invested

The need to increase capital investment and current expenditure in the course of economic restructuring is primarily related to the need to eliminate the government budget deficit, expand expenditures in the social security system and retrain workers, increase outlays for

---

[14]See *Izvestia*, June 11, 1989.

education and health care, and finance additional investments to replace obsolete equipment being completely worn out in a number of industries and at various production facilities.

Reducing the government budget deficit. The emerging market on which so many hopes are pinned will not, of course, be able to function normally with the present, profoundly disturbed state of money circulation—caused by an undue expansion of the money supply, i.e., use of printing presses to cover the government budget deficit.

The deficit in the U.S.S.R. government budget grew from an average of 20 billion rubles a year in the first half of the 1980s to 120 billion in 1988—in other words, to 14 percent of GNP. For the sake of comparison, the budget deficit in the United States does not presently exceed 3 percent of GNP, while in the OECD countries the deficit averaged 3 to 4 percent in the 1980s. The situation is aggravated by the fact that our deficit is primarily covered not by borrowing from enterprises and the public (this does not lead to an increase in the money supply and therefore does not fuel inflation), but by borrowing from the State Bank, i.e., by putting new money into circulation.

As a result, the gap between ruble demand and market supply is constantly growing, and price increases do not bridge the gap completely. Devaluation of the ruble is actually occurring in two ways: "classical" inflation expressed in price increases (at a rate that is, of course, greater than the 1 to 2 percent indicated in official statistics, but still not that great—approximately 5 to 6 percent in 1989); and growing shortages, in other words, the gap between supply and demand that is not bridged by price increases.

The overall devaluation of the ruble, that is, the drop in its purchasing power caused by inflation and growing shortages, has now probably reached 10 to 15 percent, which is a critical threshold. When a monetary unit begins to lose value at a rate above that level, a cumulative process starts—the money now begins to lose additional purchasing power because the public is willing to get rid of the devaluating bank notes; money begins circulating at a faster rate, causing it to lose value even further, and so forth.

Under these conditions, monetary circulation is thrown into a state of disorder, and the government truly loses control of the economic situation—economic levers such as prices, taxes, normative rates, interest rates, and so forth, simply stop working, since monetary income that does not confer the right to buy the things a person wants has no meaning. The idea of regulating economic life through economic incentives is discredited, and pressures are generated for a return to tough-plan discipline, to strict methods of supply by allocation, and the like. In short, to keep the idea of a market economy from dying on the vine, it is absolutely essential to restore stable monetary circulation.

The plan for 1990 calls for cutting the deficit to 60 billion rubles, compared to 92 billion in 1989, and the amount of cash put into circulation is to be reduced to 10 billion rubles, compared to 18 billion in 1989.[15] These are steps in the right direction, of course, but they are not sufficiently decisive. Pent-up consumer demand already amounts to 200 billion rubles, or half of our trade turnover.

In this situation the government should be making arrangements to take excess money out of circulation, not simply to reduce the amount of new money put into circulation. Reducing the amount of new money put into circulation will, at best, only somewhat slow, not stop, the process, already in full swing, of the collapse of the consumer-goods market. Moreover, the deficit reduction is to be achieved primarily by means of sharp cuts in production-related capital investments, cuts that threaten to cause major disproportions—but more on that later.

Increasing expenditures on social security. There is little need to prove that our social security system is hopelessly outdated and was not designed to withstand the pressures that will inevitably arise in the transition to a market economy. This transition will naturally be accompanied by a transfer of resources from some sectors and regions to others, by enterprise bankruptcies and closings, by a need to retrain millions of workers, and by price increases and greater inequality in the distribution of income.

To neutralize, to the greatest extent possible, these unavoidable costs of establishing the market, the entire system of labor training and retraining will need to be reorganized, and there will be a need to introduce government unemployment insurance, income indexing, pension adjustments, low-income family allowances, and so forth. These things, of course, will require a significant increase in budgetary outlay, but if these social-protection mechanisms are not created, economic restructuring could lead to a drop in the real income of large groups of the population, which is contrary to the principles of socialism and unacceptable for political reasons.

Increasing expenditures on education and public health. It is a known fact that investment in education, in "human capital," is an extremely important factor in economic growth—more important, perhaps, than investment in fixed assets. But unfortunately, it is also a

---

[15]See *Izvestia*, Sept. 26, 1989.

known fact that we are far behind the leading Western countries in this respect. In the 1950s the U.S.S.R. spent 10 percent of its national income on education—more than anyone else in the world. However, this indicator subsequently declined (something that has not happened in a single developed country), and today we spend only 7 percent for that purpose (the United States spends 12 percent). Even if we decide to immediately increase allocations for education, the effects will not be felt for at least 10 years. If, on the other hand, we convince ourselves that there are more important tasks to be accomplished, and we continue to put off education "until later," in 10 years we will have no workers or engineers with modern levels of training.

Here is just one example to illustrate the basic problem. Out of 135,000 Soviet schools, only 9,000 (7 percent) have one classroom equipped with computers. Plans for increasing the output of school computers constantly go unfulfilled. In the past three years (1986 to 1988), just 63,000 personal computers have been produced for school use, only 60 percent of the plan. [16] If everything remains as is, there is and will be no hope of equipping all schools with computers before the end of the century. That means that even by the year 2010 not all of those entering the work force will be trained in the "second literacy." In what year, then, will everyone working in the national economy be computer literate? In 2050?

We spend about 4 percent of our national income on health care—less than all developed countries and many developing ones as well. Out of 126 countries, we are somewhere between 60th and 70th with respect to that indicator. And although increased expenditures on health care do not affect economic growth as significantly as do expanded investments in education, obvious considerations of a humanitarian nature demand immediate modernization of health care. Central Asian maternity and children's hospitals without hot water or sewage systems; the spread of AIDS, partly because of the shortage of disposable hypodermic syringes; the incredibly high infant-mortality rate—all these examples speak for themselves.

Increasing investments to replace worn-out equipment. One paradox of all-inclusive directive planning is that while overall investments are excessive, there is an obvious shortage of investment in certain areas. Thus, in many sectors equipment is entirely worn out and should be replaced, but it is nonetheless still used in production. The retirement of fixed assets is an extremely slow affair in our industry—the standard rate of retirement was 2 to 3 percent in the 1980s, while in American manufacturing it was 4 to 5 percent. As a result, a very high

---

[16]See *Pravda*, May 13, 1989.

proportion of all production-related investment (more than three fourths, as opposed to less than half in American manufacturing) goes not to replace retired assets, but to increase total fixed assets—to build new capacity and expand existing capacity.

In Soviet industry, wear and tear on fixed assets (the ratio of accumulated depreciation to the total value of fixed assets, i.e., the ratio of net value of capital stock to its gross value) rose from 26 percent in 1970 to 30 percent in 1975, 36 percent in 1980, and 46 percent in 1988. In certain industries the equipment is so old that it has become dangerous to use it: the railroads, electric power stations, and steel industry are using equipment today that is often not just obsolete but physically worn out and should have long since been scrapped. In the petrochemical industry, almost one third of all equipment has been in use longer than its rated service life; in the automotive industry the same can be said of about 20 percent of the equipment; and so on.[17]

In other areas there is an urgent need to increase investments in the expansion of fixed assets and the creation of new capacity. Such investments are needed, for example, in housing construction and the construction of social-infrastructure facilities, in environmental protection, and in development of certain high-tech sectors.

Thus, the Soviet economy as a whole is clearly suffering from "overinvestment"—excessive capital investment. But at the same time there is a need to redirect these capital investments and change their structure, which in certain cases will entail an increase in investments, particularly in housing construction and in compensating for the retirement of fixed production assets.

Where to Get the Money

As we head into the 1990s, the total need for current and capital expenditures for the purposes discussed above can be estimated at approximately 150 to 200 billion rubles, which is equivalent to between one fifth and one fourth of our national income. The considerable complication is that these funds should be found right now, not *after* perestroika, but *in the course of* perestroika, i.e., in a period when there will inevitably be a slump in production, caused by economic restructuring itself—by conversion of defense industry and heavy industry to consumer goods production, that will be accompanied by bankruptcies, production stoppages, and so forth. Where are we to get this amount of money? Let us consider several possible alternatives.

---

[17]See N. Shmelev and V. Popov, note 13, above, pp. 145-146.

Reducing capital investments in production. At first glance, this appears the most logical and natural in light of what has been said about the bloated accumulation fund. But in actual fact, that is not the case. Naturally, a number of long-term investment projects—projects that are pretentious but useless, and even harmful (such as the plan to divert the flow of northern rivers), or that cannot hope to yield a return before the next century—must be stopped immediately (which, in part, has already been done). But putting a freeze on a multitude of other production-related construction projects is perilous, because of the danger of compounding economic disproportions in an economy that is already out of balance. After all, a planned, command economy has its own laws, and the price it exacts for breaking those laws is no less steep than the one nature exacts for breaking its laws. One such law of the planned economy is that high investment outlays are needed to support modest economic growth, because such an economy is simply unable to function without immense inventories and underutilized capacity; another law is the preferential development of producer goods, since a planned economy works more for itself than for the consumer.

If, over a period of six decades, economic growth has been ensured only by a rate of accumulation significantly higher than the one now being planned for the coming years, then a mere decree by the government or Supreme Soviet will hardly turn things around overnight. And if Group A [producer goods] has for decades grown faster than Group B [consumer goods], so that the share of total output accounted for by consumer-goods industries dropped from 60 percent in 1928 to 25 percent in 1988, and if the opposite ratio (faster growth of Group B) has only very rarely been observed, and has never been significant—if that is indeed the way things are, and not the reverse, then is it realistic to plan, for 1990, a growth rate for Group B that is 13 times that of Group A (6.7 percent and 0.5 percent, respectively)?

In other words, no doubt you can plan whatever you like, but you need to understand what the result will be. And it is not too difficult to predict the result. The planned redeployment of resources in favor of consumer-goods industries can only lead to a shortage of raw materials and supplies, energy, and equipment for the production of consumer goods themselves, with the result that their output simply will not be increased because of violations of input/output proportions at the basic level. And then investment in the production of producer goods will be required to remedy the bottlenecks.

The reduction of production-related capital investments can and should be a natural result of the transition to a market economy. It will happen of its own accord, since the market mechanism for allocation of resources is more efficient than the directive-planning method, and since, in the context of a normal market, the level of capacity use will increase, and the excessive inventories will decline.

But to speed events artificially, to hurry the process of revising the economy's structure through orders and directives from above, to attempt to accomplish, through planning, the work that only a full-fledged market can and must perform, is to ruin everything. Premature decisions (before market relations have formed) to reorient the economy toward the consumer by mandating a reduction in the accumulation fund's share of national income in favor of the consumption fund's share could break down established economic ties without forming new ties—leading to complete confusion and chaos.

Unfortunately, that train of events has already become a reality, since the plan for 1990 calls for a 25-percent cut in state capital investments in production facilities, for a reduction in the importation of certain investment-type goods (rolled ferrous metal, for example), and for a 2 percentage point drop (from 16 to 14 percent) in the share of national income devoted to production-related accumulation. On the whole, it is proposed that 15 billion rubles be shifted, in just one year's time, from production-related construction to housing construction and current consumption.[18] This means that more than a million people employed in construction (one in ten) will have to change jobs or occupations in a single year. Is that realistic? It appears that we intend to go on adhering strictly to the rules of our traditional administrative distribution game, which, in its new perestroika version, proposes to transfer resources in the opposite direction (from that of the 1930s): from industry to agriculture, from heavy to light industry, and from the military to the civilian sector. It goes without saying that the intention is most noble, but without firm reliance on the market economy, it smacks strongly of castles in the air.

Raising prices on consumer goods. Such a step could help balance the budget, since state food subsidies would be reduced. For social and political reasons, however, it is not acceptable, as the government admitted in early 1989, when it promised not to raise prices on basic foodstuffs for the next several years. For the very same reasons, there can be no recourse to either a monetary reform or a significant tax increase.

Increasing government borrowing on the internal credit market. That is undoubtedly a useful and feasible measure. The total value of outstanding state bonds in the public's hands is a paltry figure—less

---

[18]See *Izvestia*, Sept. 26, 1989.

than 25 billion rubles (9 billion in borrowings from the 1950s, and 15 billion in 3-percent bonds of 1982), and enterprises and organizations have held no state bonds whatsoever until just recently. And the volume of new-issue bonds acquired by the public in recent years has amounted to only 1 to 2 billion rubles annually.[19]

In other words, if the government were to decide to increase the interest rate paid on deposits and bonds, so that investors would at least be protected against the depreciation of their deposits as a result of inflation, it would be possible to significantly expand the volume of monetary resources enlisted through borrowing. In that way, a large part of present-day savings could be transformed from forced savings (since there is nothing to buy, and the rate of interest on deposits is low) into voluntary savings attracted by the high interest rate, and it might even be possible to stimulate an increase in savings at the expense of purchases of so-called hordable goods, which might reduce the pressure on the consumer-goods market.

In general, an expansion of internal borrowing is useful and necessary, of course, since it means a transition to normal market methods of mobilizing financial resources. However, internal borrowing does not change the overall amount of national income being utilized. It merely redistributes money, and does not make it possible to simultaneously increase both consumption and investment.

Expanding foreign borrowing. This is the preferred method. Only the use of foreign credits can quickly provide the means for offsetting the costs incurred by the radical economic reform, in order to see the economic ship through a difficult period of transition without major economic casualties—in other words, without a significant drop in the real living standard of major population groups.

Can Foreign Borrowing Be Expanded?

Let us consider the need for enlisting funds from abroad in terms of the basic equivalence used in Western macroeconomics to describe the balance of savings and investments.[20] The data that roughly charac-

---

[19]See *Pravda*, Oct. 28, 1988; *Dengi i kredit* [*Money and Credit*], No. 7, 1988, p. 7; *The U.S.S.R. National Economy in 1987* [*Narodnoye khozyaystvo SSSR v 1987 godu*], Moscow, 1988, p. 587.

[20]Gross savings—the sum of personal savings and business savings (depreciation plus retained earnings)—are equal to gross private investments, minus the government budget deficit, plus the surplus in the current-account balance of payments. In other words, the following equivalence obtains in any economy: $S = I - DG + CA$, where S is savings, I is investments, DG is the government deficit, and CA is the surplus in the current-account balance of payments. The equivalence remains valid if one substitutes net savings and net investments (i.e., gross investments minus depreciation) for gross savings and gross investments, respectively. The economic sense of the equivalence is that savings must suffice to finance investments, the government budget deficit, and exports of capital abroad; conversely, investments can be financed only out of savings, a government budget surplus, and an influx of capital from abroad.

terize that balance are presented in the table below ("roughly," because many of the needed figures are lacking in our official statistics). They convey an approximate idea of the relative amount of money (150 to 200 billion rubles) needed to finance the urgent requirements of the transitional period.

At first glance, our balance of savings and investments brings to mind the one that currently exists in the United States: An immense deficit in the central government's budget swallows up about half of all domestic savings. The difference, however, is that in the Soviet Union, domestic savings (basically in the form of forced savings by enterprises) are so great that, even with a budget deficit relatively greater than that of the United States, noncentralized capital investments can be financed here (unlike the United States) strictly from domestic sources, without a significant influx of capital from abroad.

The 45-billion-ruble surplus in the U.S.S.R.'s balance of payments (net income from foreign economic operations) is, strictly speaking, a statistical fiction. It is formed primarily from the differences in our prices for exported and imported goods (as compared to prices on the world market). The exports, which consist primarily of raw materials, cost less on the domestic market, while the imports, in which

SAVINGS AND INVESTMENTS IN THE SOVIET ECONOMY
(1987, billions of rubles)

Savings	198
Business savings	172
Depreciation	72
Retained earnings of enterprises and collective farms	100[1]
Personal savings	26
Increase in bank deposits	24
Bonds sold to the public	2
Government budget deficit	120[2]
Balance of payments (net government income from foreign economic operations)	45
Noncentralized investments	99
State Enterprises	72[2]
Collective farms	15[3]
Public, for construction of individual houses, apartments	3[3]
Change in inventories	(−1)

[1]Estimate—profits of state enterprises and collective farms after payments to the budget, net of payments from material-incentive funds and interest on loans.
[2]1988.
[3]In 1984 prices.
Calculated on the basis of *The U.S.S.R. National Economy in 1987* [*Narodnoye khozyaystvo SSSR v 1987 godu*], Moscow, 1988; *Pravda*, November 28, 1988; *Izvestia*, January 21 and September 26, 1989.

finished goods predominate, cost more. Therefore, when the state buys raw materials on the domestic market for export, sells them abroad, uses the foreign currency thus obtained to acquire finished goods abroad, and finally, sells these goods on the domestic market, it returns a significant profit. If these price disproportions were corrected by a change in domestic prices or by the imposition of reasonable import duties, then the entire foreign trade deficit, or almost all of it, would disappear. The reduction in the government's revenues from foreign trade would be offset by a reduction in expenditures subsidizing the raw-materials sectors, or by an increase in revenues from the new import duties.

Thus, in principle, the Soviet Union can increase its trade deficit and finance it with an influx of foreign capital. If that is done, if it is decided to increase consumer-goods imports and finance them with foreign loans, there will be an increase in the real consumption fund and a corresponding drop in forced savings (the public will draw money out of its savings accounts to obtain imported consumer goods). Deposits in the Savings Bank, of course, will contract, forcing it to restrict credit to other banks and to the government. But this will not require a reduction in investments, since they can be financed from the government's growing revenues from sales of consumer goods.

Thus, using foreign credits to expand consumer-goods imports makes it possible to kill two birds with one stone: to eliminate the public's forced savings by supplying goods to satisfy, at long last, the deferred consumer demand that is the cause of so much discontent, thereby increasing real consumption and raising the real living standard; and to avoid a forced reduction in production-related investments by financing them out of the government's increased revenues from consumer-goods imports. Credits can also be used to import consumer goods to support growing state expenditures on social security, on needed equipment for schools and hospitals, and for other social and production facilities. In general, of course, imports financed by loans are the easiest way to overcome present and future disproportions in the economy. The key question, however, is to what extent can we increase our international indebtedness to pay for this increase in imports.

At the beginning of 1990, according to Western estimates, the U.S.S.R.'s gross hard-currency indebtedness amounted to approximately $45 billion, and its net indebtedness (gross indebtedness minus hard-currency balances in the Soviet Union's favor in the West) came to $32 billion; its gold reserves amounted to about $25 billion, and its debt service costs accounted for slightly more than 20 percent of its hard-currency earnings from exports. In addition, the Soviet Union is a creditor of developing and socialist countries: By and large, these credits are ruble-denominated, but if the ruble becomes convertible, a portion of these credits can be used to pay off indebtedness to the West. Their dollar equivalent, at the official exchange rate, is over $140 billion.[21]

These figures are significantly at odds with the recently published official data of the U.S.S.R. State Statistics Committee, which place international indebtedness at 34 billion rubles and the ratio of debt-service payments (12 billion rubles) to hard-currency export earnings (16 billion rubles) at 75 percent, but they are nonetheless widely accepted by foreign experts. In the opinion of Soviet commentators, the high figures for the ratio of debt-service payments to exports that N. Ryzhkov cited at the First Congress of U.S.S.R. People's Deputies in the summer of 1989 can be explained by the fact that they included short-term indebtedness, which traditional international practice excludes from calculations of this sort.[22]

As it turned out, the sum of international indebtedness—34 billion rubles as of the beginning of 1989—includes the U.S.S.R.'s indebtedness in transferrable rubles (3.6 billion) and its indebtedness under clearing agreements with Yugoslavia and Finland (1.6 billion), while the indebtedness in freely convertible currency amounts to only 28.1 billion rubles.[23] That is approximately consistent with the Western assessments in dollars that are cited above. The prevailing opinion among Western experts is that the U.S.S.R. can double its debt without serious risk of experiencing a solvency crisis.

Let us accept the latter figure as a point of departure—let us assume that we really can increase our net foreign debt from $30 billion to $60 billion. Let us also allow that we can take an additional $30 billion in credit with our gold reserve as collateral. That gives us a total of $60 billion. Is that a lot or a little? Today, unfortunately, it is not a lot, although five years ago such a sum would have been quite sufficient, and we would have been able to borrow even more then, because we were in a better position with respect to payments.

Let us think back five years, to 1985, when it all began. The consumer-goods market was relatively balanced—at least it was significantly less unbalanced than it is today. The state budget deficit was a fraction of what it is today, and net foreign indebtedness was only $15 billion.[24] At that time, it would have been entirely possible to shift the economy to a market track without lowering living standards. The

---

[21]*Izvestia*, March 1, 1990. *The Soviet Economy Stumbles Badly in 1989.*

[22]*Izvestia*, June 10 and 20, 1989.

[23]*Pravitelstvennyy vestnik [Government Bulletin]*, No. 19, 1989, p. 9.

[24]The increase in our indebtedness in dollar terms in the 1985-1989 period was, to a significant extent, due to the drop in the dollar exchange rate, since a large percentage of the credits granted us were in West European currencies and yen.

costs of the transitional period could have easily been covered by foreign borrowing, and within five to seven years, perestroika would have begun recouping its own costs, since an effective market economy would have begun operating full force, and the hypertrophied, bloated accumulation fund would have been reduced to normal proportions.

Now those possibilities no longer exist. In the past five years we have made no significant progress toward a market; and just as we were five years ago, we are still only approaching radical economic reform. On the other hand, our position at the starting line has seriously deteriorated. The budgetary deficit, foreign indebtedness, and deferred consumer demand have all grown. Some of the reasons for this, of course, have been objective—the drop in world prices for petroleum and gas (our principal export items), Chernobyl, and the Armenian earthquake. But there were other factors, too, obvious blunders in the concept and implementation of the reform, inexcusable footdragging with agrarian and other changes, the senseless antialcohol campaign that deprived the budget of tens of billions of rubles—the list is too long to enumerate.

Today, unfortunately, it is no longer possible to carry out a radical economic reform as simply and with such minimal cost as it was five years ago. Even if we were to borrow $10 billion a year for the six years that we need for the new market-economy mechanism to begin working, we still will not be able to fully cover the costs of the transitional period. Given the present relationship between domestic and world prices, $10 billion in consumer-goods imports translates roughly into 100 billion rubles, which will just barely enable us to cover the budgetary deficit and balance the consumer-goods market. But it will not be enough to expand social programs and increase investments in education, health care, housing construction, and so forth. Hence we will have to forgo some things and make some sacrifices, and we will find ourselves torn again and again between raising pensions and building housing.

Moreover, our borrowing opportunities abroad are now far from what they once were. The obvious absence of perceptible economic improvement is increasingly undermining Western creditors' confidence in us. After the miners' strikes in the summer of 1989, which showed that the government is losing the initiative on the economic front and is almost unable to control the course of events, Western bankers have shifted us to the category of potentially unreliable borrowers, resulting in a marked worsening of our credit conditions (high interest rates). In addition, in late 1989 to early 1990 many Soviet enterprises and trade associations were not paying their trade debt, which completely undermined our creditworthiness.

That does not mean, however, that there is no need or way to obtain credit abroad. On the contrary, a sharp expansion of borrowing in the West, combined with a decisive and truly radical economic reform, remains our main, indeed our only, chance to carry out per-estroika in a relatively "bloodless" fashion—at a minimal cost in economic losses. True, the possibility of pulling off such a maneuver narrows increasingly with every passing month and year. Today, we can still borrow far more than token sums on favorable conditions, backing such borrowings with our gold reserves and, say, with such real assurances as, for example, a radical agrarian reform (which would enable us, as it has China, to sharply increase agricultural production and save hard currency on food imports). Tomorrow, those same funds will simply not suffice to make any noticeable improvement in the situation on the consumer-goods market. Also, there is a possibility of direct Western financial assistance.

It is not hard to imagine what will happen if the optimal scenario— radical reform in conjunction with an expansion of borrowing abroad— is once again put on the back burner, and we take the path of a planned transfer of resources from the accumulation fund to the consumption fund. Established economic ties will be broken, shortages of all goods will worsen, real incomes will begin to fall, and the country will be racked by a wave of strikes, such that the government will, for all practical purposes, completely lose control of the situation.

At that point, the only way to avert a complete collapse of the economy will be to use borrowed money for importing—a means that will undoubtedly be used. But as a result, we will fall into the "Polish trap," since several years of such living on borrowed money will increase our international debt to critical levels. There will be nothing with which to repay the debt, since the effective market economy that was lacking before will still be lacking. We will be left with only the painful and agonizing course of making the transition to a market economy by substantially lowering the real incomes of large groups of the population, and that will doubtless entail major social and political costs.

On Deepening the Reform of Foreign Economic Activities

VIKTOR BORISOVICH SPANDARYAN
AND
NIKOLAY PETROVICH SHMELEV*

The restructuring of the Soviet economy and its emergence in the front ranks of scientific and technical progress are unthinkable without our country's active engagement in international economic and technological exchange. In the long term, the external market must become a permanent alternative for us in choosing the most effective options for scientific and technological policy, capital construction, and areas of production.

Meanwhile, the present state of our foreign economic ties remains a cause for concern. An analysis of the results of the U.S.S.R.'s foreign trade from 1985 to 1987 and the data for 1988 to 1989 show that there has as yet been no significant progress in our foreign economic activities. In addition, the Soviet Union's role in international trade, which was already slight in relation to the country's importance in world economy and world politics, continues to diminish. We find ourselves increasingly on the sidelines of the integrative processes that predominate in world economic ties.

From 1985 to 1987 the U.S.S.R.'s total foreign trade, exports, and imports fell in terms of monetary value. In the process, however, the physical volume of exports grew significantly, while that of imports dropped. That was primarily the result of a worsening of our country's "terms of trade," i.e., the relationship between export and import prices. And although foreign trade turnover increased somewhat in 1988 and 1989, the value of exports continued to fall, while volume increased. The increase is attributable to a continuing rise in the cost of imports.[1]

*Spandaryan is a candidate of economics and senior research associate at the U.S.S.R. Academy of Sciences' Institute for the United States and Canada; Shmelev is a doctor of economics and department head at the institute. This article appeared in the September 1989 issue of *MEMO*; the authors have made minor changes to update it for this volume. A related article by Spandaryan and Shmelev appeared in *MEMO: New Soviet Voices on Foreign and Economic Policy*, edited by Steve Hirsch, 1989, pp. 253–273.

[1]The U.S.S.R.'s foreign trade turnover (in billions of rubles) amounted to 142.1 in 1985, 130.9

290

This is not, however, solely or even primarily a problem of worsening statistical indicators. To a certain extent, their fall can be attributed to the unfavorable state of the world energy market (energy resources account for about half the foreign currency that we earn from exports). The cause for alarm lies elsewhere.

Perestroika placed on the agenda the need for a thorough reform of our foreign-economic activity—from conceptual approach to organizational forms. A number of important decisions have been made, decisions laying the groundwork for fundamentally new approaches to development of foreign economic ties. It must be said, however, that these ties are still not being used effectively enough to help solve the country's most important and acute social and economic problems.

In our opinion, the reform of foreign economic activity is still not producing noticeable results for a number of basic reasons.

First, there has been no basic improvement in the structure of foreign trade and the priorities set for foreign economic activities. This is primarily because our economic reform has yet to produce results. It is not only restraining enterprises' general economic activities but also keeping their activity levels in check in relation to foreign economic activities.

Second, decisions reached in the area of improving foreign economic activities basically boil down to administrative and organizational measures. On the one hand, they are incomplete, while on the other hand—and most important—they are not backed by sufficiently effective economic measures.

Third, the ministries, departments, associations, enterprises, and cooperatives that have now been given the right to engage in foreign economic activities are often unable to exercise that right effectively because of lack of effective economic incentives, poor competitiveness of much of their output, insufficient knowledge of the international market's requirements and laws, and poor preparation in terms of organization and personnel.

What is the top priority in this connection? What steps must be taken right away to overcome the disarray in the foreign economic sphere and move ahead?

Begin at the Beginning

Above all, in our opinion, we must clearly define the priority areas for developing foreign economic ties in the interests of perestroika.

The lion's share of our imports is in equipment and machinery (about 40 percent of the total value of imports from 1985 to 1988). However, equipment purchased for such leading Group B [consumer-

in 1986, 128.9 in 1987, 132.1 in 1988, and 138.4 in 1989.

goods] industries as textiles, clothing, footwear, fur, food and flavorings, and tobacco amounted to only 2.5 percent of our total imports during those years. Basically, the country imported production equipment for Group A [producer-goods] industries, since our own machinery industry is overburdened and is technologically behind. Metal-cutting machine tools and forge and press equipment—the vital core and basis of machine building—accounted for only 2.2 to 2.5 percent of overall imports.

The country still spends immense sums on importation of industrial materials, basically to cover shortages caused, in many cases, by vestiges of the cost-based economy, by mismanagement, wasteful use of resources, planning errors, and supply hitches. For example, our country—the world's largest steel producer—regularly buys ferrous-metallurgy products, such as rolled metal, large-diameter pipe, oil-field pipe, specialty steels. From 1986 to 1988 alone, 11 billion rubles worth of foreign currency was spent on such products. For just a fraction of that amount it would have been possible to reconstruct Soviet metallurgy and organize production of the products that are in short supply.

One cannot help wondering why the world's largest producer of steel pipe depends on imported pipe to lay our pipelines and outfit our petroleum and natural-gas deposits—what kind of pipe do we produce and for what purpose? (Unfortunately, similar questions could be asked about products other than pipe.) As for the ordinary rolled metal that we also import, that is the result of the low yield of finished rolled metal that we obtain from the steel we smelt, and a means of covering our immensely excessive use of metal in construction and industry. Japan, whose GNP is close to our own, produces about 100 million [metric] tons of steel (one third less than we do) and not only supplies all its own needs but also exports about 30 million tons to various countries, including the U.S.S.R.

Other such examples could be cited. The sad experience of the years of stagnation attests to the fact that we will not be able to overcome the shortages if we continue attempting to compensate for the unsatisfactory performance of our own industry and of our entire system of economic management with imports paid for out of the state's pocket. Paid for, to be more precise, by the export of natural resources, and, what is more, exported today at low prices.

The required importation of grain and foodstuffs (15 to 18 percent of the value of our imports) imposes a heavy burden on our limited foreign-currency resources, and at a time when much of our own agricultural output perishes. During the 1970s and 1980s we "ate our way through" more than 150 billion rubles in that way; that figure includes 30 billion rubles the first three years of the current five-year plan. At the same time, according to the figures of the U.S.S.R. State Statistics Committee, we annually lose 22 to 25 billion rubles' worth of food grown and produced in the country! Obviously, an upswing in our agricultural production would be a radical means of improving the situation. Even a small portion of the funds expended on importation of grain and foodstuffs, if directed toward purchase of equipment and technology for storing, transporting, and processing our agricultural output, would pay heavy returns to the agroindustrial complex. It is obvious that to radically solve the food problem, we need to import more equipment and machinery for preserving and processing our agricultural products, even if that must be done at the expense of other branches of industry. Today we import equipment and materials to build gas pipelines, and then, in the final analysis, spend the revenues from the sale of the gas to buy grain and food.

Speaking on January 6, 1989, at a meeting in the CPSU Central Committee, M.S. Gorbachev stressed that a key question with regard to the present economic situation is that of overcoming the heavy legacy of the past—the state budget deficit, which influences the entire national economy.

In recent times, vigorous efforts have been made to increase production of consumer goods in our country. Reconstruction of many light-industry enterprises is already under way, in some cases with the use of foreign credits, and a number of defense-industry enterprises are being shifted to the production of consumer goods. These efforts must also be supplemented in the area of foreign economic ties, particularly in the next few years, until Soviet light industry is operating at full capacity. Efforts must not be limited to increasing imports of advanced foreign equipment and experience, but must also include direct imports of consumer goods that are in particularly great demand.

In this connection, it is hard to understand why, in 1987 and 1988, imports of consumer goods dropped by more than 8 billion rubles. Last year, purchases of fabrics from foreign countries fell by 62 million square meters, clothing by 2.3 billion rubles, and footwear by 14.3 million pairs—and that was at a time when our light industry was not fulfilling its state orders. Citing the reduction in foreign-currency resources simply will not do. After all, import of equipment (basically for Group A industries) has continued to rise, despite the fact that a significant portion of it has gotten hung up in above-normal inventories, where it physically deteriorates and becomes obsolete. As of January 1, 1990, there were 5 billion rubles' worth of such inventories.

Imports of consumer goods must be maintained at reasonable levels, and not just today, when the budget-deficit problem is so acute, but also under normal conditions, when our industry is able to meet the domestic market's basic needs and earmark some portion of output for export. A reasonable level of imports is needed both to expand the assortment of goods and for the sake of healthy competition—to avoid monopolization of certain types of products. We must not forget the advantages, particularly the long-run advantages, of utilizing the international division of labor. Do we need to make everything ourselves, without calculating the cost? The experience of many developed countries argues in favor of importing consumer goods, even when a country has a highly developed light industry of its own, and then exporting a portion of the country's own light-industry output to external markets. In 1986, imports of consumer goods (exclusive of foodstuffs and motor vehicles) accounted for 21.3 percent of U.S. imports and 6.4 percent of exports. We believe that the exchange of consumer goods with CMEA [Council for Mutual Economic Aid] member countries, and subsequently with a broader range of partners, will strengthen the contribution that foreign economic ties make to the people's well-being.

We believe that foreign economic activity must be channeled toward solving the most important and urgent social and economic problems. We need a clear-cut program to establish priorities for foreign economic activity at each stage of perestroika, and to support such activity with concrete economic and administrative measures and trade policies. For the immediate future (at least until the end of the new five-year plan), the priority areas of foreign economic activity should evidently include promoting an acceleration of scientific and technological progress and an increase in Soviet machine building, a balanced state budget, and a balanced consumer-goods and consumer-services market. For this purpose, import-export and foreign-currency plans must be radically revised, all the resources of state foreign economic policy must be brought to bear, and all elements of the national economy involved in the foreign economic sphere must be actively engaged in the effort and given a material stake in it.

It would be incorrect, in our view, if the stagnation in foreign economic ties and the limited effectiveness of the decisions that have been made to improve them were ascribed to the delays in carrying out overall economic reform. As can be seen from the experience of a number of countries—in particular, the Federal Republic of Germany and Japan, and in recent years the new industrial countries, too—foreign economic ties can be an important factor in boosting the national economy and stimulating economic growth, and an effective means of engagement in the international division of labor and in integrative world economic ties. Apparently, in developing a concept of foreign economic ties in the context of perestroika, we too must accord them a greater role in carrying out the radical economic reform.

Export is a Matter of State Importance

Widespread entrance of ministries, departments, associations, enterprises, and cooperatives into the external market cannot produce an effect without additional measures to provide economic incentives and to supply information. Those organizations need effective and multifaceted assistance from state and public organizations in all aspects of that complex activity, particularly under conditions of tough competition.

Practically all foreign states, including the United States, the EC countries, and Japan, conduct long-term comprehensive and special-purpose programs to provide every possible assistance to their entrepreneurs in foreign economic activities. They do so, first, by providing export incentives through creation of favorable economic conditions and trade policies and maintenance of ramified support systems for exporters. These countries' governments offer entrepreneurs subsidies and credit on favorable terms; they provide tax relief, insure foreign-trade operations, strive to maintain a favorable exchange rate for their national currency, assist in organizing exhibitions and in sending and hosting trade delegations, provide economic and commercial information, and help in the selection of markets and trade partners. With these widely accepted practices clearly in mind, we must see that enterprises that have obtained the right to trade on the external market enjoy conditions that are at least as favorable as, and if possible more favorable than, those of their competitors.

The most effective means of providing government incentives for exports in the United States—as, for that matter, in many other developed capitalist countries—is the use of government funds to provide favorable credit terms for promoting foreign sales of national products, particularly machinery and equipment. The U.S. Export-Import Bank pays particular attention to stimulating exports of capital equipment and transportation equipment (equipment for nuclear, thermal, and hydroelectric power stations; projects for extracting and transporting mineral and energy resources in foreign countries; entire petrochemical and metallurgical enterprises; aircraft, and others). The Export-Import Bank of Japan provides credits to promote the export of entire enterprises and complete means of transportation (ships and trains), and the carrying out of major projects in foreign countries. Many other countries also stimulate exports.

In the first half of the 1980s, 35 to 40 percent of Japan's exports, 35 percent of Britain's exports, and 30 to 35 percent of France's exports were aided by the extension of state loans on favorable terms. In the United States, the percentage was much lower (6 percent), forcing the U.S. administration to undertake a number of measures to strengthen export credits through the Export-Import Bank and other government institutions.

It is evident that we should consider creating in our country, too, a special financial institution (perhaps along the lines of the U.S. and Japanese export-import banks) to provide credit on favorable terms to Soviet enterprises and foreign importers to promote sales of capital equipment, machinery, and transportation equipment on the international market, and for carrying out projects in foreign countries.

In many countries, an important means of supporting the interests of national exporters is to provide government insurance of exporters' contracts against risks resulting from political, economic, and financial and currency instability in the world. As a rule, such insurance covers up to 100 percent of "political risk" (wars, conflicts, revolutions, cancellation of licenses) and up to 90 percent of "commercial risk" (bankruptcy of foreign entities that are parties to contracts, losses due to fluctuations in the exchange rates of foreign currencies, inflation). In the case of consumer goods, spare parts and other types of contracts that are quickly fulfilled, risk insurance is generally provided for periods of up to 180 days, and in the case of equipment and machinery exports involving long-term contracts—for periods of up to five years. In Japan, government risk insurance covers about 45 percent of exports in terms of value, in Great Britain—about 33 percent, and in the United States—only about 4 percent, since a significant percentage of the risk insurance is handled through private channels there.

We need to introduce a system of state insurance for Soviet organizations and enterprises operating in foreign markets, particularly with respect to deliveries of machinery and equipment on long-term contracts. Such insurance must provide broad coverage of the real risks in the international market. At the same time, such insurance will be a means of averting commercially unjustified risk taking.

The most common way of providing incentives for export activities is by offering various tax breaks and exemptions: postponements, reductions in and even exemptions from paying state and local taxes, agreements with foreign states to avoid double taxation, relief from paying domestic taxes on equipment and materials used for the production of export goods, and so forth. One might also include in this category such incentives as relief from paying customs duties on imported equipment, raw materials, and other materials used to produce goods for export, and the duty-free status of "free trade zones."

Widespread use is made (though without publicity) of such important state export incentives as various types of subsidies to exporters. Usually they are provided in indirect form (for example, exemption from income tax, accelerated depreciation, investment tax credits, increased tax deductions for the representational expenses involved in promoting exports, and exemption from excise taxes, real-estate taxes, value-added taxes). In the United States, widespread use is also made of direct subsidies—for example, for certain types of agricultural exports.

It seems necessary that we also work out a system of tax breaks and incentives for Soviet exporters, particularly in the areas of machinery and equipment, finished goods, and services. In light of international practice, such breaks might include reductions in and, in certain cases, exemptions from, taxes for a certain period of time (for example, the period needed to put new products intended for export into production, and to gain entrance to new markets); accelerated depreciation in cases where export products occupy a significant place in a producer's overall production; increased foreign-currency and ruble payments into enterprises' various funds; and removal of limits on enterprises' expenditure of earned foreign currency for the development of social facilities and services. We would also include the provision of temporary subsidies to encourage export of particular goods (machinery and equipment, for example) that we are particularly interested in selling abroad, but that are priced higher on the domestic than on the world market.

An extremely important function of foreign countries' government agencies is to protect the interests of national exporters and importers by means of trade policy and a supportive infrastructure. This is achieved not only by domestic measures (customs duties, licensing, quotas) but also through appropriate international (bilateral and multilateral) agreements ensuring a favorable trade-policy climate for national entrepreneurs' foreign economic activities, and protecting the national economy against unfair foreign competition. Government and public agencies in other countries facilitate the foreign economic activities of their national entrepreneurs but, as a rule, do not get involved directly in commercial activities.

Nonmaterial incentives for successful foreign economic activities are widespread. The United States has introduced awards to American companies for high achievement in exporting. Outstanding exporters are awarded orders in Great Britain. Special ("royal") prizes have been established for the small-business representatives who are most active in the foreign market.

Evidently, we too should offer every possible assistance to our exporters, particularly in a situation in which a broad range of companies and enterprises directly enter the external market. They ought to have at their disposal the full range of facilities enjoyed by their highly experienced competitors, rather than merely being granted the elementary right to receive a portion of the foreign-currency revenues they earn—revenues whose use is still restricted and often made difficult.

In this connection, we must strengthen the services available to support the foreign economic activities of Soviet organizations and enterprises that have obtained the right to enter the external market. What that means, in accordance with international practice, is an all-inclusive system for providing Soviet organizations and enterprises, through appropriate governmental and public institutions, with trade policy, economic, currency, financial, and commercial information; it also means giving them assistance in studying markets, training personnel, organizing exhibitions, hosting and dispatching commercial delegations, creating the most favorable conditions for their activities both inside the country and abroad, and so forth.

Many organizations are dealing with these questions now, but there is no unified, coordinated, and comprehensive program. A lot of duplication of efforts occurs among the various channels (for example, the GVK [State Foreign Economic Commission], the U.S.S.R. Ministry of Foreign Economic Relations, the U.S.S.R. Chamber of Commerce and Industry, the Bank for Foreign Economic Activity), but a number of important areas of foreign economic activity nonetheless remain "uncovered."

Evidently, the methodological and coordinating functions should be assigned to an appropriate governmental agency. Apart from coordinating all efforts to facilitate Soviet organizations' and enterprises' foreign economic activity, this agency could assume the task of regulating this activity in the interests of the entire state, using economic, trade policy, and administrative means. It could also draw up and carry out comprehensive programs to assist Soviet organizations and enterprises entering the foreign market. Such an agency would not only help them, but also avoid duplication of effort wherever possible, reduce unproductive expenditures, and prevent the gross errors and mistakes that inevitably result from such duplication in connection with an uncoordinated, mass entry into foreign markets.

Foreign Currency Is the Engine of Trade

All these measures for stimulating foreign economic activity are capable of yielding only limited results if the overall economic conditions for our exporters' entry into the external market and for the importation of foreign products are not normalized. The main thing here is the currency and financial aspect of the matter. Until such time as we have a reliable, objective measure for comparing internal expenditures and the results of foreign economic activity, we will be unable to rid ourselves of arbitrariness, administrative confusion, various kinds of goading, and subjective prohibitions.

It is generally conceded that an extremely important economic measure that would enable us to fundamentally transform our foreign economic ties and would open the way for the U.S.S.R.'s genuine inclusion in the international division of labor and in world economic integration processes is convertibility of the ruble. There are objective reasons why that is not possible today, and it is more than likely that we will be unable to achieve it in the near future. A great many varied opinions have been expressed recently about ways of making the transition to ruble convertibility. But they all share the recognition that the transition must be made. Obviously, a gradual transition to ruble convertibility depends on a restoration of the country's economic soundness. That process, however, can be accelerated if the development of the Soviet export base is regarded as an independent and high-priority area.

But who and what are keeping us, by way of a first step, from establishing a uniform, economically sound rate for converting the ruble into the principal freely convertible currencies? Only arrogance and contempt for economic realities are keeping us from that step, which is both necessary and natural if we have seriously decided to improve our foreign economic activity.

It is common knowledge that a currency's exchange rate is one of the most effective measures for regulating foreign economic ties. Changes in an exchange rate in one direction or another can promote the expansion or contraction of exports and imports, an increase or decrease in the price-competitiveness of export or import goods, the influx or outflow of capital, an increase or decrease in the interest that local producers and consumers have in the external market, and so forth.

Thus, for example, for a rather protracted period in the postwar era the exchange rate of the yen and the dollar and other convertible currencies was kept artificially low (and at the time, the yen was either nonconvertible or had limited convertibility). The artificially low exchange rate, combined with other economic levers (tax advantages, government subsidies, insurance) promoted vigorous development of the Japanese economy and the establishment of Japan as a major world exporter. Exportation became one of the basic components of the growth in GNP, and a powerful stimulus to development of the national economy and the strengthening of the country's currency and financial situation. Japan's economic power grew to such an extent that even now, when the yen exchange rate has risen, exports of Japanese goods remain high. Granted, such factors as high quality, technological innovation, and quality of service have assumed greater importance in maintaining the competitiveness of Japanese exports.

The sharp drop in the exchange rate of the dollar contributed to a significant increase in U.S. exports (a jump of 25 to 30 percent in 1988 over the previous year), a restoration of the competitiveness of many American goods, and a reduction in the immense trade deficit.

Even without these generally well known examples, though, it is obvious that the establishment of a ruble-conversion rate for the principal foreign currencies—a uniform rate that is economically sound and advantageous for Soviet exporters—will sharply increase the effectiveness of our exports (in ruble terms) and the level of business organizations' interest in exporting their products. To be frank, the present ruble exchange rate (about 60 kopecks to the dollar) is disadvantageous to us, to say nothing of the fact that it has no economic basis. This exchange rate makes almost all our exports a losing proposition in ruble terms, a fact that we have essentially admitted by establishing "differential foreign-currency coefficients" (for all practical purposes, a system of varying rate increments applied in the currency-conversion process) for virtually all goods. In addition, these "coefficients" do not always conform to economic reality and do not serve to make our exports truly more competitive. They are not economic levers but crutches that support a limping system of foreign-trade incentives. Meanwhile, the ruble exchange rate that was artificially established many years ago has made and is continuing to make it extremely advantageous to buy most import goods—often discouraging the development of our own capacity to produce such goods. That was particularly the case when, thanks to the increase in the price of energy, we mindlessly ate our way through our petroleum money.

A resolution of the U.S.S.R. Council of Ministers provides for a transition, beginning January 1, 1991, to the use of a new exchange rate in settling accounts in connection with foreign economic operations, and for the application, beginning January 1, 1990, and continuing until the transition to the new exchange rate, of a 100-percent increase in the exchange rate of freely convertible currencies in relation to the ruble. It is a sensible decision, but it raises a question as to why the introduction of this long-overdue and necessary measure is being put off for another two years, and why there is such foot-dragging in abandoning the ineffective system of converting actual concrete prices into Soviet rubles by means of thousands of "differentiated coefficients."

Precisely at this time, when that very resolution opens up extensive possibilities for enterprises, associations, production cooperatives, and other organizations to enter the external market, they are being forced to settle accounts through an unnatural, economically unsubstantiated system of coefficients that create various ("differentiated") conditions for different goods and organizations—in other words, a system of multiple exchange rates. Would it not be simpler to introduce exchange-rate allowances, which would be differentiated not by thousands of individual goods but by several basic groups, such as raw materials, semifinished goods, finished goods, machinery and equipment, technology and licenses, and so forth, with the allowances rising in proportion to the level of processing that products have undergone? In the meantime, carefully considered proposals for the introduction of a new exchange rate could be prepared—without waiting an additional two years.

Can it be that in this matter, as in the matter of joint enterprises, we are going to gradually, step by step (under the pressure of common sense and of international experience and practice) eliminate the contrived impediments and the ill-founded fears about its "coming to no good"? After all, the introduction of a new currency-exchange rate requires no material outlays on our part; it would merely turn right side up the settlement of accounts relating to foreign economic activities, significantly simplify that process, and create the necessary prerequisites for a gradual transition to a convertible ruble and inclusion of the U.S.S.R. in the international division of labor.

In fact, even where joint enterprises are concerned, matters have not been carried to their logical conclusion—to the point of giving them the legal form of a joint-stock company, a form that is generally accepted worldwide. That would make it possible, if necessary, to increase their capital, buy out or sell such enterprises, and so forth. Especially since we are making ever broader use of stocks in our own country. As of today, more than 1,500 joint enterprises have been registered in the U.S.S.R., but not more than a third are in operation, and the influx of foreign capital is minuscule. The reasons for this include the lack of elementary conditions for joint enterprises' activities (such as office space, modern means of communication, and a well-developed system for obtaining supplies and interacting with Soviet organizations); the bureaucratism and red tape that are involved in resolving even simple questions (for example, issuance and extension of visas); and the inadequate qualifications of Soviet personnel. Our foreign partners are increasingly outspoken about this. Obviously, an efficient system of assisting joint enterprises and providing for their needs must be quickly devised, and a high-level organization must be created with full authorization to deal with those matters. These matters cannot simply be farmed out to various departments and local authorities.

There is one more matter whose resolution is long overdue: the need to put an end to the U.S.S.R. Bank for Foreign Economic Activity's foreign-currency monopoly, which does less to promote than to impede foreign-economic turnover. It should be a real commercial bank with all the corresponding functions.

It would be useful to enlist Soviet-controlled banks abroad, such as the Moscow Narodny Bank in London and the Eurobanque in Paris, in serving the currency and financial needs of Soviet organizations and enterprises by opening branches in Moscow and other major centers. Those banks know how to operate in an efficient and modern fashion. Other Soviet banks must also be enlisted in serving foreign-economic relations. No single bank should enjoy a monopoly, since without modern, efficient, and well-defined currency and financial services—without offering clients the full range of generally accepted services and advantages—successful foreign economic activities in general, and those of Soviet organizations and enterprises in particular, are impossible.

Specialists Know All

The December 2, 1988, resolution of the U.S.S.R. Council of Ministers contains a very important provision concerning the advisability of forming various types of foreign economic organizations (such as interbranch associations, consortia, associations, joint-stock companies, trading houses) on a voluntary basis. The point of this provision is to create conditions for improving the effectiveness with which Soviet goods and services are sold on the external market, eliminate unjustified competition among Soviet exporters, reduce marketing costs, and optimize purchases abroad.

Indeed, if left unguided, the entrance into the external market of numerous state, cooperative, and other types of public enterprises, associations, and organizations is bound to be costly because of lack of experience and preparation, and in many cases the weakness as well, of certain Soviet exporters and importers with relatively limited capabilities. Does every cooperative or enterprise need to have an elaborate operation to ensure normal—in other words, in the black— foreign economic activities (commercial, financial, economic analysis, marketing and advertising services, customer-service operations)? Obviously, not all of them can afford that. Besides, is that kind of multiple duplication of effort and expenditure necessary?

Associations of exporters and importers of particular groups of goods are widely developed in most foreign countries. There are specialized and all-purpose foreign-trade middlemen at the service even of major firms, to say nothing of small and medium-sized ones.

The commissions that clients pay them are significantly less than the expenditures that each firm would have to bear if it entered the external market on its own—not to mention the experience and qualifications that the middlemen have to offer.

In a number of countries, a considerable percentage of the foreign economic activity is concentrated in the hands of a few major all-purpose trading companies (trading houses). For example, in addition to its thousands of small and medium-sized companies that serve as foreign-trade middlemen, Japan has nine extremely large universal trading companies that handle about 60 percent of the country's foreign trade, and experience has shown this arrangement to be one of the most important factors in Japan's phenomenal success in the external market. These companies (*sogo shosha*) not only assume all functions connected with carrying out and servicing foreign-economic activities but also, where necessary, play the role of creditors and organizers of consortia (for instance, in supplying complete sets of equipment and carrying out major overseas projects). They have a network of offices and daughter companies throughout the world that have close ties to the largest business associations and government agencies, know the specifics of foreign markets, and so forth.

South Korea, which has been successfully winning foreign markets, has adopted the very same system—that is, it conducts a significant portion of its foreign-economic activities through universal trading companies.

In October 1982 the United States, mindful of Japan's experience, adopted a law on export trading companies that offered American firms the possibility of creating exporting associations or joint exporting companies to sell goods and services in external markets. To that end, an exception was made to U.S. antitrust legislation. One of the law's main goals is to create favorable conditions for the export of products and services by relatively small firms. The export trading companies perform all services having to do with exporting: they prepare documents, provide insurance, warehouse goods, sell them in external markets, assist with credit and financial matters, consult on marketing problems, and so forth. Such companies are being established in the United States not only in the private sector but also under a number of state governments (Iowa, New Jersey, and Hawaii, for example), and under various public corporations (port authorities, for example).

We should take foreign countries' experience and practices into account. It might be more effective, in terms of organizational forms, to avoid creating a multitude of foreign-trade departments at enterprises and organizations, and to rely instead on the qualified services of major self-supporting, middleman-type foreign-trade associations handling a universal range of products and with their own working capital.

These associations would operate not under the U.S.S.R. Ministry for Foreign Economic Relations or the various branch ministries (on the basis of a limited, "departmental" product mix), but on an autonomous basis, independent of departmental interference and pressure.

By focusing their import-export operations on the full range of goods and services, these middleman-type associations could exercise considerable influence on foreign-trade prices, reduce the cost of commercial operations, search for markets, handle advertising, and provide efficient presale preparation and after-sale service. They could also serve as go-betweens in the search for joint-production partners, organize consortia for major projects abroad, and so forth.

Even if individual enterprises or organizations are successful in entering the external market with their products, they are going to experience difficulty in obtaining components for them or securing the services of other enterprises and agencies, and in using their earnings to import the various goods they need. They will inevitably have to turn to foreign trading intermediaries, or to several associations operating under different ministries in our own country. But if they have Soviet middlemen as reliable partners in the form of independent, self-supporting, all-purpose trading associations (provided they retain the freedom to choose whom they want to deal with), their entry into the external market will be considerably more effective.

Establishment in the various republics of self-supporting foreign-trade associations with a broad range of foreign economic activities is an important step in this direction. It is also necessary, in our view, to establish national self-supporting middleman-associations of the universal type in Moscow and other major industrial and trade centers, and to establish associations of exporters and importers by groups of goods and services, to defend their common interests and provide broad assistance to their members throughout the range of foreign economic activities.

*   *   *

The thoughts presented above make no claim to fully clarify the problems raised, and even less so, to possessing any categorical validity. Nevertheless, we believe that the proposals can help in the search for ways to bring foreign economic ties out of the doldrums and turn them into an effective tool for helping to solve perestroika's most pressing social and economic problems, and to actively enlist all elements of the national economy in foreign-economic activities.

This search has just begun. Our entire economic life and the thinking of our economic managers are still bound by the traditions and concepts of the "age of autarky," when the export of goods was viewed as something imposed by necessity, unhealthy, and regrettable, while importation was seen as something that was possibly desirable, but was hard to come by and extraordinary by its very nature. One must bear in mind that, for an entire historical period, having a "Great Wall of China" around our country was regarded as an ideal, albeit an unattainable one. In recent decades these deep-rooted attitudes were reinforced by a structure of foreign economic ties that was truly absurd for a great industrial power—a structure based predominantly on the exchange of its natural resources for grain, meat, pipe, and rolled steel, and marked by a constantly falling share of equipment and consumer durables in exports.

To this must be added two other factors that had also, so to speak, engraved themselves on our national psychology: a blind, unthinking feeling of hostility toward foreign competition, and profound suspicion toward any and all forms of active foreign participation in our economic life. It turned out, in fact, that this protracted absence of foreign competition in our domestic market and our inability to compete in external markets because of our cumbersome administrative-command system became one of the principal causes of our deepening scientific, technological, and economic backwardness; and that our disdain for the possibilities of importing capital became yet another artificial limit on the development of our economic potential.

The modern-day "opening up" of national economies, a process which has already encompassed not only the industrial world but the developing world as well, is by no means dictated by some set of abstract, spiritual ideals. It is dictated by urgent necessity, economic rationality, and the tough demands of survival under conditions of the present-day race for scientific and technological progress. The traditional motto, "export or die," is joined today by the no less categorical and no less imperative motto, "import or die" (death, in these terms, meaning locking oneself into backwardness and remaining apart from integrative processes in the development of world economic ties). And that is not just so many words—it is the reality of life itself. Without competing with other world producers, and without enlisting foreign technical and financial resources in the development of its own economic potential, not a country in the world can hope to succeed. Those with historical promise are those that have assimilated this truth, not those that are hunkering down behind their national fences in hopes of sitting out the changes taking place in the world.

Of course, one cannot expect a country to emerge from protracted autarky or to break into demanding and highly saturated world markets overnight. It will take time to carry out serious structural transformations, to put the economy on the basis of full cost accounting and create a free market in producer goods inside the country, to organically fuse the domestic and external elements of the new economic mechanism, and finally, to make the transition to ruble convertibility—and thereby to the opening of our economic borders in fact, rather than merely on paper. Even now, however, one begins to hear voices, frightened by the signs of chaos in our foreign-economic sphere, asking: "Shouldn't we turn back?" These voices are apparently proceeding on the assumption that we can never cope with the tasks that other countries in this world are already accomplishing or have accomplished, that for some mystical national reasons, fate itself has decreed that we sit forever behind our wall.

No, there is no turning back for us. The present disarray in the foreign-economic sphere can be overcome only if we move forward. There is no denying that the foreign-economic problems we face are difficult. But they are solvable if we stay the course.

The Foreign Economic Relations of the U.S.S.R.'s Agroindustrial Complex: The Need for Perestroika

ANDREY YEVGENYEVICH SIZOV*

Today it cannot be said that there is any sort of diversity in the foreign transactions of the country's agroindustrial complex. They mainly come down to foreign food purchases paid for with oil export revenues, a practice that was developed in the first half of the 1970s. The petroruble euphoria is a thing of the past. Yet food imports have increased and continue to be used to "patch" the holes in the country's domestic market. They account for about 20 percent of all Soviet imports, an exceptional figure. Not only does such a phenomenon not exist in a single developed country, it is not even known in most Third World countries. Foreign purchases place an excessively heavy burden on the country's economy. Of the 16 billion rubles in hard-currency revenue anticipated for 1989, more than 5 billion (that is, one third) will go for importation of grain and foodstuffs. [1]

The strain in the domestic food market is so intense, and our dependence on foreign purchases so great, that it is impossible to solve the food import problems by simply reducing its volume. On one hand, the mix of imports must be fundamentally changed to eliminate imbalances in the country's food complex and improve the population's diet. On the other hand, extensive use must be made of all the forms of foreign economic relations that have been developed by the world community. This is all inseparable from development of a foreign economic food policy, a policy which for all practical purposes does not at present exist. Without one, it will hardly be possible to carry out an effective agrarian policy as a whole, or for that matter, to accomplish the specific tasks required to saturate the country's food market.

*Candidate of economics and senior research associate at the U.S.S.R. Academy of Sciences' Institute of World Economy and International Relations [IMEMO]. This article appeared in the March 1990 issue of *MEMO*.
[1]*Izvestia*, June 10, 1989.

Paradoxes of Importation

What do we import and why? At the CPSU Central Committee's May 1982 plenary session, at which the Food Program was adopted, L.I. Brezhnev answered that question as follows: "in the past few years, especially because of poor harvests, we have been forced to purchase grain, meat, and a number of other products abroad. This has been done in the interests of the people. We have no intention in the future, either, of rejecting what foreign trade can offer for the purposes of supplementing our food resources—naturally, with due consideration for economic feasibility."[2]

So it turns out that we imported because our climate was unsuitable and foreign purchases were economically justifiable, and therefore we would continue to import—for the good of the people, of course. As for those who were not entirely convinced that the importation of foodstuffs was being carried out exclusively in their interest, a unanimous chorus of interpreters of the Food Program explained in layman's terms: The well-being of Soviet people was steadily increasing, and their diet was being improved through a rise in the consumption of livestock products, and it was common knowledge that the production of such products required feed grain and high-protein feeds. And so the state had to purchase them overseas. As for the population's needs for bread and bakery products, the U.S.S.R. State Statistics Committee assured us that they were being fully satisfied by domestic production.

So it turns out that we are all to blame for the fact that the country has become a major importer of foodstuffs and will probably remain one for a long time to come. If we ate bread and pasta, everything would be fine, and there would be no need for foreign purchases. Yet once we started to consume more meat, milk, and eggs, the need for imports immediately arose. It turns out that the departments that put their energy into arguing the need to allocate hard currency for foreign purchases instead of concerning themselves with the development of the country's domestic food complex are not to blame at all.

It is indeed true that, according to the figures of the U.S.S.R. State Statistics Committee, in the 1980s we started to consume more meat and dairy products than we had a decade before. Yet these are not bananas and pineapples, but *meat and dairy* products, whose production we are fully capable of increasing at home. After all, we have 1.3 hectares of pastureland and 0.8 hectares of cropland per capita, com-

---

[2]*Materials of the CPSU Central Committee's May 1982 Plenum [Materialy mayskogo Plenuma TsK KPSS 1982 goda]* Moscow, 1982, p. 14.

pared to 0.18 and 0.25 hectares respectively in Western Europe, and 1.0 and 0.8 hectares in the United States. Yet they export and we import. And not just feed grain, but a great deal more.

From 1972 through 1988 expenditures on grain imports rose by a factor of 3.2. By item, expenditures on imports rose by factors of 3.4 for wheat, 9.2 for meat and meat products, 7.4 for vegetable oil, 14.1 for sugar, and 43.8 for butter![3] Translated into terms of our food consumption's dependence on imports, every second kilogram of sugar, every third kilogram of vegetable oil, every third loaf of bread, and every second package of pasta products is purchased abroad or produced from imported raw materials.[4]

These are all products that ought to be produced in our own country, yet they account for more than 70 percent of the U.S.S.R.'s food imports. From the viewpoint of any economist, this situation utterly goes against common sense. After all, most countries of the world clearly divide imported goods into those that are competitive and those that are not competitive with a country's domestic products. Throughout the world, governments attempt to regulate the importation of competitive goods (through quotas, tariffs, and nontarriff barriers) and encourage development of domestic production. It was a deliberate foreign food policy that turned the EC countries in a short time from grain importers into the world's second leading grain exporters. We, on the other hand, for all intents and purposes, have for many years been investing billions in hard currency to support Western farmers, while ignoring the needs of our country's agricultural sector for the importation of machinery and equipment. Hard currency cannot be found, for example, for purchasing the small-scale farm machinery that is so essential for farmers working under leasing arrangements, who could already be providing additional food production today.

In effect, the structure of the agroindustrial complex's imports duplicates the imbalances in the complex itself. We primarily import agricultural raw materials (grain, sugar, and oil seeds). Moreover, they are raw materials that our own agriculture produces. Yet we spend only one fourth to one third as much on the importation of machinery and equipment for agriculture, processing, and storage facilities. Purchases abroad of this agricultural raw material reach 50 million [metric] tons annually, of which 30 to 40 million tons are grain. All this must be stored and processed, a difficult task given our extremely

[3]Calculated on the basis of *U.S.S.R. Foreign Trade* [*Vneshnyaya torgovlya SSSR*] for the relevant years.
[4]*Izvestia*, Dec. 14 and June 16, 1989.

backward storage and processing facilities. It can be accomplished only if a considerable portion of our agroindustrial complex's processing capacity is shifted to processing imported raw material, at the price of worsening the conditions for the storage and processing of our own. The result is that the intolerable losses, recurring year after year, of domestic agricultural products are in many respects the direct result of the additional burden placed on the agroindustrial complex by the importation of millions of tons of agricultural raw materials. Such imports not only do nothing to help eliminate the imbalances in the country's own agroindustrial complex, but to the contrary, aggravate them further.

At the same time, from a financial standpoint the predominance of agricultural raw materials in the mix of imports is simply a money-losing proposition. Given the present imbalance in feed rations, which results in excessively high unit costs for the production of livestock products (from 50 percent to 100 percent higher than in the United States), and the present-day purchase prices of those products, the yield from the importation of feed grain is actually negative. Thus, a dollar spent for the purchase and importation of American corn used in hog raising produces 1.5 to 2 rubles' worth of final product at state retail prices. And taking budget subsidies into account, this amounts to a net loss for the state coffers of 2 to 2.5 rubles per kilogram of pork. It is perfectly obvious that such a use of hard currency has little to do with attempts to balance the country's consumer market, and only intensifies inflationary tendencies.

At the same time, we do everything possible to economize on importation of a wide range of food products that we lack the conditions for producing. The point is not just that many of them could considerably increase budget revenues. For example, a dollar spent on importing bananas, lemons, or coffee brings the state, respectively, 3 rubles, 5.5 to 6.6 rubles, or 7 to 8 rubles, which in today's situation does far more to help improve the situation in the market and in the financial sector than the importation of grain. But another aspect of the problem, which has direct bearing on people's health, is also important.

Despite considerable shortages in the country's food supply, 30 percent of the population is overweight due to excessive consumption of fatty and starchy foods. This is a serious factor in the risk of arteriosclerosis, heart disease, and cancers. On the other hand, vitamin deficiencies, especially during the winter, reach 70 percent. They are especially dangerous for children, who pay for them with poor vision, tooth decay, diathesis, rickets, and other diseases. It appears that we are importing agricultural raw materials that increase the production of animal fats that undermine our health. On the other hand, the food products needed to improve that health are regarded, at best, as of less importance.

Yet in all the developed countries food importation is an important means of balancing the population's diet. For example, consumption of citrus fruits in the Federal Republic of Germany, Sweden, and Canada (that is, in countries where they are not produced at all) is from 21 to 28 kilograms a year per capita, compared to 2 kilograms in our country. We consume 200 grams of other tropical fruits, while "they" consume 50 to 60 times as much. These, of course, are averages. Considering the way in which imported goods are distributed in our country, children in many regions know of oranges, bananas, and pineapples only from pictures. Most of our consumers have never even heard of many other fruits that are available to the ordinary consumer in the West (avocadoes, kiwis, papayas).

Can it be that our country's consumer is inferior? Wouldn't he like to improve and diversify his diet? Of course he would! The figures of the All-Union Institute for Market and Demand Research indicate that our countrymen clearly "rank" their dietary requirements. They would prefer foods that contribute most to a healthy diet. Of the families surveyed, 63 percent would like to consume more fruits and 57 percent would like to consume more fish and cultured milk products; next come cheese, fruit and vegetable juices, sausages, vegetables, vegetable juices, poultry, canned fruits, and only then, meat (34 percent).

A few words about exports. Our exportation of foodstuffs is insignificant, yet we sell fairly large amounts of the means of production used in the agroindustrial complex. These include mainly mineral fertilizers, fuel, and lubricants, although by no means do we have a surplus of them. Farm machinery is constantly standing idle on collective and state farms because of fuel and spare part shortages. This results in unharvested crops and millions of rubles in losses. On the average, our fields receive only 40 percent of the recommended amount of mineral fertilizers, while we export millions of tons of them. Estimates show that only about 22 percent as much grain is acquired with the hard currency earned from exporting mineral fertilizer as could have been additionally harvested by using that same fertilizer for grain crops in our country.[5] We fail to harvest about 30 million tons of grain annually because of the protraction of the harvest period, which is chiefly due to a shortage of fuel.

This sort of exportation could be compared to a "distress sale" and is very closely connected to our importation of foodstuffs. We sell since we lack the hard currency to pay for purchases of agricultural products,

[5]*Pravda*, Sept. 8, 1988.

while the requisite conditions for expanding domestic agricultural production in terms of materials and equipment are constantly being undermined because we export necessities.

Thus, the existing structure of our agroindustrial complex's foreign ties is at odds with the objectives both of increasing the efficiency of agricultural production and food processing, and of improving the Soviet people's diet. It is absolutely clear that today there are no grounds for saying that the U.S.S.R.'s agroindustrial complex participates in an effective way in the international division of labor. The reliance on imports as a means of supplementing food resources has made us exceptionally dependent on external supplies, especially of food grain. And let's not try to explain the import policy by a desire to increase meat consumption in step with higher incomes of the population. The reasons are entirely different and are directly connected with a bureaucratic interest in imports, an interest that for a long time contributed to the distortions in the country's grain industry.

Grain Hostages

In the 1980s an average of about 18 million [metric] tons of wheat was imported into the country annually; this amounted to one fifth of world imports of that grain. One immediately wonders whether production drops of food grain have been so great as to force us to resort to such large-scale importation of wheat. No, the problem is not unreliable weather. Even in years of drought and poor crops we harvest 70 to 75 million tons of wheat, and in a normal year we harvest at least 80 to 85 million tons. The United States, for example, harvests 55 to 60 million tons (in the poor year of 1988, only 49 million tons), while the EC countries taken together harvest 70 to 75 million tons.

Yet our consumption of food grain is about 130 kilograms per capita, and only about 38 million tons of wheat a year is needed to provide for that.

So what is the problem? It is that an increasingly large part of the wheat that is grown and harvested in the U.S.S.R. is unfit for baking. This is in a country that once prided itself on its grain. "Our durum wheats are especially renowned," the well-known economic geographer V. Den wrote in the 1920s. "They are unparalleled in the world and are the pride of Russian agriculture. The reason for their high quality lies in the exceptionally favorable soil and climatic conditions one finds for wheat crops in our country."[6] It was Russian varieties that provided the basis for Canadian and American wheats. And as late as the 1960s our export grain was highly valued on the world market.

---

[6]V. Den, *Course in Economic Geography* [*Kurs ekonomicheskoy geografii*], Moscow, 1928, p. 206.

Changes for the worse happened when we shifted to the regular mass importation of grain (with a view, of course, to "economic expediency").

The bureaucratic apparatus quickly acquired a taste for imports. For some people they opened a "window" to Europe and America; others were allowed to calmly produce wheat that was unfit for making bread; and still others were enabled to receive bonuses and rewards for fulfilling and overfulfilling plan assignments for processing imported grain. Matters got to the point that in the 1980s the Ministry of Grain Products produced annually nearly a million tons of flour more than the country could consume. How did that happen? "Flour production," complained A. Budyk, former U.S.S.R. Minister of Grain Products, "is determined for us by the State Planning Committee, while the Ministry of Trade distributes it."[7]

In short, import purchases immediately made it possible for our departments to live without anxiety. The State Planning Committee could plan how much flour had to be produced and how much grain had to be imported for that purpose; the State Agroindustrial Committee could pass off mediocre output for high-quality output; the Ministry of Grain Products evade the issues of organizing the effective processing and storage of domestically produced grain (and why?—"the outside world will come to the rescue"), while calmly processing grain into flour, despite its surplus in the market. The Grain Exports Foreign Trade Association became, in effect, the Grain Imports Foreign Trade Association, which signed contracts not with domestic grain producers, but with American, West European, Argentinean, and Australian grain companies, justifying this practice by referring to orders "from above." Everyone was about his business. It was pointless to look for anyone who was out of the picture.

For everything to function smoothly in this well-organized departmental chain, foreign purchases needed to be put on a planned, and hence stable, footing. This problem was solved fairly simply—by concluding long-term intergovernmental grain purchase agreements, first with the United States, then with Canada, Argentina, and others. In effect, this meant that the Soviet Union was undertaking certain commitments to import grain (in the 1980s, about 15 to 20 million tons annually), regardless of the state of affairs in either grain farming or the national economy as a whole. Such agreements, in effect, let our suppliers know in advance that the U.S.S.R. would continue to remain a major importer. It was truly priceless information for Western grain

---

[7]*Izvestia*, April 22, 1988.

companies, especially when supply exceeded demand on the world market. And our own bureaucrats also know in advance: good harvest or bad, the grain will come in all the same.

This was all packaged in the form of "guaranteed foreign sources for supplementing the country's food resources." Let us not analyze too deeply the consequences of the U.S. government's partial embargo of grain shipments to the U.S.S.R. in 1980—an embargo imposed despite the existence of a grain agreement. It seriously complicated the country's hard-currency and general economic situation and stressed how dependent we were on imports. The main thing is that, by largely relieving the departments of the problems of producing, procuring, and processing of domestic grain, the large-scale, regular importation of grain created the conditions for stagnation and decline in the production of high-quality grain, and for preserving distortions in economic relations between grain purchasers and grain producers.

Following the growth in imports, domestic purchases of grain fit for food purposes began to decline. In the second half of the 1960s (that is, before the beginning of large-scale imports), domestic purchases averaged 41 million tons of baking wheat annually; in the 1970s they averaged 36 million tons; and in the 1980s they averaged only 24 million tons. Domestic purchases of durum wheat were even worse: From 1966 to 1970 they averaged 3 million tons annually; in the 1970s, 2 million tons; and in the 1980s, 1.1 million tons.[8] Moreover, the quality of durum wheat has declined significantly. In the past few years only a little more than half of the domestic durum wheat purchased has been classified as high quality.

A vicious circle developed. The increase in imports that took place before the mid-1980s made it possible to pay less and less attention to the quality of food-grain, which is persuasively shown by the drop in purchases of baking wheat. And that made the importation of such grain increasingly essential. Consequently, the departments shored up the whole mechanism of the organization of import purchases with social and political arguments that, from every indication, were hard for any political leader to resist. After all, a sharp curtailment of foreign purchases would immediately threaten the supply of bread to the country's population, especially the big industrial centers. Without suspecting it, we became hostages of sorts to our own departments, and they, by organizing the importation and processing of foreign grain, practically turned into our bread-winners. They did so, of course, at our expense, and a growing expense at that.

[8]*Soviet Agriculture* [*Selskoye khozyaystvo SSSR*], Moscow, 1988, p. 217.

In the meantime, farms continue to feed bread wheat and even durum wheat to livestock. This is not some paltry amount but 13 to 16 million tons of high-quality bread wheat and 1.3 to 1.5 million tons of durum wheat—that is, magnitudes that almost perfectly match our imports. Not only does this mean that livestock is, in effect, grazing on baking grain for which we have to pay hard currency, but it also inflates the unit cost of livestock products.

Let us not hasten to condemn our collective and state farms for this. They are simply forced to operate in a world of fun-house mirrors in which the abnormal looks perfectly normal. Thus, after selling their grain to the monopolistic purchasers, agricultural enterprises have to pay from 50 percent to 100 percent more for low quality mixed feed that they acquire from the same purchasers.

Nothing of this sort exists in any developed food economy. In the United States, for example, a substantial portion of feed (about 40 percent) is prepared directly on the farms themselves. On the other hand, there are about 1,500 companies in the commercial feed sector, with the largest (Ralston Purina Co.) accounting for only 5 percent of total feed production.[9] The existence of a large number of companies, along with the widespread production of concentrated feeds directly on farms, rules out any monopolistic manipulation of prices that occurs in our country. In recent years the average price of concentrated feeds was approximately two thirds that of food-quality wheat. Baking wheat is also distinguished everywhere from wheat used for feed, which is also less expensive. In our country, however, the pricing system is such that farms that produce inferior common wheat (for example, in the Moscow region) receive a higher price than farms that produce high-quality baking wheat but enjoy more favorable natural conditions. That is, it is not the consumer value but the cost to the farms that serves as the basis for the pricing system: where that cost is higher, the price is higher.

The U.S.S.R.'s situation as a grain purchaser was partially relieved by the drop in world prices that occurred prior to mid-1988. Moreover, the rivalry among grain exporters that sharply intensified during that period created a situation in which our trading partners, particularly the United States and the EC, started to offer us substantial price reductions. In the past two years the average price reduction in purchases of American wheat was $35 a ton, or 25 to 30 percent of the export price.[10] Things even got to the point that the French minister of agriculture accused the United States of helping the Rus-

[9]Calculated on the basis of: *Harvard Business School. British Petroleum—An Unconventional Player*, 1988, pp. 7, 24.

[10]*U.S.S.R.: Agricultural and Trade Report*, U.S. Department of Agriculture, Washington, 1989, p. 48.

sians build up their nuclear potential! Of course, what won't you say when a more powerful competitor starts to crowd you out of an attractive market. But if one follows that logic, the EC, which offers export subsidies for sales not just of grain but also of meat and dairy products, has invested no less than the United States in the "strengthening" of our defense.

Today all that is becoming a thing of the past. On one hand, the sharp decline in the world export resources that occurred in the second half of 1988 as the result of the drought in the United States and Canada changed market conditions in an unfavorable direction for us. Prices for grain, especially wheat, shot upward. In 1988 they were $125 to $130 a ton, today they are about $170 a ton. That is for ordinary baking wheat. Canadian high-quality durum wheat is 30 percent higher, on the average. On the other hand, in the course of multilateral negotiations that have been taking place within the GATT framework, an agreement in principle has been reached to freeze subsidies for the exportation of agricultural goods, and to gradually roll them back. Therefore, although price reductions are still offered, they are offered with increasing difficulty and on a lower scale. Only the intervention of U.S. President Bush allowed us to receive them in May 1989 when purchasing a regular lot of American wheat. The amount of the reduction was only $8.50 a ton.

The food import situation is becoming increasingly serious if one considers our extremely strained overall foreign economic situation. No increase in export earnings can be foreseen in the near future. Exports of traditional commodities (fuel and gold) are physically limited, and it will take a long time to establish any significant exports of finished products to the Western countries.

Hence the need to take prompt steps aimed at reducing imports of agricultural products, on the basis of which parasitical attitudes have flourished. But we already find ourselves drawn too deeply into the crater of foreign dependency. Resolutions calling to "improve," "perfect," or "increase" efficiency (which imply that in general everything is fine, nearly perfect, and even efficient, and only has to be slightly improved) will not accomplish much here.

Foreign Economic Relations and Current Agrarian Policy

It is fundamentally wrong to lay responsibility for the impasses and distortions in our foreign economic relations exclusively on our foreign trade institutions, as some public-affairs writers have done. Such a course of events was programmed in the early 1970s by the system of bureaucratic command management, which made it possible to pass off departmental interests as state interests. From that standpoint, the fact that grain importation grew from a sporadic occurrence (as it was in the mid-1960s) into a systematically planned phenomenon was highly typical and predictable. At the same time, the growth in food imports up to the mid-1980s also resulted from the absence of a foreign food policy as an important part of overall agricultural policy.

The integral development of the country's food complex requires the coordination of domestic and foreign food policies. Key decisions determining the dimensions and structure of foreign trade operations should be concentrated in a single agency, which could be the U.S.S.R. Council of Ministers' State Commission for Food and Procurements. The Commission's proposals would be considered by the U.S.S.R. Supreme Soviet's Agrarian and Food Committee, which would approve or disapprove the proposals on the basis of the requirements for developing the agroindustrial complex.

I think that such an approach would make it possible to bring together the allocation of ruble and hard-currency funds appropriated for food purchases and for development of the agroindustrial complex, and to channel such funds first into improving the branches of our agrarian sector that produce substitutes for imports, rather than into purchasing new shipments of agricultural products abroad.

A first, timid step has been taken in providing incentives for import substitution. I have in mind the U.S.S.R. Council of Ministers' resolution on the partial payment for grain with hard currency. But the total amount of grain that was purchased for hard currency from our state and collective farms in 1989 was insignificant—only 223,000 tons. One reason was the low level of purchase prices (40 to 60 gold rubles per ton, which is approximately half the current world prices.). Nonetheless, the Grain Exports Foreign Trade Association, which is supposed to handle domestic hard-currency purchases, does not consider these prices too low. And as an argument, it cites foreign-trade wheat prices in 1987 and 1988. Granted, it says nothing about two "minor" circumstances. The first is that world prices during that period were at a record low because of overproduction of grain. The second is that the Soviet Union received large price reductions on grain imports from the United States and the EC. In effect, the departments set the lowest possible price, which has nothing in common with setting prices that would stimulate import substitution. But they can still claim that they are implementing the resolution of the U.S.S.R. Congress of People's Deputies.

It is probably unnecessary to reinvent the wheel. Many countries have fairly rich experience in solving such problems. For example, wide use is made of guaranteed minimum prices, which are set at the level of 80 to 95 percent of the average world price, calculated on the basis of the past several years. There are other solutions, as well. In our country, however, only one solution has come into play—an administrative-apparatus solution that not only will not enable us to reduce our dependence on imports, but will not provide savings of hard currency by relying on domestic purchases, because of their paltry amounts.

Moreover, despite official assurances that no restrictions will be placed on a farm's use of the hard currency it earns,[11] such restrictions do exist: An agricultural enterprise can spend the money it has earned only through foreign trade organizations of the U.S.S.R. Ministry of Foreign Economic Relations. Such so-called service means, for all intents and purposes, that part of the money earned goes to maintain the foreign trade bureaucracy for its middleman services. What the quality of those services is, how effective they are, and whether they are needed at all by any specific farm become purely hypothetical questions. They need not be answered, since agricultural enterprises have no choice. So a seemingly progressive measure aimed at lessening the country's dependence on food imports proves, in practice, to be a measure that works toward preserving state agencies' monopolistic position.

Therefore, establishment of foreign trade associations that are genuinely self-supporting and are removed from departmental control is a necessary condition for creating an effective import-substitution mechanism. The state would conclude contracts with them, possibly even on a competitive basis, while fulfillment of the contracts would be the prerogative of the foreign trade organizations themselves. They themselves should decide from whom they buy—domestically or abroad—primarily on the basis of economic considerations, while they would receive part of any hard currency they saved in the process for use at their own discretion. Only under such conditions can one expect that the foreign trade organizations will find not just Western partners, but their own Soviet partners, from whom they could buy to their mutual benefit, and without any directives to do so from above.

In the activities of these self-supporting foreign trade enterprises, a place should be found for collective and state farms, individual farmers who lease or own their land, agroindustrial associations, and agricultural firms. Their participation as stockholders would make it possible to move toward the organization of modern-type production and trading firms with facilities for the initial processing, transportation, and storage of agricultural products. Such firms could provide a framework in which the necessary organizational and economic conditions would be created to allow development of companies that can handle a diversity of commodities and can restructure their purchases

---

[11]*Pravitelstvennyy vestnik* [*Government Bulletin*], No. 17, 1989, p. 9.

in short order in response to changing market conditions. This is especially important in the importation of products that form a single technological chain (for example, feed grain, high-protein additives, and meat products).[12]

At the same time, such foreign trade associations are also needed to revive the export potential of a number of branches of agriculture. This pertains especially to grain production. I think that combining economic incentives with organizational measures to restructure the work of foreign trade organizations would make it possible to reduce foreign wheat purchases by 2 to 3 million tons a year. This would enable us to virtually quit importing it entirely in five to seven years. That period is also optimal in terms of our external commitments (the existence of long-term intergovernmental agreements on grain purchases). At the same time we should, without further delay, create the conditions for entering foreign markets for rye and rye products. Rye bread is assuming an increasingly prominent place in modern concepts of a "healthy diet." We should not be afraid to advertise it aggressively, but, using such advertisement to the fullest advantage, should strive to occupy leading positions in this market that is still relatively undeveloped by competitors.

Some of the hard currency that is saved should be used to provide further incentives for development of import replacements in the country's agrarian sector. Some of it should be used for temporarily expanding foreign purchases of meat products and increasing importation of fresh and processed vegetables and fruits, coffee, tea, and other tropical products. In other words, it is hardly possible to reduce hard-currency expenditures within the context of the country's food complex. On the other hand, it is simply essential to ensure that those expenditures are effectively used to saturate the domestic food market, improve the structure of consumption, and stimulate domestic production.

However, today the traditional "foreign-trade" approach to restructuring the agroindustrial complex's external ties is no longer capable of answering all the questions. This is especially true with respect to the problems of modernizing the processing industry. In the 1980s domestic purchases accounted for 45 to 50 percent of all deliveries of equipment for the food-processing industry [the *pishchevaya* industry, which includes fresh meat, fish, and dairy products, but not,

---

[12]An analysis of the movement of world prices for agricultural commodities shows that when prices for feed resources rise rapidly, the increase in meat prices is considerably "softer" and exhibits a certain time lag. Moreover, when feed prices surge sharply, many livestock farms are forced to reduce the size of their herds, which increases the supply of meat on the market and restrains price increases.

for example, fresh produce—*Trans.*].[13] At present, imported equipment accounts for about 33 percent of all production equipment in some branches of the food-processing industry; 43 percent of all production equipment in bakeries and pasta plants; and from 55 to 65 percent of such equipment in the fruit-and-vegetable, oils, and tea industries. Nonetheless, this has not made our table any richer. The assortment remains worse than meager. There are extremely few so-called convenience products (ready for direct consumption, or requiring little preparation time). The food-processing industry remains the most backward sector of the overall food complex, a fact which in many cases nullifies any progress in producing agricultural products themselves. Of the existing 56,000 processing enterprises, only 11,000, or 19 percent, meet modern standards; 38,000 are in need of modernization; and the rest have production facilities that should be written off as completely unfit for further use. At the same time, according to the former U.S.S.R. State Agroindustrial Committee, in 1988 inventories of uninstalled imported equipment were valued at 570 million rubles.[14]

In short, it is a familiar picture. A considerable amount is purchased, but the yield from it is minimal. The process of installing imported equipment drags out for years; production lines are often set up without all the required components; and a considerable amount of equipment lies around in warehouses or in the open, becoming unfit for use.

In this connection, it is possible that some of the money spent for importing equipment for the food-processing industry might be reallocated to develop cooperation with foreign agribusiness firms. Many of them have technologies for processing food raw materials that are of particular interest to us, since using them would potentially enable us to reduce our agricultural imports by making efficient use of local resources. Thus, foreign experience shows that the demand for sugar can be substantially reduced by producing sugar substitutes obtained from processing grains and potatoes. It was dynamic growth in the production of low-calorie sweeteners that caused the consumption of refined sugar to drop by nearly 40 percent in the United States in the 1980s. Technologies for producing bread products from common wheat have been widely employed in the West European countries (in our country such wheat is used chiefly for feeding livestock), which has allowed them to substantially cut back on imports of durum wheat. Many foreign companies have gained valuable experience in the production of feed additives that substantially increase the efficiency of feeds; and so forth.

---

[13]*U.S.S.R. Industry* [*Promyshlennost SSSR*], Moscow, 1988, p. 129.
[14]*Izvestia*, Jan. 12, 1989.

However, we can hardly count on establishing joint enterprises with Western firms in these areas. The experience of negotiations with ADM (Archer Daniels Midland Co.), which is one of the world's leading corporations in the processing of feed grain and oil-bearing seeds, showed that the company had absolutely no interest in the joint production and marketing of high-protein products. Most of the world's agricultural markets are highly competitive, and the appearance of a new seller threatens a further intensification of competition. It is absolutely clear that the major Western firms will not undertake to create a new competitor of their own accord. Yet we often, in effect, insist that they do so, in the naive belief that our provision of manpower and a plot of land with a "box" on it is sufficient grounds for a Western partner to let us in on its technologies and allow us access to foreign markets through its marketing channels.

Under these conditions, a more promising form of cooperation might be licensing agreements, which can be highly diverse: from simple or "pure" licensing, to a comprehensive agreement on industrial cooperation in which licensing becomes the core of a broad contractual package. Another possible way to attract Western food-industry corporations to cooperate with Soviet enterprises is through consortia in which a foreign partner's costs and profits would be paid out of the export earnings of "hard currency producing" Soviet enterprises operating in different industries.

It is also worth considering granting the status of import-substitution enterprise to foreign food-processing companies and agribusinesses, whose profits from the sale of output produced in the Soviet Union would be converted into hard currency. This would be a powerful incentive for the establishment of joint enterprises in the processing industry. We would gain not only the modern food products that are so badly needed today, but also access to the technologies for producing them. It is perfectly possible that this sort of arrangement would prove much more efficient than the agonizingly complicated process of retooling defense enterprises for the production of food-processing equipment, a process which initial results show to be costly and relatively inefficient.

Modern forms of foreign economic relations can also contribute to increased supplies of tropical produce, for which the unsatisfied demand is simply immeasurable. In addition to traditional foreign trade operations, serious consideration should be given to actively establishing joint enterprises in Third World countries themselves. However, this idea has been raised extremely timidly, and only with respect to the so-called countries of socialist orientation (Vietnam and Ethiopia). The chief difficulty in developing joint enterprises in the agricultural sector in Third World countries is our extremely poor knowledge of local natural and socioeconomic conditions, as well as our lack of the required managerial experience. It seems that establishing joint enterprises on the basis of third-party cooperation involving Western firms that have experience operating in the developing countries would be a way to eliminate these obstacles.

* * *

Indisputably, what has been said deals only with certain aspects (albeit, in our view, extremely important ones) of our foreign food policy. The formulation and implementation of that policy are directly connected with the elaboration of measures for the economic regulation of foreign ties, the arsenal of which is extremely meager today. But it is fairly obvious that this policy cannot be narrowly specific and oriented toward individual departments and their related economic branches. It should be organically connected with the country's domestic food policy. If it continues to be reduced merely to questions of organizing imports, we will scarcely break out of the vicious circle of food poverty and dependency.